DATA AND APPLICATIONS SECURITY XVII

Status and Prospects

IFIP – The International Federation for Information Processing

IFIP was founded in 1960 under the auspices of UNESCO, following the First World Computer Congress held in Paris the previous year. An umbrella organization for societies working in information processing, IFIP's aim is two-fold: to support information processing within its member countries and to encourage technology transfer to developing nations. As its mission statement clearly states,

> *IFIP's mission is to be the leading, truly international, apolitical organization which encourages and assists in the development, exploitation and application of information technology for the benefit of all people.*

IFIP is a non-profitmaking organization, run almost solely by 2500 volunteers. It operates through a number of technical committees, which organize events and publications. IFIP's events range from an international congress to local seminars, but the most important are:

- The IFIP World Computer Congress, held every second year;
- Open conferences;
- Working conferences.

The flagship event is the IFIP World Computer Congress, at which both invited and contributed papers are presented. Contributed papers are rigorously refereed and the rejection rate is high.

As with the Congress, participation in the open conferences is open to all and papers may be invited or submitted. Again, submitted papers are stringently refereed.

The working conferences are structured differently. They are usually run by a working group and attendance is small and by invitation only. Their purpose is to create an atmosphere conducive to innovation and development. Refereeing is less rigorous and papers are subjected to extensive group discussion.

Publications arising from IFIP events vary. The papers presented at the IFIP World Computer Congress and at open conferences are published as conference proceedings, while the results of the working conferences are often published as collections of selected and edited papers.

Any national society whose primary activity is in information may apply to become a full member of IFIP, although full membership is restricted to one society per country. Full members are entitled to vote at the annual General Assembly, National societies preferring a less committed involvement may apply for associate or corresponding membership. Associate members enjoy the same benefits as full members, but without voting rights. Corresponding members are not represented in IFIP bodies. Affiliated membership is open to non-national societies, and individual and honorary membership schemes are also offered.

DATA AND APPLICATIONS SECURITY XVII

Status and Prospects

IFIP TC11 / WG11.3 Seventeenth Annual Working Conference on Data and Applications Security
August 4–6, 2003, Estes Park, Colorado, USA

Edited by

Sabrina De Capitani di Vimercati
Università degli Studi di Milano
Italy

Indrakshi Ray
Colorado State University
USA

Indrajit Ray
Colorado State University
USA

SPRINGER SCIENCE+BUSINESS MEDIA, LLC

Library of Congress Cataloging-in-Publication Data

A C.I.P. Catalogue record for this book is available from the Library of Congress.

Data and Applications Security XVII: Status and Prospects
Edited by Sabrina De Capitani di Vimercati, Indrakshi Ray, and Indrajit Ray

DOI 10.1007/978-1-4020-8070-8

Printed on acid-free paper.
www.springer.com/mycopy

Contents

Contributing Authors

Vijayalakshmi Atluri is an Associate Professor of Computer Information Systems in the MS/IS Department at Rutgers University. She received her B.Tech. in Electronics and Communications Engineering from Jawaharlal Nehru Technological University, Kakinada, India, M.Tech. in Electronics and Communications Engineering from Indian Institute of Technology, Kharagpur, India, and Ph.D. in Information Technology from George Mason University, USA. Her research interests include Information Systems Security, Database Management Systems, Workflow Management and Multimedia.

Jean Bacon is a Reader in Distributed Systems at the University of Cambridge Computer Laboratory and a Fellow of Jesus College.

Ed Ball is at present a Senior Research Fellow in the Information Systems Institute, University of Salford. He has over 30 years of research experience in Electronic Engineering and telecommunications. Projects he has worked on include the RACE Catalyst, and Vantage projects (ATM over satellite) and the ACTS IMMP (Multi-Media) Trumpet (Telecommunications management) projects. He has over 100 published papers and consultancy reports.

Steve Barker is a Lecturer in Computer Science at King's College, London, UK. His research interests include role-based access control policy formulation and temporal authorization methods.

Elisa Bertino is professor of database systems in the Department of Computer Science and Communication of the University of Milan where she is currently the chair of the Department and the director of the DB&SEC laboratory. She has been a visiting researcher at the IBM Research Laboratory (now Almaden) in San Jose, at the Microelectronics and Computer Technology Corporation, at Rutgers University, at Purdue University, at Telcordia Technologies. Her main research interests include security, privacy, database systems, object-oriented technology, multimedia systems. In those areas, Prof. Bertino has published more than 200 papers in major refereed journals, and in proceedings of international conferences and symposia. Elisa Bertino is a Fellow member of IEEE and a member of ACM and has been named a Golden Core Member for her service to the IEEE Computer Society.

Joachim Biskup is a professor at the University or Dortmund. He is head of the ISSI (Information Systems and Security) working group, researching on of various aspects of information systems and security in computing systems.

David Chadwick is Professor of Information Systems Security at the University of Salford and the leader of the Information Systems Security Research Group. He specialises in X.509, and how it might be used to convert traditional paper based processes to run securely over the Internet. Particular research topics include policy based authorisation, the management of trust and the delegation of authority. He is the BSI representative to X.509 standards meetings, and is the author of a several Internet Drafts, RFCs and Global Grid Forum documents. Research projects include: distributed programmable authorisation, TrustCom (a 6th Framework IP), TrustHealth 2, ICE-CAR, PERMIS, PKI Challenge, Intelligent Computation of Trust, and Electronic Prescription Processing.

Shiping Chen is a doctoral student in Center for Secure Information Systems, George Mason University, Fairfax, Virginia. His research interests include information security, security policy, and formal methods.

Sun S. Chung is currently a Ph.D. candidate in Computer Science at CWRU. Her research interests are in Database Security, Database Encryption and Multimedia Query Processing. Currently she is working on query processing techniques over the encrypted database.

Marco Cremonini is a research associate at the Department of Information Technology of the University of Milan. His main interests include network and web application security, distributed systems and information protection.

Ernesto Damiani is a professor at the Department of Information Technology of the University of Milan. His main research interests include distributed and object oriented systems,semi-structured information processing and soft computing. He is the Vice-Chair of the ACM Special Interest Group on Applied Computing(SIGAPP).

Steven A. Demurjian is a professor of Computer Science at the University of Connecticut with research interests of software requirements specification, reusability and refactoring for component-based systems, and RBAC/MAC models and security solutions for distributed environments. Dr. Demurjian has over 100 publications, in the following categories: 1 book, 1 edited book, 8 journal articles, 19 book chapters, and 72 refereed articles.

Paul Douglas is a lecturer in Computer Science at Westminster University, London, UK. His research interests include distributed database systems and deductive database applications.

Csilla Farkas is an assistant professor in the Department of Computer Science and Engineering and Director of the Information Security Laboratory at the University of South Carolina. Csilla Farkas received her Ph.D. from George Mason University, Fairfax. In her dissertation she studied the inference and aggregation problems in multilevel secure relational databases. Dr. Farkas R current research interests include information security, data inference problem, cyber crime, and security and privacy on the Semantic Web. Dr. Farkas is a recipient of the National Science Foundation Career award. The topic of her award is "Semantic Web: Interoperation vs. Security - A New Paradigm of Confidentiality Threats". Dr. Farkas actively participates in international scientific communities as program committee member and reviewer.

Elena Ferrari is professor of database systems at the University of Insubria at Como, Italy. She has also been on the faculty in the Department of Computer Science of the University of Milano, Italy, from 1998 to March 2001. She received a PhD. in Computer Science from the University of Milano, in 1997. Elena Ferrari has been a visiting researcher at George Mason University, Fairfax (VA) and at Rutgers University, Newark (NJ). Her main research interests include database and web security, temporal and multimedia databases. In those areas, Prof. Ferrari has published several papers in all major refereed journals, and in proceedings of international conferences and symposia. Elena Ferrari is a member of ACM and the IEEE Computer Society.

Ehud Gudes is currently a professor in computer science at Ben-Gurion university in Israel, and his current research interests are: Knowledge and databases, Data Security and Data mining. A native of Israel, he received his Bsc and Msc from the Technion - Israel Institute of Technology, and his PhD in Computer and Information Science from the Ohio State University in 1976. Following his Phd, he worked both in academia (Penn State University, Ben-Gurion University,), where he did research in the areas of Database systems and Data security, and in Industry (Wang Laboratories, National Semiconductors, Elron, IBM Research), where he developed Query languages, CAD Software, and Expert systems for Planning and Scheduling. He has published over 50 papers in the above general areas, and was the the chair of three international conferences, including IFIP WG11.3 2002.

Hakan Hakan Hacıgümüş received his M.S. and Ph.D. degrees in Computer Science from the University of California, Irvine. Currently, he is currently working at the IBM Almaden Research Center, San Jose, CA as a Research Staff Member. He is a recipient of an IBM Ph.D. fellowship in 2000, 2001, and 2002. His research interests include On-Demand Service Provisioning Models, Privacy and Security in Databases, Grid Computing, and e-Business Infrastructures.

Mahantesh Halappanavar is a PhD student in the Department of Computer Science at the Old Dominion University. He holds a bachelors degree in Engineering from Karnataka University, India and a Masters degree in Computer Science from Old Dominion University, Norfolk. His present work includes design of alternate architectures and performance enhancements for PKI. His research interests include information security, distributed systems, and systems programming.

Michael Hitchens received the B. Math. Degree from Newcastle University, Australia, in 1986 and the Ph.D. degree in Computer Science from the same university in 1991. He is a senior lecturer in the Department of Computing at Macquarie University. He has also worked at the universities of Sydney and Western Sydney. His current areas of research interest include security for large distributed systems, models and languages for access control, security for wireless networks, security for distributed file systems, authorization management and security protocols.

Sarath Indrakanti received Bachelor of Applied Science (major in Computing) degree from the University of Western Sydney, Australia in 2001. He is currently a Ph.D. student with the Information and Networked Systems Security Group in the Department of Computing, Macquarie University, Australia working on Secure Authorization for Web Services.

Bala Iyer, IBM Distinguished Engineer, is the manager of the Advanced Technology Development group at the IBM's Silicon Valley Lab, earned his Masters and PhD from Rice University, winning the Best Thesis Award at the university. In the past has worked as a Member of Technical Staff at Bell Labs in Murray Hill, NJ and as a Research Staff Member at IBM TJ Watson Research Center, NY. He has devoted the last 15 years to R&D for IBM Data Management products. Bala is the co-architect of IBM z-Series server's hardware compression facility, and compression software support in IBM's DB2, IMS and VSAM software products. Bala has contributed in numerous other areas including, the data grid, data security and privacy, application service provisioning, storage for Life Science, e-business, ERP application performance, data mining, multidimensional analysis, SQL optimization, database performance, high performance sorting and synchronization algorithms for scalable database clustering, analytical performance modeling, high speed network switching, and computer network architecture.

Sushil Jajodia is the BDM International Professor of Information Technology and the director of Center for Secure Information Systems at the George Mason University, Fairfax, Virginia. His research interests include information security, temporal databases, and replicated databases.
The URL for his web page is http://csis.gmu.edu/faculty/jajodia.html.

Rajat Kumar joined Microsoft in 2000 as a Principal Technology Specialist in the Dotcom Group, and has also served as the Program Manager for the academic and research community in Australia. He works with researchers to identify and coordinate possible opportunities and projects with Microsoft Research in various areas such as Web Services and multimedia technology. He was previously a senior technology leader at an Internet solutions firm where he designed large-scale Internet systems for corporate clients.

Thomas Leineweber is research assistant at the ISSI working group at the University of Dortmund since mid-2000. He performs research on computer security, especially on access control.

Peng Liu is an assistant professor in the school of IST, PSU. His research interests are network and database security, and systems survivability.

Charles U. Martel received the B.S. degree in Computer Science from MIT in 1975 and the Ph.D. degree in Computer Science from the University of California at Berkeley in 1980. Since 1980 he has been on the Computer Science faculty at the University of California at Davis, where he is currently a Full Professor. He has worked on algorithms for parallel and distributed systems, scheduling, graph theory and network algorithms, and more recently, security algorithms. As a five time world bridge champion, he also has an interest in computer bridge playing programs.

Pietro Mazzoleni is a PhD student at the University of Milan, Italy. He has been visiting researcher at Rutgers University, Newark (NJ) and Vrije University, Amsterdam (The Netherlands). His main research interests include databases and access control into highly distributes information systems, multimedia and cultural heritage application. In those areas, Pietro Mazzoleni has published several papers in major refereed journals, and in proceeding of international conferences.

Sharad Mehrotra is currently associate professor in the Information and Computer Science Department at the University of California, Irvine and Director of the RESCUE Project, funded through the NSF large ITR grant, that aims at developing information technology solutions to improve crisis response. He received his Ph.D. in Computer Science in 1993 and subsequently worked at MITL, Princeton as a scientist from 1993-1994. From 1994-1998 he was an Assistant Professor in the Computer Science department and at the Beckman Institute at the University of Illinois at Urbana-Champaign. He specializes in the area of database management and is an author of about 100 research publications some of which have made pioneering contributions to the field. Prof. Mehrotra's research is currently funded by NSF through four active projects and through the KDD consortium.

Ken Moody is a Reader in Distributed information Management and a Fellow of King's College.

Ravi Mukkamala received the PhD degree from the University of Iowa in 1987 and the MBA degree from the Old Dominion University in 1993. Since 1987, he has been with the Department of Computer Science at Old Dominion University, Norfolk, Virginia, where he is currently a professor. His research interests include distributed systems, data security, performance analysis, and PKI. His research has been sponsored by NRL, DARPA, NASA, and CISC.

Peng Ning is an assistant professor of Computer Science at North Carolina State University. He received his PhD degree in Information Technology from George Mason University in 2001. Prior to his PhD study, he received an ME degree in Communication and Electronic Systems in 1997, and a BS degree in Information Science in 1994, both from University of Science and Technology of China. Peng Ning is a founding member of the NCSU Cyber Defense Laboratory. He is also a member of the ACM, the ACM SIGSAC, the IEEE, and the IEEE Computer Society.

Glen Nuckolls received his PhD in September of 2003 from the University of California at Davis under Charles Martel. His dissertation research developed a number of new techniques for efficient database query authentication. He received an MS in Mathematics from Auburn University and a BA in Mathematics from Grinnell College. Currently Dr. Nuckolls is a lecturer in the Computer Science department at the University of Texas at Austin.

Martin Olivier is a Professor in the Department of Computer Science at the University of Pretoria, South Africa. He is also Research Coordinator at the School of Information Technology of the University of Pretoria. His research interests include privacy and security in distributed systems.

Sylvia L. Osborn received her PhD from the University of Waterloo. Since 1977 she has been a faculty member in the Computer Science Department at the University of Western Ontario in London, Ontario, Canada. Her current research interests are in role-based access control, object-oriented databases, and database integration.

Oleksandr (Sassa) Otenko is a Research Fellow at the University of Salford and a member of the PERMIS development team.

Gultekin Ozsoyoglu is presently a professor in Computer Science at Case Western Reserve University. He published in database, security, multimedia computing, and real-time computing conferences and journals such as ACM Transactions on Database Systems, IEEE Transactions on Software Engineering, IEEE Transactions on Knowledge and Data Engineering, and Journal of Computer and System Sciences. He has served in program committees, panels and chairs of database conferences such as ACM SIGMOD, VLDB, IEEE Data Engineering.

Brajendra Panda is an associate professor in Computer Science and Computer Engineering Department at the University of Arkansas. His research interests include Database Systems, Computer Security, and Defensive Information Warfare.

Jaehong Park is a post doctoral fellow at the Laboratory for Information Security Technology (LIST), Department of Information and Software Engineering, George Mason University. His research interests are access control models and digital rights management.

Jörg Parthe is a research assistant at the ISSI working group at the University of Dortmund since mid-2002. He performs research on computer security, especially on access control.

Charles E. Phillips is a Lieutenant Colonel in the U.S. Army, a Ph. D. Candidate from the Univ. of Connecticut, and a Military Academy Instructor with the Dept. of EE&CS, West Point, NY. His research areas of interest are RBAC/MAC models, security solutions for distributed environments, and information assurance in coalition warfare. LTC Phillips has 11 publications: 4 book chapters and 7 refereed articles.

Prahalad Ragothaman was a graduate student in Computer Science and Computer Engineering Department at the University of Arkansas when this research was performed. He is currently working at Oracle, India.

Boris Rozenberg received his Bsc from the Ben-Gurion University. He is currently a MSc student in computer science at Ben-Girion university in Israel, and his current research interests are Data Security and Data mining.

Pierangela Samarati is a professor at the Department of InformationTechnology of the University of Milan. Her main research interests are in data and application security, information system security, access control policies, models and systems, and information protection in general. She is the Chair of the IFIP Working Group 11.3 on Data and Application Security.

Mikhail Sahalayev is a postgraduate research student at the University Of Salford. His primary work is focused on Certificate retrieval for OpenLDAP. He also has a MSc in Applied Mathematics and Complex Systems Modeling degree from Sumy State University, Ukraine. Mikhail coauthored several Internet Drafts and conference papers.

Ravi Sandhu is a professor in Department of Information and Software Engineering, George Mason University, the director of Lab for Information Security Technology (LIST), and the Chief Scientist of NSD Security. His research areas are access control models, database security, network security, and distributed system security.

David A. Singer is currently a professor in Mathematics at CWRU. His research interests are in geometry, especially Riemannian geometry, dynamical systems, and variational problems. At present his work concerns finite- and infinite-dimensional integrable Hamiltonian systems arising from geometric problems. His current teaching interest is Cryptology, the mathematics of secure communications.

Anna Cinzia Squicciarini is a PhD Student at the University of Milan, Italy. She received a degree in Computer Science from the university of Milan in July 2001 with full marks. During autumn 2002 Anna Cinzia has been a visiting researcher at Swedish Institute of Computer Science, Stockholm. Her main research interests include trust negotiations, privacy and, recently, models and mechanisms for privilege and contract management in virtual organizations.

Andrei Stoica is a Ph.D. candidate at the University of South Carolina. He received the B.S. in Computer Science from Polytechnica University of Bucharest, Romania in 1997 and the M.S. in Computer Science and Engineering from the University of South Carolina in 2000. He is a graduate research assistant in the Information Security Laboratory, USC. His research interests include information systems security, optical networks, and large-scale system design.

Stuart Stubblebine is a computer scientist with both practical and theoretical expertise in security and privacy technology. Dr. Stubblebine is a founder and consultant with Stubblebine Consulting providing security expertise in design, analysis, and evaluation for many Fortune 500 companies. Also, Dr. Stubblebine conducts sponsored research for Stubblebine Research Labs in the areas of security and privacy technology. Additionally, Dr. Stubblebine is affiliated as a professional researcher with University of California - Davis. Dr. Stubblebine has published numerous of conference and journal papers. He is an associate editor for the ACM Transactions on Information and System Security. He listed as an inventor on a numerous patents. Previously, Dr. Stubblebine worked for Bell Labs, and University of Southern California. He earned his Ph.D. degree in Electrical Engineering from University of Maryland in 1992, and his MS degree from University of Arizona in Electrical Engineering in 1988. His BS was a double major in computer science and mathematics from Vanderbilt University in 1983. Please see www.stubblebine.com for additional information and links to full papers.

T.C. Ting is emeritus professor of Computer Science at the University of Connecticut, with research interests of mutual exclusion and security constraints, RBAC/MAC models and security solutions for distributed environments, and networks and internetworking. Dr. Ting has given keynote addresses at many major security conferences and is on the editorial boards of the International Journal on Computer Standards and Interfaces and International Journal on Data and Knowledge Systems.

Vijay Varadharajan received the B.S degree in Electronic Engineering from Sussex University, UK, in 1981 and Ph.D. degree in Computer and Communication Security in the U.K in 1984, which was sponsored by BT Research Labs. He is the Microsoft Chair and Professor of Computing at the Macquarie University and the Director of Information and Networked System Security Research. He is also the Technical Board Director of Computer Science, Australian Computer Society. He has been a member of the Board of Advisors in Trusted Computing Platform Association (TCPA) and is on the Microsoft Trustworthy Computing Academic Advisory Board (TCAAB). He was responsible for worldwide Security Research at corporate Hewlett-Packard Labs based in Europe at HP Labs., UK. Prior to HP, he was a Research Manager at British Telecom Research Labs. U.K. His current areas of research interest include security in high speed networks, security for large distributed systems, security policies and management in distributed applications, Internet security, secure electronic commerce and payment models, secure mobile agents, wireless security, security models and architectures and security protocols.

He Wang is a Ph.D. student in the Computer Science department at the University of Western Ontario, London, Canada. He received his M.Sc. and B.Sc. degrees in Computer Science from the University of Western Ontario. He also accepted his B.Sc. degree in Microbiology Engineering from Shandong University, Jinan, China. His research interests include security of databases, operating systems and applications.

Duminda Wijesekera is an assistant professor in the Department of Information and Software Engineering at George Mason University, Fairfax, Virginia. In the past, he has worked in quality of service, multimedia systems and program verifications. His current interests are in information security and formal methods.

Dingbang Xu received a Master degree in computer science from Tsinghua University, China in 2001. Currently, he is a PhD student in North Carolina State University. His interests include information security, database management systems and distributed applications. Currently he is working in the area of intrusion detection, more specially, intrusion alert correlation.

Jianyong Zhang is a Ph.D student in the Department of CSE, PSU. His research interests are self management in storage systems and database systems.

Xinwen Zhang is a doctoral student in Lab for Information Security Technology (LIST), Department of Information and Software Engineering, George Mason University. His research interests are access control models and technologies, digital right management policies, and distributed systems security.

Preface

This volume contains the papers selected for presentation at the 17th IFIP WG 11.3 Working Conference on Database and Application Security. The Conference was held on 4-6 August 2003, in Estes Park, CO, USA. It describes original research results and innovative practical developments that pertain to maintaining security and privacy in database systems and applications.

In response to the call for papers, 49 papers were submitted to the conference. These papers were evaluated on the basis of their significance, novelty, and technical quality. Each paper was reviewed by at least three members of the Program Committee. The Program Committee meeting was held electronically. Of the papers submitted, 26 were selected for presentation at the conference. The papers cover a wide range of topics: Information Warfare, Information Assurance, Security and Privacy, Authorization and Access Control in Distributed Systems, Access Control Models and Technologies, and Security Technologies for the Internet. The papers not only demonstrate the richness of the discipline but also outlines directions for future research in Data and Applications Security.

An event like this just does not happen; it depends on the volunteering efforts of a lot of individuals, as well as on the support of the local co-organizers and of the sponsoring institutions. We thank the authors for submitting high quality papers to this conference. We are grateful to the program committee for reviewing and selecting the best papers. We are especially indebted to Indrajit Ray, Colorado State University, U.S.A., who served as the General Chair of the Seventeenth Annual IFIP WG 11.3 Conference, and to Pierangela Samarati, Chair, IFIP WG 11.3. We acknowledge the institutional support provided by Colorado State University and the financial assistance provided by Air Force Research Laboratory, Rome, NY.

Sabrina De Capitani di Vimercati and **Indrakshi Ray**
(Program Chairs)

Conference Committees

Conference Chairs

General Chair: *Indrajit Ray*, Colorado State University, U.S.A.
Program Chairs: *Sabrina De Capitani di Vimercati*, U. of Milan, Italy
Indrakshi Ray, Colorado State University, U.S.A.

Program Committee

Gail-Joon Ahn, University of North Carolina at Charlotte, U.S.A.
Vijay Atluri, Rutgers University, U.S.A.
Elisa Bertino, University of Milan, Italy
Joachim Biskup, University of Dortmund, Germany
Csilla Farkas, University of South Carolina, U.S.A.
Eduardo Fernandez-Medina, University of Castilla-La Mancha, Spain
Ehud Gudes, Ben-Gurion University, Israel
Sushil Jajodia, George Mason Univeristy, U.S.A.
Carl Landwehr, National Science Foundation, U.S.A.
Peng Liu, Pennsylvania State University, U.S.A.
Ravi Mukkamala, Old Dominion University, U.S.A.
LouAnna Notargiacomo, Oracle Corporation, U.S.A.
Marta Oliva, Universitat de Lleida, Spain
Martin Olivier, University of Pretoria, South Africa
Sylvia Osborn, University of Western Ontario, Canada
Pierangela Samarati, University of Milan, Italy
Ravi Sandhu, NSD Security and George Mason University, U.S.A.
Sujeet Shenoi, University of Tulsa, U.S.A.
David Spooner, Rennselaer Polytechnic Institute, U.S.A.
T.C. Ting, University of Connecticut, U.S.A.
Bhavani Thuraisingham, NSF and MITRE Corp., U.S.A.
Reind P. van de Riet, Vrije Universiteit, The Netherlands
Duminda Wijesekera, George Mason University, U.S.A.

External Referees

Qijun Gu
Meng Yu
Wanyu Zang

IFIP WG11.3 Chair

Pierangela Samarati, University of Milan, Italy

I

INFORMATION WARFARE

REMOTE COMPUTER FINGERPRINTING FOR CYBER CRIME INVESTIGATIONS

Jon Novotny, Dominic Schulte, Gavin Manes and Sujeet Shenoi
Center for Information Security, University of Tulsa, Tulsa, Oklahoma 74104, USA

Abstract This paper describes a novel tool for remotely "fingerprinting" computers used in criminal activity. The tool employs network scanning and machine identification techniques to acquire a fingerprint of a computer over the Internet. The fingerprint includes identifying information about the operating system, banners, enumerations and services. Once the computer is seized, it is connected to a closed network and scanned again to produce a second fingerprint to check against the original. Two scenarios – one related to investigating pedophiles and the other involving an illegal website – are examined. Legal issues pertaining to the use of computer fingerprinting in criminal investigations are also discussed.

Keywords: Computer Forensics, Digital Evidence, Computer Fingerprinting

1. Introduction

The goals of a criminal investigation are to acquire evidence of illegal activity and to conclusively establish the role of the suspect. In a cyber crime investigation, it is necessary to identify the devices (computers, cell phones, PDAs, etc.) used in the illegal activity and to establish that the suspect used those devices in the crime [20].

Networked computers are increasingly used in illegal activities [6]. For example, Internet chat rooms are often used by pedophiles to reach potential victims: according to one survey, 19% of young people between the ages of ten and seventeen who used the Internet at least once a month received unwanted sexual solicitations [13].

Law enforcement agents sometimes pose as minors in chat rooms to catch pedophiles [2,11]. In a typical scenario, an undercover detective and suspect meet in a chat room, communicate using chat room applications and/or direct messaging (e.g., e-mail), and arrange a sexual liaison at which time the pedophile is arrested [17]. The evidence includes recorded chat room conversations and direct messages, which demonstrate an intent to engage in sex with the "minor"

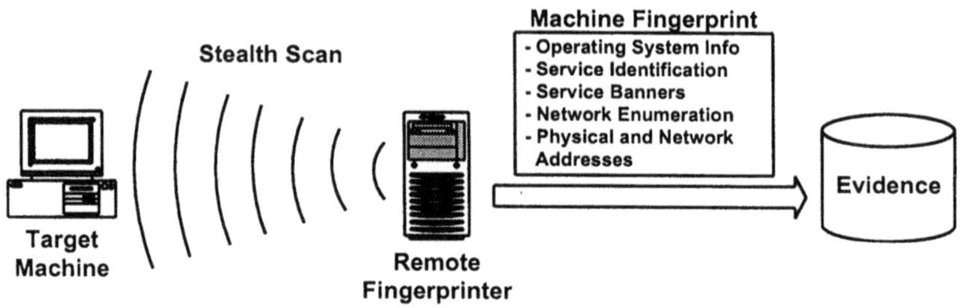

Figure 1. Remote machine fingerprinting.

and the details of the rendezvous [12]. The suspect is tied to this evidence when he/she is arrested at the rendezvous point.

Remote fingerprinting can be used to obtain evidence that the suspect's computer was the one used to communicate with the undercover detective. This "machine fingerprint" includes identifying information about the operating system, banners, enumerations and services of the suspect's computer. After the suspect is arrested and his/her computer is seized, it is scanned again to produce a new fingerprint. Matching the new fingerprint with the remotely acquired one can help establish that the seized computer was used in the crime.

The remote fingerprinting strategy is presented in Figure 1. The fingerprinting tool employs network scanning techniques [1,7,8] to acquire a fingerprint of a target machine over the Internet. The fingerprint is cryptographically sealed along with other electronic evidence (e.g., chat room and and e-mail transcripts). While it is preferable that the target machine be configured to permit network scans, it is possible to obtain useful identifying information even when it employs network defense mechanisms.

2. Network Scanning Tools

The hacker community was the first to use network-based machine exploration. Their goal was to identify hosts with specific vulnerabilities that could be exploited. Interestingly, generalized versions of early hacker tools are at the core of current strategies for mapping networks, identifying machines and discovering vulnerabilities – all intended to secure computing assets. Popular tools like Nmap [5] and ENUM are in fact the direct result of ideas, scripts and programs originally developed by hackers.

Nmap is an open source utility for network exploration and security auditing [5,8]. It transmits IP packets in carefully designed sequences to identify network hosts, open ports, services, operating systems and versions, packet filters, and firewalls, among other information. Nmap, however, has two shortcomings. First, Nmap was not developed to uniquely identify single machines; rather, it offers a broad view of multiple machines to locate common attributes. Second,

Nmap is not appropriate for cyber investigations because it does not ensure the accuracy and integrity of the data it acquires. Indeed, this limitation is true for all the tools discussed in this section.

ENUM, along with the more recent ShareScan and Netcat tools, can enumerate NetBIOS and Samba information, including network shares, user accounts and password policies. The Unix `finger` command similarly provides information about network/host users, including full name, default shell and login times.

Two other popular tools are Nessus [16] and LANGuard [10]. Nessus uses a set of plug-ins to test for the presence of various services and their vulnerabilities. It can distinguish between an SMTP server running on port 25 and port 3005; however, it uses a brute force approach that requires frequent updates. The LANGuard scanner can identify operating systems and obtain operating system specific information. It also enumerates NetBIOS groups on hosts running Microsoft operating systems and SNMP properties on network printers.

Although current network scanning tools gather useful information about target machines, no single tool provides all the desired capabilities and ensures information integrity, which is required for remote fingerprinting. What is needed is a comprehensive, reliable tool for remote machine fingerprinting that will meet the rigorous standards of evidence.

3. Remote Fingerprinting System

The remote fingerprinting system refines existing network scanning techniques to acquire a fingerprint of a target machine over the Internet. All machine-specific information constituting a fingerprint is available without authentication or is available anonymously, and can be acquired by any machine connected to the Internet. No intrusion into personal data, including files and their contents, is attempted. When a machine connects to the Internet, it uses various protocols (TCP, UDP, etc.) and ports (1-65535) and applications running on these ports (`ftp` 21, `telnet` 23, etc.). This information and data gathered from the network stack and active services are used to produce a fingerprint. All the information gleaned is time-stamped, cryptographically sealed and stored in an evidence container (e.g., hard disk).

Network enumeration is the most intrusive technique used by the fingerprinter, as it potentially provides a list of files and computer settings. Note, however, that an enumeration only yields the list of resources that the user has chosen to share with other computers. Storing a hash value of the resource list instead of the list itself can mitigate the intrusiveness of this technique; fingerprint comparison would then check the stored hash value.

Remote machine fingerprinting has three components: open port identification, operating system detection and service analysis (Figure 2). Service

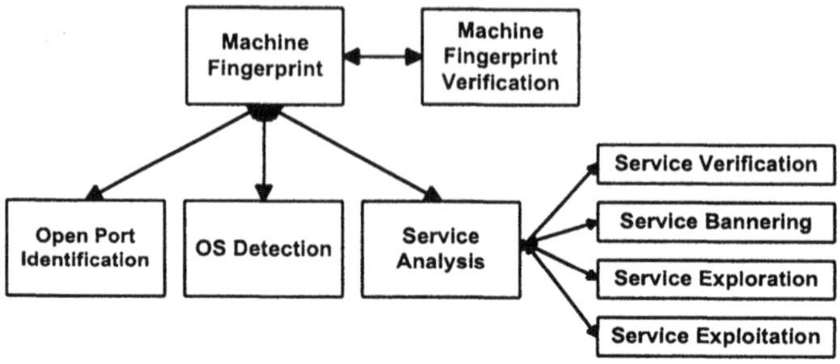

Figure 2. Machine fingerprint components.

analysis has four subcomponents: service verification, service bannering, service exploration and service exploitation. One or more of these components can constitute a machine fingerprint. Obviously, incorporating more components produces a better (more detailed) fingerprint.

3.1. Open Port Identification

Open ports are identified using a specially designed Java-based host port mapping tool. The list of open ports provides a foundation for operating system detection and service analysis.

The port mapping tool uses the full connect and SYN stealth techniques to identify open ports [8]. The full connect technique attempts to open a Java socket with the remote port, which requires a full TCP handshake. The SYN stealth technique transmits the initial SYN packet in the TCP handshake and waits for a SYN-ACK packet. SYN scanning requires fewer packets (it is faster) and can go undetected (half-open connections are less likely to be logged than full TCP connections). The port mapper efficiently scans all 65,535 ports, alert to the fact that users "hide" certain services in uncommon port ranges to avoid detection.

3.2. Operating System Detection

The TCP stack of a target machine is probed by transmitting a set of seven TCP packets. The responses are analyzed to infer operating system (OS) information.

TCP packets transmitted to the target machine vary slightly in their control bits and whether they are sent to open or closed ports [9,15]. The responses to these packets are dependent upon the TCP stack of the target machine, and help identify the OS, often down to version and/or kernel build.

TCP/IP stack analysis relies on two closely related facts. First, network protocol specifications are evolutionary in nature. For example, explicit congestion notification (ECN) proposed in RFC 3168, gives routers the ability to notify

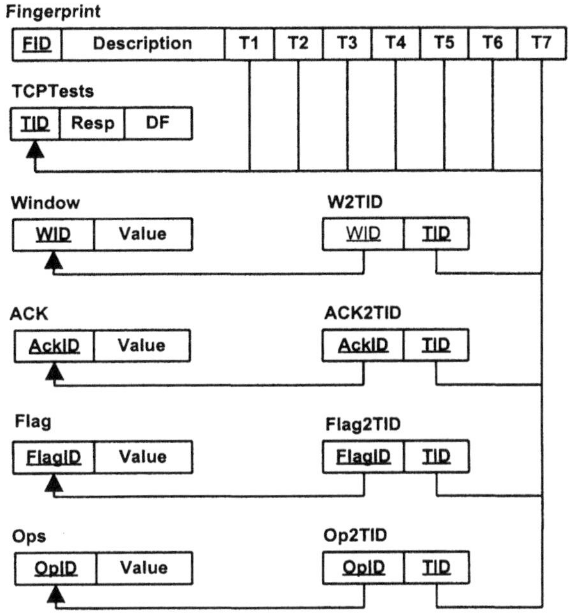

Figure 3. Operating system identification.

sending and receiving parties of persistent network congestion using certain IP and TCP header fields [18]. ECN is now filtering its way into network OSs, and is being used by some (not all) implementations. Checking the ECN field distinguishes OSs that use it from those that do not. Second, vendors often view protocol standards as recommendations, resulting in implementation variations. One example is the use of reserved space within packets, where some vendors evidently interpret reserved to mean "saved for vendor use." Such variations help differentiate between OS specific network protocol implementations.

Figure 3 displays the database schema used in OS detection. The main table (Fingerprint) links each of the individual tests into a single fingerprint, which identifies the OS based on the test results. The other nine tables are used to store the defining attributes of a response packet, like Window Size and TCP control bits. These tables are linked using the test identifier (TID) attribute, where each TID represents a unique response received from the probe packets. This organization improves efficiency because many responses are identical according to our criteria.

3.3. Service Analysis

Service-related information is acquired by service analysis, which includes service verification, service bannering, service exploration and service exploitation, and uses the list of open ports provided by the port mapping tool as its starting point. Analyzing the network services offered by the target machine provides information which differentiates the machine and is an important component of its fingerprint.

Service verification confirms the identity of services, regardless of their port numbers. This guards against cases where users mask possibly malicious intentions by hiding common services on uncommon ports. Verification is implemented using finite state machines. By focusing on RFC and vendor (e.g., ssh.com) specifications, service verification is only a matter of identifying and encoding core commands and responses. Figure 4 presents the finite state machine used for POP3 service verification.

Service banners provide a wealth of information about a machine and its users [9]. Default banners for `telnet` and `ftp` may identify the operating system down to its kernel build. Personalized banners, e.g., call signs and computer names, provide valuable identifying information. The service bannering utility connects to the available services and captures all the information offered before authentication, e.g., identifiers, greetings and prompts.

The service enumeration utility lists anonymously available data provided by a service or services. The data may include files represented in tree form from an `http` server or an `ftp` service, usernames, drives and directories on a machine, SMTP server settings, operating system password policies, routing tables, printer trays and paper types.

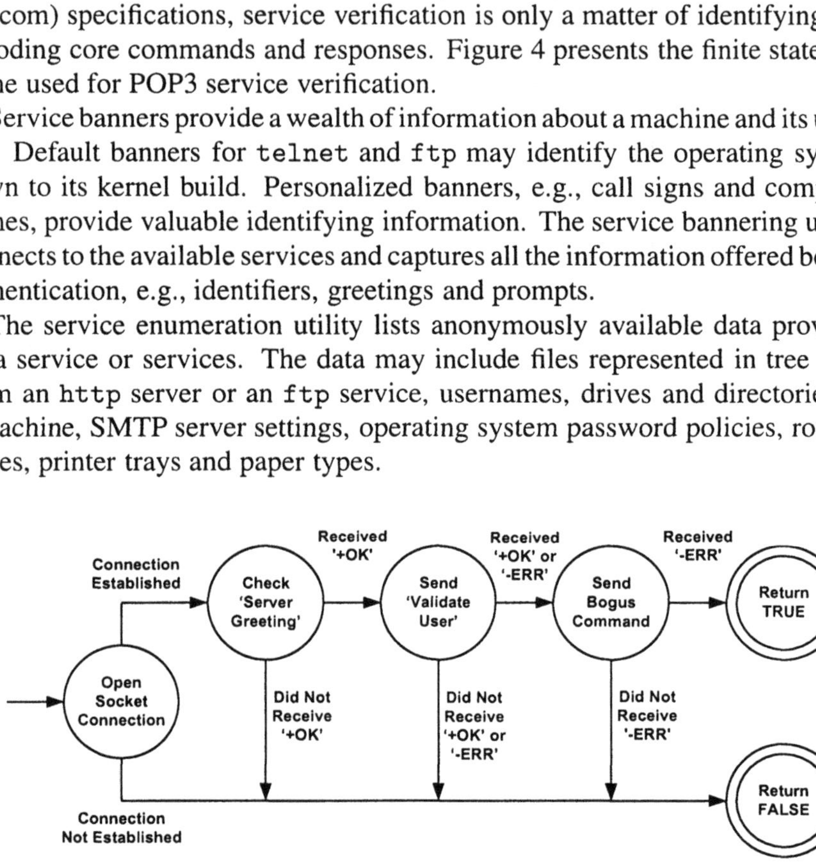

Figure 4. POP3 service verification.

Service exploitation has limited (if any) investigative applications as it potentially involves illegal activity. This technique works by identifying and exploiting vulnerabilities to obtain private information.

3.4. Fingerprinting Results

Identifying specific machines in networks driven by standardization and interoperability is difficult. However, malicious individuals often mask their identities and activities, e.g., by hiding chat room or file sharing services on uncommon ports, by modifying service banners, or by employing network security

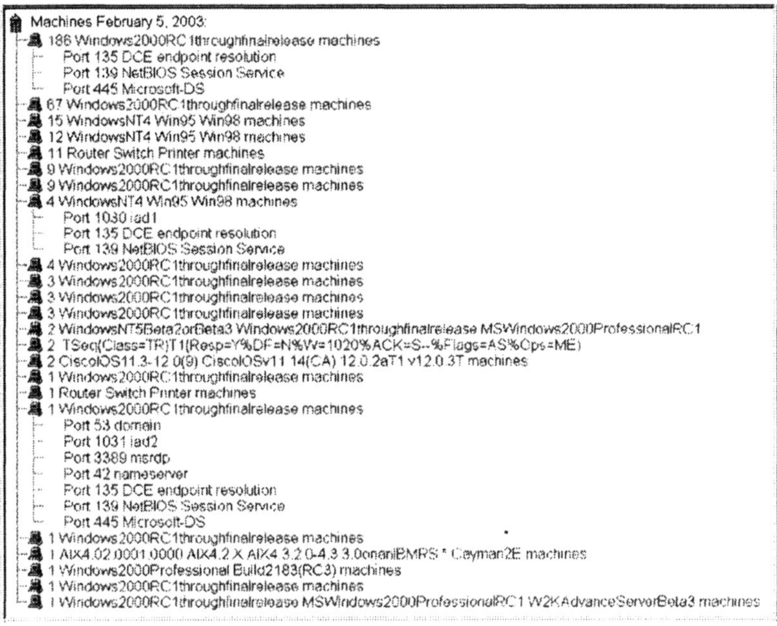

Figure 5. Fingerprint results for a production network.

mechanisms. The remote fingerprinter thrives on the uniqueness introduced by such actions.

Figure 5 summarizes the results of remote fingerprinting performed on a production network of 340 computers. Only two components – commonly used (2,048) open ports and operating system – are considered. More than 50% of the machines have identical profiles based on the two fingerprint components. Even so, eight machines are uniquely identified, and many more are grouped with three or fewer other machines with the same fingerprint. This is significant because computers used in illegal activities would likely fall in one of the smaller fingerprint groups or be uniquely identified. Indeed, when additional identifying components are used, the uniqueness of fingerprints is even greater.

4. Investigative Scenarios

The fingerprinting technique can be used to good effect in a variety of investigations. Two common scenarios, one related to investigating pedophiles and the other involving an illegal website, are discussed.

Children are increasingly exposed to pedophiles on the Internet [6,11]. In the past, pedophiles would prey on children at school playgrounds, parks and neighborhoods; now they target children from the privacy of their own homes. According to one survey [13], 19% of young people between the ages of ten and seventeen who used the Internet at least once a month received unwanted sexual solicitations.

Pedophiles frequently use Internet chat rooms to reach potential victims [6,17]. The chat room conversations and e-mail exchanges may escalate to meetings intended to consummate the online relationships. Sometimes these meetings progress beyond sexual abuse and rape, including kidnapping and murder [13].

One strategy used by law enforcement to apprehend online pedophiles is illustrated in Figure 6. An undercover detective posing as a minor communicates with a suspect in an Internet chat room. The detective builds a relationship with the suspect through repeated chat room communications and via direct messages (e.g., e-mail or instant messages). During the communications, the detective arranges a liaison with the suspect. Often, the detective asks the suspect to bring something (e.g., stuffed animals, alcoholic beverages or sexual paraphernalia). The item requested in Figure 6 is Duff Beer. When the suspect is apprehended at the rendezvous point with the requested items, there is evidence that the suspect was the individual who communicated with the undercover detective in the chat room.

The evidentiary strategy can be viewed as completing the triangle in Figure 6. First, all chat room conversations and direct messages, including the request to bring Duff Beer, must be captured and sealed as evidence. This evidence is acquired using chat room logging tools, monitoring software or by simply videotaping over the detective's shoulder [12,17]. Then, it is necessary to tie the suspect's computer (after it has been seized) to the sealed chat room transcripts (side 1 in Figure 6). Next, the suspect must be linked to the seized computer (side 2).

The remote fingerprinter and a simple chat room monitoring tool help complete sides 1 and 2 of the evidence triangle. The chat room monitor logs conversations and direct messages, and the remote fingerprinter links the suspect's machine to the recorded transcripts. Matching the remotely acquired fingerprint with that of the seized computer establishes that the suspect's computer was used for the online communications. Side 3 of the triangle is established when the suspect is arrested at the meeting place with the items (e.g., Duff Beer) that were specifically requested by the detective in the logged communications.

Another potential application of remote fingerprintering involves acquiring information about a website host, e.g., one offering child pornography or one belonging to a suspected terrorist group. In such a case, the fingerprinter can be used to identify the web server for when it is eventually seized.

Remote fingerprinting has many other applications. In all cases, it is important that the fingerprint be sealed (e.g., using MD5 hashing) like other electronic evidence [20]. Moreover, chain-of-custody and evidence storage standards must be guaranteed [20,22,23].

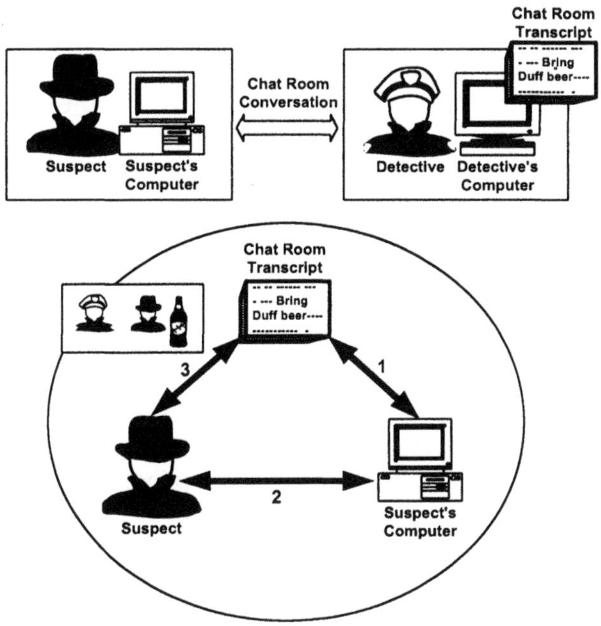

Figure 6. Pedophile investigation.

5. Legal Issues

No evidence acquisition technique or tool should be employed without examining the legal implications. This section considers the admissibility of remote fingerprinting evidence and the legality of its use by law enforcement.

5.1. Admissibility of Evidence

Admissibility refers to the principles determining whether or not particular items of evidence may be admitted into a court of law [22]. In the United States, Supreme Court decisions and the Federal Rules of Evidence (F.R.E.) define the criteria for the admissibility of novel scientific evidence [20,22].

In the landmark 1993 judgment, Daubert v. Merrell Dow Pharmaceuticals, the Supreme Court cast upon trial judges the duty to act as gatekeepers charged with preventing junk science from entering the courtroom [14]. To assist judges in this role, the decision specified four factors: testing, peer review, error rates and acceptability in the relevant scientific community. The Daubert case emphasized that a judge's inquiry is a flexible one, and its focus must be solely on principles and methodology, not on the conclusions that they generate. Although other cases have recognized that not all four Daubert factors apply to every type of expert testimony (see, e.g., Kumho Tire Co. v. Carmichael; Tyus

v. Urban Search Management), the factors can be helpful in estimating the admissibility of evidence produced by remote fingerprinting [14].

It is also necessary to consider issues related to F.R.E. requirements. In Rule 702, the requirements state: "If scientific, technical or other specialized knowledge will assist the trier of fact to understand the evidence or to determine a fact in issue, a witness qualified as an expert by knowledge, skill, experience, training, or education, may testify thereto in the form of an opinion or otherwise, if (1) the testimony is based upon sufficient facts or data, (2) the testimony is the product of reliable principles and methods, and (3) the witness has applied the principles and methods reliably to the facts of the case" [14].

Thus, the reliability of scientific evidence is supreme in determining its admissibility. This rule guides the use of DNA evidence in federal courts [14]. For example, since 1987 - when DNA evidence was first used in a criminal case - the evidence has generally been admitted in federal courts when it can be verified that DNA testing has been reliably applied. In the majority of cases in which DNA evidence has not been admitted, the reasons were that scientific techniques were not applied properly and/or chain-of-custody standards were not met.

Remote fingerprinting is obviously not as mature as human fingerprinting or DNA testing. As with these techniques, the technology should advance with time to become sufficiently reliable. But unlike human fingerprinting and DNA testing, remote fingerprinting may not provide a "unique" identification. Rather, we believe that a remote fingerprint – properly acquired and preserved – would constitute one more indication that the seized machine was used in the illegal activity.

5.2. Federal Law

If law enforcement fails to respect the privacy of individuals in its investigations, evidence will be suppressed and criminals will escape prosecution [3,20]. More importantly, the citizenry's confidence in government will be eroded.

U.S. federal law governing law enforcement's acquisition of electronic evidence in criminal investigations has two primary sources: the Fourth Amendment to the U.S. Constitution, and the statutory privacy laws in the Wiretap Statute (18 U.S.C. Sections 2510-22), the Pen/Trap Statute (18 U.S.C. Sections 3121-27) and the Electronic Communications Privacy Act (ECPA) of 1986 (18 U.S.C. Sections 2701-2712) [19,22]. The ECPA regulates how the government can obtain stored account information from network service providers; remote fingerprinting does not involve such information, therefore the ECPA is not relevant to this discussion.

5.2.1 The Fourth Amendment. The Fourth Amendment limits the ability of government agents to search and seize evidence without a warrant. We consider the constitutional limits on warrantless searches in cases involving computers. According to the Supreme Court, a warrantless search does not violate the Fourth Amendment if: (i) the government's conduct does not violate a person's "reasonable expectation of privacy," or (ii) the search falls within an established exception to the warrant requirement [4,22,23].

The most relevant exception to the warrant requirement pertaining to remote fingerprinting is plain view. To rely on this exception, "the agent must be in a lawful position to observe and access the evidence, and its incriminating character must be immediately apparent" [22]. The exception merely permits an agent to seize evidence that he/she is authorized to view under the Fourth Amendment.

The Fourth Amendment also restricts the government's use of innovative technology to obtain information about a target [4,22]. In Katz v. United States, the Supreme Court ruled that a search is constitutional if it does not violate a person's "reasonable" or "legitimate" expectation of privacy [22]. Therefore, in the case of remote fingerprinting, it is important to assess whether or not an individual with a computer connected to the Internet has a reasonable expectation of privacy regarding his/her services and bannering information.

Kyllo v. United States is also relevant [22]. In this case, the Supreme Court held that the warrantless use of a thermal imager to reveal the relative amounts of heat released from the various rooms of a suspect's home was a search that violated the Fourth Amendment. In particular, the Court held that where law enforcement "uses a device that is not in general public use, to explore details of the home that would previously have been unknowable without a physical intrusion, the surveillance is a 'search' and is presumptively unreasonable without a warrant." Use by the government of innovative technology, such as remote fingerprinting, which is not in general use to obtain information from a suspect's computer may implicate the Kyllo ruling. This suggests that law enforcement may not employ remote fingerprinting without a warrant.

The Supreme Court, however, restricted its holding in the Kyllo case to the use of technology to reveal information about "the interior of the home" [22]. Therefore, it can be argued that the Kyllo case would not apply to the use of the remote fingerprinter because the information gathered would metaphorically lie outside the home, within the public domain of the Internet.

5.2.2 The Wiretap and Pen/Trap Statutes. The Wiretap Statute (18 U.S.C. Sections 2510-2522), generally known as "Title III," is the most important federal statute governing real-time electronic surveillance in federal criminal investigations [21,22]. Title III broadly prohibits the "interception" of oral communications, wire communications and electronic communications. Failure to comply with this statute may result in civil and criminal liability, and in the suppression of evidence. However, Title III contains an exception permitting law enforcement officers to intercept communications in which they are a party to the communication. This "under color of law" exception makes Title III a relative non-issue for remote fingerprinting [22].

The Pen/Trap Statute (18 U.S.C. Sections 3121-3127) governs the use of pen registers and trap and trace devices to collect address information and other non-content information for wire and electronic communications [22]. Because law enforcement officers are legally permitted to access the entire communication by the "under color of law" exception to Title III when they are party to the communication, it is reasonable to assume that they would be permitted to intercept the address information as well. Therefore, the Pen/Trap Statute would not pose a barrier to law enforcement officers using the remote fingerprinter.

5.3. State Law

In addition to the applicable federal statutes, state law must also be considered. Although the "under color of law" exception to Title III may permit law enforcement officers to intercept communications in which they are one of the parties to the communication, not all state wiretap laws have this same exception. Indeed, some state wiretap laws require the consent of all parties to a communication. Because state law varies considerably in this regard, we recommend that law enforcement officers be familiar with the particular state laws in effect where an investigation takes place, aware that remote fingerprinting may require a warrant.

6. Conclusions

As the scope and magnitude of cyber crime increase and the specter of cyber terrorism rears its head, it is imperative to design sophisticated forensic tools for acquiring evidence that will help identify, apprehend and prosecute suspects. Remote fingerprinting is a novel technique for identifying computers on the Internet. The machine fingerprint, which includes detailed information about the operating system, banners, enumerations and services, may not provide a "definitive" identifier like a human fingerprint or DNA sample. Still, a remote machine fingerprint, legally acquired and properly preserved, is one more objective indication that a seized computer was used in a crime.

References

[1] M. Andress. Network scanners pinpoint problems. *Network World*, February 2, 2002.

[2] B. Bell. Secrets and lies: News media and law enforcement use of deception as an investigative tool. *University of Pittsburgh Law Review*, 60:745-837, 1999.

[3] K. Connolly. *Law of Internet Security and Privacy*. Aspen, New York, 2003.

[4] M. Elmore. Big brother where art thou? Electronic surveillance and the Internet: Carving away Fourth Amendment privacy protections. *Texas Tech Law Review*, 32:1053-1083, 2001.

[5] R. Farrow. System fingerprinting with Nmap. *Network Magazine*, November 5, 2000.

[6] Federal Bureau of Investigation. *A Parent's Guide to Internet Safety*. www.fbi.gov, 2002.

[7] J. Forristal and G. Shipley. Vulnerability assessment scanners. *Network Computing*, January 8, 2001.

[8] Fyodor. The art of port scanning. www.insecure.org, 1997.

[9] Fyodor. Remote operating system detection via TCP/IP stack fingerprinting. www.insecure.org, 2002.

[10] GFI Software. LANGuard Network Security Scanner. www.gfi.com.

[11] J. Leonard and M. Morin. Stalking the web predator. *Los Angeles Times*, January 17, 2002.

[12] A. Meehan, *et al.* Packet sniffing for automated chat room monitoring and evidence preservation. *Proceedings of the 2001 Workshop on Information Assurance and Security*, 285-288, 2001.

[13] K. Mitchell, D. Finkelhor and J. Wolak. Risk factors for and impact of online sexual solicitation of youth. *Journal of the American Medical Association*, 285(23):3011-3014, June 20, 2001.

[14] A. Moenssens, editor. Amendments to the Federal Rules of Evidence. www.forensic-evidence.com, 2003.

[15] J. Nazario. Passive system fingerprinting using network client applications. Crimelabs Security Group. www.crimelabs.net, January 19, 2001.

[16] Nessus. Documentation. www.nessus.org.

[17] J. Novotny, *et al.* Evidence acquisition tools for cyber sex crimes investigations, *Proceedings of the SPIE Conference on Sensors and C3I Technologies for Homeland Defense and Law Enforcement*, 4708:53-60, 2002.

[18] K. Ramakrishnan, S. Floyd and D. Black. The addition of explicit congestion notification (ECN) to IP. RFC 3168, September 2001.

[19] E. Sinrod, *et al.* Cyber-crimes: A practical approach to the application of federal computer crime laws. *Santa Clara Computer and High Technology Law Journal*, 16:177-232, 2000.

[20] P. Stephenson. *Investigating Computer-Related Crime*. CRC Press, Boca Raton, Florida, 1999.

[21] R. Strang. Recognizing and meeting Title III concerns in computer investigations. *United States Attorneys' Bulletin*, 49(2):8-13, 2001.

[22] U.S. Department of Justice. *Searching and Seizing Computers and Obtaining Electronic Evidence in Criminal Investigations*. www.cybercrime.gov, 2002.

[23] R. Winick. Searches and seizures of computers and computer data. *Harvard Journal of Law & Technology*, 8:75-128, 1994.

IMPROVING DAMAGE ASSESSMENT EFFICACY IN CASE OF FREQUENT ATTACKS ON DATABASES

Prahalad Ragothaman and Brajendra Panda
Department of Computer Science and Computer Enginering, University of Arkansas, Arkansas, USA

Abstract: *A database log is the primary resource for damage assessment and recovery after an electronic attack. The log is a sequential file stored in the secondary storage and it can grow to humongous proportions in course of time. Disk I/O speed dictates how fast damage assessment and recovery can be done. To make the process of damage assessment and recovery more efficient, segmenting the log based on different criteria has been proposed before. But the trade off is that, either segmenting the log involves a lot of computation or damage assessment is a complicated process. In this research we propose to strike a balance. We propose a hybrid log segmentation method that will reduce the time taken to perform damage assessment while still segmenting the log fast enough so that no intricate computation is necessary. While performing damage assessment, we re-segment the log based on transaction dependency. Thus during repeated damage assessment procedures, we create new segments with dependent transactions in them so that the process of damage assessment becomes faster when there are repeated attacks on the system.*

Key words: Database log, damage assessment, log segmentation, transaction dependency

1. Introduction

Ever since the dawn of the Internet, there have been reports of unauthorized entry into computer systems and rendering them inconsistent and unstable. There are many methods to protect a system from such attacks but savvy hackers always find newer ways to break into a system and use it maliciously. Several intrusion detection mechanisms have also been developed. But those methods do not detect an intrusion as soon as it occurs. This results in the damage caused by the malicious user to spread throughout the system in an exponential manner. In course of time, the system may become so unstable that we have to shut the entire system down in order to bring it back to a consistent state. This is highly unacceptable in time critical database systems where valid users must have access to data at every, and all times. Hence the next best solution to the problem would be to design fast and efficient damage assessment and recovery algorithms to be used during the post intrusion detection scenario.

Traditional logging mechanisms as described in [2], [5], and [3], record only the "write" operations of a transaction. A traditional log does not suffice to recover a database from an attack, as it does not contain the "read" operations of the transaction. Read operations are essential to establish dependences among transactions and data items.

To expedite the process of damage assessment and recovery after an attack, the log can be segmented based on certain criteria. That way, when an attack is detected, we can skip large portions of the log, which, we are sure, does not contain malicious or affected transactions.

Several log segmentation approaches have been devised. Notable among them are the transaction dependency based approach [8], the data dependency based approach [10], and segmenting based on certain criteria like fixed number of transactions, time window for transactions to commit and space for committed transactions [11]. In this research, we propose to devise a hybrid method of log segmentation that uses the approaches presented in [8] and [11] so that damage assessment and hence recovery can be expedited.

The rest of the paper is organized as follows. In section 2, the prior work and the motivation behind this research are described. In section 3, description of log re-segmentation with accompanying cases and algorithms are presented. In section 4, the damage assessment model using the re-segmented log is described. Section 5 presents the simulation results. Section 6 concludes the paper.

2. Prior Work and Motivation

In [4], the researchers have proposed several guidelines for trusted recovery. Amman et al. [1] followed a transaction dependency approach that uses relationships among transactions to identify and repair damage in the database. Panda and Giordano [9] adopted a data dependency approach to recover from malicious attacks. Reordering transactions for efficient recovery has been discussed by Liu et al. [6]. A distributed recovery approach has been offered by Liu and Hao in [7]. But all of these approaches scan a sequential log file, which is very huge. Log segmentation techniques using transaction dependency and data dependency were presented in [8] and [10] respectively. These methods segment the log file in such a way that all dependent transactions (or dependent data-items in the case of data dependency segmentation) are stored in one segment. By doing so, it can be made sure that we do not have to scan a large portion of the log when an attack is detected.

But a major drawback in these approaches is that they use valuable system resources to perform intricate computation to determine dependences among transactions or data-items while the execution of the transactions is still on. Also, there is a chance of a segment growing too large because too many transactions or data-items may be dependent on one another. Different segments have a chance of merging into one segment and ultimately it could be one huge segment, as big as the log itself. This defeats the purpose of log segmentation. In [11] researchers have presented methods of segmenting the log based on number of transactions, a time window for transactions to commit and fixed space for committed transactions. In the first method, a segment is formed after a fixed number of transactions commit. In the second approach, there is a time window provided for transactions to commit. All transactions that committed in that time frame form one segment. In the third method, the space for a segment remains fixed. All committed transactions that fit into that segment are stored. Transactions are not allowed to span from one segment to another. Thus the size of each segment is kept under control and running the risk of a segment growing too big is avoided in all these three approaches. Also, each of these methods uses very little computation while segmenting the log. However, a significant amount of computation has to be done to determine the dependences among the segments during damage assessment. In scenarios where attacks are quite frequent, this method may not yield the fastest solution to recover a database.

In this research, we present a hybrid method of log segmentation that uses the techniques provided in [11] and [8]. We propose to further segment a log already segmented based on any of the three approaches described in [11] based on transaction dependency approach as described in [8]. We shall do the re-segmentation while assessing damage during subsequent attacks on the database. By doing so, we intend to achieve a significant improvement in terms of time required during damage assessment while still keeping the log segmentation algorithm simple enough so that the time for execution of transactions is not hindered.

3. Hybrid Log Segmentation

Our model is based on the following assumptions: (a) Transaction operations are scheduled in accordance with the rigorous two-phase locking protocol as defined in [3], (b) Read operations are also recorded in the log file, (c) Intrusion is detected using one of the intrusion detection techniques and the *id* of the attacking transaction is available, (d) The log is never purged, and (e) Blind writes are not allowed. Below, a list of definitions is presented that are helpful in understanding the research and the algorithms.

Definition 1: Transaction T_j is said to be dependent on transaction T_i if T_j read one or more data items that was previously written by the committed transaction T_i.

Definition 2: A *tuft* is a group of transactions that adheres to any one of the three models presented in [11]. The transactions in a *tuft* are stored in the chronological order in which they committed. It is represented as Γ_i where 'i' denotes the *tuft* number.

Definition 3: A *read_items* list is a list of all the data items that were read by all the transactions in a segment.

Definition 4: A *write_items* list is a list of all the data items that were written by all the transactions in a segment.

Definition 5: A *tuft_table* is a table that contains the transaction number and the tuft in which it is present.

Definition 6: An *affected_items* list contains all the data items that were written either by a malicious or an affected transaction.

Definition 7: A transaction is said to be affected if it updates the value of a data item using the value of another data item that was previously written by either a malicious or another affected transaction.

Definition 8: A "size-controlled-segment" is a segment that was created using one of the three approaches described in [11]. In other words, we choose to call a *tuft* as a size-controlled-segment.

Definition 9: A "size-un-controlled-segment" is a segment that was created using transaction dependency.

The log segmented based on any of the three approaches described in [11] can be pictorially represented as shown in Figure 1.

Figure 1: Log Segments before Re-segmentation

Re-segmenting the log begins after an attack is detected and the attacking transaction is available. The process is done during the damage assessment phase. Let us assume that an attack was detected in Γ_2. It has been shown that scanning of transactions in Γ_1 is unnecessary because none of the transactions in Γ_1 read a data item written by any of the transactions present in Γ_2. Rigorous two-phase locking protocol ensures this. The attacking transaction in Γ_2 is determined using the *tuft_table*. All transactions in all the segments until the last affected segment, i.e. the segment that has the last affected transaction in it, are scanned. A new segment is started with the first malicious transaction in it. To determine the dependency among transactions, we intersect the "write" set of the malicious transaction with the read set of the transaction to be scanned. There are two cases, as discussed below, depending upon the results of the intersection.

3.1 The result is not a null set

The transaction is affected. That particular transaction is stored in the newly formed segment that contains the malicious transaction and other affected transactions. The data items that were written by the transaction are appended to the *affected_items* list. Thus all malicious and affected transactions will be present in one segment at the end of the damage assessment phase and all affected data items in the *affected_items* list.

3.2 The result is a null set

This means that the transaction did not read any affected data. The "read" and the "write" sets of the transaction are stored in a new *read_items* list and *write_items* list respectively. We can be sure that the transaction is not dependent on any other transaction in any of the other size-un-controlled segments that were formed. Hence a new segment is created and the operations of the transaction are stored in it.

During subsequent scanning of transactions, the "read" items of that transaction is intersected with all the *write_items* lists and *affected_items* list available to determine if there is a dependency between the transaction and the segments. By doing so, it is checked whether the transaction read a data item that was previously written by another transaction. If the result of all the intersections is a null set, it means that transaction is completely independent of all other transactions scanned so far. A new segment is created and the operations of that transaction are stored in it. Also, a new *read_items* list and a *write_items* list is started as in the previous case and the "read" set and the "write" set of the transaction are stored into the respective lists.

If on the other hand, the result of the intersection of the "read" set of the transaction with two or more *write_items* lists is not a null set, it means that the transaction is dependent upon two or more transactions that are present in two different segments. In such a case, those two segments are merged and the operations of the current transaction are stored in the merged segment. The *read_items* list and the *write_items* list are also merged and the "read" set and the "write" set of the transaction are stored into the appropriate lists.

If the transaction is dependent on only one of the segments that have been formed, it is added to the end of the segment upon which it is dependent. The "read" set and the "write" of the transaction are stored into the appropriate lists. Thus one or more size-un-controlled segments will be present in parallel between Γ_1 and the last affected segment. Each size-un-controlled segment will have its own *read_items* list and a *write_items* list. A pictorial representation of a re-segmented log is shown in Figure 2.

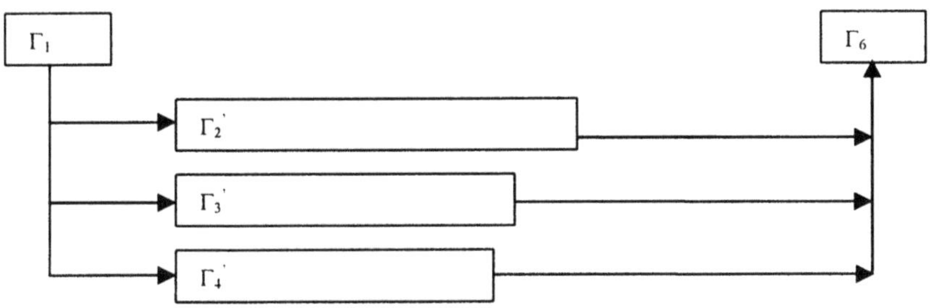

Figure 2: Log Segments after Re-Segmentation

Some segments may be larger or smaller than others depending on how many transactions are present in that segment. Each of the newly formed segments Γ_2', Γ_3', and Γ_4' will contain transactions that are dependent on one another. When an attack is detected, only the segment containing the malicious transaction has to be scanned since all affected transactions would be present in that segment alone. All other size-un-controlled segments can be safely avoided. We present an algorithm for log re-segmentation in the following section.

3.3 Algorithm for log re-segmentation during damage assessment

1. Determine the position of the attacking transaction using the *tuft_table*. Let us assume that the transaction, say T_i, is present in Γ_i.
2. Set *affected_items* = write_set(T_i); *read_items* = read_set(T_i).
3. Start new segment Γ_i'.
4. For each transaction, say T_j, that appears after the attacking transaction T_i, in Γ_i until the last transaction in the last affected *tuft*, say Γ_j, where j > i

    If (*affected_items* $\cap$ read_set(T_j) != ϕ)

Add T_j to Γ_i'; Add the write set of T_j to *affected_items*; Add read_set(T_j) to *read_items*.

Else

Intersect the write set of T_j with all available *read_items* list. If none are available, start a new size-un-controlled-segment, add the operations of T_j in the segment, start a new *read_items* list and a *write_items* list and add the read_set and write_set of T_j into the respective lists. Continue from step 3.

If the result of all the intersections is a null set

Start a new size-un-controlled-segment, say Γ_j', and add the operations of T_j.

Start a new *read_items* list and a *write_items* list and add the read set and the write set of T_j into the respective lists.

If the result of the intersection is not a null set with only one of the segments

Add the operations of T_j into that segment.

Update the appropriate *read_items* list and the *write_items* list.

If the result of the intersection is not a null set with more than one of the segments

Merge the segments into one single segment.

Add the operations of T_j into the merged segment.

Merge the appropriate *read_items* list and *write_items* list and add T_j's read and write items into the respective lists.

As it is evident in the above method, there is the risk of having to manage a segment that is too large because various segments might get merged to form one big segment. Eventually this segment might end up being as big as the log itself. In order to avoid this scenario, a new method to segment the log in a hybrid manner is proposed. In this approach, pointers are provided to link the information flow from one segment to another instead of merging the segments together. Thus after subsequent damage assessment on the database, the log can pictorially be represented as shown in Figure 3.

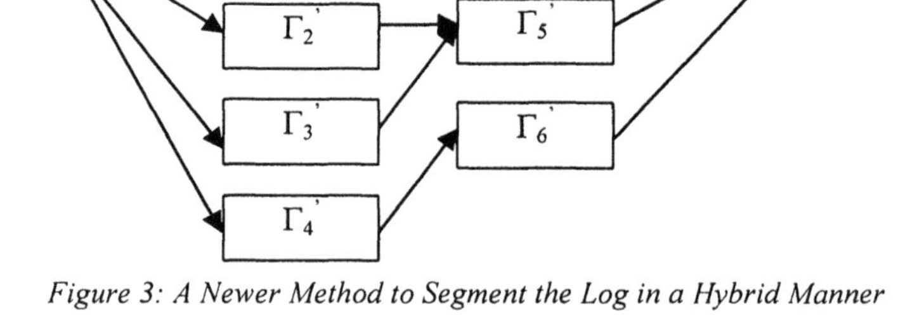

Figure 3: A Newer Method to Segment the Log in a Hybrid Manner

Let us consider the segments as shown in Figure 1. Assume that an attack was detected in Γ_2. As mentioned before, none of the transactions that are present in Γ_1 need to be scanned as they are not affected. Damage assessment is carried out as mentioned before and all the cases hold true here too. Let us assume that the first set of parallel segments are formed and they are named as Γ_2', Γ_3' and Γ_4'. During subsequent scanning of transactions from other size-controlled segments, it is assumed that a transaction read data items that were written by transactions from two different size-un-controlled segments making that transaction dependent on two different segments. From Figure 3, it is evident that a transaction present in Γ_5' read data items written by transactions in Γ_2' and Γ_3'. Thus pointers are established from these two segments to Γ_5' to show that there is an information flow from both Γ_2' and Γ_3' onto Γ_5'. Thus during subsequent damage assessment procedures, the pointers can be checked and the information flow can be obtained. An algorithm to segment the log using the new hybrid log segmentation approach is given below.

3.4 Algorithm for log re-segmentation using the new method of hybrid log segmentation

1. Determine the tuft, say Γ_i, where attacking transaction, say T_i, is present.
2. Set *affected_items* = write_set(T_i); *read_items* = read_set(T_i); Start new segment Γ_i'.
3. For each transaction, say T_j, that appears after the attacking transaction T_i, in Γ_i until the last transaction in the last affected *tuft*, say Γ_j, where j > i

    If (*affected_items* $\cap$ read_set(T_j) != ϕ)

        Add T_j to Γ_i'; Add the write set of T_j to *affected_items*; Add read_set(T_j) to *read_items*.

    Else

        Intersect the write set of T_j with all available *read_items* list.

        If none are available, start a new size-un-controlled-segment, add the operations of T_j in the segment, start a new *read_items* list and a *write_items* list and add the read_set and write_set of T_j into the respective lists. Continue from step 3.

            If the result of all the intersections is a null set

                Start a new size-un-controlled-segment, say Γ_j', and add the operations of T_j.

                Start a new *read_items* list and a *write_items* list and add the read set and the write set of T_j into the respective lists.

            If the result of the intersection is not a null set with only one of the segments

                Add the operations of T_j into that segment.

Update the appropriate *read_items* list and the *write_items* list.
If the result of the intersection is not a null set with more than one of the segments
Establish pointers between the two segments.
Retain the *read_items* list and *write_items* list as it is.

4. Damage Assessment Using the Re-Segmented Log File

There are two cases to consider during damage assessment process when an attack is detected after re-segmentation. They are explained based on the segments shown in Figure 3.

4.1 An attack is detected in Γ_1 or in any of the size-controlled segments that were ignored when damage assessment was done the first time

The operations of all the transactions from the point of attack in Γ_1 until the point where the size-un-controlled segments start are scanned. The "write" set of the first malicious transaction in Γ_1 is added to the *affected_items* list. The *affected_items* list is then intersected with the "read" set of transactions that appear after the malicious transaction in all the *tufts* until the size-un-controlled-segments start. The log gets re-segmented with all dependent transactions in one segment. Cases similar to those described in the previous section hold good here too. Thus new sets of parallel size-un-controlled segments are formed. Dependency between each of the newly formed size-un-controlled-segments and the existing size-un-controlled segments is then established. It has to be noted that the segments will not be merged as described in the previous section. Instead, pointers will be established to determine information flow. An algorithm to assess damage for the case discussed is given below.

4.1.1 Algorithm for damage assessment for the case described above

1. Let the first attacking transaction in Γ_1 be T_i. Add the write_set of T_i to the *affected_items* list. Start a new size-un-controlled-segment, say Γ_1' and add the operations of T_i in Γ_1'.
2. For every transaction that appears after T_i, say T_j, until the last transaction before the size-un-controlled-segment starts, do
   If (*affected_items* $\cap$ read_set(T_j) != ϕ)
      Add write_set(T_j) to *affected_items*; Add the operations of T_j to Γ_1'.
   Else

Intersect the read_set of T_j with all available *read_items* lists that were formed for the newly created size-un-controlled-segments.
If none are available, start a new size-un-controlled-segment and add the operations of T_j to that segment. Start new *read_items* list and *write_items* list and update them accordingly.
If the result of all the intersections is a null set
Start a new size-un-controlled-segment and add the operations of T_j.
Start a new *read_items* list and a *write_items* list and add the read set and the write set of T_j into the respective lists.
If the result of the intersection is not a null set with only one of the segments
Add the operations of T_j into that segment.
Update the appropriate *read_items* list and the *write_items* list.
If the result of the intersection is not a null set with more than one of the segments
Establish appropriate pointers between segments.
Record the "read" items and the "write" items in the appropriate lists.

4.2 An attack is detected in any of the size-un-controlled segments

In this case, all the size-controlled segments that appear prior to the segment in consideration and all other size-un-controlled-segments that were formed with the current segment can be safely ignored, as there would be definitely no dependency between those segments. Thus, the damage assessment process begins by scanning each transaction after the first malicious transaction in the current segment. This is followed checking every size-controlled-segment and size-un-controlled-segment that appears after the first scanned segment until the last affected segment in the log file. With the help of pointers from one segment to another, we can determine the information flow and thus know what segments need to be scanned after the current one. If there are pointers from a segment leading to two different segments, both the segments have to be scanned after the current segment is scanned. Similarly, if two different pointers from two different segments lead to one single segment, then that segment must be scanned twice while assessing damage. If the result is not a null set, it means that segment is affected and one or more transactions in that segment have read a data item that was previously written by a malicious or affected transaction. An algorithm for this case is presented below.

4.2.1 Algorithm for damage assessment for the case described above

1. Identify the size-un-controlled-segment where the malicious transaction is present. Let us assume it is Γ_i'. All other size-un-controlled-segments parallel to Γ_i' can be ignored. Identify the malicious transaction, say T_i, in Γ_i.
2. Append the write_set of T_i and all other transactions in the same segment to the *affected_items* list.
3. For each segment, say Γ_j, that appears after the current segment until the last affected segment, do

    If (*affected_items* $\cap$ *read_items*(Γ_j) != ϕ)

      If Γ_j is a size-un-controlled segment

        Merge Γ_i' and Γ_j.

        Merge the respective *read_items* list and *write_items* list.

        Append the *write_items* list to the *affected_items* list.

      If Γ_j is a size-controlled-segment then for each transaction, say T_k in Γ_j

        If (*affected_items* $\cap$ *read_items*(T_k) != ϕ)

          Append operations of T_k to Γ_i'.

          Append the read_set and write_set of T_k to appropriate *read_items* list and *write_items* list.

        Else

          Intersect the read_set of T_k with all available *write_items* lists of size-un-controlled-segments that were recently created.

          If the result of the all the intersections is a null set or if no size-un-controlled-segments were recently formed

            Create a new size-un-controlled segment with the operations of T_k in it.

            Start a new *read_items* list and a *write_items* list and add the read_set and write_set of T_k to the appropriate list.

          If the result of the intersection is not a null set with only one segment

            Append the operations of T_k and its read_set and write_set to the segment, the *read_items* list and *write_items* list respectively.

          If the result of the intersection is not a null set with more than one segment

            Establish pointers between the appropriate segments.

In the case when an attack is detected in any of the size-controlled-segments that appears after all the size-un-controlled segments, the scenario is similar to that described in section 3.

5. Simulation and Results

A "C" program was developed to simulate a database log file that conforms to the rigorous two-phase locking protocol. The log was segmented using the fixed number of transactions approach with 50 transactions in each tuft. The algorithms developed in this research were then implemented into a program and applied on the segmented log file. Table 1 shows some of the parameters used to draw the chart depicted in Figure 4.

Table 1: Values of Parameters for Chart Shown in Figure 4

Total number of transactions	500
Total number of data items	5000
Maximum data items accessed by a transaction	30

The values obtained under the "traditional approach" legend were determined by assuming an attacking transaction having transaction *id* 150, and then determining how many bytes of data are read from the log while performing damage assessment without having a segmented log. The "number" legend shows the number of bytes read from a log segmented based on the number of transactions and assuming an attacking transaction with transaction *id* 150 too. The third legend, which is "Hybrid 1", shows the number of bytes read from a log which was re-segmented based on the hybrid approach presented in this research. An attacker was assumed and damage assessment was done once and a log segmented based on the hybrid approach was obtained. With this log, and the same attacking transaction, the algorithm was implemented again but the log was not segmented as it is proposed in this research. The number of bytes read was determined. This process was carried out several times by changing the seed of the program thus obtaining a new log file. An average of all the runs was calculated and the chart was obtained.

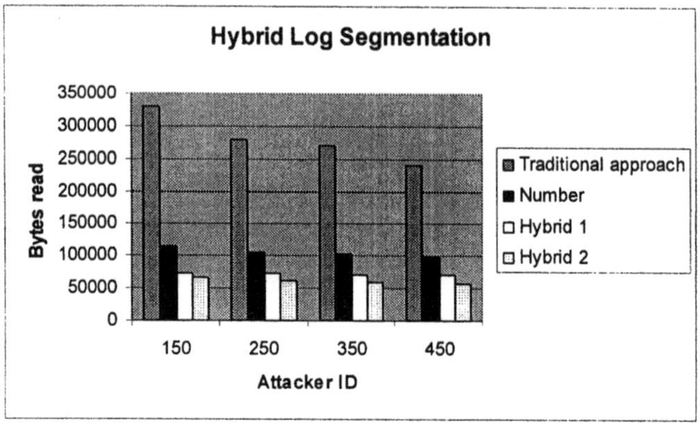

Figure 4: Comparison of Various Damage Assessment Procedures with the Hybrid Approach Using the Values Shown in Table 1

"Hybrid 2" shows the number of bytes read by the damage assessment program when it was implemented as proposed in this research. An attacking transaction with transaction *id* 50, was assumed to be stored in a log that is segmented based on the number of transactions. Damage assessment was performed and a log segmented based on the hybrid approach was obtained. With this log as reference, four different attacking transactions with ids 150, 250, 350 and 450 were assumed. Each time an attack was assumed, damage assessment was done and while doing so, the log was re-segmented based on transaction dependency using the pointer method that was discussed earlier. An average of all the runs was taken. Subsequently, attackers 150, 250, 350 and 450 were assumed and each time the same procedure was carried out. A different log was obtained each time by changing the seed in the program. Figure 5, shows a graph obtained using parameters given in Table 2.

Table 2: Values of Parameters for Chart Shown in Figure 5

Total number of transactions	500
Total number of data items	5000
Maximum data items accessed by a transaction	40

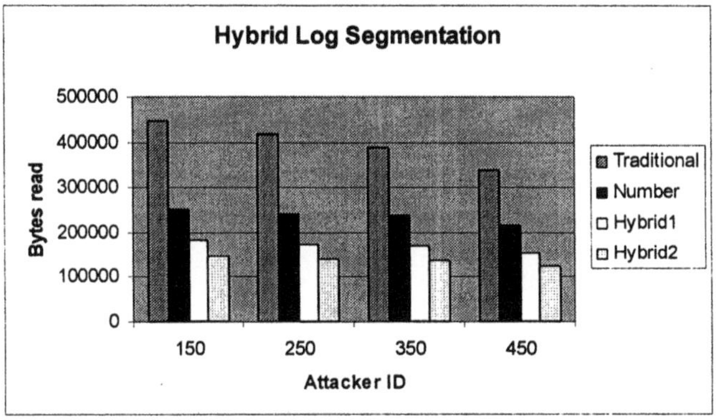

Figure 5: Comparison of Various Damage Assessment Procedures with the Hybrid Approach Using the Values Shown in Table 2

6. Conclusion

In this research, we have presented methods of re-segmenting an already segmented log based on transaction dependency for much faster damage assessment and hence recovery. We have overcome the shortcomings of the previous work where we observed that damage assessment would be more time consuming when compared to other log segmentation approaches like transaction dependency and data dependency while still being much faster had there been no segmentation at all. The model that we have presented here will work best in scenarios where attacks are more frequent. The segmented log will be re-segmented again based on transaction dependency thus limiting damage to only one segment. The process of re-segmenting is done while performing damage assessment and thus system resources will not be wasted. Different cases were observed while re-segmenting and assessing damage using the re-segmented log. Each case was discussed in detail and algorithms were provided to handle the cases separately. The algorithms were implemented in a simulation model and the results were discussed. It was also shown that our model performs better during damage assessment than when the log is not segmented at all or when the log is segmented using number of transactions. The model is also expected to perform similarly well on a log segmented based on either time or space.

Acknowledgement

This work has been supported in part by US AFOSR under grant F49620-01-10346. The authors are thankful to Dr. Robert. L. Herklotz for his support, which made this work possible.

References

[1] P. Amman, S. Jajodia, C. D. McCollum, and B. Blaustein, Surviving Information Warfare Attacks on Databases, *Proceedings of the 1997 IEEE Symposium on Security and Privacy*, May 1997.

[2] P.A. Bernstein, V. Hadzilacos, and N. Goodman, *Concurrency Control and Recovery in Database Systems*, Addison-Wesley, 1987.

[3] R. Elmasri and S. B. Navathe, *Fundamentals of Database Systems, Third Edition*, Addison-Wesley, 2000.

[4] S. Jajodia, C. D. McCollum, and P. Amman, Trusted Recovery, *Communications of the ACM*, 42(7), pp. 71-75, July 1999.

[5] H. F. Korth, A. Silberschatz, and S. Sudarshan, *Database System Concepts, Third Edition*, McGraw-Hill International Edition, 1997

[6] P. Liu, P. Ammann, and S. Jajodia, Rewriting Histories: Recovering from Malicious Transactions, *Distributed and Parallel Databases*, 8(1), pp. 7-40, January 2000.

[7] P. Liu and X. Hao, Efficient Damage Assessment and Repair in Resilient Distributed Database Systems, *Proceedings of the 15th Annual IFIP WG 11.3 Conference on Database and Application Security*, July 2001.

[8] B. Panda and S. Patnaik, A Recovery Model for Defensive Information Warfare, *Proceedings of the 9th International Conference on Management of Data*, p. 359-368, Hyderabad, India, December 1998.

[9] B. Panda and J. Giordano, Reconstructing the Database After Electronic Attacks, *Database Security XII: Status and Prospects*, S. Jajodia (editor), Kluwer Academic Publishers, 1999.

[10] B. Panda and S. Tripathy, Data Dependency Logging for Defensive Information Warfare, *Proceedings of the 2000 ACM Symposium on Applied Computing*, p. 361 – 365, Como, Italy, March 2000.

[11] P. Ragothaman, and B. Panda, Modeling and Analyzing Transaction Logging Protocols for Effective Damage Assessment, *Research Directions in Data and Applications Security*, E. Gudes and S. Shenoi (editors), Kluwer Academic Publishers, 2003.

II

INFORMATION ASSURANCE

DELIVERING SERVICES WITH INTEGRITY GUARANTEES IN SURVIVABLE DATABASE SYSTEMS*

Jianyong Zhang, Peng Liu
jzhang@cse.psu.edu, pliu@ist.psu.edu, Pennsylvania State University

Abstract Current database survivability technologies focus on maintaining data integrity and availability in the face of attacks. They are very limited in satisfying differentiated information assurance requirements of various database services under sustained attacks. This paper takes the first steps towards delivering database services with information assurance guarantees. In particular, (a) we introduce the concept of Quality of Integrity Assurance(QoIA) services; (b) we present a data integrity model which allows customers or applications to quantitatively specify their integrity requirements on the services that they want the database system to deliver; and (c) we present an algorithm that can enable a database system to deliver a set of QoIA services without violating the integrity requirements specified by the customers on the set of services. Our approach can deliver integrity guarantees to database services, though sometimes some availability loss could be caused. Our approach can be easily integrated into our Intrusion Tolerant Database System(ITDB).

Keywords: Database Security, Survivability, QoIA Services

1. Introduction

Despite authentication and access control, data contained in a database can be corrupted by authorized insiders due to operational mistakes or malicious intent, or by outside attackers who have assumed an insider's identity. Although substantial research is done on how to survive data corruption attacks [10, 3, 2, 8, 5, 7], with a focus on maintaining data integrity and availability in the face of attacks (i.e., *state-oriented* survivability), existing database survivability technologies are very limited in satisfying differentiated information assurance requirements of various database services under sustained attacks.

* This work is supported by NSF CCR-TC-0233324, and by the Defense Advanced Research Projects Agency (DARPA) and Air Force Research Laboratory, Air Force Material Command, USAF, under agreement number F20602-02-1-0216.

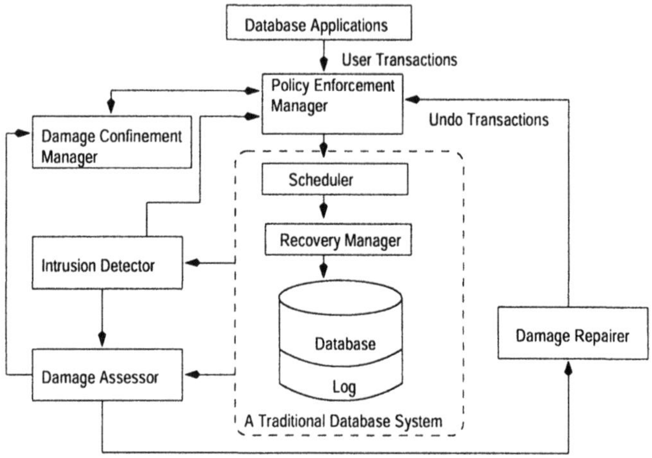

Figure 1. A Survivable Database System Architecture

We call database services associated with a specific level of information assurance requirements a *QoIA* (Quality of Information Assurance) service. We say a QoIA service is *delivered* if the assurance requirements of the service are satisfied when the service is executed.

The concept of QoIA services is closely related to the concept of database *trustworthiness* (or assurance), which has two important aspects: one is the extent to which we trust that the database *state* is valid and not corrupted. We call this aspect *state trustworthiness*, which is the focus of state-oriented survivability. The other is the extent to which we trust that the services delivered by the database system are not corrupted or distorted. We call this aspect *service trustworthiness*, which concerns the database system's capacity in delivering QoIA services. State trustworthiness represents the System Security Officer's(SSO's) view of the database's trustworthiness, while service trustworthiness represents the services' or the users' view of the database's trustworthiness. Service trustworthiness is very desirable because it directly addresses how users' businesses are affected by attacks. The goal of this paper is to develop a novel service-oriented survivability scheme that can deliver QoIA database services.

The need to deliver QoIA services can be further justified by a fundamental limitation of a survivable database system we have developed recently, called ITDB [9, 2, 8, 7]. The ITDB architecture is shown in Figure 1. When a malicious transaction B_i is detected, ITDB can locate every transaction affected by B_i (via damage assessment) and repair each corrupted data object without stopping the execution of new transactions on-the-fly. However, in many cases damage assessment and repair could be slower than damage spreading so the database can become even worse (in terms of integrity) during on-the-fly repair. The inability of damage assessment and repair in healing the database on-the-fly indicates the utility of multiphase damage confinement [7], which will first quickly confine every data object that could have been corrupted as soon as a malicious transaction B_i is identified during the confining phase, then try to unconfine the data objects that are actually not corrupted but mistakenly confined during several unconfining phases. To ensure that no new transaction will spread the damage (by B_i) after B_i is detected, ITDB does not allow any access to a confined data object.

A serious limitation of multiphase damage confinement is that substantial availability could be lost. Since the confining phase needs to instantly confine every data object corrupted by B_i, there is no time for the confining phase to precisely locate the set of corrupted data objects, so a lot of data objects can be mistakenly confined, especially when the detection latency is long. Thus during the repair time window from the time when B_i is identified to the time when every object corrupted by B_i is repaired, many database services which need to access a confined object could be denied or delayed.

Therefore, to provide more availability, it can be very beneficial to continue delivering services that need to access a confined data object during the repair time window. However, since a confined data object could have been corrupted, so when a service of a user Alice wants to access a confined object x, she takes the risk that the service could be distorted, and the SSO takes the risk that the service could spread the damage. It is not surprising that whether we should take the risks is dependent on whether we can satisfy the QoIA requirements of Alice on the service. If Alice's QoIA requirements can be satisfied, then Alice's risk is removed, and the SSO's risk can be compensated by the availability gain. Moreover, to minimize the SSO's risk, the SSO can extend the confinement control to cover the data objects updated by a QoIA service.

The discussion above indicates the need to deliver QoIA services. To develop a survivable database system that can deliver QoIA services, we must solve three fundamental problems: (a) How can we model data objects' integrity levels? How can we quantitatively assess or estimate data objects' integrity levels? (b) What is "QoIA"? How can we specify QoIA requirements? (c) How to deliver QoIA services? In this paper, we take the first steps towards solving these problems.

The rest of the paper is organized as follows. In Section 2, we present a data object integrity model that allows us to specify QoIA requirements. We propose a set of valuable strategies to satisfy users' QoIA requirements in Section 3. In Section 4, we present an algorithm to allow a survivable database system to deliver services with integrity guarantees. The related work is summarized in 5. We conclude the paper in Section 6.

2. Modeling QoIA Requirements in an ITDB System

In this section, we will formally model several aspects of quantitative QoIA specification. First, we will define some basic terms.

A database is a set of data objects (objects for short). It is denoted as: $DB = \{o_1, o_2, \ldots, o_n\}$. A database provides a set of services to its users. *A service* is a set of database transactions (transactions for short). It is denoted as: $S = \{T_1, T_2, \ldots, T_k\}$. In this paper, we will simplify the service definition, and assume that each service just includes one transaction. A user is a business customer who accesses the database and changes the database state through services.

2.1. The Model of Integrity of Data Objects

In ITDB, when attacks occur, some data objects will be corrupted. We define integrity in a way different from integrity constraints. In our paper, integrity means whether data objects are *good* or corrupted.

An Intuitive Model of Integrity of Data Objects. Intuitively, we can model the integrity of data objects as the following: a data object is associated with an integrity value, which is either of two values: G or B. G means that the data object is good, and B means that the data object is corrupted. The integrity variable $I(o,t)$ is defined for an object o at time t, and $I(o,t) \in \{G, B\}$. This variable can capture all information of one data object's integrity property.

However, in a real ITDB system, the previous model is not practical, because it assumes that the system knows which objects are corrupted and which are not at every point of time, but it is almost impossible for the ITDB system or a SSO to have that knowledge. We will analyze the survivability process from attack detection to damage repair to show why this is almost impossible.

Figure 2 shows the confinement timeline and the database state transition diagram when one malicious transaction occurs in an ITDB system. A malicious transaction B_i starts at time T_{mal_s}, and commits at time T_{mal_c}. At time T_{detect}, ITDB detects that this transaction is malicious, and starts the process of damage confinement, damage assessment and damage repair. This process continues until time T_{repair} when every object corrupted by B_i is repaired. We denote the period of time from T_{mal_s} until T_{detect} as the *detection time window*, and denote the period of time from T_{detect} until T_{repair} as the *repair time window*. In this process, the database has three distinct states. Before time T_{mal_s}, all data objects in the database are good, which is state $S1$. Within the detection time window, some data objects are corrupted by the malicious transaction. Since the malicious transaction is not identified by the ITDB system, ITDB still regards all the data objects as good objects. This is state $S2$. Within the repair time window, ITDB has detected the malicious transaction. Here we assume

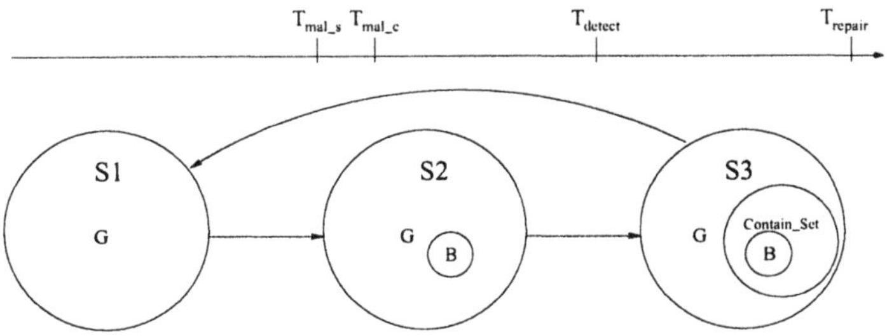

Figure 2. The Confinement Timeline and Data Objects State Transition Diagram for One Malicious Transaction

that ITDB first confines every object that is either in B_i's write set or written after time T_{mal_c} by other transactions, and then deny new transactions' access to the data objects in the *containment set* (In ITDB, after the confining phase is done, all the objects that are confined are conceptually held in this set). Then the database is in state $S3$. After time T_{repair}, the database transits back to state $S1$.

In state $S3$, there are four kinds of data objects from the ITDB's perspective: (1) Good data: the data objects outside of the containment set. (2) Unknown bad data: the data objects in the containment set that have been corrupted, but ITDB doesn't know that they are corrupted. (3) Unknown good data: the data objects in the containment set that have not been corrupted, and ITDB is not sure that they are good. (4) Known bad data: the data objects in the containment set that have been corrupted, and ITDB knows that they are corrupted.

From the above analysis, we can find that the above data integrity model is not practical, since the assumption is not true in a real system that the system knows each data object's exact integrity value in any time. Thus we need to give a more practical model to data object integrity.

In this paper, we focus on the model and specification aspects about how to access the confined data objects in state $S3$. How to deliver QoIA service in state $S2$ is out of the scope of this paper.

A Practical Model of Integrity of Data Objects. From the previous analysis, we find that ITDB has incomplete knowledge about integrity values of many data objects in the containment set within the repair time window. Because of this uncertainty, if users are provided services in this period, they may have to take risk of accessing corrupted data objects. Our idea is to use a probability based integrity model to quantitatively assess this risk.

In this model, each data object has also two integrity values, which are G or B. G means that the data object is good, and B means that the data objects is corrupted.

In order to assess the risk, we have to estimate which data objects are good in the containment set, since we can not get exact information about it. Assume that we have a good estimator to estimate probabilities that data objects in the containment set are good in the repair time window. (In the later section, we will have a more detailed discussion about how to do estimation.) We denote the probability that a data object o_i is good at time t as $G(o_i, t)$. We call $G(o_i, t)$ as o_i's *integrity level*, and $0 \leq G(o_i) \leq 1$. Integrity level of a data object o_i indicates that the frequency of o_i is good when a specific attack pattern occurs. For example, when a malicious transaction B_0 occurs, $G(o_i, t) = 90\%$, which means that if the bad transaction B_0 occurs 100 times, the times when o_i is good is 90.

For example, for an object o, when the database is in states $S1$ or $S2$, $G(o, t) = 100\%$. When a malicious transaction is detected at time T_{detect}, $G(o, t)$ is estimated as 40%. At time $T^o_{identify}$, o is identified as damaged, then $G(o, t) = 0\%$. In the time T^o_{repair}, o is repaired, so $G(o, t)$ is updated to 100% again. Thus o's integrity level is:

$$G(o,t) = \begin{cases} 100\% & t < T_{detect} \text{ or } T \geq T^o_{repair} \\ 40\% & T_{detect} \leq t < T^o_{identify} \\ 0\% & T^o_{identify} \leq t < T^o_{repair} \end{cases}$$

This model is more practical than that of the intuitive model, since in many cases We can use the (transaction) history to get good estimations about data object integrity levels, and moreover the SSO can use additional semantic information and workload characteristics to improve such estimations. Finally, it should be noted that the intuitive integrity level model is a special case of this model. If at each time t, we let $G(o, t)$ have only two values: 100% or 0%, then this model will generate the same kind of integrity levels as the intuitive model.

2.2. The QoIA Requirement Model

Based on the data object integrity model, we can specify QoIA requirements. For each user, his/her QoIA requirements are the requirements on service trustworthiness. Since a service is composed of a set of transactions, to specify QoIA requirements, we need to model a transaction's trustworthiness at first.

A transaction's input and output are shown in Figure 3. A transaction (a) has a set of input arguments, called the *input* of the transaction, (b) reads a set of data objects, called the *readset* of the transaction, and (c) writes a set of data objects, called the *writeset* of the transaction. We denote a transaction T's input as I_T, its readset as R_T, and its writeset as W_T.

We assume that the input to a transaction is not corrupted and the execution of the transaction is not distorted. Hence, the transaction's trustworthiness is only related to its readset. How to handle malicious inputs is out of the scope of this paper.

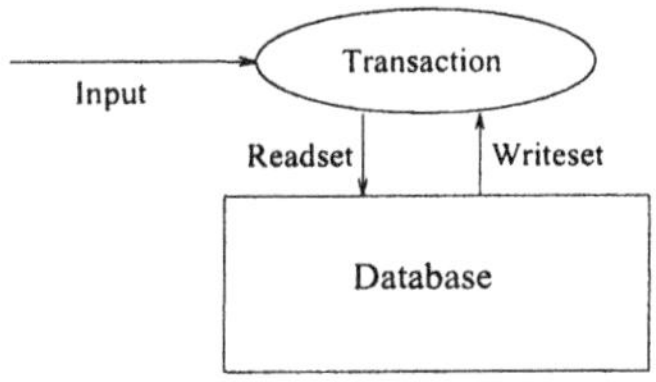

Figure 3. A Transaction's Input and Output Graph

Transaction T's QoIA requirements: for a data object o_i in T's readset, a lowest bound of integrity level is specified and denoted as $th(o_i^r, T)$, where $o_i^r \in R_T$. This requirement means $G(o_i^r, T) \geq th(o_i^r, T)$ at any time.

Next we will define *a user u's QoIA requirements*: for a service S_k that u uses, the QoIA requirements of u on S_k are specified for each transaction that belongs to this service. In particular, a lowest bound of integrity level for each transaction T_j that belong to S_k is specified. We denote it as $th(o_i^r, T_j, S_k)$, and this requirement means that $G(o_i^r, T_j, S_k) \geq th(o_i^r, T_j, S_k)$ should be held at any time, in which $o_i^r \in R_{T_j}$.

In our framework, $th(o_i^r, T_j, S_k)$ can be specified by users or by an agent program. The mechanism to specify it will be our future work. Now we have specified a user's QoIA requirements. The next issues are how ITDB systems can satisfy all users' QoIA requirements, and what strategies can be used to deliver QoIA services.

3. Strategies to Satisfy Users' QoIA Requirements

3.1. How to Estimate Data Objects' Integrity Level?

When a malicious transaction B_i is committed, the objects in W_{B_i} are the initial corrupted data objects. And then in the detection time window, the corruption will be spreading to other data objects through the new transactions' execution. This spreading is related to W_{B_i} and new transactions' arrival pattern and access pattern, thus we can use previous history to predict the future. The idea is to do prediction based on a probabilistic object affecting pattern. For each object o_x, we can use the previous history to estimate the probability that another object o_y is affected by o_x, directly or indirectly. Then we can construct an affected object set for o_x. This set includes every object that can be affected by o_x and the probability that this object is good when o_x is corrupted by a malicious transactions B ($o_x \in W_B$). For example, the affected object set can be as the following: $\{(o_1, p_1), (o_1, p_1), \ldots, (o_n, p_n)\}$, $o_j, 1 \leq j \leq n$ is the data object that has been affected by o_x in the history, and p_j is the probability estimation that o_j is good when o_i is corrupted by a malicious transaction. When a malicious transaction B is detected, we can check the affected object set of the data objects that belong to W_B. For example, suppose B's writeset $W_B = \{o_1^w, o_2^w, \ldots, o_m^w\}$, the affected object set of o_i^w is $A(o_i^w)$, $1 \leq i \leq n$.

If a data object o belongs to affected sets $A(o^w_{i1}), A(o^w_{i2}), \ldots, A(o^w_{il})$, and its tuples are $(o, p_{i_1}), (o, p_{i_2}), \ldots, (o, p_{i_l})$, $1 \leq i_1, i_2, \ldots, i_l \leq m$, we can set $G(o,t) = min\{p_{i_1}, p_{i_2}, \ldots, p_{i_l}\}$, t is time from current time until the ITDB identifies whether o is good.

3.2. How Can Transactions Affect Data Objects' Integrity Levels?

First, we want to present the propagation rule.

Propagation rule: if transaction T's readset is $\{o^r_1, o^r_2, \ldots, o^r_m\}$, then for each data object $o^w_j \in W_t$, its integrity level $G(o^w_j) = min\{G(o^r_1), G(o^r_2), \ldots, G(o^r_m)\}$.

The propagation rule is a syntactic rule, and it produces conservative results. If we use semantic analysis, for example, data flow analysis, we can get more accurate and optimistic results. The issue to do semantic analysis is out of the scope of this paper.

Not all transactions propagate damage (caused by a malicious transaction). We call the transactions that propagate damage as spreading transactions.

Spreading transaction: During a repair time window, if a new transaction's readset includes some data in the current containment set, and the writeset is not empty, it is called a spreading transaction.

The other transactions are non-spreading transactions. They include read-only transactions and the transactions that don't access objects in a containment set.

Spreading transactions can spread corruption to new data objects (when data objects in their writesets are out of the containment set) or increase data objects' corruption probability (when data objects in their writesets are in the containment set). This will affect the capability of the ITDB to satisfy all users' QoIA requirements.

3.3. Strategies in Making Decisions about Denying a Spreading Transaction

Within a repair time window, if a spreading transaction comes, a decision has to be made about whether to deny its execution or not. Consider the following objectives when making such a decision.

- **Throughput rule**: execute as many transactions as possible that access objects in the containment set.

- **Spreading rate rule**: guarantee that the damage spreading rate is low. The damage spreading rate can be defined in several ways, for example, it can be measured by the number of data objects newly corrupted within one second.

The throughput rule aims to maximize ITDB's availability in delivering QoIA services. In contrast, the spreading rate rule aims to (a) minimize the amount of damage spreading that could be caused by the QoIA services that access a confined data object, and (b) minimize the number of services that need to be undone later. Note that if a transaction allowed to access a confined data object is found affected and involved in spreading the damage, it will be undone, and the user that submits the service will finally lose the availability of this service. In the following, we will use an example to show the idea. Suppose when an ITDB system detects a malicious transaction B, it will enforce the initial confinement instantly and the resulted containment set is C_0. For an object $o \in C_0$, suppose before o is repaired, a sequence of transactions will arrive at the ITDB system and ask to access o. Suppose these transactions are: $(T_1, 0.9)$, $(T_2, 0.6, 0.6)$, $(T_3, 0.8, 0.8)$,-$(T_4, 0.9)$, $(T_5, 0.8, 0.8)$, $(T_6, 0.7, 0.7)$, $(T_7, 0.9)$. The tuple $(T_1, 0.9)$ means that T_1 will not write to o (i.e., it is a read-only transaction), and its requirement on o's integrity level is 0.9. The tuple $(T_2, 0.7, 0.7)$ means that (a) T_2 will write to o; (b) T_2's requirement on o's integrity level is 0.7; (c) T_2 will change o's integrity level to 0.7 after T_2 commits; and (d) T_2's writeset includes only o. Other tuples have similar meanings.

When T_1 arrives, we assess and found that o's integrity level is 0.9. For this sequence, we can do an offline analysis based on the complete knowledge about what transactions will arrive following T_1 to get an optimal execution sequence that enforces the two rules. With the constraint that a transaction can be executed only if its QoIA requirements can be satisfied, the following execution sequences are possible: (1) T_1, T_2; (2) T_1, T_3, T_5, T_6; (3) T_1, T_4, T_5, T_6; (4) T_1, T_4, T_7. According to the throughput rule and the spreading rule, we can find the optimal execution sequence is sequence (3).

The above example handles only one object. For multiple objects, similar offline analysis can be done. With offline analysis, we can make optimal decisions in terms of the two rules about whether or not to deny a QoIA service. However, in the real world, in many cases we have to make such decisions online without complete knowledge about the transactions that will arrive in the future. The decision is related to the future transactions' arrival patterns and access patterns, and also related to their readsets and writesets. It is clear that without complete knowledge about these affecting factors, it is impossible to make optimal decisions when delivering QoIA services. Hence, from now on, we will focus on near-optimal decision making using heuristics. In particular, we want to use the history to do some predictions about what could happen in the future, then make decisions based on the prediction. The prediction is basd on some heuristics. We propose a simple method to deal with this problem:

- First, in order to enforce the spreading rate rule, we set a lowest bound or threshold for the integrity levels of all the data objects in the containment set. We denote this threshold as G_0. For example, if we set $G_0 = 70\%$, then for each object o in the containment set, $G(o) \geq 70\%$ should be always satisfied.

- We want to use the history to judge if we will let a spreading transaction be executed. Our simple scheme is based on the following heuristic: if there are a lot of new spreading transactions arriving, then there will be many similar type transactions bound to arrive later. Our idea is that if there are at least DENY_SIZE spreading transactions that have been denied, this kind of spreading transactions will be permitted to execute next time if the QoIA requirement is satisfied and the lowest threshold G_0 is satisfied. DENY_SIZE is a parameter to specify the number of spreading transactions that the ITDB can deny execution at most. For example, in the previous example, if we set DENY_SIZE$= 2$, then the execution sequence will be T_1, T_3, T_5. DENY_SIZE can be adjusted according to previous repair history.

The above is only an example heuristic based method. Good heuristics need to adapt to different workloads. Developing and evaluating new heuristics for different situations will be one of our future work.

4. QoIA Aware Damage Confinement and Repair Algorithm

In this section, a QoIA-aware damage confinement and repair algorithm will be proposed. We only focus on how to integrate our QoIA management framework into the original ITDB algorithms [9]. In order to provide QoIA services, a new module QoIA manager will be added, and the modules of the Confinement Executor, the Unconfinement Executor, which both belong to the Damage Confinement Manager, and the Damage Repair will be modified. Since QoIA services may spread the damage, for spreading transactions, we will confine objects of their writesets to control probably damage spreading.

4.1. Data Structures

In the ITDB, each object is associated with a *time stamp*, denoted by ts_x. ts_x indicates when x is updated. The ITDB's log includes all read and write operations of the transactions. (Refer to the paper [9] about the techniques for getting read information.) ITDB maintains *D_SET* and *U_SET* that are used in the damage containment and repair stage. D_SET maintains each object that the Damage Repair has identified it corrupted, and U_SET maintains the set of objects that have been unconfined by the Unconfinement Executor. And ITDB uses the *confinement time window* to enforce time stamp based confinement control.

In this algorithm, we will add three new data structures:

- *STT*: a spreading transaction table that is an array of records. Each record has six fields: (1) a transaction id; (2) a start time of this transaction; (3) the commit time of this transaction; (4) a transaction type (used by the type based unconfinement phase [7]); (5) a list of input arguments of this transaction (used to materialize a transaction's readset and writeset [7]); (6) a log sequence number of this transaction's commit record in the log file (used to find all the operations of this transaction, since all the operation log entries of a transaction are chained together in the log). STT records each spreading transaction's information in the repair period.
- *I_SET*: an array of tuple $(o, G(o))$, $G(o)$ is o's integrity level. After the QoIA manager assesses an object' integrity level, we put the tuple $(o, G(o))$ to I_SET.
- *S_SET*: an array of data objects. This array keeps all spreading transactions' writesets. This set is a new spreading set after initial confinement. In order to control damage leakage, we will still contain this set. Thus the intersection of S_SET and U_SET is empty, since objects in U_SET have been unconfined.

4.2. QoIA Manager

The QoIA Manager is a component to stay between the Policy Enforcement Manager and the Database Scheduler(refer to Figure 1), and it maintains the global data structure STT and the local data structure I_SET. The Damage Confinement Manager and Damage Repairer modules will access STT.

In the repair time window, when a new transaction arrives, the QoIA Manager will check if the system can satisfy the QoIA requirements of the user who submits the transaction. If it makes the decision that this transaction can be executed, it forwards this transaction to the scheduler; else, it denies this transaction, and sends a response to the user. Thus the QoIA manager is responsible to: (1) Assess an object's integrity level if a new transaction will access this object. (2) Evaluate if a new transaction's QoIA requirement is satisfied. (3) Make the decision whether to deny a new transaction or not. (4) Maintain STT, I_SET.

Algorithm 1 [QoIA Control]
/* it only executes in the repair period. And the Confinement Executor maintains the confinement time window $[t1, t2]$. For an object o, if $t1 \leq ts_o \leq t2$, and $o \notin$ U_SET, or if $o \in S\_SET$, then o is confined. */
while (a new transaction T arrives)
{
for each object $o_i^r \in R_T$
// In the transaction T, o_i^r's QoIA requirement is $Q(o_i^r)$

{
    if (o_i^r is confined)
    {
        if (o_i^r is in I_SET) retrieve its integrity level as $G(o_i^r)$.
        else estimate its integrity level as $G(o_i^r)$,
            and add the tuple $(o_i^r, G(o_i^r))$ in I_SET.
        if $Q(o_i^r) < G(o_i^r)$ deny this transaction's execution,
        and go to while statement.
    }
}
use the strategies proposed in Section 3 to make the decision about whether this transaction can be executed. If it is permitted to be executed, then the QoIA Manager forwards it to the Scheduler.}

For a spreading transactions T_s, after T_s is committed, for each object $o_i^w \in W_{T_s}$, a tuple $(o_i^w, G(o_i^w))$ is added in I_SET, and o_i^w is added in S_SET. Then the record of T_s is added in STT, and if $o_i^w \in U\_SET$, then remove it from U_SET. If it is aborted, there is nothing to do.

4.3. Modifications to the Damage Confinement Manager and the Damage Repairer

One of the main differences between QoIA services and original ITDB services is: in QoIA services, Transactions can access confined data, so it can spread damage in order to deliver QoIA services. We have to modify the Damage Confinement Manager and Damage Repairer to handle this situation.

In the Damage Confinement Manager, all transactions that each unconfinement phase has to handle include the transactions in the confinement time window $[t1, t2]$ and the transactions in STT. All containment data objects that each unconfinement phase has to handle include the objects whose updated time stamps are within the period of $[t1, t2]$ and the objects in S_SET. In QoIA aware situation, the Damage Confinment Manager has to handle more transactions and more objects with the similar algorithm with the original one.

The Damage Repairer has the similar modification as that of the Damage Confinement Manager. Besides original transactions and objects that it has to handle, it will also handle transactions in STT, and repair corrupted objects in S_SET. After an object o is repaired, the Damage Repairer will remove o from S_SET if $o \in$ S_SET, and change the confinement time window to $[ts_o, t2]$, which means the log before time ts_o has been repaired. For a transaction $T \in STT$, after T is repaired or identified as good, T will be removed from STT.

Since the QoIA service probably spreads damage, we need to make sure that repair procedure can terminate. It is easy to detect the repair termination, since we only need to check whether STT is empty and the length of confinement time window is 0. Then the termination problem is: how can we make sure that repair can terminate?

In our algorithm, we can easily control the damage spreading rate. We can use sizes of STT and S_SET to dynamically change the parameter DENY_SIZE and G_0 (the lowest threshold for all contained objects' integrity level). By changing DENY_SIZE and G_0, the damage spread rate can be controlled. Thus we can make sure that repair can terminate.

4.4. Performance Issues

With the strategies that we proposed previously, it is easy to integrate the Algorithm 1 to the ITDB prototype. Through analysis of Algorithm 1, we can find that the algorithm has little impact to the ITDB's performance.

In the algorithm, three additional data structures are added. Within the repair time window, the number of spreading transactions is denoted as N_{t_s}. We assume that a spreading transaction's writeset and read objects in the containment set are small, then the space complexity of all STT, I_SET, and S_SET is $O(N_{t_s})$.

The algorithm is enforced only during the repair time window. It only handles transactions that will access some confined objects. If damage spreads, the Damage Confinement Manager and Repairer will have additional work, but we can control the damage spreading rate. This is a tradeoff between additional repair time because of damage spreading and the gained availability through delivering QoIA services during the repair time window.

5. Related Work

With a focus on data confidentiality, traditional database security technologies, such as authorization [6], inference control [1], multilevel secure databases [12], and multilevel secure transaction processing [4], cannot tackle data corruption attacks. Although database survivability is a relatively new topic, there is already substantial work in this field. Some database attack recovery work is done in [11]. In [3], a color scheme for marking damage and a notion of integrity suitable for databases that are partially damaged are used to develop a fault-tolerant mechanism to survive database attacks. Their approach assumes that each data object has an (accurate) initial damage mark, while our approach will dynamically estimate and adjust the integrity levels of a lot of objects whenever a new malicious transaction is identified.

In [9], a comprehensive survivable database system (i.e., ITDB) is developed, where several valuable database survivability techniques are developed, such as on-the-fly attack recovery [2], attack isolation [8] and multiphase damage containment [7]. However, all these techniques focus on how to maintain data integrity and availability under sustained attacks, and they are limited in delivering QoIA services.

6. Conclusions

This paper takes the first steps to deliver database services with information assurance guarantees. In particular, (a) we introduce the concept of QoIA services; (b) we present a data integrity model which allows customers or applications to quantitatively specify their integrity requirements on the services that they want the database system to deliver; and (c) we present an algorithm that can enable a database system to deliver a set of QoIA services without violating the integrity requirements specified by the customers on the set of services.

In our future work, first, we want to develop the efficient strategies to estimate data objects' integrity level; second, we want to extent and generalize our integrity model to deal with other situations, such as, the integrity model for data objects in state $S2$; third, we want to implement a prototype to evaluate our design.

References

[1] M. R. Adam. Security-Control Methods for Statistical Database: A Comparative Study. *ACM Computing Surveys*, 21(4), 1989.

[2] P. Ammann, S. Jajodia, and P. Liu. Recovery from malicious transactions. *IEEE Transactions on Knowledge and Data Engineering*, 15(5):1167–1185, 2002.

[3] P. Ammann, S. Jajodia, C. D. McCollum, and B. T. Blaustein. Surviving Information Warfare Attacks on Databases. In *Proceedings of the IEEE Symposium on Security and Privacy*, pages 164–174, Oakland, CA, May 1997.

[4] V. Atluri, S. Jajodia, and B. George. *Multilevel Secure Transaction Processing*. Kluwer Academic Publishers, 1999.

[5] D. Barbara, R. Goel, and S. Jajodia. Using checksums to detect data corruption. In *Proceedings of International Conference on Extending Data Base Technology*, Mar 2000.

[6] P. P. Griffiths and B. W. Wade. An Authorization Mechanism for a Relational Database System. *ACM Trans. Database Syst.*, 1(3):242–255, Sept. 1976.

[7] P. Liu and S. Jajodia. Multi-phase damage confinement in database systems for intrusion tolerance. In *Proc. 14th IEEE Computer Security Foundations Workshop*, June 2001.

[8] P. Liu, S. Jajodia, and C. McCollum. Intrusion confinement by isolation in information systems. *Journal of Computer Security*, 15(7):1373–1380.

[9] P. Liu, J. Jing, P. Luenam, Y. Wang, L. Li, and S. Ingsriswang. The design and implementation of an self-healing database system. Technical report, School of Info Sciences and Technology, Penn State University, 2002. submitted for publication.

[10] J. McDermott and D. Goldschlag. Storage jamming. In D. Spooner, S. Demurjian, and J. Dobson, editors, *Database Security IX: Status and Prospects*, pages 365–381, 1996.

[11] B. Panda and J. Giordano. Reconstructing the database after electronic attacks. In *Proceedings of the 12th IFIP 11.3 Working Conference on Database Security*, July 1998.

[12] R. Sandhu and F. Chen. The multilevel relational (mlr) data model. *ACM Transactions on Information and Systems Security*, 1(1), 1998.

CERTIFYING DATA FROM MULTIPLE SOURCES

Glen Nuckolls
Department of Computer Science
University of Texas, Austin
nuckolls@cs.utexas.edu

Chip Martel
Department of Computer Science
University of California, Davis
martel@cs.ucdavis.edu

Stuart G. Stubblebine
Stubblebine Research Labs
8 Wayne Blvd., Madison, NJ 07940
stuart@stubblebine.com

Abstract

Data integrity can be problematic when integrating and organizing information from many sources. In this paper we describe efficient mechanisms that enable a group of data owners to contribute data sets to an untrusted third-party publisher, who then answers users' queries. Each owner gets a proof from the publisher that his data is properly represented, and each user gets a proof that the answer given to them is correct. This allows owners to be confident that their data is being properly represented and for users to be confident they are getting correct answers. We show that a group of data owners can efficiently certify that an untrusted third party publisher has computed the correct digest of the owners' collected data sets. Users can then verify that the answers they get from the publisher are the same as a fully trusted publisher would provide, or detect if they are not. The results presented support selection and range queries on multi-attribute data sets and are an extension of earlier work on Authentic Publication which assumed that a single trusted owner certified all of the data.

1. Introduction

Many settings require data from multiple sources to be combined into a single online database. A combined data set offers the convenience of a single source for queries and support for query types that are dependent on the overall data set. These benefits come at the cost of introducing new security concerns. Principal among them is the need to ensure the honesty of the party who collects the data and provides answers to users' queries. In order to assure accurate answers to queries, we need to prevent inadvertent and malicious data corruption.

In this paper we provide a formal framework and specific implementations which address the problems that arise when an untrusted third party publisher collects and organizes data from many different data owners and then provides answers to user queries on the combined data set. We focus on achieving the two closely related goals of providing a third-party publisher with **efficient** mechanisms to:

(1) Assure data owners that their data will be accurately represented in answers to user queries.

(2) Assure users that the answers to their queries are accurate.

MOTIVATION AND APPLICATIONS. Sites which provide provably accurate data have many important applications including consumer, financial, medical and government settings. Many of these applications draw from multiple sources for their content and, as the Internet expands, the need for accurate data will only increase. As data becomes more valuable, the motivation for dishonest data representation increases and thus the need for mechanisms to prevent it.

A product pricing engine provides a simple and familiar example where a number of data owners, here retailers, contribute data to an untrusted publisher, the pricing engine. If a user asks for a list of all digital cameras matching a given description, they want to know that they have the cheapest listing and that everything in the list is a legitimate. The retailers also want to be sure that the pricing engine is not excluding or misrepresenting their products in favor of other retailers.

In this situation, we want the retailer to be confident that the pricing engine is returning all of his products which match the users description. More generally, we want a retailer to be sure that all of his products that match the query are returned to the user. The user also should be confident that all of the returned data is from legitimate sources. We want to achieve these goals without forcing a retailer or consumer to spend large amounts of extra resources to ensure data integrity.

Our solutions provide mechanisms to support multi-attribute queries which expands the range of database applications.

EXTENDING AUTHENTIC PUBLICATION. There are many possible ways to assure data integrity. Our solutions are an extension of prior work on Authentic Publication [6] which allows untrusted third party publishers to provide users with query answers and short proofs that the answer given is correct. Merkle trees [13, 14] provided the original basis for this work. Since our results extend Authentic Publication to multiple owners, we briefly recap the basic construction. Our example uses a binary search tree, for a data set D, with the values stored at the leaves. The tree is digested using a cryptographic hash function as follows: Starting at the leaves, the digest value of a leaf is the hash of its data value. The digest value of an internal node is the hash of the digest values of its (two) children. The overall digest value of the tree is just the digest value at the root. With this digest value, an efficient proof, of size $O(\log |D|)$ can be given that a data item is or is not in the set.

Authentic Publication has this initial setup: (1) A trusted owner digests the data (e.g. with a binary search tree); (2) the data is given to one or more untrusted publishers; (3) the digest is distributed to the users. Users now send queries to an untrusted publisher, and the publisher returns an answer and a proof that the answer is the same as would be given by the trusted owner. Efficient protocols based on the Merkle tree approach [6] and general methods for producing them [12] exist for a wide range of query types and were proved to be secure in [12] as long as the publisher can't find a collision in the hash function. This approach has many advantages including scalability, since anyone can be a publisher, efficiency, since it uses efficient hash computations, and security, since there are no secret keys used in the proofs to be compromised.

MULTIPLE OWNER SETTING. We want to extend the advantages of Authentic Publication to the multiple owner setting. However, with no single trusted source and limited communication among the owners, there are new challenges. Now, not only does the publisher need to convince the user that the digest used in verification is a valid one, he must also convince each owner. One possible solution has the publisher give the entire collected data set to each owner, who then computes the digest on his own, more or less replicating the single owner Authentic Publication protocol. However, each owner must now deal with the entire database, and we want each owner's work to depend only on the size of his own data set. There are significant difficulties presented by this since each owner only sees a part of the data and digest structure being verified. Since the publisher is not trusted, we must also prevent him from creating and including his own values in the data set and digest. We now give a high level view of our protocols:

Consider a situation in which a set of n data owners $O_1, O_2, \ldots, O_n$ wish to combine their respective data sets $D_1, D_2, \ldots, D_n$ to support multiple queries for many users U. Assume that a third party publisher P collects and combines the sets, and provides the answers to users' queries. The publisher needs to convince each owner that his data set is correctly included and each user that her answer is accurate. A typical sequence of events is in figure 1 as follows:

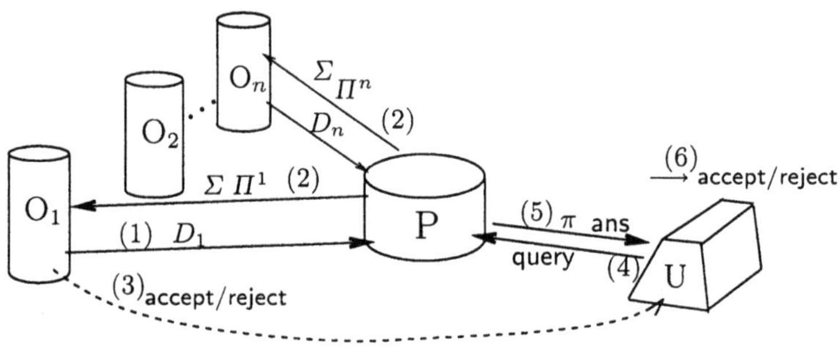

Figure 1. Typical protocol execution.

1 The owners O_i send their data sets D_i to the publisher P.

2 P collects the data sets and computes a digest Σ of the combined data set $D = \bigcup_{i=1}^{n} D_i$, and for each owner, a proof Π^i that the data set D_i is correctly included in Σ. Π^i and Σ are sent to each owner. Σ is also made available to the users.

3 Each owner evaluates his proof and either accepts or rejects, notifying any users of this result and the digest value Σ.

4 A user U sends query to P.

5 P computes an answer ans and a proof π that ans is correct, returning these to U.

6 U evaluates ans and π, and either accepts or rejects.

We assume that each owner and user receives the same value for Σ, whether or not it is accurate. We also assume that every party has access to the hash function H which is used to produce the digest and in the verification procedures. With multiple owners, we can either assume that all owners are trusted to complete the protocol, or that some owners are untrusted, and may conspire with the publisher or other untrusted owners. We outline the results in each case. We will also consider settings where a trusted third-party collects owner approvals of the digest Σ. This reduces the need for owner-user interactions, and for the user to know the details of which owner's contributed to the data set.

GOALS. When an untrusted party collects data for (re)publication there are a variety of guarantees users and data owners might desire. Perhaps the strongest is that the answer to any query is exactly the same as would have been given by a trusted data collector who correctly acquired the owners' data. In the Trusted owners section below we discuss achieving this strong result for multi-attribute queries.

An important, but weaker goal would be to assure an owner (and users) that all his data will be correctly included, but the answer might also include bad data from other, or non-existent owners (e.g. for a selection or range query). An additional goal is to assure the owner that no data items not in his data set will be falsely reported as his. We show this is possible for a broader range of settings.

TRUSTED OWNERS. For a collection of n trusted owners, we provide an efficient protocol that an untrusted publisher can use to compute a digest value Σ for a binary search tree storing the owners' combined data set. The publisher provides a proof to each owner, proportional in size to each owner's data set (and the log of the combined set), that Σ is valid. If each owner accepts their proof, and there is no collision found in the hash function, then Σ is exactly what a fully trusted publisher would have produced for the owners' combined data. We achieve this using a *count certified search tree* which we define and use to support the protocol. The count certified search tree supports, among other query types, authentication of answers to selection and range queries. Users can query the Publisher many times based on Σ, just as in the single owner Authentic Publication setting. We also extend this result to digests of multi-dimensional range trees which allows a richer set of multi-attribute queries (e.g. return all digital cameras which have 1-3 mega-pixels, cost \$250-\$400 and weigh at most 6 ounces). The results in this setting are given in section 2.

UNTRUSTED OWNERS. If some owners cannot be trusted to follow the protocol, and might be conspiring with the publisher, we still want to guarantee each honest owner that if he approves the digest of a publisher, then his data will be properly included in answers to queries. As before, each owner gets a proof of size proportional to his individual data set (and the log of the entire data set). If an owner approves this proof, then he can be confident that any answer a user accepts will contain exactly those data items from his data set which satisfy the user's query. This works for selection, range, and multi-dimensional range queries (e.g. in our digital camera example above, a retailer who approved the digest value of a publisher could be confident that all of his cameras which fit the user's criteria would be returned). We also provide new, efficient mechanisms to prevent false data attribution. An honest owner O can be sure that the publisher cannot return a data item which is claimed to belong to O, but is not in O's data set.

1.1. Background and Related Work

Data authentication has been used for time-stamping [9] and micro-payments [4]. The work in this paper is an extension of earlier work on Authentic Publication [6]. The techniques used in Authentic Publication are based on the original work by Merkle [13, 14] and refinements by Naor and Nissim [15] for certificate revocation.

Devanbu and Stubblebine showed how to create authenticated versions of stacks and queues in [7], and Maniatis and Baker [11, 10] present similar methods for authenticating B-trees and using them for secure data repositories. In [6], we introduced the general idea of authentic data publication, and showed how to securely answer a broader range of queries. This work is extended to authentic publication of XML documents in [5] using authenticated tries, and in [12] we introduced a general model and framework for Authentic Publication for a wide range of query types by defining a general class of authenticated data structures. Goodrich, Tamassia, Triandopoulos and Cohen applied this to a wide range of geometric data structures in [8].

The above approaches share a common theme of leveraging the trust provided by a few digest values from a trusted party over multiple hashes to efficiently protect the integrity of the digested content. All of these methods rely on a single trusted owner to compute the digest. Our scheme avoids this limitation, but extending these results to a more complex distributed setting introduces new challenges to maintaining efficient data authentication. Nonetheless, our protocols incur essentially the same computational effort as in the non-distributed setting.

Two recent papers have started to reduce the need for a single trusted data owner. Buldas, Laud and Lipmaa [2] presented a scheme for accountable certificate management. Though the focus and setting are different from ours, they achieve some similar results. They show how an untrusted party can compute a digest of a set of certificates and, for a given certificate, prove that it is or is not a member of the set. Using an *authenticated search tree*, they show that unless an adversary finds a collision in the hash function, no contradictory proof can be given. This is almost the same as our result in the untrusted owner setting described in section 3 for selection queries. Our results, however, describe extensions to more complex queries and methods to prevent data which is falsely attributed to an owner. In [3], Buldas, Roos and Willemson provide some detail for a solution to "interval" or single dimensional range queries, but do not address the issue of proofs to owners showing that data is correctly represented. They describe as an open problem the extension of authentication techniques to multi-dimensional range trees. We solve this open problem using a *count certified search tree* which is an enhanced version of their authenticated search tree. Our mechanisms guarantee that the untrusted third party has computed the digest of a search tree just as a fully trusted party would. This is a stronger guarantee which allows a richer range of queries in our setting.

2. Implementations for Trusted Owners

Suppose a Publisher wants to collect data from n data owners, store this data in a Binary Search Tree (BST) and then compute a digest of the data. We present an efficient and secure protocol which allows the n owners to determine that the digest computed is the same as the digest which would be computed by a trusted party with access to the owners' joint data set. We extend this to digests of Multidimensional range trees (MDRTs) to efficiently answer multi-attribute queries.

We assume throughout the paper that all data items d have a value $\mathsf{key}(d)$ which is unique. It is possible that two data owners may each have data items with the same local key values. By adding a unique owner identifier to the local key values, the new global key value $\mathsf{key}(d)$ is again unique. We give a somewhat informal description of our results in this section to focus on the main ideas. A more formal treatment (along with the proofs) is given in the full version [16].

2.1. Owner Certification of a Binary Search Tree

We consider a setting with n owners with data sets $D_1 \ldots D_n$. We let D denote this combined data set and let N be the total number of items. For the protocol to produce a correct result, the true value of N must be used in the Owner verification. We discuss ways to ensure that each Owner knows the correct value of N in section 2.4.

Following the protocol outlined in the introduction, our goal is to allow an untrusted Publisher who knows D to construct a binary search tree and its digest Σ, then efficiently prove to the owners (using the proofs π^i) that their data is correctly represented in a tree which has digest Σ. Once we establish that the digest Σ correctly represents D, the Publisher can answer queries from users and provide proofs just as in single owner Authentic Publication. If all parties follow the protocol correctly, then all owners will accept their proofs for Σ. The following theorem states that our *Owner BST certification protocol* is secure.

Theorem 1 *For a set of n owners with data sets $D_1 \ldots D_n$, where N is the number of data items in $D = \bigcup_{i=1}^{n} D_i$, if each Owner correctly executes the BST certification protocol and accepts his proof for the digest Σ and the data count N, then either Σ is a valid digest of a BST for D, or the Publisher has found a collision in the hash function used.*

The Publisher can compute the digest Σ and all proofs in $O(N \log N)$ time, and Owner i can verify his proof in $O(|D_i| \log N)$ time.

Thus the verification time for an owner i is nearly linear in the size of the set D_i. The full details of the proof of Theorem 1 are in the full paper [16]. However, the next two subsections, describe the digesting scheme and sketch how the publisher proves to the owners that their data is correctly represented.

2.2. The Count Certified Search Tree

Since each owner only sees a small part of the tree, we need a stronger digesting scheme than is used in a standard Merkle tree. A *count certified search tree* is a binary search tree, storing data values at the leaves and split values at internal nodes and is digested using the following scheme. The *count* associated with a node v of the tree (denoted $\mathsf{count}(v)$) is the number of data items stored in the leaves of the subtree rooted at v. We also let $\mathsf{split}(v)$ be the split value and $\mathsf{digest}(v)$ be the digest value. Our digesting scheme uses a collision-resistant hash function H. The digest value of a leaf is just the hash of its associated data value. For an internal node v with children u and w,

$$\mathsf{digest}(v) = \mathsf{H}(\mathsf{split}(v), \mathsf{count}(u), \mathsf{count}(w), \mathsf{digest}(u), \mathsf{digest}(w)).$$

We note that the BST structure is only a logical structure which the protocol must use for digesting and proofs. The publisher need not physically implement his database this way. For example, prior results show that a logical BST can be used with a physical B-tree implementation [11, 10, 12].

2.3. Proofs to Owners

We sketch how the Publisher proves to an owner O_i with data set D_i that this data is properly represented. Details are presented in [16]. For each data item d in D_i the Publisher's proof essentially simulates a search for data item d: the proof is a sequence of five tuples of values followed by d. The first five tuple contains the five values used to compute the digest value Σ of the root r of the (claimed) BST with left child u and right child w: $\mathsf{split}(r)$, $\mathsf{count}(u)$, $\mathsf{count}(w)$, $\mathsf{digest}(u)$, $\mathsf{digest}(w)$.

The owner hashes these five values to get a result x, and rejects unless $x = \Sigma$. If $x = \Sigma$, he uses the root's split value to determine if the search should go left, $d \leq \mathsf{split}(r)$, or right, $d > \mathsf{split}(r)$. If the search goes left, the next five values of a correct proof hash to $\mathsf{digest}(u)$.

This digest value is known from the first five values in the proof. Thus we can check that the second five values in the proof hash to $\mathsf{digest}(u)$, and we can also check that the counts match (the second five values should include the number of leaves in the left and right subtrees of u; the sum of these should match $\mathsf{count}(u)$, the number of leaves in the subtree at u, which was given in the first five values of the proof).

The verification process continues until, in the final step, we should reach a leaf whose value is d and which has an associated count of one.

In [2, 12] they also use split values to simulate a search however, our use of the counts is new. The split values make sure that no data values are missing. The counts make sure that no extra data items have been included. At each step of the proof the owner checks that the sizes of the next two subtrees along the path sum to the size of their parent. To make the whole process work, we also need to check that the size of the root (the sum of the counts of its two subtrees) matches N, the total size of the data set. We discuss these issues in more detail in the next section.

2.4. Implementation Issues and Assumptions

So far we have concentrated on the owner-publisher procedures and their proofs, but not the underlying communication mechanisms necessary to carry out the protocols. Theorem 1 shows that if all n owners follow the protocol correctly and approve their proofs for the digest value Σ and for the correct data count value N, then users can be confident that the digest Σ is for a BST which represents the combined data set. We now address the related issues of how to ensure that a User:

1 knows all Owners approve the digest Σ for the correct value of N.

2 gets the digest Σ.

This will partly depend on what we assume the user knows about the n owners and what the owners know about each other. At one extreme we can assume a user knows the identity of all participating owners along with the owners' public keys, and thus could expect to see a signed approval from each owner. At the other extreme, a user may know none of the participating owners, but may relay on a trusted third party "moderator" to determine an appropriate set of owners to participate. In between, a user may know of some owners they want involved, but expect other owners to contribute as well.

USING A TRUSTED MODERATOR. A trusted *Moderator* reduces the information both users and owners need about the set of owners. This is like an online Better Business organization which accepts owners who agree to follow the protocols. After an owner gets a correct proof for a digest value Σ, he sends a signed message to the Moderator: his approval, the digest, the size of his data set, the claimed total size of the entire data set, and the Publisher's web address. Once the Moderator gets an approval from all owners, it is easy to check that all owners approved the same digest and that the total of the individual sizes of the data sets matches the global data set size. The digest Σ for that Publisher can then be approved and posted (or, the Publisher gets a signed approval from the Moderator which can be given to users).

With this scheme a user can get answers and have confidence that the digest they are using is correct without knowing anything in advance about the set of owners. They only need to know about (and trust) the Moderator, who can then provide a signed approval of the digest Σ to the Publisher who passes this on to the Users. Thus, the Moderator has much less overhead than the Publisher since he does not directly deal with the Owners' data sets (just a single acknowledgment per owner) and also need not deal directly with Users.

ELIMINATING THE TRUSTED MODERATOR USING PKI. If we assume that users know which owners are involved and the owners' public keys, we can eliminate the need for a trusted Moderator. In this case, the publisher can give the user each owner's signed accept/reject response to Σ. The response would contain Σ and the count value each owner verified. The User would only need to know that the true count value was used to be confident that the Publisher's computed digest is accurate. Any number of assumptions could be made that ensure that the correct data count value N is used, but a simple and reasonable assumption is that at least one Owner knows N. The User simply checks that all Owners agree on the count value. Even if no Owner initially knows N, there are a number of efficient methods that a set of Owners could use to determine N. Any such method is sufficient to ensure the correctness of the Publisher computed digest value.

2.5. Multi-dimensional Range Trees

For a database containing a set of N r-tuples, an r-dimensional range query has the form $(l_1, u_1), \ldots, (l_r, u_r)$. The answer is the set of points with all coordinates satisfying the corresponding range $\{(x_1, \ldots, x_r) : l_i \leq x_i \leq u_i \text{ for } 1 \leq i \leq r\}$. These r-tuples can be efficiently found using a *multidimensional range tree* (MDRT) in time $O(\log^r N + k)$ where k is the number of r-tuples in the answer set [1]. This important setting allows us to support multi-attribute queries. In a 2D MDRT each data item d is stored in $\log N$ ordinary BSTs (all tied together in a larger data structure). Thus for each data item d an owner i gets a proof Π_d^i which has $\log N$ proofs similar to those used for a data item in the BST setting. The proof also has additional information tying the $\log N$ pieces together. Extending this result to higher dimensions, we get the following theorem:

Theorem 2 *For a set of n owners with data sets $D_1 \ldots D_n$, where N is the number of data items in $D = \bigcup_{i=1}^{n} D_i$, if each Owner correctly executes the MDRT certification protocol and accepts his proof for the digest Σ of an r-dimensional range tree, then either Σ is the digest of an r-dimensional range tree over D or the Publisher has found a collision in the hash function* H.

The Publisher can compute the digest Σ and all proofs in $O(N \log^r N)$ time, and Owner i can verify his proof in $O(|D_i| \log^r N)$ time.

3. Protocols for the Untrusted Owners Setting

In this setting there may be "untrusted owners" who may not follow the protocol. These owners may conspire with the publisher or other untrusted Owners to present false results.

An owner does not see the publisher's entire database, so cannot depend on the accuracy of data other than his own. However, an owner still wants assurance that any of his data that matches a query will be properly included in the answer, and that data not in his data set cannot be falsely attributed to him. We continue to assume that all data items have an identifier for the owner. Assuming no collisions in the hash function are found, we show how to achieve the following guarantee for an honest owner when a user submits a single or multi-dimensional range query: if an owner O_i accepts the publisher's proof for D_i and the user accepts the proof for the answer given to a query, then the data in the answer attributed to O_i is exactly what O_i should have returned if he had answered the query only on his data set D_i. Removing the assumption that all participating owners are trusted motivates our focus on individual owners in the relaxed security statement.[1] We can also extend this result to multi-dimensional range queries in a fairly straightforward way. We state the one-dimensional result formally in theorem 3.

Theorem 3 *Let* $\mathsf{F}([a,b], D)$ *be a function which returns answers to one dimensional range queries on the collection of data sets* D*. If an owner* O_i *correctly executes the Owner BST certification protocol and accepts the proof of the digest* Σ *and the user correctly accepts the answer returned by the publisher, denoted* $\widetilde{\mathsf{ans}}$*, then either* ***1)*** $\mathsf{F}([a,b], D_i) = \widetilde{\mathsf{ans}} \cap D_i$ ***or*** ***2)*** *the Publisher has found a collision in the hash function.*

3.1. Preventing Falsely Attributed Data

We frequently want to prevent a dishonest publisher from giving the user data which is attributed to an honest owner, but is not in the owner's data set. We can prevent such "false attribution" by adding an additional mechanism to our protocols.

We describe a variation of our results in the untrusted setting where each data element is checked efficiently using a single hash computation. In the new approach, each data owner securely combines each data element with a secret value to form a means to authenticate the origin of that data element, the owner commits to the secret, and later the owner reveals the secret so that users can use the secret to authenticate the origin of the data elements. More specifically the protocol is as follows.

1 Each owner, O_i ,generates a secret random number, k_i.[2]

2 O_i computes a message authentication code (MAC), $h_{k_i}(d)$, for each data element $d \in D_i$. The MAC is the hash of each data element d using a hash function keyed with the unrevealed random number k_i.[3]

3 O_i passes each of his data elements and its corresponding message authentication code to the publisher. Also, O_i passes a commit-

---

[1] In the presence of untrusted owners, and thus untrusted data, answers to queries which depend on the entire data set are no longer reliable. For example, the minimum of the data values is not useful since spurious data values could cause skewed results.

[2] The size of k_i should be chosen, with respect to the message authentication function in the next step, to be sufficiently large to prevent a variety of attacks on the system.

[3] Note that we assume that $\mathsf{key}(d)$ makes it easy to determine the claimed owner of the data element, so the user can efficiently identify the k_i of the owner. Otherwise, the user would have to check each k_i of all possible owners to determine the owner.

ment to k_i of the form $salt_i, h_{k_i}(salt_i)$. The publisher now builds the Count Certified BST using as leaf values the pairs $(d,\ h_{k_i}(d))$ which are still ordered by $\mathsf{key}(d)$.

4 After receiving the inputs from all owners, the publisher commits to the root hash Σ of the combined database, the list of data owners, and the commitments of each data owner, [4]
$\Sigma_{pub} = (\Sigma, O_1 \ldots O_j, [salt_1, h_{k_1}(salt_1)], \ldots, [salt_j, h_{k_j}(salt_j)])$.

5 O_i checks that the root hash properly reflects his data values essentially as in the prior section, and that $(salt_i, h_{k_i}(salt_i))$ is correct. He then reveals k_i to the publisher along with his signed acceptance of Σ_{pub}. The publisher can now make the tuples (O_i, k_i) available to the users in query responses along with O_i's signed acceptance of Σ_{pub}. To verify the authenticity of a data element which appears to belong to O_i, the user confirms that O_i signed Σ_{pub} and checks that k_i corresponds to the O_i's secret commitment.[5] Finally, the user verifies the message authentication code on the data element using the corresponding k_i.

It takes $O(1)$ effort to check $d \in D_i$ due to the hash commitment scheme and so for selection and range queries with T answers, verification now takes $O(\log N + T)$ time and space for a 1D range query and for r-dimensional range queries, verification takes $O(\log^r N + T)$.

4. Conclusion

One main limitation of our scheme is the need for users to know who has approved the digest. This is likely to make updates harder and introduces extra overhead for the user and owners. In addition, we would like to extend our results to a wider class of query types, as was done for the single owner case in [12].

Acknowledgments

The authors would like to thank Phil Rogaway for his excellent suggestions in the preliminary development of this work. Matt Franklin

[4]We might also want to include a time as part of Σ_{pub} as this would give the user evidence of the freshness of the values used in query answers. Even stronger would be to provide a time interval during which the values are presumed valid. Note that we typically assume that the data used in these applications does not change quickly, so precise clock synchronization is not required.

[5]Note, these steps need to be performed at most once per publication since notes corresponding to successful verification might be cached with the user.

and Prem Devanbu also provided valuable feedback for this paper. This work was supported by NSF grant CCR 85961.

References

[1] M. D. Berg, M. V. Kreveld, M. Overmars, and O. Schwarzkopf. *Computational Geometry.* Springer, New York, 2000.

[2] A. Buldas, P. Laud, and H Lipmaa. Eliminating counterevidence with applications to accountable certificate management. *Journal of Computer Security*, 10:273–296, 2002.

[3] A. Buldas, M. Roos, and J. Willemson. Undeniable replies for database queries. In *Proceedings of the Fifth International Baltic Conference on DB and IS*, volume 2, pages 215–226, 2002.

[4] S. Charanjit and M. Yung. Paytree: Amortized signature for flexible micropayments. *Second Usenix Workshop on Electronic Commerce Proceedings*, 1996.

[5] P. Devanbu, M. Gertz, A. Kwong, C. Martel, G. Nuckolls, and S. G. Stubblebine. Flexible authentication of xml documents. In *Proceedings of the 8th ACM Conference on Computer and Communications Security (CCS-8)*, pages 136–145, 2001.

[6] P. Devanbu, M. Gertz, C. Martel, and S. G. Stubblebine. Authentic publication over the internet. *Journal of Computer Security*, 3(11):291–314, 2003.

[7] P. Devanbu and S. Stubblebine. Stack and queue integrity on hostile platforms. *IEEE Transactions on Software Engineering*, 26(2), 2000.

[8] M. Goodrich, R. Tamassia, N. Triandopoulos, and R. Cohen. Authenticated data structures for graph and geometric searching. Technical report, Center for Geometric Computing, Brown University, 2002.

[9] S. Haber and W. S. Stornetta. How to timestamp a digital document. *J. of Cryptology*, 3(2), 1991.

[10] Petros Maniatis and Mary Baker. Enabling the archival storage of signed documents. In *Proceedings of the USENIX Conference on File and Storage Technologies (FAST 2002)*, pages 31–45, Monterey, CA, USA, January 2002. USENIX Association.

[11] Petros Maniatis and Mary Baker. Secure history preservation through timeline entanglement. In *Proceedings of the 11th USENIX Security Symposium*, San Francisco, CA, USA, August 2002.

[12] C. Martel, G. Nuckolls, P. Devanbu, M. Gertz, A. Kwong, and S. Stubblebine. A general model for authentic data publication. To appear in *Algorithmica*, `http://truthsayer.cs.ucdavis.edu/pubs.html`.

[13] R.C. Merkle. Protocols for public key cryptosystems. In *Proceedings of the IEEE Symposium on Security and Privacy*, pages 122–134. IEEE Computer Society Press, 1980.

[14] R.C. Merkle. A certified digital signature. Advances in Cryptology–Crypto '89, *Lecture Notes in Computer Science*, 435:218–238, 1990.

[15] M. Naor and K. Nissim. Certificate revocation and certificate update. *Proceedings of the 7th USENIX Security Symposium*, 1998.

[16] G. Nuckolls, C. Martel, and S. Stubblebine. Certifying data from multiple sources. Available at `http://truthsayer.cs.ucdavis.edu/pubs.html`.

ENSURING THE INTEGRITY OF ENCRYPTED DATABASES IN THE DATABASE-AS-A-SERVICE MODEL*

Hakan Hacıgümüş
IBM Almaden Research Center
650 Harry Road, San Jose, CA 95120, USA
hakanh@acm.org

Bala Iyer
IBM Silicon Valley Lab.
San Jose, CA 95141, USA
balaiyer@us.ibm.com

Sharad Mehrotra
Department of Information and Computer Science
University of California, Irvine, CA 92697, USA
sharad@ics.uci.edu

Abstract In the database-as-a-service model, a service provider hosts the clients' data and allows access to the data through the Internet. Database-as-a-service model offers considerable benefits to organizations with data management needs by allowing them to outsource their data management infrastructures. Yet, the model introduces many significant challenges, in particular that of data privacy and security. Ensuring the integrity of the database, which is hosted by a service provider, is a critical and challenging problem in this context. We propose an encrypted database integrity assurance scheme, which allows the owner of the data to ensure the integrity of the database hosted at the service provider site, in addition to the security of the stored data against malicious attacks.

*This work was supported in part by NSF grant CCR 0220069 and an IBM Ph.D. Fellowship.

Keywords: database, security, privacy, integrity, authentication, encryption, cryptography, e-services, application service provider model

1. Introduction

Rapid advances in networking and Internet technologies have fueled the emergence of the "software-as-a-service" model, also referred as the Application Service Provider (ASP) model, for enterprise computing. Successful examples of commercially viable software services include rent-a-spreadsheet, electronic mail services, general storage services, disaster protection services. *Database-as-a-Service* (DAS) model [11, 8, 9], inherits all the advantages of the ASP model by allowing organizations to leverage data management solutions provided by the service providers, without having to develop them on their own. It alleviates the need for organizations to purchase expensive hardware and software, deal with software upgrades, and hire professionals for administrative and maintenance tasks. Instead, the new model allows third party database service providers the capability to seamlessly host data from diverse organizations and take over these tasks. By outsourcing, organizations can concentrate on their core competencies instead of sustaining a large investment in data management infrastructures. Increasingly, large companies are outsourcing their IT departments and sometimes their entire data centers to specialized service providers [6, 5].

NetDB2 system [11], which is being developed at IBM in cooperation with University of California, Irvine, is an instantiation of DAS model. The system has been deployed on the Internet and under constant use for over two years.

Among the others, *data privacy* and *security* are the most significant challenges in the DAS model. In the DAS model, the user data is stored at the service provider (ASP) site. The ASP stores the client's data and the client poses queries against that database and the ASP (or the server) responds back to the client with results of the queries. Most companies and individuals view their data as an asset. The theft of intellectual property already costs organizations great amount of money every year [4]. Therefore, first, the owner of the data needs to be assured that the data is protected against malicious attacks from outside of ASP. In addition to this, recent studies indicate that 40% of those attacks are perpetrated by the insiders [4]. Hence, the second and more challenging problem is the privacy of the data when even the ASP itself is not trusted by the owner of the data. First problem is examined in [11] and the second one is studied in [8], which explores how SQL queries can be executed over encrypted data.

In this paper, we look at another important issue that arises in the context of the second problem stated above. Although the client's data is protected against both outsiders and the ASP with data encryption techniques, how can the client ensure the integrity of the database, which belongs to the client but is under the control of the ASP? Our preliminary work on this issue appears in [10]. That work does not provide efficient schemes to ensure the table-level integrity. Here we present efficient incremental techniques to ensure the table-level integrity and discuss the applicability of the schemes in real database environments. The previous work also fails to assess the performance implications of the integrity assurance schemes. In this paper, we experimentally evaluated the performance of the schemes we propose by using the standard benchmark queries.

We view the integrity problem in two dimensions. First, when the client receives a record from the sever, how can the client ensure the integrity of the record? That is, how can the client verify that the data has not been changed in an unauthorized way? Second, the client needs to assure the integrity of whole table stored at the server site. This problem is more pronounced in dynamic environments, where the update rate of the database is high. In such environments, the client needs efficient mechanisms, which will require minimal computational resources that are limited at the client site. While entailing minimal computational resources, preferred solution is a mechanism that can be automated requiring minimum human involvement. In this paper, we present such a solution to ensure the integrity of hosted databases.

Integrity problems may arise both from malicious or non-malicious circumstances. Malicious threats may originate from misbehaving server or some other adversary who breaks into the system. Active and replay (restore) attacks, as described in [12], are the typical examples for those kinds of threats. Non-malicious threats can also have many sources. One example for those is system failures. ASP may experience a system breakdown and may not be able to recover all user data from on-line and/or archive sources. In those cases, the client does not have any verification mechanism to detect the integrity of the original data. In the course of NetDB2 project, we have particularly observed the need for addressing data integrity problems raised from second group of sources, namely; non-malicious threats.

To address these issues, we propose two-level encrypted database integrity scheme, which consists of *Record-Level Integrity* and *Table-Level Integrity* concepts. Those are developed in the context of the DAS model and described in Section 3.2 and Section 3.3, respectively. We note that, the techniques we present in this paper are not specific to either the DAS

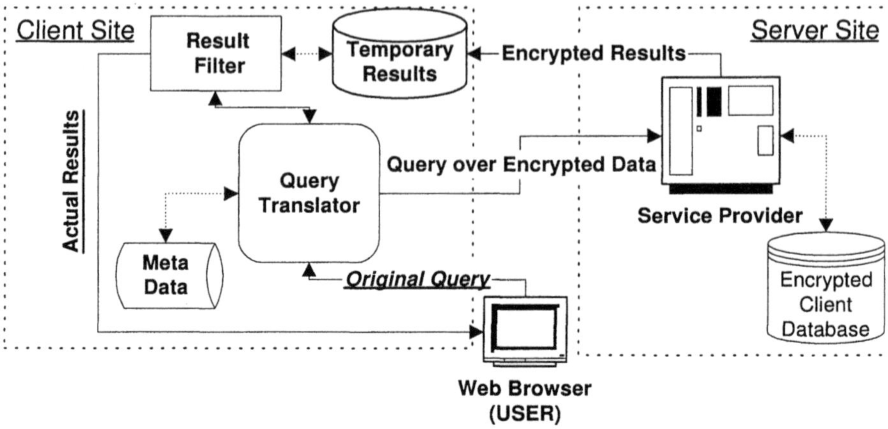

Figure 1. Database-as-a-Service architecture

model or the encrypted databases but have wider applicability to any relational data that is subject to integrity issues. Once implementation of these techniques is in place, the system can automatically detect the integrity violations and intrusions.

The rest of the paper is organized as follows. Section 2 provides background on the DAS model and the encrypted database storage model. Section 3 presents our solution to encrypted database integrity by discussing the record-level and the table-level integrity techniques. Section 4 gives our experimental results on queries from the TPC-H benchmark. We conclude the paper in Section 5.

2. Background

2.1. Database-as-a-Service Model

The system we use in this study is based on the architecture proposed and described in [8] and [9]. The basic architecture and the control flow of the system are shown in Figure 1. It is comprised of three fundamental entities. A *user* poses the query to the client. A *server* is hosted by the service provider that stores the encrypted database. The encrypted database is augmented with additional information (which we call the index) that allows certain amount of query processing to occur at the server without jeopardizing data privacy. A *client* stores the

Table 1. Relation *emp*

eid	*ename*	*salary*	*addr*	*did*
23	Tom	70K	Maple	40
860	Mary	60K	Main	80
320	John	23K	River	35
200	Sarah	55K	River	10

Table 2. Encrypted version emp^S of relation *emp*

RID	*etuple*	eid^{id}	$ename^{id}$	$salary^{id}$	eid^f	$ename^f$
1	=*?Ew@R*((¡¡=+,-...	2	19	81	@R*...	¡(*...
2	b*((¡¡(*?Ew@=l,r...	4	31	59	E:q!,...	=+,...
3	w@=W*((¡¡(*?E:,j...	7	59	22	@Aw*...	¿(]...
4	ffTi* @=U(¡?G+,a...	8	49	59	hRs(...	?@Q=...

data at the server. Client[1] also maintains *metadata* for translating user queries to the appropriate representation on the server, and performs post-processing on server query results. From the privacy perspective, the most important feature is, the client's data is always stored in encrypted form at the server site. The server never sees the unencrypted form of the data, and executes the queries directly over encrypted data without decrypting it. We fully studied the query processing techniques, which allow this process, in [8].

2.2. Encrypted Database Storage Model

We briefly summarize how the client's data stored at the server in an encrypted fashion.[2] Following this we introduce our extensions to the model to implement data integrity techniques.

For each relation $R(A_1, A_2, \ldots, A_n)$, we store, on the server, an encrypted relation: $R^S(etuple,\ P_1^{id}, P_2^{id}, \ldots, P_i^{id},\ F_1^f, F_2^f, \ldots, F_j^f)$, where $1 \leq i \leq n, 1 \leq j \leq n$. Here, an *etuple* stores an encrypted string that corresponds to a tuple in relation R. Each attribute P_i^{id} stores the partition index for corresponding attribute A_i that will be used for

[1]Often the client and the user might be the same entity.

[2]We will not repeat here all of the details of storage model, since they are thoroughly discussed in [8]. Rather, we only provide necessary notations to explain the constructs we develop in this work.

query processing at the server. F_j^f represents the encrypted form of the attribute value of corresponding attribute A_j.

For example, consider a relation *emp* given in Table 1 that stores the information about the employees. The *emp* table is mapped to a corresponding table, shown in Table 2, at the server: $emp^S(RID, etuple, eid^{id}, ename^{id}, salary^{id}, eid^f, ename^f)$.

RID represents record identifier, which we will use in Section 3.3. The second column *etuple* contains the string corresponding to the encrypted tuples in *emp*. For instance, the first tuple is encrypted to "=*?Ew@R*((¡¡=+,-. . . " that is equal to $\mathcal{E}_k(1, 23, Tom, 70K, Maple, 40)$, where $\mathcal{E}$ is a deterministic encryption algorithm with key k. Any deterministic encryption technique such as AES [1], Blowfish [14], DES [7] etc., can be used to encrypt the tuples. The third column corresponds to the index on the employee ids.[3] The sixth column represents the individually encrypted values employee ids.

3. Encrypted Database Integrity

We study the integrity of a database at two different granularity levels, 1) Integrity of the records, 2) Integrity of a table. We call the former as *Record-Level Integrity* and the latter as *Table-Level Integrity*.

3.1. Preliminaries

In this subsection we provide necessary definitions and concepts that we use in the rest of the section. Our definitions are based on [12, 15].

- A *hash function* is a function h, which has, as a minimum, the following properties: 1) *Compression*, meaning h maps an input x of arbitrary finite bitlength to an output $h(x)$ of fixed bitlength n and 2) *Ease of computation*, meaning given h and an input x, $h(x)$ is easy to compute.
- A *one-way function* is a function f that for each x from the domain of f, it is easy to compute $f(x)$, but it is computationally infeasible to find any x such that $y = f(x)$. A hash function $h(x)$ is *collision resistant* if it is computationally infeasible to find any two distinct inputs x, x' where $h(x) = h(x')$.
- The *manipulation detection codes (MDCs)* are one-way collision resistant hash functions that provide a *representative image* or *hash* of a message.

[3] Details of creation of those index values can be found in [8].

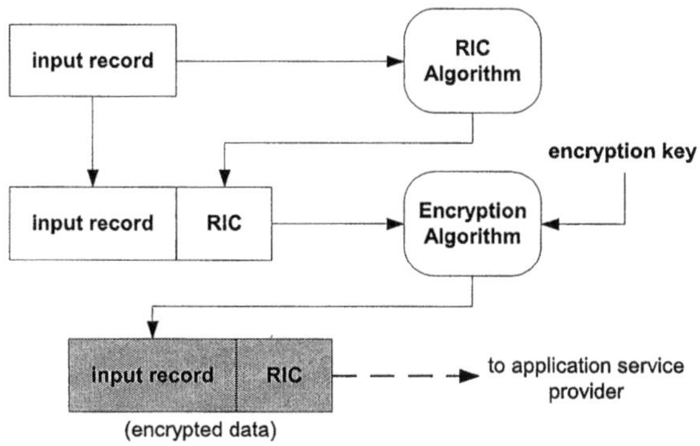

Figure 2. Record-level integrity with RICs

• The *data integrity*, in general, can be defined as a property, which guarantees that the data has not been manipulated in an unauthorized manner since the time it was created by an authorized source. MDCs provide this level data integrity in combination with data encryption.

As we will see, we need to expand this definition to satisfy data integrity requirements in the DAS model. This definition only provides data integrity for individual records stored in the database at the server site. In addition to that, we want to ensure the integrity of tables in an efficient way.

3.2. Record-Level Integrity

The record-level integrity represents that the content of a record has not been manipulated in an unauthorized manner. Although it may not be apparent, data encryption does not provide data integrity automatically. The owner of the decryption key can decrypt the encrypted messages, which were encrypted with the same key. But this does not guarantee that the encrypted message has not been manipulated by the adversary. The discussion of how encrypted messages can be manipulated undetectably can be found in [12]. This motivates the need for data integrity measures over encrypted data.

To provide record-level integrity we propose a scheme based on *Record Integrity Codes (RICs)*. RICs are specially computed representative images for each record with certain security and uniqueness measures. Figure 2 shows the procedure that provides record-level data integrity. The client has a record r that will be inserted into the database, which is maintained by the application service provider or simply the server. The client first computes the hash code of the record $H = h(r)$ by using a hashing algorithm, which produces *Record Integrity Code* (RIC). This can be any algorithm, which satisfies the security requirements given before. Here we use MDCs for this purpose. After this step, the client concatenates the hash code H with the original record text r and encrypts them together by using any deterministic encryption algorithm $\mathcal{E}$ with secret key k, i.e., the client computes ciphertext $C = \mathcal{E}_k(r \parallel h(r))$, where $\parallel$ represents concatenation. The client inserts ciphertext C as an *etuple* into the database.

Whenever the client requests a record, the server sends back the corresponding *etuple* in encrypted form. To verify the integrity of the record, the client first decrypts the *etuple* recovering r' and H', which is the RIC, parts. Since only the client has the secret key k for encryption algorithm no one else can decrypt. Then the client independently computes $h(r')$ of received record r' and compares that with the hash code H'. If they are equivalent, this verifies that the received record is authentic and has data integrity, i.e., has not been manipulated in an unauthorized manner.

3.3. Table-Level Integrity

In the previous section we discussed mechanisms that enable the client to test the integrity of individual the records returned by the server. In this section, we study schemes, which allow the client to validate the integrity of the table(s).

The integrity of a table may be compromised by an adversary by modifying, adding, or deleting some or all of the records. An unauthorized modification on records can be detected by the record-level integrity techniques, when they are queried by the client. However, the record-level integrity is not enough to detect unauthorized addition and/or deletion of records in any case.

To successfully detect such modifications, we propose a mechanism, which creates a signature for each table. Those signatures can be thought of the fingerprints of the corresponding tables. They are created, updated, and stored at the client site in a secure way. Hence, an adversary cannot re-compute the signature and verification of the signature the would detect the unauthorized modifications. Considering our focus on security, the signatures should be resilient against various cryptographic attacks.

In addition to that, we make note of another important issue regarding the computation of the signatures. The client should re-compute the signature when he inserts/deletes a record from a table. This is an extra overhead for the client and can be significant in terms of system resources at the client site and network traffic. Undoubtedly, a highly preferred alternative would be a scheme, which allows incremental updates on the signatures instead of requiring the processing of all of the existent records.

3.3.1 Incremental Signatures. To achieve the incremental updates on signatures, we make use of specialized schemes, XOR MACs, introduced by Bellare et al. [3, 2], in the context of incremental cryptography [2]. The main idea is; when there is a change in a document D, to construct mechanisms to reflect "only the changes" on the cryptographic transformation (in our case the signatures) of the document D without processing all the document from scratch. Hence, such an incremental algorithms run time would be proportional to the number of changes but not proportional to the document length. Formal definition of XOR scheme we use in this study is given in [3] as follows:

f_1 is a pseudorandom function (PRF) with secret key k_1 and f_2 is a pseudorandom permutation (PRP) with secret key k_2. $Rand(\cdot)$, called randomizer, is an algorithm, which given a string x picks a random k-bit string r and returns $x \parallel r$. The message that will be authenticated is $D = D_0 \parallel D_1 \parallel \ldots \parallel D_n \parallel D_{n+1}$, where D_0 is a special start symbol and D_{n+1} is a special end symbol. Then the tag of the message is computed in three steps:

1 Randomize: Let $R_i = Rand(D_i) : 0 \leq i \leq n$

2 Chain: Let $h = \oplus_{i=0}^{n} f_1(R_i, R_{i+1})$

3 Tag: Let $T = f_2(h)$

In our system setup, D_i's are defined as the database records r_i of the table and the tag T corresponds to the signature S of the table. [3] discusses possible instantiation alternatives for PRF f_1, such as using DES, MD5, or both. The instantiation of f_2 can be handled in a similar way as a block-cipher can be viewed as a PRP. For simplicity, we assume that size of a database record is equal to block size of the block-cipher. If record size is larger, then it can be processed as multiple blocks. If it is smaller than the block size, the standard padding techniques can be used. Security of the scheme also analyzed thoroughly in [3] against the various types of attacks.

Insert: We use the record identifiers (RIDs) to keep track of the index of the records r_i in the algorithm. Note that, although the RIDs are stored in the clear at the server, they are also included in the *etuples* in the encrypted form. (See Section 2.2) Therefore, even the server manipulates the RIDs, the client can always recover the original ones by decrypting the *etuples*. We assume that the RIDs are always non-decreasing unique numbers. (Most of commercial database systems already provide table definitions to create this type of ids.)

Assume that the current signature of a table is S and the RID of the last record is i. If the client inserts a new record r_{i+1} (i.e., RID=$i+1$), then the new signature S' is computed as follows:

1 The client recovers hash value h as $h = f^{-1}(S)$

2 The client moves the special end record one position forward by assigning $R_{i+2} = R_{i+1}$ (Note that here R_{i+1} is not the randomized form of the new record being inserted but the randomized form of the special end record.)

3 The client computes $R_{i+1} = Rand(r_{i+1})$

4 The client updates the hash value by:

$$h' = h \oplus f_1(R_i, R_{i+2}) \oplus f_1(R_i, R_{i+1}) \oplus f_1(R_{i+1}, R_{i+2})$$

5 The client computes the new signature $T' = f_2(h')$

Delete: Deletions are reflected on the signature in an incremental way as follows. Assume that the current signature of a table is S and the client wants to delete a record r_i (i.e., RID=i), then the new signature S' is computed as follows:

1 The client recovers hash value h as $h = f^{-1}(S)$

2 The client updates h by:

$$h' = h \oplus f_1(R_{i-1}, R_{i+1}) \oplus f_1(R_{i-1}, R_i) \oplus f_1(R_i, R_{i+1})$$

3 The client computes the new signature $T' = f_2(h')$

Incrementing requires five calls to the PRF. This is a significant saving as compare to computing the signature from scratch, which would require one call for each record in the table.

3.3.2 Application of the Incremental Signatures. We have presented the incremental signature computation formally. The scheme uses the RIDs as record indexes, which are also employed in the computation steps. Now, we will discuss the realization of the scheme in database applications.

The insertion operation does not pose any difficulty. Since the RIDs are always incrementing unique numbers, the client inserts a new record with a new RID and updates the signature of the table. On the other hand, deletion operation requires some more work.

In typical database applications, the users usually don't query the records with their RIDs. As an example, if we want to delete a record of an employee whose employee id is 123 from `employee` table, a typical query would be:

```
DELETE FROM employee WHERE eid = 123
```

To execute this deletion, the client runs two queries to obtain the RIDs and the *etuples* required to compute the updated signature.

The first query retrieves the RID of the record being deleted as follows:

SELECT rid,etuple FROM employee WHERE $\texttt{eid}^f$ = $\mathcal{E}$(123)

Let us assume that the RID of the corresponding record is 345, then the second query retrieves the RIDs of two records, whose RIDs are the immediate predecessor and successor of the RID of the record being deleted.[4]

```
(SELECT rid,etuple FROM employee
   WHERE rid < 345 ORDER BY rid DESC FETCH FIRST ROW ONLY)
UNION
(SELECT rid,etuple FROM employee
   WHERE rid > 345 ORDER BY rid ASC FETCH FIRST ROW ONLY)
```

After running this query, the client would have enough information to update the signature of the table.

We used equality predicate in the WHERE clause of the query for this example. We note that, if the query has inequality predicates then the approach should be different. In that case, the client could use partition indexes (See Section 2.2) instead of the field-level encrypted values to obtain the necessary information.[5] What the client needs are RIDs and corresponding *etuples* in any case. Therefore, the queries should be reformulated accordingly to retrieve that information by utilizing partition indexes.

We also note that SQL update operations can be implemented as the combination of delete and insert.

[4]SQL queries given below have been executed on IBM DB2 v8.1.
[5]Query processing with partition indexes is fully discussed in [8].

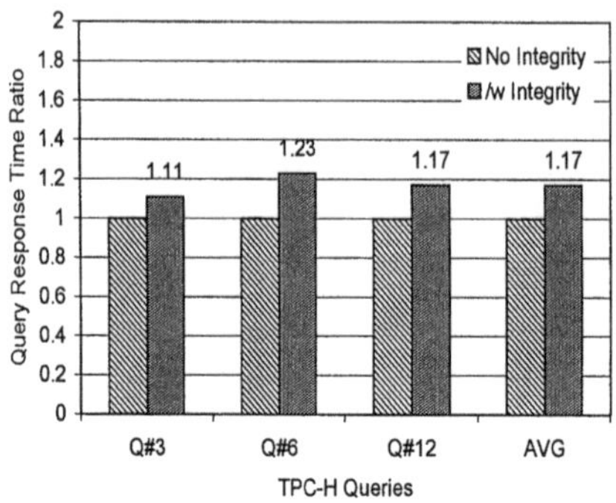

Figure 3. Server response time

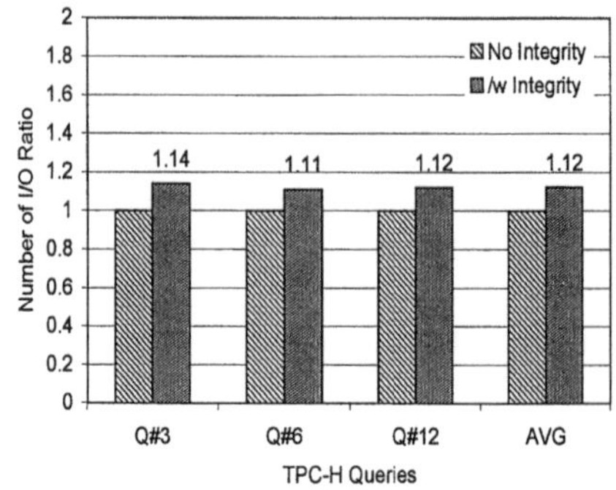

Figure 4. Server I/O performance

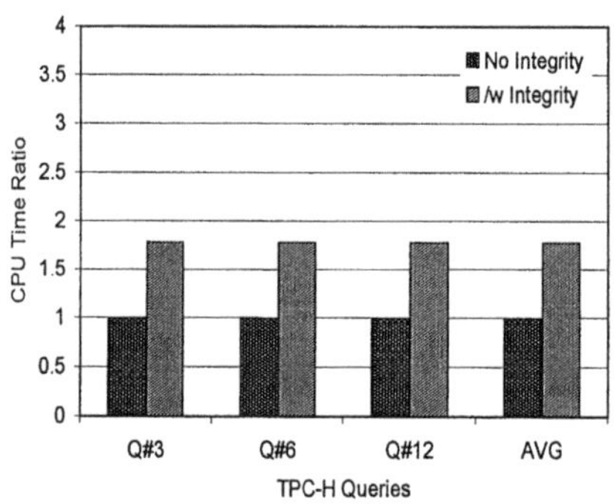

Figure 5. Client response time

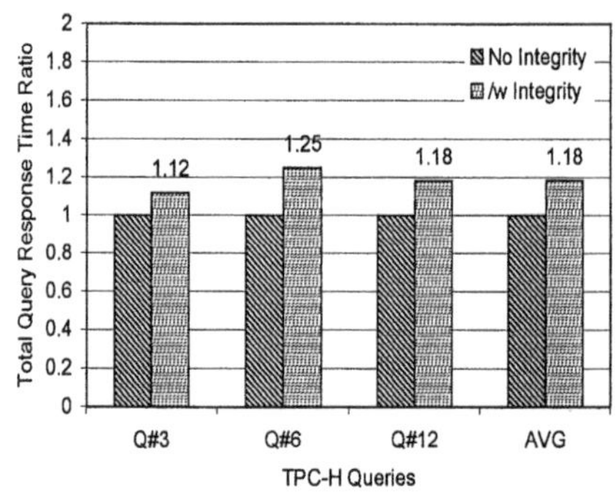

Figure 6. Total query response time

4. Experimental Evaluation

We have conducted experiments to evaluate the overhead introduced by the record-level integrity schemes that we have presented. Our results showed that the overheads are not significant. We used the standard TPC-H benchmark [16] queries, specifically Q#3, Q#6, Q#12 from TPC-H suite. The TPC-H database was created in scale factor 1, which corresponds to 1GB in size. To implement the integrity schemes, we used the AES block cipher [1] as the encryption algorithm, and the MD5 message digest [13] as the one-way hash function. The experiments were executed on a server, which had a Pentium III-750MHz CPU, 256MB RAM, Windows 2000 OS, and IBM DB2 UDB v8.1.

To provide the detailed analysis, we report the results for the server side queries, the client side queries, and the total query elapsed times. In all figures, we compare two cases, namely; the case, where there is no integrity scheme is deployed and the case, where the record-level integrity schemes we have presented are implemented.

Figure 3 shows the overhead in server side query response times. On the average the increase is 17%. Figure 4 presents the increase in the number of I/Os executed at the server site. The increase, 12% on the average, is mainly due to the increase in the tuple sizes. The tuple sizes increase as a result of inclusion of the RICs into the records and it is reflected to server side query response time.

Figure 5 shows the measurements for client side query CPU time. It increased, constantly for all queries, by 70%. The overhead is due to the increased number of bytes that are decrypted and the validation of the integrity of the tuples by the client. The total query response time, which is presented in Figure 6, showed 18% increase on the average, which did not constitute significant overhead.

5. Conclusions

We have studied the crucial problem of encrypted database integrity in the context of database-as-a-service model. We have proposed two-level encrypted database integrity scheme, which consists of *Record-Level Integrity* and *Table-Level Integrity* concepts, as a solution to this problem. Our scheme is combined with encrypted database storage model. Consequently, the resultant system provides the security of the stored data against the malicious attacks as well as the database integrity features, which ensure the authenticity and the validity of the data stored at the service provider site.

References

[1] AES. Advanced Encryption Standard. *National Institute of Science and Technology, FIPS 197*, 2001.

[2] Mihir Bellare, Oded Goldreich, and Shafi Goldwasser. Incremental cryptography: The case of hashing and signing. *Lecture Notes in Computer Science*, 839:216–233, 1994.

[3] Mihir Bellare, Oded Goldreich, and Shafi Goldwasser. Incremental cryptography and application to virus protection. In *STOC*, pages 45–56, 1995.

[4] Computer Security Institute. CSI/FBI Computer Crime and Security Survey. *http://www.gocsi.com*, 2002.

[5] ComputerWorld. J.P. Morgan signs outsourcing deal with IBM. Dec. 30, 2002.

[6] ComputerWorld. Business Process Outsourcing. Jan. 01, 2001.

[7] DES. Data Encryption Standard. *FIPS PUB 46, Federal Information Processing Standards Pub.*, 1977.

[8] H. Hacıgümüş, B. Iyer, C. Li, and S. Mehrotra. Executing SQL over Encrypted Data in Database Service Provider Model. In *Proc. of ACM SIGMOD*, 2002.

[9] H. Hacıgümüş. Privacy in Database-as-a-Service Model. *Ph.D. Thesis, Department of Information and Computer Science, University of California, Irvine*, 2003.

[10] H. Hacıgümüş, B. Iyer, and S. Mehrotra. Encrypted Database Integrity in Database Service Provider Model. In *Proc. of Certification and Security in E-Services (CSES'02), IFIP 17th World Computer Congress*, 2002.

[11] H. Hacıgümüş, B. Iyer, and S. Mehrotra. Providing Database as a Service. In *Proc. of ICDE*, 2002.

[12] D. R. Menezes, P. C. van Oorschot, and S. A. Vanstone. *Handbook of Applied Cryptography.* CRC Press, 1997.

[13] R. Rivest. The MD5 Message-Digest Algorithm. *RFC 1321*, 1992.

[14] Bruce Schneier. Description of a new variable-length key, block cipher (blowfish), fast software encryption. In *Cambridge Security Workshop Proceedings*, 1994.

[15] D. R. Stinson. *Cryptography: Theory and Practice.* CRC Press, 1995.

[16] TPC-H. *Benchmark Specification,* `http://www.tpc.org/tpch`.

ADAPTING QUERY OPTIMIZATION TECHNIQUES FOR EFFICIENT ALERT CORRELATION*

Peng Ning and Dingbang Xu
Department of Computer Science
North Carolina State University
{ pning, dxu } @ncsu.edu

Abstract Intrusion alert correlation is the process to identify high-level attack scenarios by reasoning about low-level alerts raised by intrusion detection systems (IDSs). The efficiency of intrusion alert correlation is critical in enabling interactive analysis of intrusion alerts as well as prompt responses to attacks. This paper presents an experimental study aimed at adapting main memory index structures (e.g., T Trees, Linear Hashing) and database query optimization techniques (e.g., nested loop join, sort join) for efficient correlation of intensive alerts. By taking advantage of the characteristics of the alert correlation process, this paper presents three techniques named *hyper-alert container, two-level index,* and *sort correlation.* This paper then reports a series of experiments designed to evaluate the effectiveness of these techniques. These experiments demonstrate that (1) hyper-alert containers improve the efficiency of order-preserving index structures (e.g., T Trees), with which an insertion operation involves search, (2) two-level index improves the efficiency of all index structures, (3) a two-level index structure combining Chained Bucket Hashing and Linear Hashing is the most efficient for streamed alerts with and without memory constraint, and (4) sort correlation with heap sort algorithm is the most efficient for alert correlation in batch.

Keywords: Intrusion detection, intrusion alert correlation, query optimization

1. Introduction

Traditional intrusion detection systems (IDSs) focus on low-level attacks or anomalies, and raise alerts independently, though there may be logical connections between them. In situations where there are intensive intrusions, not only will actual alerts be mixed with false alerts, but the amount of alerts will also

*This work is partially supported by the National Science Foundation under grants CCR-0207297 and ITR-0219315, by the U.S. Army Research Office under grant DAAD 19-02-1-0219. The authors would like to thank the anonymous reviewers for their valuable suggestions.

become unmanageable. As a result, it is difficult for human users or intrusion response systems to understand the alerts and take appropriate actions.

To assist the analysis of intrusion alerts, several alert correlation methods (e.g., [6, 15]) have been proposed recently to process the alerts reported by IDSs. As one of the methods, we have developed an alert correlation technique using prerequisites and consequences of attacks [11]. Intuitively, the prerequisite of an intrusion is the necessary condition for the intrusion to be successful, while the consequence of an intrusion is the possible outcome of the intrusion. Based on the prerequisites and consequences of different types of attacks, our method correlates alerts by (partially) matching the consequence of some previous alerts and the prerequisite of some later ones.

We have implemented an offline intrusion alert correlator based on our approach, and the initial experiments indicate that our approach is promising in constructing attack scenarios and differentiating true and false alerts [11]. However, our solution still faces some challenges. In particular, we implemented the previous intrusion alert correlator as a DBMS-based application [11]. Involving a DBMS in the alert correlation process provided enormous convenience and support in intrusion analysis; however, relying entirely on the DBMS also introduced performance penalty. For example, to correlate about 65,000 alerts generated from the DEFCON 8 CTF data set, it took the alert correlator more than 4 minutes. Such performance is clearly insufficient to be practical, especially for interactive analysis of intensive alerts. Our timing analysis indicates that the performance bottleneck lies in the interaction between the intrusion alert correlator and the DBMS. Since this implementation completely relies on the DBMS, processing of each single alert entails interaction with the DBMS, which introduces significant performance penalty.

In this paper, we address this problem by performing alert correlation entirely in main memory, while only using the DBMS as the storage of intrusion alerts. We study several main memory index structures, including Array Binary Search [2], AVL Trees [1], B Trees [3], Chained Bucket Hashing [8], Linear Hashing [10], and T Trees [9], as well as some database query optimization techniques such as nested loop join and sort join [7] to facilitate timely correlation of intrusion alerts. By taking advantage of the characteristics of the alert correlation process, we develop three techniques named *hyper-alert container, two-level index,* and *sort correlation*, which further reduce the execution time required by alert correlation.

We performed a series of experiments to evaluate these techniques with the DEF CON 8 CTF data set. The experimental results demonstrate that (1) hyper-alert containers improve the efficiency of index structures with which an insertion operation involves search (e.g., B Trees, T Trees), (2) two-level index improves the efficiency of all index structures, (3) a two-level index structure combining Chained Bucket Hashing and Linear Hashing is most efficient for correlating streamed alerts with and without memory constraint, and (4) sort correlation with heap sort algorithm is most efficient for alert correlation in batch. With the most efficient method, the execution time for correlating the alerts generated from the DEF CON 8 CTF data set is reduced from over four minutes to less than one second.

The remainder of this paper is organized as follows. To be self contained, the next section briefly describes our alert correlation method. Section 3 presents our adaptations of the main memory index structures and some join methods. Section 4 reports our implementation and experimental results. Section 5 discusses the related work, and Section 6 concludes this paper and points out some future research directions.

2. An Overview of Alert Correlation

This section briefly describes our model for correlating alerts using prerequisites and consequences of intrusions. Further details can be found in [11].

The alert correlation model is based on the observation that in series of attacks, the component attacks are usually not isolated, but related as different stages of the attacks, with the early ones preparing for the later ones. To take advantage of this observation, we correlate alerts using prerequisites and consequences of the corresponding attacks. Intuitively, the *prerequisite* of an attack is the necessary condition for the attack to be successful, while the *consequence* of an attack is the possible outcome of the attack if it is successful. We identify the prerequisites (e.g., existence of vulnerable services) and the consequences (e.g., discovery of vulnerable services) of each type of attacks and correlate detected attacks (i.e., alerts) by matching the consequences of previous alerts and the prerequisites of later ones.

We use predicates as basic constructs to represent prerequisites and consequences of attacks. For example, we may use the predicate *UDPVulnerableToBOF* (*VictimIP, VictimPort*) to represent the discovery of a vulnerable UDP service. We use a *hyper-alert type* to encode our knowledge about each type of attacks. A *hyper-alert type T* is a triple (*fact, prerequisite, consequence*) where (1) *fact* is a set of attribute names, each with an associated domain of values, (2) *prerequisite* is a logical formula whose free variables are all in *fact*, and (3) *consequence* is a set of logical formulas such that all the free variables in *consequence* are in *fact*. Intuitively, the *fact* component of a hyper-alert type gives the information associated with the alert, *prerequisite* specifies what must be true for the attack to be successful, and *consequence* describes what could be true if the attack indeed happens. For brevity, we omit the domains associated with attribute names when they are clear from context.

Given a hyper-alert type *T* = (*fact, prerequisite, consequence*), a *hyper-alert (instance) h of type T* is a finite set of tuples on *fact*, where each tuple is associated with an interval-based timestamp [*begin_time, end_time*]. The hyper-alert h implies that *prerequisite* must evaluate to True and all the logical formulas in *consequence* might evaluate to True for each tuple. The *fact* component of a hyper-alert type is essentially a relation schema (as in relational databases), and a hyper-alert is a relation instance of this schema. A hyper-alert *instantiates* its *prerequisite* and *consequence* by replacing the free variables in *prerequisite* and *consequence* with its specific values. Note that *prerequisite* and *consequence* can be instantiated multiple times if *fact* consists of multiple tuples.

To correlate hyper-alerts, we check if an earlier hyper-alert *contributes* to the prerequisite of a later one. Specifically, we decompose the prerequisite of a hyper-alert into parts of predicates and test whether the consequence of an earlier hyper-alert makes some parts of the prerequisite True (*i.e.*, makes the prerequisite easier to satisfy). If the result is positive, then we correlate the hyper-alerts. In our formal model, given an instance h of the hyper-alert type T = (*fact, prerequisite, consequence*), the *prerequisite set (or consequence set, resp.) of* h, denoted $P(h)$ (or $C(h)$, resp.), is the set of all such predicates that appear in *prerequisite* (or *consequence*, resp.) whose arguments are replaced with the corresponding attribute values of each tuple in h. Each element in $P(h)$ (or $C(h)$, resp.) is associated with the timestamp of the corresponding tuple in h. We say that hyper-alert h_1 *prepares for* hyper-alert h_2 if there exist $p \in P(h_2)$ and $C \subseteq C(h_1)$ such that for all $c \in C$, $c.end\_time < p.begin\_time$ and the conjunction of all the logical formulas in C implies p.

We use a *hyper-alert correlation graph* to represent a set of correlated hyper-alerts. Specifically, a *hyper-alert correlation graph* $CG = (N, E)$ is a connected graph, where N is a set of hyper-alerts and for each pair $n_1, n_2 \in N$, there is a directed edge from n_1 to n_2 in E if and only if n_1 prepares for n_2. Figure 1 shows one of the hyper-alert correlation graphs discovered in our experiments with the 2000 DARPA intrusion detection evaluation data sets [11]. Each node in Figure 1 represents a hyper-alert. The numbers inside the nodes are the alert ID's generated by the IDSs.

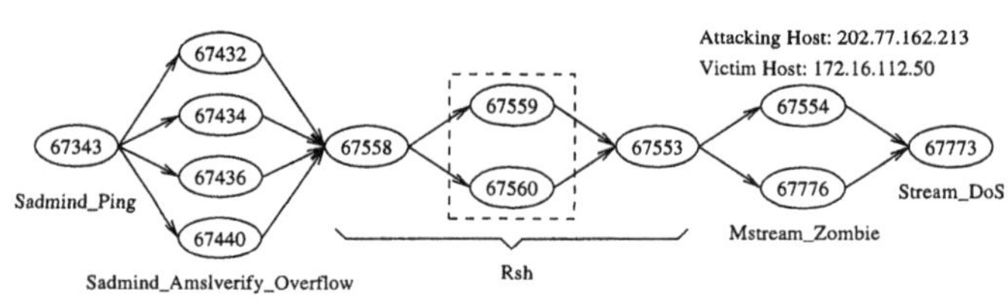

Figure 1. A hyper-alert correlation graph

We have implemented an intrusion alert correlator using our method [11], which is a Java application that interacts with the DBMS via JDBC. In this implementation, we expand the consequence set of each hyper-alert by including all the predicates implied by the consequence set. We call the result the *expanded consequence set* of the hyper-alert. The predicates in both prerequisite and expanded consequence sets of the hyper-alerts are then encoded into strings called *Encoded Predicate* and stored in two tables, *PrereqSet* and *ExpandedConseqSet*, along with the corresponding hyper-alert ID and timestamp. Both tables have attributes *HyperAlertID*, *EncodedPredicate*, *begin_time*, and *end_time*, with meanings as indicated by their names. As a result, alert correlation can be performed using the following SQL statement:

```
SELECT DISTINCT c.HyperAlertID, p.HyperAlertID
FROM PrereqSet p, ExpandedConseqSet c
WHERE p.EncodedPredicate = c.EncodedPredicate AND c.end_time < p.begin_time
```

As discussed earlier, one problem of the intrusion alert correlator is its efficiency because of its dependence on, and intensive interaction with the DBMS. In this paper, we address this problem by performing alert correlation entirely in main memory, while only using the DBMS as the storage of intrusion alerts. In the following, we study how to improve performance of alert correlation by adapting database query optimization techniques, including various main memory index structures.

3. Adapting Query Optimization Techniques

The essential problem in this work is how to perform the SQL query in the previous section efficiently. One option is to use database query optimization techniques, which have been studied extensively for both disk based and main memory databases. However, alert correlation has a different access pattern than typical database applications, which may lead to different performance than traditional database applications. In addition, the unique characteristics in alert correlation give us an opportunity for further improvement. Thus, in this section, we seek ways to improve alert correlation by adapting existing query optimization techniques.

In our study, we study the suitability of the following main memory index structures: Array Binary Search [2], AVL Trees [1], B Trees [3], Chained Bucket Hashing [8], Linear Hashing [10], and T Trees [9]. We do not describe them here, since the related information can be found in the references. For comparison purpose, we also implement a naive, sequential scan method, which simply scans in an (unordered) array for the desired data item.

3.1. Correlating Streamed Intrusion Alerts

We first study alert correlation methods that deal with intrusion alert streams continuously generated by IDSs. With such methods, an alert correlation system can be pipelined with IDSs and produce correlation result in a timely manner.

Figure 2 presents a nested loop method that can accommodate streamed alerts. (As the name suggests, nested loop correlation is adapted from nested loop join [7].) It assumes that the input hyper-alerts are ordered ascendingly in terms of their beginning time. The nested loop method takes advantage of main memory index structures such as Linear Hashing. While processing the hyper-alerts, it maintains an index structure $\mathcal{I}$ for the instantiated predicates in the expanded consequence sets along with the corresponding hyper-alerts. Each time when a hyper-alert h is processed, the algorithm searches in $\mathcal{I}$ for each instantiated predicate p that appears in h's prerequisite set. A match of a hyper-alert h' implies that h' has the same instantiated predicate p in its expanded consequent set. If h'.EndTime is before h.BeginTime, then h' prepares for h. If the method processes all the hyper-alerts in the ascending order of their beginning time, it is easy to see that the nested loop method can find all and only the prepare-for relations between the input hyper-alerts.

Outline of Nested Loop Correlation
Input: A list H of hyper-alerts ordered ascendingly in their beginning times.
Output: All pairs of (h', h) such that both h and h' are in H and h' prepares for h.
Method:

Maintain an index structure $\mathcal{I}$ for instantiated predicates in the expanded consequence sets of hyper-alerts. Each instantiated predicate is associated with the corresponding hyper-alert. Initially, $\mathcal{I}$ is empty.

```
for each hyper-alert h in H (accessed in the given order)
    for each instantiated predicate p in the prerequisite set of h
        Search the set of hyper-alerts with index key p in I. Let H' be the result.
        for each h' in H'
            if (h'.EndTime< h.BeginTime) then output (h', h).
    for each p in the expanded consequence set of h
        Insert p along with h into I.
end
```

Figure 2. Outline of the nested loop alert correlation methods

The nested loop correlation method has different performance if different index structures are used. Thus, one of our tasks is to identify the index structure most suitable for this method. In addition, we further develop two adaptations to improve the performance of these index structures. Our first adaptation is based on the following observation.

Observation 1 *Multiple hyper-alerts may share the same instantiated predicate in their expanded consequence sets. Almost all of them prepare for a later hyper-alert that has the same instantiated predicate in its prerequisite set.*

Observation 1 implies that we can associate hyper-alerts with an instantiated predicate p if p appears in the expanded consequence sets of all these hyper-alerts. As a result, locating an instantiated predicate directly leads to the locations of all the hyper-alerts that share the instantiated predicate in their expanded consequence sets. We call the set of hyper-alerts associated with an instantiated predicate a *hyper-alert container*.

Using hyper-alert containers does not always result in better performance. There are two types of accesses to the index structure in the nested loop correlation method: insertion and search. For the index structures that preserve the order of data items, insertion implies search, since each time when an element is inserted into the index structure, it has to be placed in the "right" place. Using hyper-alert container does not increase the insertion cost significantly, while at the same time reduces the search cost. However, for the non-order preserving index structures such as Linear Hashing, insertion does not involve search. Using hyper-alert containers would force to perform a search, since the hyper-alerts have to be put into the right container. In this case, hyper-alert container decreases the search cost but increases the insertion cost, and it is not straightforward to determine whether the overall cost is decreased or not. We study this through experiments later.

Observation 2 *There is a small, static, and finite set of predicates. Two instantiated predicates are the same only if they are instantiated from the same predicate.*

Observation 2 leads to a *two-level index structure*. Each instantiated predicate can be split into two parts, the predicate name and the arguments. The top-level index is built on the predicate names. Since we usually have a static and small set of predicate names, we use Chained Bucket Hashing for this purpose. Each element in the top-level index further points to a second-level index structure. The second-level index is built on the arguments of the instantiated predicates. When an instantiated predicate is inserted into a two-level index structure, we first locate the right hash bucket based on the predicate name, then locate the second-level index structure within the hash bucket (by scanning the bucket elements), and finally insert it into the second-level index structure using the arguments.

3.2. Correlating Intrusion Alerts in Batch

Some applications allow alerts to be processed in batch (e.g., forensic analysis with an alert database). Though the nested loop method discussed earlier is still applicable, there are more efficient ways for alert correlation in batch.

Figure 3 presents a sort correlation method, which is adapted from sort join [7]. The sort correlation method achieves good performance by taking advantage of efficient main memory sorting algorithms. Specifically, it uses two arrays, A_{pre} and A_{con}. A_{pre} stores the instantiated predicates in the prerequisite sets of the hyper-alerts (along with the corresponding hyper-alerts), and A_{con} stores the instantiated predicates in the expanded consequence sets (along with

Outline of Sort Correlation

Input: A set H of hyper-alerts.

Output: All pairs of (h', h) such that both h and h' are in H and h' prepares for h.

Method:

Prepare two arrays A_{pre} and A_{con}, each entry of which is a hyper-alert associated with a key field. Each array is initialized with a reasonable size, and reallocated with doubled sizes if out of space. Existing content is copied to the new buffer if reallocation happens.

```
for each h in H
    for each p in the prerequisite set of h
        Append h to A_pre with key = p.
    for each p in the expanded consequence set of h
        Append h to A_con with key = p.
Sort A_pre and A_con ascendingly in terms of the key field (with, e.g., heap sort).
Partition the entries in A_pre and A_con into maximal blocks that share the same
  instantiated predicate. Assume A_pre and A_con have B_pre and B_con blocks, resp.
i = 0, j = 0.
while (i < B_pre and j < B_con) do
    if (A_pre.B_i.Predicate < A_con.B_j.Predicate) then
        i = i + 1.
    else if (A_pre.B_i.Predicate > A_con.B_j.Predicate) then
        j = j + 1.
    else for each h in A_pre.B_i and each h' in A_con.B_j
            if h'.EndTime < h.BeginTime then output (h', h).
        i = i + 1, j = j + 1.
end
```

Figure 3. The sort correlation method

the corresponding hyper-alerts). This method then sorts both arrays in terms of the instantiated predicate with an efficient sorting algorithm (e.g., heap sort).

Assume both arrays are sorted ascendingly in terms of instantiated predicate. The sort correlation method partitions both arrays into blocks that share the same instantiated predicate, and scans both arrays simultaneously. It maintains two indices, i and j, that references to the current blocks in A_{pre} and A_{con}, respectively. The method compares the instantiated predicates in the two current blocks. If the instantiated predicate in the current block of A_{pre} is smaller, it advances the index i; if the instantiated predicate in the current block A_{con} is smaller, it advances the index j; otherwise, the current blocks of A_{pre} and A_{con} share the same instantiated predicate. The method then examines each pair of hyper-alerts h' and h, where h' and h are in the current block of A_{con} and A_{pre}, respectively. If the end time of h' is before the beginning time of h, then h' prepares for h.

It is easy to see that the sort correlation method can find all pairs of hyper-alerts such that the first prepares for the second. Consider two hyper-alerts h and h' where h' prepares for h. There must exist an instantiated predicate p in both the expanded consequence set of h' and the prerequisite set of h. Thus,

p along with h' must be placed in the array A_{con}, and p along with h must be placed in the array A_{pre}. The scanning method (lines 9–16) will eventually point i to p's block in A_{pre} and j to p's block in A_{con} at the same time, and output h' prepares for h. Therefore, the sort correlation can discover all and only pairs of hyper-alerts such that the first prepares for the second.

We also study the possibility of adapting two-index join and hash join methods [7] to improve the performance of batch alert correlation. However, our analysis indicates they cannot outperform nested loop correlation due to the fact that alert correlation is performed entirely in main memory.

A naive adaptation of two-index join leads to the following method: Build two index structures for the instantiated predicates in the prerequisite sets and the expanded consequence sets, respectively. For each instantiated predicate p, locate the hyper-alerts related to p in both index structures, and compare the corresponding timestamps. However, this method cannot perform better than the nested loop method. The nested loop method only involves insertion of instantiated predicates in the expanded consequence sets and search of those in the prerequisite sets. In contrast, the above adaptation requires insertion of instantiated predicates in both prerequisite and expanded consequence sets, and search of instantiated predicates in at least one of the index structures.

A possible improvement over the naive adaptation is to merge the two index structures. We can associate two sets of hyper-alerts with each instantiated predicate p, denoted $H_{pre}(p)$ and $H_{con}(p)$, and build one index structure for the instantiated predicates. $H_{pre}(p)$ and $H_{con}(p)$ consist of the hyper-alerts that have p in their prerequisite sets and expanded consequence sets, respectively. After all the instantiated predicates in the prerequisite or the consequence set of the hyper-alerts are inserted into the index structure, we can simply scan all the instantiated predicates, and compare the corresponding timestamps of the hyper-alerts in $H_{pre}(p)$ and $H_{con}(p)$ for each instantiated predicate p. However, each insertion of an instantiated predicate entails a search operation, since the corresponding hyper-alert has to be inserted into either $H_{pre}(p)$ or $H_{con}(p)$. Thus, this method cannot outperform the nested loop method, which involves one insertion for each instantiated predicate in the expanded consequence sets, and one search for each instantiated predicate in the prerequisite sets. A similar conclusion can be drawn for hash join.

Another possibility to have a faster batch correlation is to use Chained Bucket Hashing. Since the number of alerts is known beforehand, we may be able to decide a relatively accurate hash table size, and thus have a better performance than its counter part for streamed alerts. We study this through experiments later.

3.3. Correlating Intrusion Alerts with Limited Memory

The previous approaches to in-memory alert correlation have assumed that all index structures fit in memory during the alert correlation process. This may be true for analyzing intrusion alerts collected during several days or weeks; however, in typical operational scenarios, the IDSs produce intrusion alerts continuously and the memory of the alert correlation system will eventually be exhausted. A typical solution is to use a "sliding window" to focus on alerts that are close to each other; at any given point in time, only alerts after a previous time point are considered for correlation.

We adopt a sliding window which can accommodate up to t intrusion alerts. The parameter t is determined by the amount of memory available to the intrusion alert correlation system. Since our goal is to optimize the intrusion alert correlation process, we do not discuss how to choose the appropriate value of t in this paper. Each time when a new intrusion alert is coming, we check if inserting this new alert will result in more than t alerts in the index structure. If yes, we remove the oldest alert from the index structure. In either case, we will perform the same correlation process as in Section 3.2. It is also possible to add multiple intrusion alerts in batch. In this case, multiple old alerts may be removed from the index structure. Note that though choosing a sliding *time* window is another option, it doesn't reflect the memory constraint we have to face in this application.

Using a sliding window in our application essentially implies deleting old intrusion alerts when there are more than t alerts in the memory. This problem appeared to be trivial at the first glance, since all the data structures have known deletion algorithms. However, we soon realized that we had to go through a little trouble to make the deletion efficient. The challenge is that the index structures we build in all the previous approaches are in terms of instantiated predicates to facilitate correlation. However, to remove the oldest intrusion alerts, we need to locate and remove alerts in terms of their timestamps. Thus, the previous index structures cannot be used to perform the deletion operation efficiently. Indeed, each deletion implies a scan of all the alerts in the index structures.

To address this problem, we add a *secondary data structure* to facilitate locating the oldest intrusion alerts. Since the intrusion alerts are inserted as well as removed in terms of their time order, we use a queue (simulated with a circular buffer) for this purpose. Each newly inserted intrusion alert also has an entry added into this queue, which points to its location in the *primary index structure* in terms of the instantiated predicates. Thus, when we need to remove the oldest intrusion alert, we can simply dequeue an alert, find its location in the primary index structure, and delete it directly. Indeed, this is more efficient than the generic deletion method of the order preserving index structures (e.g., AVL Trees), since deletion usually implies search in those index structures.

4. Experimental Results

We have implemented all the techniques discussed in Section 3 in Java, with JDBC to connect to the DBMS. We performed a series of experiments to compare these techniques. All the experiments were run on a DELL Precision Workstation with 1.8GHz Pentium 4 CPU and 512M bytes memory. The alerts used in our experiments were generated by a RealSecure Network Sensor 6.0 (`http://www.iss.net`), which monitors an isolated network in which we replayed the network traffic collected at the DEF CON 8 CTF event. We summarize the results in this section; further details can be found in [12].

Nested-Loop Correlation without Memory Constraint. Our first set of experiments is intended to evaluate the effectiveness of hyper-alert container in nested loop correlation. According to our analysis, hyper-alert container may reduce the execution time if we use the order-preserving index structures. We compared the execution time for Sequential Scan, Array Binary Search, and Linear Hashing, with or without hyper-alert container. Our results show that hyper-alert containers reduce the execution time for Array Binary Search, but increases the execution time for Sequential Scan significantly, and Linear Hashing slightly. Figure 4(a) shows some results obtained in the experiments.

Our second set of experiments is to evaluate the effectiveness of two-level index structure in the nested loop correlation method. Our results indicate that two-level indexes reduce execution time for all index structures. Figure 4(b) shows the improvement of two-level index for B Tree and Linear Hash.

Our next goal is to find out which index structure (with or without the two adaptations) has the best performance for nested loop correlation. Our results show that two-level Linear Hashing (without hyper-alert container) achieves the best performance. Figure 4(c) shows the top three fastest methods, two-level Array Binary Search with hyper-alert container, two-level AVL Tree, and two-level Linear Hashing.

Batch Correlation without Memory Constraint. Our evaluation here is to determine whether any method can achieve better performance than nested loop correlation with two-level Linear Hashing, the best method for correlating streamed alerts. Besides two-level Linear Hashing, we tested Chained Bucket Hashing and the sort correlation methods because of their potential to outperform two-level Linear Hashing. To further examine the impact of the time order of input hyper-alerts, we examined the timing results with ordered and unordered input (in terms of their timestamps). With unordered input, an algorithm must insert all of the instantiated predicates in the expanded consequence sets before it processes any instantiated predicate in the prerequisite sets.

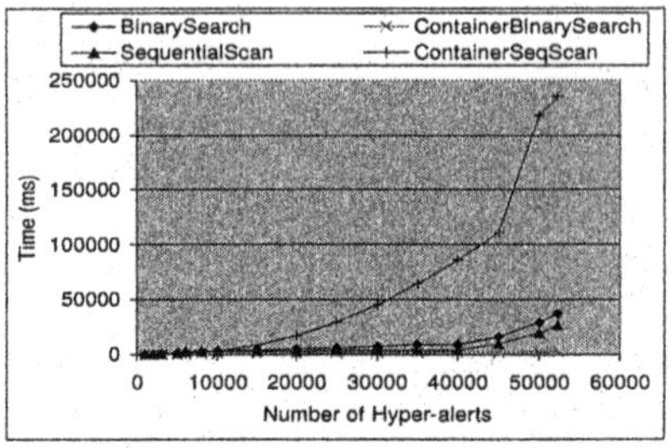

(a) Hyper-alert containers

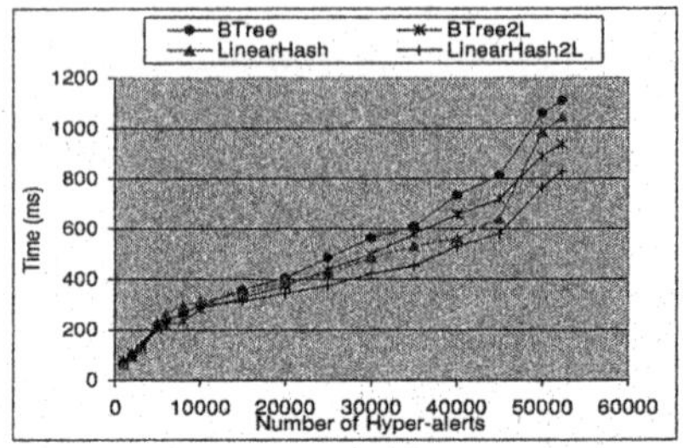

(b) Two-level indices

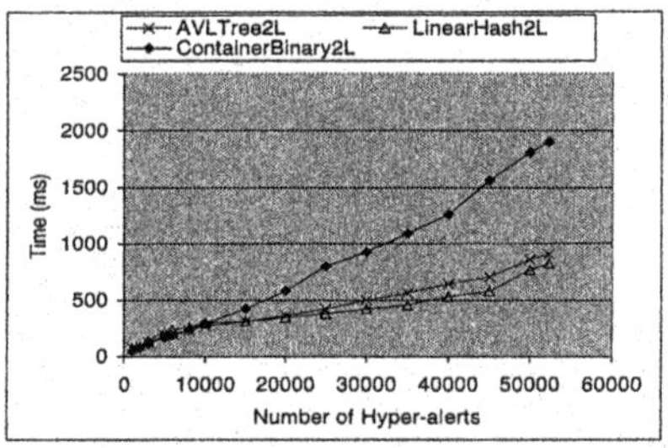

(c) Efficient two-level indices

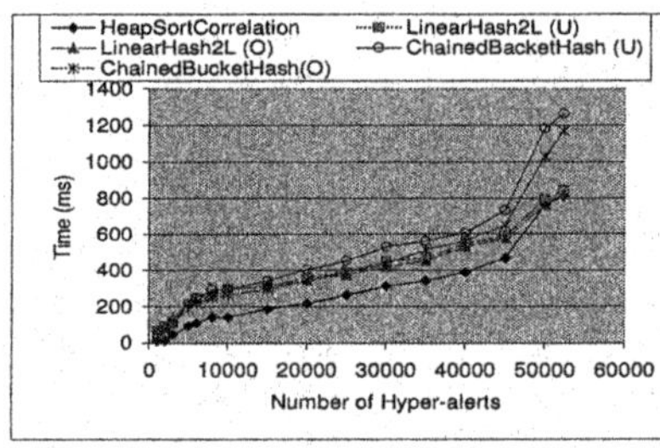

(d) Efficient batch correlation

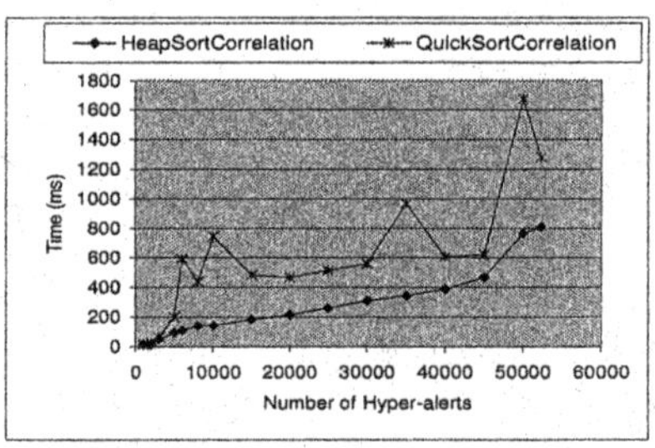

(e) Impact of sorting algorithms

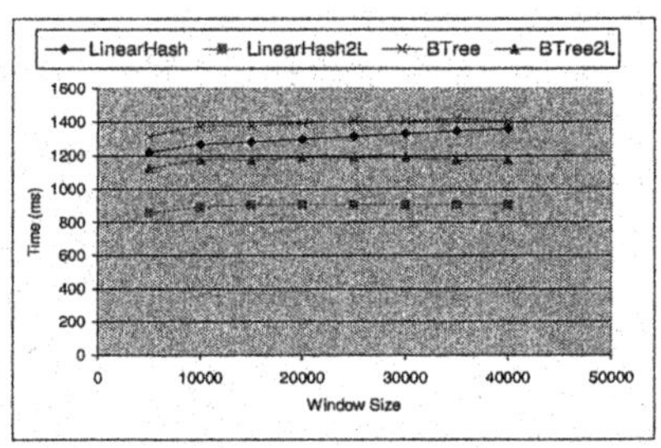

(f) With memory constraint

Figure 4. Experimental results

Figure 4(d) shows the timing results of these methods. Surprisingly, Chained Bucket Hashing has the worst performance. Our further investigation reveals that there is a highly uneven distribution of hyper-alerts in the buckets, which lead to this bad performance. Having ordered input only reduces the execution time slightly for nested loop correlation with both two-level Linear Hashing and Chained Bucket Hashing. Finally, sort correlation with heap sort achieves the best performance among these methods.

We also study the impact of different sorting algorithms on the execution time of sort correlation. We compare two sorting algorithms, heap sort and quick sort. Heap sort has the least complexity in the worst case scenarios, while quick sort is considered the best practical choice among all the sorting algorithms [4]. Figure 4(e) shows the timing results of both algorithms: Sort correlation with quick sort performs significantly worse (and most unstable) than the heap sort case.

Nested-Loop Correlation with Memory Constraint. Our last set of experiments is focused on evaluating the efficiency of different indexing structures when there is memory constraint. The results indicate that two-level Linear Hashing is the most efficient and the two level index structure improves the performance for all four methods. Figure 4(f) shows some timing results obtained with varying sliding window sizes.

5. Related Work

The result in this paper is a continuance of our previous work [11], which has been described earlier. Our method was initially developed to address the limitations of JIGSAW [14]. Our method has several features beyond JIGSAW, including the ability to deal with missing detections and alert aggregation. The work closest to ours is the alert correlation method by Cuppens and Miege [5]. This approach also correlates alerts using partial match of prerequisites (pre-conditions) and consequences (post-conditions) of attacks. However, our method allows alert aggregation during and after correlation, while their approach treats alert aggregation as an individual stage before alert correlation.

Several other alert correlation methods have been proposed. Spice [13] and the probabilistic alert correlation method [15] correlate alerts based on the similarities between alert attributes. Though they are effective in correlating some alerts (e.g., alerts with the same source and destination IP addresses), they cannot fully discover the causal relationships between alerts. Another type of alert correlation methods (e.g., the data mining approach [6]) bases alert correlation on attack scenarios specified by human users or learned through training data sets. These methods are restricted to *known* attack scenarios. We consider these results complementary to ours.

6. Conclusions and Future Work

In this paper, we studied main memory index structures and database query optimization techniques to facilitate timely correlation of intensive alerts. We developed three techniques named *hyper-alert container, two-level index,* and *sort correlation* by taking advantage of the characteristics of the alert correlation process. The experimental study demonstrated that (1) hyper-alert containers improve the efficiency of order-preserving index structures, with which an insertion operation involves search, (2) two-level index improves the efficiency of all index structures, (3) a two-level index structure combining Chained Bucket Hashing and Linear Hashing is most efficient for streamed alerts with and without memory constraint, and (4) sort correlation with heap sort algorithm is the most efficient for alert correlation in batch. Our future work includes incorporating the efficient methods in this paper into the intrusion alert correlation toolkit and developing more techniques to facilitate timely interactive analysis of intrusion alerts.

References

[1] A. Aho, J. Hopcroft, and J.D. Ullman. *The Design and Analysis of Computer Algorithms*. Addison-Wesley, 1974.

[2] A. Ammann, M. Hanrahan, and R. Krishnamurthy. Design of a memory resident DBMS. In *Proc. of IEEE COMPCON*, February 1985.

[3] D. Comer. The ubiquitous B-Tree. *ACM Computeing Surveys*, 11(2):121–137, 1979.

[4] T. H. Cormen, C. E. Leiserson, and R. L. Rivest. *Introduction to Algorithms*. The MIT Press, 1989.

[5] F. Cuppens and A. Miege. Alert correlation in a cooperative intrusion detection framework. In *Proc. of the 2002 IEEE Symposium on Security and Privacy*, May 2002.

[6] O. Dain and R.K. Cunningham. Fusing a heterogeneous alert stream into scenarios. In *Proc. of the ACM Workshop on Data Mining for Security Applications*, November 2001.

[7] H. Garcia-Molina and J. Widom J. D. Ullman. *Database System Implementation*. Prentice Hall, 2000.

[8] D. Knuth. *The Art of Computer Programming*. Addison-Wesley, 1973.

[9] T. J. Lehman and M. J. Carey. A study of index structure for main memory database management systems. In *Proc. of the 12th Int'l Conf. on Very Large Databases*, pages 294–303, August 1986.

[10] W. Litwin. Linear hashing: A new tool for file and table addressing. In *Proc. of the 6th Conf. on Very Large Data Bases*, pages 212–223, Montreal, Canada, October 1980.

[11] P. Ning, Y. Cui, and D. S Reeves. Constructing attack scenarios through correlation of intrusion alerts. In *Proc. of the 9th ACM Conf. on Computer and Communications Security*, pages 245–254, November 2002.

[12] P. Ning and D. Xu. Adapting query optimization techniques for efficient intrusion alert correlation. Technical Report TR-2002-13, NCSU Computer Science, August 2002.

[13] S. Staniford, J.A. Hoagland, and J.M. McAlerney. Practical automated detection of stealthy portscans. *Journal of Computer Security*, 10(1/2):105–136, 2002.

[14] S. Templeton and K. Levitt. A requires/provides model for computer attacks. In *Proc. of New Security Paradigms Workshop*, pages 31 – 38, September 2000.

[15] A. Valdes and K. Skinner. Probabilistic alert correlation. In *Proc. of the 4th International Symposium on Recent Advances in Intrusion Detection (RAID 2001)*, pages 54–68, 2001.

III

SECURITY AND PRIVACY

COLLABORATIVE PRIVACY PRESERVING FREQUENT ITEM SET MINING IN VERTICALLY PARTITIONED DATABASES

Ehud Gudes and Boris Rozenberg
Department of Computer Science, Ben-Gurion University, Beer-Sheva, Israel

Abstract: Privacy concerns have become an important issue in Data Mining. This paper deal with the problem of association rule mining from distributed vertically partitioned data with the goal of preserving the confidentiality of each individual database. Each site holds some attributes of each transaction, and the sites wish to work together to find globally valid association rules without revealing individual transaction data. This problem occurs, for example, when the same users access several electronic shops purchasing different items in each. We present two algorithms for discovering frequent item sets and analyze their security, privacy and complexity properties.

Key words: item set, association rule, privacy

1. INTRODUCTION

Data mining technology has emerged as a means for identifying patterns and trends from large quantities of data. Mining encompasses various algorithms such as clustering, classification, and association rule mining. Traditionally, all these algorithms have been developed within a centralized model, with all data being gathered into a central site, and algorithms being run against that data. Privacy concerns can prevent this approach. There may not be a central site with authority to see all the data, or if the data is partitioned among several sites, sites may not want to disclose to each other their individual database, even if they are willing to disclose some information in order to enable the extraction of globally valid knowledge. Clearly if all participating sites are willing to share their data, or trust a third party to do the mining, the privacy problem is solved. We deal here with the problem that each site tries to protect the confidentiality of its database, without compromising most of the knowledge discovery process. Informally, the problem is to mine association rules across two databases, where the columns in the table are at different sites, splitting each row. The problem was first discussed by Vaidya and Clifton in [3] (called here VDC). Their algorithm requires the intensive use of secure computation and may also have the potential of inferring some information of the individual databases, as will be discussed in Section 2.2, and this motivated our algorithms. Generally, the mining of association rules is divided into two phases: finding frequent item sets with support above a threshold, and finding rules with confidence above a threshold . In this paper we present two algorithms for solving the first problem. The problem of computing the rules can be solved similarly but is not addressed in this paper. The first algorithm is a two-party algorithm which requires a third party, but may also work instead with secure computation. The second is an asymmetric n-party algorithm, which does not require a third party or secure computation. In our protocols, one database is designated the master, and the initiator of the protocol, the other database is the slave. There is a join key present in both databases and the remaining attributes are present in one database or in the other, but not in both. The algorithms are based on two basic ideas. The first idea is the use of fake transactions. In spite of the existence of fake transactions it is possible to compute correctly the frequent item sets. The second idea is not to fix a precise measure of support but rather an approximate measure only, which can be made as precise as needed with a trade-off of the potential amount of inferred private information.

The rest of the paper is structured as follows. Section 2 presents the background and related work. In particular, Section 2.1 reviews the secure computation of a scalar product of two vectors (based on [6]), which we shall use in our algorithm for computing secure intersection of two sets, and Section 2.2 reviews the VDC algorithm [3] and discusses its potential problems. Section 3 presents the two algorithms, and some examples of their use. Section 4 discusses the privacy, security and complexity of the algorithms, and Section 5 is the conclusions and future work section.

2. BACKGROUND

Agrawal and Srikant [1] have proposed the first algorithm for discovering all significant association rules between items in a large database of transactions. However, this work did not address privacy concerns. Later the authors proposed a procedure in which some or all the numerical attributes are perturbed by a randomized value distortion, so that both the original values and their distributions are changed. The proposed procedure then performs a reconstruction of the original distribution. This reconstruction does not reveal the original values of the data, and yet allows the learning of decision trees. Another paper shows a reconstruction method, which does not entail information loss with respect to the original distribution.

When the data is partitioned among several sites, there are algorithms that assume that all required data is available or can be sent to a central site. Then the existing data mining algorithms for centralized data mining model are executed. Another approach for distributed data mining runs the existing data mining algorithms for centralized data mining model at each site independently and combines the results [2]. But this will often fail to achieve a globally valid result. As pointed in [3], The issues that can cause a disparity between local and global results include:

a) Values for a single entity may be split across sources. Data mining at individual sites will be unable to detect cross-site correlations.
b) The same item may be duplicated at different sites, and will be over-weighted in the results.
c) Data at a single site is likely to be from a homogeneous population, hiding geographic or demographic distinctions between that population and others.

To overcome the above problems, algorithms were proposed for partitioned data between sites. The algorithms that were proposed for horizontally partitioned data (i.e. each site contains basically the same columns). Some of them use cryptographic techniques to minimize the amount of disclosed information or a special architecture. This architecture contains sites that sequentially add noise to the original data, compute the answer with noise and remove the noise from the answer. All these methods work with the assumption that no collusion occurs between the sites and the sites follow the protocol precisely.

The main work on vertically partitioned data is that by VDC [3], which we will discuss later in this section.

There has been much work addressing Secure Multiparty Computation. It was first investigated by Yao[4], and later, after Goldriech proved existence of a secure computation for any function[5] some algorithms based on his Circuit Evaluation Protocol have been proposed. But the general method, which is based on Boolean circuits, is inefficient for large inputs. Atallah and Du [6] proposed a more efficient technique for some cases of multi-party computation problem. One of them is the Two-Party Scalar Product Protocol. VDC uses a similar but more efficient protocol for secure product computation as the basis for their algorithm for privacy preserving association rules mining [3]. We will discuss this in more detail later.

This paper uses the general approach suggested by VDC, but proposes two new algorithms to deal with vertically partitioned data. It also does not provide a zero-knowledge solution, but it discloses less amount of information than [3], and may be more practical in some cases.

2.1 M.J.Atallah and W.Du Scalar Product Protocol

Inputs: Alice has a vector $X = (x_1, x_2, \ldots, x_n)$, and Bob has a vector $Y = (y_1, y_2, \ldots, y_n)$.
Outputs: Alice (but not Bob) gets $X \bullet Y + v$ where v is random scalar known to Bob only.

1 Alice and Bob agree on two numbers p and m, such that p^m is so large that conducting p^m additions is computationally infeasible.

2 Alice generates m random vectors, $V_1, \ldots, V_m$, such that $X = \sum_{j=1}^{m} V_j$.

3 Bob generates m random numbers $r_1, \ldots, r_m$, such that $v = \sum_{j=1}^{m} r_j$.

4 For each $j = 1, \ldots, m$ Alice and Bob conduct the following sub-steps:

4.1 Alice generates a secret random number $k, 1 \leq k \leq p$.

4.2 Alice sends $(H_1, \ldots, H_p)$ to Bob, where $H_k = V_j$, and the rest of H_i's are random vectors. Because k is a secret number known to Alice only, Bob does not know the position of V_j.

4.3 Bob computes $Z_{j,i} = H_i \bullet Y + r_j$ for $i = 1, \ldots, p$.

4.4 Using the 1-out-of-N Oblivious Transfer protocol [8,9], Alice gets $Z_j = Z_{j,k} = V_j \bullet Y + r_j$, while Bob learns nothing about k.

5 Alice computes $u = \sum_{j=1}^{m} Z_j = X \bullet Y + v$

As we'll see in Section 3, we could use the above algorithm to compute the size of the intersection of two sets, however a straightforward use by using binary vectors as membership vectors is not secure enough. This will be explained further in Section 3.1.

2.2 The VDC algorithm [3].

The algorithm uses the apriori-gen function to generate all candidate itemsets. For each found itemset, the algorithm calculates the support as follows:

$L_1 = \{\text{large 1-itemsets}\}$
for ($k = 2$; $L_{k-1} \neq \emptyset$; k++) do begin
  C_k = apriori-gen(L_{k-1})
  for all candidates $c \in C_k$ do begin
    if all attributes in c are entirely at A or B
      that party independently calculates *c.count*
    else
      let A have l of the attributes and B have the remaining m attributes.
      construct X on A 's side and Y on B 's side where $X = \prod_{i=1}^{l} A_i$ and $Y = \prod_{i=1}^{m} B_i$
      compute $c.count = X * Y = \sum_{i=1}^{n} x_i \cdot y_i$
    end if
    $L_k = L_k \cup c \mid c.count \geq \text{minsup}$
  end
end
Answer = $\cup_k L_k$

Suppose we want to compute if a particular 5-itemset is frequent with site A having 2 of the attributes and site B having 3 attributes. i.e. A and B want to know if the itemset $I = \{A_a, A_b, B_a, B_b, B_c\}$ is frequent. A creates a new vector X of cardinality n where $X = A_a * A_b$ (component multiplication) and B creates a new vector Y of cardinality n where $Y = B_a * B_b * B_c$. The Scalar product of X and Y provides the (in)frequency of the itemset . The scalar product is computed using a different method of secure computation than the one presented in [6]. As we'll see later we use a minor modification of the algorithm in [6], but we could have used the method of [3] as well.

The VDC algorithm has some problems. First the method requires communication of the two sites, for each item set computation. As we shall see, this is not required in our algorithm. The second problem is that this method may disclose information in certain cases, because in this algorithm each site learns the exact support of each item set. This is explained next.

Assume that site A learns the exact support for some itemset. With this knowledge, A learns the probability that an item in the set supported by A has a property in B, computed as the ratio of the actual support to A 's support. For example, in the case when we have a support value of 5% for an itemset *ab*, and exactly 5% of the items on A have item *a*, A knows that at least those same items on B have property b. This occurs always when the global support equals A's support, not just when A's support is at the threshold.

As we shall see, our algorithm discloses such information in less number of cases. Only when the global support is exactly equal to the threshold and to one of the parties' support value, it discloses the same amount of information as VDC. When the global support value is larger than the threshold, it discloses less information than VDC, and when the support value is less than the threshold, it discloses almost no information.

3. THE ALGORITHMS

We first present the definition of the problem, and the ideas, which are common to both algorithms and then, the two algorithms.

The association rule mining problem can be formally stated as follows [7]: Let $I = \{i_1, i_2, \ldots, i_m\}$ be a set of literals called items. Let D be a set of transactions, where each transaction T is a set of items such that $T \subseteq I$. Associated with each transaction is a unique identifier, called its TID. We say that transaction T contains X, a set of some items in I, if $X \subseteq T$. An association rule is an implication of the form, $X \Rightarrow Y$, where $X \subset I$, $Y \subset I$, and $X \cap Y = \phi$. The rule $X \Rightarrow Y$ holds in the transaction set D with confidence c, if c% of the transactions in D that contain X also contain Y. The rule $X \Rightarrow Y$ has support s in the transaction set D, if s% of the transactions in D contain $X \cup Y$. Item set X is called large if its support is greater then or equal to the minimal support threshold. Our goal is to find all large itemsets (as noted in the introduction, the problem of finding the rules can be solved similarly, but is outside of the scope of this paper.).

In a vertically partitioned database we have the following situation. There are two databases, DB1 and DB2. In both databases, the domain of the TIDs is the same. We are only interested in large item sets, which contain attributes from both databases. In both databases there are TIDs which are not present, however for those TIDs which are not null, TIDs (DB1) $\cap$ TIDs(DB2) is close to size(DBi), which enables a real-life mining of globally frequent item set. The problem is to find large item sets without each site revealing its own database.

Both algorithms follow the basic collaborative Apriori algorithm. However, before applying the algorithm there is a pre-processing stage that populates the individual databases with fake transactions. After this action, each party can send the resulted database to the opposite party to calculate the frequent itemsets in the resulted database. In the first algorithm the two parties are symmetric. In the first phase one is designated as a master, which initiates the protocol and will get the results, and the other as a slave, which only contributes its information but will not do any global computations. The master is looking for all large itemsets according to its own real transactions, and check whether the found itemsets are present in the *slave* real transactions. This is done with the help of a third untrusted party (this party is not trusted with the database, but it is trusted with computations). The parties change roles at the end of the phase.

In the second algorithm, there are n slaves and one master. The master computes the globally valid item sets and tells the results to the slaves.

We assume without loss of generality that the number of transactions in each database is equal to N – some number that depends on area of business, and the TIDs range from 1 to N. When fake transactions are introduced, they use "unoccupied" TIDs. When information between the parties is shared, then only information in which some attributes are real (in one of the databases) is of use. That is, a fake transaction whose corresponding TID in the other database is empty, is not considered at all. Its important to note that when each site computes large itemsets it doesn't know whether the attributes corresponding to his real transaction, are real or not!

3.1 Algorithm 1

Preparing phase (executed by two parties):

1 Construct database with fake transactions (Simply put randomly 1 in non existing transactions).
2 Send to the third Party all your real TID.
3 Receive from third Party whether mining is possible (See the Third Party execution phase). If it is then continue.
4 Send the database from one party to the opposite party and receive its database.
5 Build the global database (TIDs from step 1, and attributes from the two databases).
6 Build local true database (LTDB - contains the local real transactions only, but with possibly fake attributes from the other party).

Master's Execution phase:

1 find LL_1 – all large 1-itemsets in the local database from 6.
2 for each $l \in LL_1$:
2.1 send LID = {TID | l present in transaction
with id = TID} to third Party
2.2 receive from third Party Ok or Not
3 end
4 $GL_1 = \{l \in LL_1 \mid \text{third Party said Ok}\}$
5 for ($k = 2$; $GL_{k-1} \neq \phi$; k++)

5.1 C_k = apriori-gen(GL_{k-1})
5.2 for all transaction $t \in$ LTDB
5.2.1 C_t = subset(C_k , t)
5.2.2 for all candidates $c \in C_t$
5.2.2.1 *c.count* ++
5.2.3 end
5.3 end
6 $LL_k = \{c \in C_k \mid c.count \geq \text{minsup}\}$
7 for each $l \in LL_k$
7.1 send LID = {TID | l presents in transaction with id = TID} to third Party
7.2 receive from third Party Ok or Not
8 end
9 GL_k = { $l \in LL_k$ | third Party said Ok}
10 end
11 send to third Party "Master Finished"
12 Answer = $\cup_k GL_k$
13 reverse roles and execute algorithm again

Third Party execution phase:

1 receive from the two parties their real TID (TID1,TID2)
2 send to the two parties (|TID1 $\cap$ TID2| $\geq$ minsup)
3 if (|TID1 $\cap$ TID2| $\geq$ minsup)
3.1 while (Master not finished) do
3.1.1 receive set of TID's from Master (MTID, |MTID| $\geq$ minsup)
3.1.2 if [|MTID $\cap$ TID2| $\geq$ minsup] then
3.1.2.1 send "Ok" to Master
3.1.3 else
3.1.3.1 send "NotOK" to Master
3.1.4 end if
3.2 end while
4 else
4.1 send "NotOK" /* mining is not possible! not enough overlap! */
5 end if
6 end

Slave execution phase:

1 Execute preparing phase.
2 Wait for master to finish.

3.1.1 Secure computation

Instead of a third party, one may use secure computation. The main problem is overcoming the "0,1" problem. Let us discuss it in more detail.

To compute the intersection size of two sets of TIDs (from a common domain), one can use binary vectors where a 1 indicates membership and a zero indicates non-existence. The scalar product of these two vectors is the size of intersection. For example in Algorithm1, the master creates a vector $X = (x_1, x_2, \ldots, x_n)$ such that $x_i = 1$ if transaction with ID = i is a real transaction of the Master and contains the checking item set l, and $x_i = 0$, if transaction number i is a fake transaction or does not contains an itemset l, and the Slave generates a vector $Y = (y_1, y_2, \ldots, y_n)$ similarly. However, if one uses Attallah and Du's protocol [6] directly, there may be a compromise of information. This can be demonstrated as follows:

Suppose one party knows some data values, the equations can be solved to reveal all values. For example, if X is represented as $V_1 = (0,0,1)$, $V_2 = (0,1,0)$, $V_3 = (0,1,1)$, $Y = (1,1,1)$ and $r_1 = 4$, and the first party gets:

$y_3 + r_1 = 7$

$y_2 + r_1 = 5$

$y_2 + y_3 + r_1 = 7$

Since y_1 was eliminated by the "zeroes", the first party now has 3 equations with 3 unknowns. Which it can solve to disclose both the y's and the r.

To reduce this possibility in our protocol, we can restrict the Master not use the value "0" in the representation of vector X, and for the Slave not to reuse the r-values sent once.

The following method explain, how we can divide the vector X into m random vectors $V_1, \ldots, V_m$:

The Master generates m random vectors from Z_p^n such that $X = \sum_{j=1}^{m} V_j \mod p$

Now, the Master and the Slave can perform a Scalar Product Protocol as is, to find the size of the intersection of vectors X and Y. For example, assume the Master creates vector $X = (x_1, x_2, \ldots, x_{10}) = (1,1,0,0,0,1,1,0,1,0)$ and the Slave generates the vector $Y = (y_1, y_2, \ldots, y_{10}) = (1,1,0,1,0,1,1,0,0,1)$. Suppose the Master and the Slave agree on the number $m = 3$ and p =11 in the protocol. Now, the Master generates following random vectors:

$V_1 = (1,2,3,4,5,6,7,8,9,10)$

$V_2 = (2,3,4,5,5,7,8,9,1,10)$
$V_3 = (9,7,4,2,1,10,8,5,2,2)$

Now, the Master and the Slave can perform a Scalar Product Protocol as is, to find the size of the intersection of vectors X and Y without having the danger of eliminating Ys because of the "0"s. Note, that only the Slave knows the size of the intersection, and it can send to Master "Ok" if this size $\geq$ minimal support.

3.2 Algorithm 2

In this algorithm we do not use a third party and instead let each slave compute the intersection itself. However, since the slaves have no knowledge of the other databases, their inference from this computation is very limited.

We assume that we have one Master and n Slaves. The Master starts the computation with the first Slave and waits for the last Slave for a positive or a negative result.

Execution phase for each Slave:

1 receive a set of IDs (or "NOT OK") from your left neighbour.
2 if received "NOT OK"
2.1 send "NOT OK" to your right neighbour.
2.2 go to 1
3 else
3.1 intersects the set with your own real IDs and test.
4 if result $\geq$ minimal support
4.1 send resulted SetOfIds to your right neighbour
5 else
5.1 send "NOT OK" to your right neighbor.
5.2 go to 1
6 end if

Now we can describe the algorithm, which is quite similar to Algorithm 1.

Master's preparing phase:

1 Send to your right neighbor all real TIDs. Receive from your left neighbor whether mining is possible. If it is, then continue.
2 Build the global database (TID = TID1 $\cup$ TID2,... $\cup$ TIDn and the attributes from the n databases (i.e. each slave sends the database with fake transactions to the master).
3 Build local true database (LTDB - contains the local real transactions only).

Master's execution phase:

1 find LL_1 – all large 1-itemsets in the local database from 4.
2 for each $l \in LL_1$:
2.1 LID = {TID | l present in transaction with id = TID}
2.2 send LID to the right neighbor
2.3 receive from left neighbor Ok or Not
3 end
4 $GL_1 = \{l \in LL_1 \mid$ Slave said Ok$\}$
5 for ($k = 2$; $GL_{k-1} \neq \phi$; k++)
5.1 C_k = apriori-gen(GL_{k-1})
5.2 for all transaction $t \in$ LTDB
5.2.1 C_t = subset(C_k , t)
5.2.2 for all candidates $c \in C_t$
5.2.2.1 *c.count* ++
5.2.3 end
5.3 end
5.4 $LL_k = \{ c \in C_k \mid c.count \geq \text{minsup}\}$
5.5 for each $l \in LL_k$
5.5.1 LID = {TID | l presents in transaction with id = TID}
5.5.2 send LID to the right neighbor
5.5.3 receive from left neighbor Ok or Not
5.6 end
5.7 $GL_k = \{ l \in LL_k \mid$ Slave said Ok$\}$
6 end
7 Answer = $\cup_k GL_k$
8 send Answer to all Slaves

Note that in this case we may also use secure computation, but if the number of databases is greater than 2, this is not really necessary, since each slave may not be able to infer much anyway. This is because when n>2, each slave not only does not know the exact size of the final intersection, but also does not know which exact item set the master is currently testing!

4. ANALYSIS

4.1 Correctness

The two algorithms use the apriori-gen function to generate all candidates to be large itemset. On each iteration k, a large k-item sets that was found by the Master according to its true transactions only, was checked by another site. So, all existed large itemsets where found.

4.2 Security analysis

The security of the approach depends on the algorithm and the method. In algorithm 1 and a Third party, it depends on the integrity of the third party. In algorithm 2, on the integrity of each of the slaves.

If we use secure computation, then the security of our approach is based on the security of the scalar product protocol, which is based on the inability of the slave side to solve $p * m$ equations with $n+m$ unknowns, which requires that $n>m\ (p\text{-}1)$. Since the master does not get the result of the scalar product, just an "OK" answer, it cannot use the linear equations methods anyway.

Computing support for each candidate item set requires one run of the component scalar product protocol. Again, the slave is secured by the same bound, since at each run the master sends it a different intersection set (with different random components).

4.3 Disclosed information

In both algorithms, neither the Master nor the Slave learns the exact support for an item set. They only know, whether some item set is frequent or not. This decreases the probability that the Master or Slaves will learn that a set of items on another site has a given property and it occurs only when the global support value is above or equal to the threshold value, and is also equal to the Master's or Slave's support. For example, if *a* is an item from the Master's database, and *b* is an item from the Slave's database, the threshold support is 5%, and the global support is greater or equal 5%, and item set *{a,b}* is present in exactly 5% of the real Master's transactions, then the Master knows that the same transactions are real transactions of the Slave.

In the case when the item set *{a,b}* is present in more then 5% (support threshold) of transactions in the Master's database, say 7%, and *{a,b}* is still a global large item set, the Master knows, that at least $5/7$ transactions of the Slave are real transactions, but he is not sure even which are real transactions and which are fake. When the support of a tested item set is less than the support threshold, very little information is disclosed to the master and almost none to the slave.

Note that the master in either Algorithm1 or Algorithm2 never knows the support value, whether we use a third party or secure computation. When we use secure computation, or in Algorithm2 with only 2 parties, the slave does know the exact value of support, but it cannot do anything with it since it doesn't know which item set the master is currently testing! So knowing the size of the product does not give him much information!

As was explained in Section 2.2, in VDC, in contrast, the Master learns the probability that an item in the set supported by Master has a property in the Slave's database, computed as the ratio of the global 1 support to the Master's support, whether the *item set is frequent or not*!

One important point that we want to stress here is that if the participants don't know the number of fake transactions, then this number has no effect on the amount of disclosed information. It can only affect the performance (redundant computations) of the algorithm!

One problem which can occur in our algorithms, although unlikely, is that some specific value will be disclosed when the database has a large number of overlapping entities. For example, suppose the Master's real IDs are $I_m = \{1,2,3,4,5,6\}$, and the Slave's real IDs are $I_s=\{1,2,3,4\}$ and minsupp = 4. Assume the Master asks the Slave whether $|I_1 \cap I_s| \geq$ minsupp and gets answer "YES" (I_1 - subset of I_m and $I_1=\{1,2,3,4,5,6\}$). Next question is whether $|I_2 \cap I_s| \geq$ minsupp and he gets the answer "NO" (I_2 - subset of I_m and $I_2=\{1,2,3,5,6\}$). The Master can come to the conclusion that transaction with ID = 4 is a real transaction of the Slave, and at least 2 transactions from {1,2,3,5,6} are fake. Allowing approximate answers as follows can reduce this possibility.

4.4 The Support approximation method

Let us assume that the Master and the Slave agree on *ac* – approximation coefficient. In both algorithms, whoever compute the intersection size, the third party or the slave, instead of checking whether it is greater or equal than the minimal support, it does the following. It generates a random number c, such that (minsup - ac) $\leq$ c $\leq$ minsup, and sends "Okey" to the Master if the size of above intersection $\geq$ c, and "No" in the other case.

Now, for every tested item set, this approximation will use a new value of c. Thus, even for overlapping item sets it will be quite difficult to discover facts such as demonstrated above. This property decreases the exactness of the solution, since it only guarantees that the support will be above minimal-support – ac, but it discloses less information to the opposite side, and decreases the ability of any side to guess the real transactions of the opponent.

Using the above example, the Master cannot distinguish between the following two cases:

C = 3 during the first intersection calculation and C = 4 during the second intersection calculation when {1,2,3} are real transactions of the Slave.

C = 2 during the first intersection calculation and C = 3 during the second intersection calculation when {1,2} are real transactions of the Slave.

On the other hand, if the Master asks the Slave the same question a large number of times, it increases its chance of guessing the correct size of the intersection. This since if ac is not large, the average result will give out some information. To reduce this possibility, we can restrict the Master to check each set only once.

5. CONCLUSIONS AND FUTURE WORK

We presented two algorithms for discovering all large item sets in vertically distributed databases, without the sources revealing their individual transaction values. We compared these algorithms to the previously known algorithm by Vaidya and Clifton [3] and show that it is possible to achieve good security and privacy with complexity cost small enough.

In the future, we will develop precise algorithms for producing rules and not only frequent item sets. We also plan to further investigate the privacy/performance tradeoffs both analytically and experimentally and test these tradeoffs with different support values.

REFERENCES

1. R. Agrawal and R. Srikant. Fast algorithms for mining association rules. In Proceedings of the 20th International Conference on Very Large Data Bases, Santiago, Chile, Sept. 12-15 1994.
2. A.Prodomidis, P.Chan, S.Stofo. Meta-learning in distributed data mining systems: Issues and approaches, chapter 3. AAAI/MIT Press, 2000.
3. J.Vaidya, C.Clifton. Privacy Preserving Association Rule Mining in Vertically Partitioned Data. In Proceedings of SIGKDD 2002, Edmonton, Alberta, Canada.
4. A.C.Yao. How to generate and exchange secrets. In Proceedings of the 27th IEEE Symposium on Foundations of Computer Science,.1986, pages 162-167.
5. O.Goldreich, S.Micali, A.Wigderson. How to play any mental game – a completeness theorem for protocols with honest majority. In Proceedings, 19th ACM Symposium on the Theory of Computing, pages 218-229, 1987.
6. W.Du and M.J.Atallah,. Secure multi-party computational geometry. In proceedings of the 7th International Workshop on Algorithms and Data Structures, Providance, Rhode Island, 2001.
7. R.Agrawal, T.Imielinski, A.M.Swami. Mining association rules between sets of items in large databases., In Proceedings of the 1993 ACM SIGMOD International Conference on Management of Data, pages 207-216, Washington, 1993.
8. G.Brassard, C.Crepeau, J.Robert. All-or-nothing disclosure of secrets. In Advances in Cryptology-Crypto86, Springer Lecture Notes in Computer Science, volume 263, 1986.
9. I.Even, O.Goldreich, A.Lempel. A randomized protocol for signing contracts. Communications of the ACM, Vol 28:637-647, 1985.

PRIVACY UNDER CONDITIONS OF CONCURRENT INTERACTION WITH MULTIPLE PARTIES

Martin S Olivier

Department of Computer Science, University of Pretoria, South Africa

http://mo.co.za

Abstract This paper explores the possibility to represent the privacy policies of an individual, as well as the processing steps of those who (concurrently) process the data, using a simple process algebra, FSP. The approach leads to the identification of two major classes of privacy policies: aggregation policies and quantitative policies. Automated analysis (with the LTSA tool) of such policies, in combination with the actions of parties that process personal information allows the automated discovery of possible breaches of privacy.

It is demonstrated that addressing the breaches often involves tradeoffs, such discontinuing interaction with some parties, so that policies are no longer violated.

1. Introduction

Personal privacy has, in some respects, been an evasive topic in Computer Science. While it has become entrenched in phrases such as *Security and Privacy*, it is often difficult to establish what *privacy* adds to the notion that is not already covered under the rubric of *security*. The one clear exception is the association between *privacy* and *anonymity*: If privacy is a form of security for the individual, then anonymity guarantees privacy. Anonymity, however, is not a panacea: Not only are anonymity and accountability incompatible, but a tradeoff between anonymity and privacy implies a tradeoff between privacy and freedom — freedom of speech [23] and freedom to act; the degree to which actions and utterings can be observed, stored and matched in a digital environment would constrain such actions to a significant extent if one's only option to perform them with a reasonable amount of privacy were to perform them anonymously.

Having said this, it is important to realise that sharing of personal information with others always carries some risk. There are very few guarantees that personal information, once shared, will be treated in confidence and used in the manner in which it was intended. This risk is not without benefit, however: society depends on information about individuals being available. Society's need for accountability justifies individuals carrying identity cards and passports. This need justifies the requirement that cars are fitted with licence plates. This need also justifies (responsible) use of blacklists for services where individuals moved outside society's reasonable expectations of how individuals should behave under certain circumstances.

If total anonymity (for total privacy) is not the only option, the question becomes one of how much privacy can be achieved by how much reserve? Unfortunately, privacy and reserve (with many other such notions) are notoriously difficult to quantify. It seems that the best approximation to this is some (formal) model that enables one to reason about specific tradeoffs.

P3P [29] provides a first step in this direction. P3P allows both the user and the service provider to represent (aspects of) their privacy policy. These policies are then compared and, only if the policies are compatible, is the individual's information shared. No attempt, however, is made to correlate information shared with a number of parties. Arguably, when multiple parties are involved, privacy risks for the combined case are significantly higher than the sum of the individual risks. This is amongst others due to the possibility of correlating ('matching') and aggregation of information by the various parties.

This paper explores the possibility to achieve some indication of the tradeoffs that occur when an individual interacts with multiple parties and wishes to maintain privacy according to some personal policy. The activities of parties with whom an individual deals are formally modelled. Next, the activities that have privacy implications are highlighted using the same formal modelling technique. Finally, the individual's privacy policy is represented using the same technique. In this privacy policy undesirable states are indicated. Reachability analysis is then used to check the possibility of reaching such undesirable privacy states. The individual can now decide how to react to such a possible breach of privacy.

A simple process algebra, FSP [22], is used to model the activities of those parties with whom the individual interacts and the individual's privacy policies. The LTSA tool [22] is used to perform the reachability analysis.

The approach followed in this paper still offers many challenges, not the least of which is the complexity of appropriately modelling something as intangible as privacy. This complexity will specifically impact on the possibility of practical application of the proposed approach. This paper has a more modest goal than attempting to give a comprehensive solution to the stated problem; its goal is rather to explore the notions involved in addressing the problem and thereby help set the stage for a solution (if a practical solution does exist).

The paper is structured as follows. Section 2 gives some background about privacy. Section 3 introduces modelling the actions of parties with whom the individual deals as well as the individual's privacy policy. Next, section 4 uses reachability analysis to identify privacy policies and considers courses of action the individual may pursue to address such problems. Section 5 ties up some loose ends after which section 6 concludes the paper.

2. Background

Privacy is a complex issue. This is already evident if one only focusses on technical issues — the main concern of this paper. It seems that technical work has been done in five areas regarding privacy, namely anonymity, private communication, inference control, organisational safeguards and personal control. Each of these is briefly considered below. For an introduction to non-technical aspects of privacy see [4, 8, 9, 18, 23, 27, 31, 40].

Anonymity work in privacy is based on the fact that observation of one's actions in Cyberspace is easier, and records tend to persist for longer. Work done to achieve anonymity (or pseudonymity) include onion routing [13] and Crowds [30] — both of which hide the origin of messages flowing through a network — and anonymous proxies (such as web anonymizers and anonymous remailers [5, 11, 21]) — that hide the IP-address and other identifying details of the client from the server. In this regard, it is worth noting Chadwick's point [6] that anonymity is not only a bad idea on the Internet (due to its incompatibility with accountability), but also that most of these solutions actually provide a pseudonymous solution.

The second area — privacy of personal communications — has primarily been addressed by encryption. This is evidenced by, for example, the name of the popular encryption product, PGP: Pretty Good *Privacy* [12].

The third aspect of (technical) privacy that has received some attention is that of statistical inference. This has been achieved by modifying data in ways that are statistically insignificant [35] and by limiting statistical queries over such data to queries that include a sufficient number of entries so that inferences cannot be made about individual cases [7] and removing identifying information from such entries [33, 36]. In the last case, it is interesting to note that removing obviously identifying information (such as names, identity numbers, etc) is not sufficient and a more extensive sanitising of data is required [33, 36].

In the case of organisational safeguards, most work done on security is relevant, but not specific to privacy. Specific privacy safeguards will focus on protection of the individual's information against inadvertent (or even intentional) misuse by the organisation or those associated with the organisation. It may be approached by implementing checks and balances to ensure that personal information is not misused. This can, amongst others, be ensured by recording the purpose for which personal data has been collected, recording the privacy policy applicable at the time of data collection, recording personal preferences, and other similar privacy-related information. Additionally, an access monitor then controls all accesses to such data by ensuring that access attempts are compatible with all the security information recorded earlier, as well as other privacy considerations at the time of collection and/or at the time of use. A number of solutions to achieve this have been proposed [3, 10, 19, 1, 2, 20, 26]. A common reservation about such solutions is the doubt that businesses will voluntarily implement them. The business case for such solutions have been argued in a number of places [2, 14, 15, 16, 17, 20, 23, 28, 39]. The essence of these arguments is that these technologies make business sense because they will help to attract customers and to build a relationship of trust with new and existing customers, yielding a (mutually) beneficial associasion. Such technologies can also help to prevent costly privacy-related accidents. Products that have been introduced in this area include IBM's Tivoli Privacy Manager [38] and PrivacyRight's TrustFilter [28]. Note should also be taken of IBM's Enterprise Privacy Architecture [15, 19].

The importance of organisational safeguards for the current paper is the fact that they provide a degree of assurance that organisations will indeed honour their privacy commitments as expressed in their privacy policies. When such technologies are properly installed and regularly audited, personal control becomes more dependable.

The final privacy aspect to be addressed here is indeed that of personal control. The best-known example here is P3P [29] where the individual controls whether information should be divulged to an organisation, given the organisation's privacy policy. Also in this category is the work done by Teepe et al [37] that establishes what information an individual will need to divulge during the course of a workflow process before the individual initiates the workflow. This enables the individual to know whether participation in a workflow will become too sensitive, before divulging some private information as part of a process. The current paper also addresses this aspect (personal control) of the privacy problem.

The relationships between the technologies considered above has been investigated elsewhere [24], where it has been shown that a fully ordered relationship exists between them, that was then formalised as the Layered Privacy Architecture (LaPA).

The use of a process algebra to model aspects of security is not new [32]. Also privacy (specifically anonymity) has been modelled using a process algebra [32, 34]. In these cases, the goal is to model security protocols and determine whether specific security properties (secrecy, authentication, non-repudiation and anonymity) hold for these protocols as required. In our case it is not security protocols that will be modelled, but business processes. We will also not be primarily concerned about whether specific properties hold, but whether an arbitrary (user-specifiable) privacy policy can be violated.

3. Modelling actions and privacy

3.1. Behaviour of parties

If the actions of some party with whom an individual wants to interact are known, it is relatively easy to model the actions of that party in FSP. To illustrate, the actions of a shop may be

```
SHOP = (address.request -> pack -> ship -> address.release ->
   SHOP).
```

Here the `pack` and `ship` actions are assumed to be primitives that have no real impact on the privacy of the individual. In contrast `address.request` and `address.release` are actions that were chosen to indicate that the shop acquires the customer's address somehow and deletes it afterwards.

Even the simple definition of a SHOP holds a number of challenges. Firstly, the question arises about who should define the actions of the SHOP. The end-user may not have access to the internal operation of the SHOP and may therefore not be able to model the SHOP accurately. A better solution would therefore be for the SHOP to model its own actions and publish that as part of its privacy policy. This, however, would require a standardised nomenclature (or ontology) — a problem that we ignore given the explorative nature of this paper. A second problem introduced by the SHOP publishing its own actions as part of a privacy policy would be knowing which of its actions are relevant for a diverse population of individuals, each with his or her own privacy policy. It is possible to address this by expecting the SHOP to publish a relatively detailed account of its actions, and where the individual then selects only those that are appropriate to his or her privacy policy. The following FSP statement expresses that only `address.request` and `address.release` are relevant to the individual:

```
SHOP = (address.request -> pack -> ship -> address.release ->
   SHOP)
   @{address.{request,release}}.
```

It is also possible to model temporal retention of data for audit purposes, as follows

```
SHOP = (address.request -> pack -> ship -> waitFiveYears ->
   address.release -> SHOP).
```

However, this paper does not consider such temporal constraints. What the paper does consider are cases where information is retained until some action leads to its deletion. This is illustrated by the following definition of INSURER:

```
INSURER = (insurancedata.request -> INSURED),
```

```
INSURED = (claim -> process -> payout -> INSURED |
   cancel -> insurancedata.release -> INSURER).
```

Here the insurance data is retained until the policy is cancelled by an explicit `cancel` action.

For the sake of illustration below, one further class of organisations is introduced here:

```
MARKETER = (address.request -> sendmail -> address.release ->
   MARKETER).
```

Finally, the instances of these categories of organisations are defined and specified as processes that execute concurrently. For our purposes `a` and `d` are `INSURER`s, `b` is a `SHOP` and `c` is a `MARKETER`:

```
||ORGANISATIONS = (a:INSURER || b:SHOP || c:MARKETER ||
   d:INSURER).
```

3.2. Categories of parties

Now that the behaviour of parties has been specified, and some instances of those parties have been defined, it becomes possible to identify categories of organisations so that it will be possible to specify privacy policies in terms of such categories, rather than specific parties (although specification of privacy policies in terms of such specific parties will not be precluded).

The first category is one that inherently holds a negative connotation:

```
SPAMMER = (address.request -> spam -> SPAMMER).
```

The intention here is that, whenever a party identified as a `SPAMMER`, performs an `address.request` action, it becomes possible for the `SPAMMER` process to perform the `spam` action, that will be used below in the policies section to specify a privacy policy to limit the actions of spammers.

The second category to be used in this paper is not inherently value laden; it will be used to identify financial institutions and specifically identify the points at which they request and release information. `FINANCIAL` accomplishes this:

```
FINANCIAL = ({address,insurancedata}.request -> finreq ->
   {address,insurancedata}.release -> finrel -> FINANCIAL).
```

This definition incorporates a rudimentary form of categorising data: `address` is assumed to be part of `insurancedata`, and when either is requested, the `finreq` (*financial request*) action becomes enabled. Similarly, when either is released, the `finrel` (*financial release*) action becomes enabled.

Unfortunately, given the nature of the process algebra used, these trigger actions (`spam`, `finreq` and `finrel`) will automatically be enabled for those parties who are not placed in the respective categories. (For example, if `a` is not identified as a `SPAMMER` in this section, `a.spam` will automatically be enabled in the policies section below, because there is no `a.spam` in the category section here (yet) for which it will have to 'wait'.) In order to avoid this, it is necessary to introduce 'opposites' for the categories already introduced:

```
NOTSPAMMER = NOTSPAMMER +{spam}.
NOTFINANCIAL = NOTFINANCIAL +{finreq, finrel}.
```

In both of these cases the trigger actions do not form part of the process descriptions but the alphabets of the processes are extended with these actions; they therefore inherently cannot occur in these processes and will therefore not be enabled in the policies section below.

All that remains in this section is to combine the various instances of parties with their respective categories. A possible combination looks as follows:

```
||CATEGORIES =
   ({c}:SPAMMER || {a,b,d}:NOTSPAMMER ||
   {a,d,b}:FINANCIAL || {c}:NOTFINANCIAL)
```

3.3. Privacy policies

Once the parties and categories have been modelled, the policies can be modelled.

In some cases (possible) occurrence of the trigger action will violate privacy and therefore needs to be indicated as such:

```
property CHECKSPAM = (spam -> ERROR).
```

Another possible policy is to limit the number of occurrences of one's information in different databases. The following policy limits one's information to two financial institutions:

```
const MaxFin = 2
property CHECKFIN = CHECKFIN[0],
CHECKFIN[i:0..MaxFin] = (
   when (i<MaxFin) finreq -> CHECKFIN[i+1] |
   when (i==MaxFin) finreq -> ERROR |
   when (i>0) finrel -> CHECKFIN[i-1] |
   when (i==0) finrel -> ERROR).
```

These examples suffice for the initial discussion and now it is possible to combine the various policies:

```
set AllProc = {a,b,c,d}
||POLICIES = (AllProc::CHECKSPAM || AllProc::CHECKFIN).
```

Finally the parties, categories and policies can be combined:

```
||SYSTEM = (ORGANISATIONS || CATEGORIES || POLICIES).
```

4. Discussion

A reachability analysis of the system described above can now be performed to see if the ERROR state can be reached. If it can, a trace to this state will illustrate how it is possible to violate the individual's privacy policy. As is clear from the simple examples given above, it is indeed possible to violate the policy. A safety analysis with LTSA produces the following trace:

```
Depth 2 -- States: 4 Transitions: 27 Memory used: 7356K
Trace to property violation in POLICIES.{a,b,c,d}::CHECKSPAM:
        c.address.request
        c.spam
```

This indicates the (obvious) problem that the individual's CHECKSPAM policy can be violated if c requests the individual's address leading to the possible execution of the trigger action spam by c.

This simple example illustrates one of the major points of this paper: Once a possible breach of privacy has been identified, it is, in general, up to the individual to deal with the possible breach. The individual may, for example, avoid the breach by no longer dealing with c. The individual may also investigate the reasons why he or she has identified c as a spammer. If it possible to accept the amount of junk mail c sends, it may warrant reclassifying c as a NOTSPAMMER. To further elaborate on this last point, suppose that b is classified as a SPAMMER, but in our agreed upon interaction (as specified by the FSP definition of b's behaviour) b does not send any mail. If we accept the specified descriptions as true of actual behaviour (a point that we already noted earlier in the paper), the individual may decide to phrase the SPAMMER category in terms of the mail action rather than (or in addition to) the address.request action, as follows:

```
SPAMMER = (mail -> spam -> SPAMMER).
```

or

```
SPAMMER = (address.request -> mail -> spam -> SPAMMER).
```

Given such a trigger action definition, b would not violate the policy even if b were identified as a SPAMMER. In other words, thinking about the semantics of actions may lead to a redefinition of a trigger action or a privacy policy that would avoid the conflict. These options are in addition to the options of no longer dealing with the party involved in the breach of a privacy policy, or renegotiating the interaction with that party.

Once the SPAMMER violation has been addressed in any of the above manners, a reachability analysis with LTSA leads to the following trace:

```
Depth 6 -- States: 570 Transitions: 3756 Memory used: 8463K
Trace to property violation in POLICIES.{a,b,c,d}::CHECKFIN:
        a.insurancedata.request
        b.address.request
```

```
d.insurancedata.request
a.finreq
d.finreq
b.finreq
```

What this shows is the (again obvious) result that the maximum number of financial institutions that are allowed to simultaneously hold the individual's information can be exceeded (as illustrated here, when a, b and d simultaneously hold some of the individual's information).

Resolving the violation may again be considered by stopping interaction with any of the parties involved (a, b or d), changing the categorisation (for example deciding that b is not a financial institution after all) or changing the policy (by, for example, setting MaxFin equal to three). For example, changing classification of b to NOTFINANCIAL yields the following safety results from LTSA:

```
Depth 25 -- States: 16384 Transitions: 93184 Memory used: 8082K
No deadlocks/errors
```

The question that needs to be addressed now, is one on the nature of privacy violations that can be modelled (and detected) using the approach described in this paper. While it is clearly possible to check privacy violations from a single party (such as that represented by the CHECKSPAM policy above) the clear power of the technique lies in detecting (and addressing) privacy violations that arise from the interaction of many parties that are concurrently active and processing one's data. Before turning our attention to that, it is worth noting that single-party violations need not be as simple as the CHECKSPAM policy above: it is also possible to have a policy that monitor's the party's acquisition of personal information over time and flags the point at which the amount of collected information exceeds some threshold. The details of how this can be done will be clear after the multi-party scenario has been discussed below.

One type of privacy policy for which the described approach holds potential, is that of computerised matching. Suppose that some party m has access to the individual's medical records, while another, t, has access to the individual's tax records. If the individual is concerned that m and t might use their access to match the data to learn more about the individual, the individual can set up a privacy policy that, while permitting the two parties to access his or her information, does not allow them to do it simultaneously. To do this, suppose that appropriate categories have been created to cause suitable medicalreq, medicalrel, taxreq and taxrel trigger actions. Then the following policy will specify the non-matching requirement:

```
property CHECKMATCH = (taxreq -> HASTAX | medicalreq ->
   HASMED),
HASTAX = (taxrel -> CHECKMATCH | medicalreq -> ERROR),
HASMED = (medicalrel -> CHECKMATCH | taxreq -> ERROR).
```

with POLICIES now defined as

```
||POLICIES = (AllProc::CHECKSPAM || AllProc::CHECKFIN ||
   t,m::CHECKMATCH).
```

Prevention of computerised matching is clearly a special case of what may be termed an *aggregation* policy — where the individual wants to prevent simultaneous processing of a set of personal data items that, when aggregated, may form a more comprehensive image of the individual (whether it is true or false) than the individual data items would have. Definition 1 formalises this notion.

Definition 1 (Aggregation policies) *Let $\mathbb{A}$ be the set of all personal attributes of an individual and $\mathbb{P}$ the set of all parties with whom the individual interacts. Let $A \subseteq \mathbb{A}$ be a set of personal attributes about some individual. Let $P \subseteq \mathbb{P}$ be a set of those parties that occasionally process the attributes in A. Let $proc_i(p) \subseteq A$, with $p \in P$ indicate the set of attributes being processed by some party p at some instant i. An aggregation policy for A over P specifies that no instant i exists for which*

$$\bigcup_{p \in P} proc_i(p) = A$$

Note that the case where $|P| = 1$ is the special case alluded to above when single-party policies were briefly considered.

While the class of aggregation policies can indeed include a range of specific policies, it does not include the case that was used to introduce the modelling of properties above, where some financial information was limited to a specific number of instances or occurrences amongst a set of financial institutions. That case is formally defined in definition 2

Definition 2 (Quantitative policies) *Let $\mathbb{A}$ again be the set of all personal attributes of an individual and $\mathbb{P}$ the set of all parties with whom the individual interacts. Let $A \subseteq \mathbb{A}$ be some set of personal attributes and $P \subseteq \mathbb{P}$ some set of parties with whom the individual interacts. Let $n \geq 0$ be an integer. A quantitative policy for A over P specifies that*

$$|\{p \in P | proc_i(p) \cap A \neq \emptyset\}| \leq n$$

where $proc_i$ has the same meaning it had in definition 1.

Again note that the 'spamming policy' used above is a special case of a quantitative policy for which $n = 0$. When $n = 1$ the privacy policy for a document implies that the document should be treated like a paper-based document: it could be at different parties, but not simultaneously. For $n > 1$ the choice of n in general seems to be arbitrary, with a lower value of n simply specifying a higher degree of privacy (with its concomitant costs).

5. Tying up loose ends

One of the fundamental assumptions of this paper is that is is possible to specify the behaviour of parties with whom one interacts and then 'know' that they will stick to that behaviour. The notion that it is possible to specify real-world behaviour in a compact manner seems plausible but needs to be tested with real-world examples. This is, however, left to future research.

The requirement that parties will stick to a given behaviour, once that behaviour has been formalised in a policy, is also a complex issue, with psychological, social, ethical, technical and (possibly) other dimensions. This paper accepts that policies are routinely used to specify behaviour and that mechanisms exist in society to audit adherence to a policy and legal, societal and other sanctions can be used guarantee a reasonable degree of compliance. However, apart from the remarks made earlier about organisational safeguards, it is outside the scope of the current work to consider compliance with policies in practice.

A more pressing issue for the current work is the nature of interaction specified in the policies. Information was typically requested by some action (for example, `address.request`) and released afterwards (for example, `address.release`). The assumption was that data was to be provided when the request occurs and deleted later when the release occurs. This, however, does not accurately reflect practices in the real world. Since a customer database is an asset owned by a company, it is unlikely to destroy parts of it the moment it is no longer required for purposes of the transaction conducted. With the emergence of data mining the value of such data increases and the chances of voluntary deletion decreases. One possible route to explore is social pressure to enforce deletion, which is a viable option if society is indeed better served by such a practice than by permanent archiving — an aspect that is not explored in the current paper.

A more viable approach seems to be the following: If parties who process personal information are willing to change their behaviour such that they send out a request to process the information about an individual that they already have on record, it becomes possible to specify privacy policies in terms of not only data acquisition and release, but also in terms of processing. This would require the parties responsible to specify such points in their behaviour where they start and stop processing data; in the case of a `claim` in our earlier example, behaviour might be specified as follows:

```
INSURED = (claim -> insurancedata.beginprocessing -> process ->
   payout -> insurancedata.endprocessing -> INSURED |
   cancel -> insurancedata.release -> INSURER).
```

While this approach is again against the spirit of the current paper, in that it expects a behaviour change from parties who process information rather than only focussing on the individual's ability to control his or her private information, this behaviour change clearly enhances the individual's possibilities of taking control: If this is implemented, the individual will be able to specify privacy policies much more precisely; computerised matching, for example, can be controlled even if a party holds two pieces of information that should not be matched — simultaneous possession is less of a concern if simultaneous processing can be excluded. While consideration of such policies is well within the scope of the current paper, a lack of space precludes a detailed discussion here.

It is also worth noting that expecting a party to indicate its intention to begin processing a personal data attribute (and possibly to be blocked at that point by a privacy policy) need not be a practical major concern: It is possible to establish trusted third parties that store individuals' privacy policies and grant or deny semaphores based on the appropriate policy. (See the version of this paper published in the preproceedings for more information on the use of such semaphores in this context.) Again, availability and fault-tolerance issues for such third parties will not be considered in the current paper.

6. Conclusion

This paper considered the possibility of representing personal privacy policies using a process algebra. Simple examples were used to illustrate two major classes of privacy policies: aggregation policies and quantitative policies. Automated analysis of the examples were used to identify the tradeoffs an individual has to make when enforcing such privacy policies.

A number of open problems were introduced in the paper and will not be repeated here. One interesting implication of the approach has not yet been considered: If many individual privacy policies are modelled and publicly available, a party that processes private data can begin to measure the effects of its own processes in the light of known privacy constraints; it potentially becomes possible to measure how a certain action will constrain or enhance business processes. This, however, also needs to be left for future research.

References

[1] S. B. Adler, E. F. Bangerter, K. A. Bohrer, J. Brown, N. Howard, J. Camenisch, A. M. Gilbert, D. Kesdogan, M. P. Leonard, X. Liu, M. R. McCullough, A. C. Nelson, C. C. Palmer, C. S. Powers, M. Schnyder, E. Schonberg, M. Schunter, E. van Herreweghen, and M. Waidner. Using an object model to improve handling of personally identifiable information. United States Patent Application 20030004734, January 2003.

[2] R. Agrawal, J. Kiernan, R. Srikant, and Y. Xu. Hippocratic databases. In *28th Int'l Conf. on Very Large Databases (VLDB), Hong Kong*, 2002.

[3] P. Ashley, S. Hada, G. Karjoth, and M. Schunter. E-P3P privacy policies and privacy authorization. In *Proceedings of the ACM workshop on Privacy in the Electronic Society*, pages 103–109. ACM Press, 2003.

[4] D. Brin. *The Transparent Society — Will Technology Force us to Choose between Privacy and Freedom?* Perseus Books, Reading, MA, 1998.

[5] M. A. Caloyannides. Encryption wars: Shifting tactics. *IEEE Spectrum*, 37(5):46–51, 2000.

[6] D. Chadwick, M. S. Olivier, P. Samarati, E. Sharpston, and B. Thuraishingham. Privacy and civil liberties. In E. Gudes and S. Shenoi, editors, *Research Directions in Database and Application Security*, pages 331–346. Kluwer, 2003.

[7] G. T. Duncan and S. Mukherjee. Microdata disclosure limitation in statistical databases: Query size and random sample query control. In *IEEE Computer Society Symposium on Research in Security and Privacy*, pages 278–287, Oakland, CA, USA, May 1991.

[8] A. Etzioni. *The Limits of Privacy*. Basic Books, New York, NY, 1999.

[9] A. Etzioni. Medical records — enhancing privacy. preserving the common good. *Hastings Center Report*, 23(2):14–23, 1999.

[10] S. Fischer-Hübner and A. Ott. From a formal privacy model to its implementation. In *21st National Information Systems Security Conference*, Arlington, VA, USA, October 1998.

[11] E. Gabber, P. B. Gibbons, D. M. Kristol, Y. Matias, and A. Mayer. Consistent, yet anonymous, web access with LPWA. *Communications of the ACM*, 42(2):42–47, February 1999.

[12] S. Garfinkel. *PGP: Pretty Good Privacy*. O'Reilly, 1995.

[13] D. M. Goldschlag, M. G. Reed, and P. F. Syverson. Onion routing. *Communications of the ACM*, 42(2):39–41, February 1999.

[14] S. Hunt. Market overview: Privacy management technologies. Giga Information Group, February 2003.

[15] IBM. Enterprise privacy architecture: Securing returns on e-business. Executive brief, IBM, 2001.

[16] IBM. Privacy in a connected world. White paper, IBM, May 2002.

[17] IDcide. IDcide introduces corporate privacy compliance software. Press release, February 2001. `http://www.idcide.com/pages/press_releas.htm#6`.

[18] D. G. Johnson. *Computer Ethics*. Prentice Hall, third edition, 2001.

[19] G. Karjoth, M. Schunter, and M. Waidner. Privacy-enabled services for enterprises. Research Report RZ 3391 (# 93437), IBM Research, 2002.

[20] G. Karjoth, M. Schunter, and M. Waidner. Platform for Enterprise Privacy Practices: Privacy-enabled management of customer data. In R. Dingledine and P. Syverson, editors, *Privacy Enhancing Technologies: Second International Workshop, PET 2002, San Francisco, CA, USA, April 14-15, 2002, Revised Papers*. Springer, 2003.

[21] G. Lawton. Is technology meeting the privacy challenge? *IEEE Computer*, 34(9):16–18, 2001.

[22] J. Magee and J. Kramer. *Concurrency — State Models & Java Programs*. Wiley, 1999.

[23] M. S. Olivier. Database privacy. *SIGKDD Explorations*, 4(2):20–27, 2003.

[24] M. S. Olivier. A layered architecture for privacy-enhancing technologies. In J. H. P. Eloff, H. S. Venter, L. Labuschagne, and M. M. Eloff, editors, *Proceedings of the Third Annual Information Security South Africa Conference (ISSA2003)*, pages 113–126, Sandton, South Africa, July 2003.

[25] M. S. Olivier. Privacy under conditions of concurrent interaction with multiple parties. In S. de Capitani di Vimercati, I. Ray, and I. Ray, editors, *Proceedings of the Seventeenth*

Anual IFIP WG11.3 Working Conference on Database and Application Security, pages 103–117, Estes Park, Colorado, USA, August 2003 (Preproceedings).

[26] M. S. Olivier. Using organisational safeguards to make justifiable decisions when processing personal data. In J. H. P. Eloff, P. Kotzé, A. P. Engelbrecht, and M. M. Eloff, editors, *IT Research in Developing Countries (SAICSIT 2003)*, pages 275–284, Sandton, South Africa, September 2003.

[27] E. F. Paul, F. D. Miller, and J. Paul, editors. *The Right to Privacy*. Cambridge University Press, Cambridge, 2000.

[28] PrivacyRight. Control of personal information — the economic benefits of adopting an enterprise-wide permissions management platform. White Paper, 2001. http://www.privacyright.com/info/economic.html.

[29] J. Reagle and L. F. Cranor. The platform for privacy preferences. *Communications of the ACM*, 42(2):48–55, February 1999.

[30] M. K. Reiter and A. D. Rubin. Anonymous web transactions with Crowds. *Communications of the ACM*, 42(2):32–48, February 1999.

[31] A. Rosenberg. Privacy as a matter of taste and right. In E. F. Paul, F. D. Miller, and J. Paul, editors, *The Right to Privacy*, pages 68–90, Cambridge, 2000. Cambridge University Press.

[32] P. Ryan, S. Schneider, M. Goldsmith, G. Lowe, B. Roscoe, and G. Lower. *Modelling and Analysis of Security Protocols*. Addison Wesley, 2000.

[33] P. Samarati. Protecting respondents' identities in microdata release. *IEEE Transactions on Knowledge and Data Engineering*, 13(6):1010–1027, 2001.

[34] S. Schneider and A. Sidiropoulos. CSP and anonymity. In *Proceedings of European Symposium on Research in Computer Security*, number 1146 in Lecture Notes in Computer Science, pages 198–218. Springer-Verlag, 1996.

[35] D. Stamate, H. Luchian, and B. Paechter. A general model for the answer-perturbation techniques. In *Seventh International Working Conference onScientific and Statistical Database Management*, pages 90–96, Charlottesville, VA, USA, Sep 1994. IEEE.

[36] L. Sweeney. Datafly: A system for providing anonymity in medical data. In T. Y. Lin and S. Qian, editors, *Database Security XI: Status and Prospects*, pages 356–381. Chapman & Hall, 1998.

[37] W. Teepe, R. P. van de Riet, and M. S. Olivier. Workflow analyzed for security and privacy in using databases. In B. Thuraisingham, R. P. van de Riet, K. R. Dittrich, and Z. Tari, editors, *Data and Applications Security — Developments and Directions*, pages 271–282. Kluwer, 2001.

[38] Tivoli Software. Enable your applications for privacy with IBM Tivoli Privacy Manager for e-business. Technical discussion, IBM, July 2002.

[39] Tivoli Software. IBM Tivoli Privacy Manager for e-business. Commercial brochure, IBM, 2002.

[40] R. Whitaker. *The End of Privacy — How Total Surveillance is Becoming a Reality*. New Press, New York, NY, 1999.

CORRELATED DATA INFERENCE

Ontology Guided XML Security Engine

Csilla Farkas
Information Security Laboratory
University of South Carolina *
farkas@cse.sc.edu

Andrei G. Stoica
Information Security Laboratory
University of South Carolina
stoica@cse.sc.edu

Abstract In this paper we examine undesired inferences in distributed XML documents. An undesired inference is a chain of reasoning that leads to protected data of an organization or an individual, using only intentionally disclosed information. We propose a framework, called Ontology guided XML Security Engine (Oxsegin), to detect and prevent undesired inference attacks. Oxsegin uses the Correlated Inference Algorithm to detect sensitive associations that may exist at a lower security levels. The system operates on the DTD's of XML documents to identify data associations and the corresponding security classifications. Oxsegin uses an ontological class-hierarchy to identify associations with two or more conflicting classifications. A Security Violation Pointer (SVP) is assigned to a set of tags that contribute to the conflicting classification. The likelihood of a detected security violation is measured by a confidence level coefficient attached to the SVPs.

Keywords: XML security, ontology based inference attack, data aggregation, correlated data inference, multi-level XML security

*This work was partially supported by the National Science Foundation under Grants IIS-0237782 and DUE-0112874

1. INTRODUCTION

Information systems have become a fundamental part of our everyday life. During the last few years the number of distributed applications using eXtensible Markup Language (XML) increased and the concept of Semantic Web emerged [15]. XML query languages [1, 17], supported by ontologies [11, 9, 8, 16, 2], enable semantic-based information processing without human assistance.

Unfortunately, techniques that support interoperation may also lead to unintended data disclosures. While individual data units are usually carefully analyzed not to disclose any confidential information, correlated data may allow unintended disclosure of confidential information. Current research in XML security follows two main trends: (i) Document Instance Security for digital signatures [5] and encryption [18] and (ii) Access Control Models for multi-level XML documents [3, 10, 4, 6, 14]. These techniques, however, do not consider the security implications of automated correlation of large amount of machine-understandable data that may lead to undesired inferences.

Intuitively, an undesired inference occurs when a user is able to infer non-permitted information from intentionally disclosed data and available metadata, such as ontologies. This inference threat is similar to the inference problem in traditional databases, where the ontology corresponds to the external domain knowledge. However, traditional inference control techniques are insufficient to provide protection against undesired inferences due to (i) the dynamic nature of the Web, (ii) the large amount of information to be processed, and (iii) the fact that the owner of the sensitive information does not have control over all publicly available data that may lead to undesired inferences. Up to date, small-scale data availability and the lack of automated data correlation tools limited the threat of unwanted inferences via external domain knowledge. The impact of automated XML document correlations from large distributed databases using ontologies has not been yet fully addressed from the information security point of view.

Our research targets the security impact of the ontology enhanced XML processing tools over large, distributed XML databases. We show that it is possible to use ontologies to mount specific data inference attacks on XML data. We develop techniques to detect and prevent attacks due to coexistence of sensitive association at a lower security level. To prevent these attacks, we propose the Ontology guided XML Security Engine (Oxsegin). Oxsegin is a probabilistic engine that computes security violation pointers over those tags that lead to low-level duplicates of sensitive associations.

The rest of the paper is organized as follows: Section 2 presents an example of ontology-guided attack using public domain data. Section 3 describes the architecture and functionality of Oxsegin. Section 4 gives the technical details for the correlated data inference process in the security engine. Finally we conclude and propose future research in Section 5.

2. ONTOLOGY-BASED ATTACKS IN XML DATABASES

Undesired inferences in multilevel secure databases have been studied extensively (see [12] for an overview). The inference problem is to detect and remove inference channels that lead to disclosure of unauthorized data by combining authorized data and metadata. In Web environment, where correlated data may come from several, independent sources, only a small portion of publicly available data is under the control of the owner of the sensitive information. This work focuses on detecting replicated data associations with different security requirements.

We assume that organizational data repositories contain both public (e.g., available from the Web) and confidential (e.g., available only to some of the users) data . To prevent undesired data disclosure, it is required that the security consequences of the release of new public data are evaluated before the release. That is, to determine whether unauthorized users will be able to combine the new information with other publicly available data to gain access to confidential data. Ontologies support semantic-based data integration, thus extend upon purely syntax-based data integration.

To illustrate a possible inference attack, consider the document fragment (Table 1.a) part of a database carrying information for upcoming air-shows. This document provides information such as the address and driving directions to military bases (Base_X) where an air-show is held. The second document fragment (Table 1.b), extracted from a local State Division for Health Administration, shows a map of drinking water basins within a given state. Finally, the third fragment (Table 1.c), is part of a sensitive document, containing data about the locations of the water sources for several military bases, including Base_X. The security requirement of the military is that the information about the water reservoirs of military bases should only be accessible by authorized users. The air-show information (fragment 1) is available on-line and the drinking water basins information (fragment 2) is outside of the military protection domain and publicly available. Indeed, our example is based on data available on existing Web site but we replaced the real data with fictional values.

a. Air-show information	b. Drinking water basins	c. Critical Infrastructure
<?xml version="1.0"?>	<?xml version="1.0"?>	<?xml version="1.0"?>
<show> ... **P**	<waterMap> ... **P**	<infrastructure> ... **S**
<fort>Base_X	<district>District_Y	<base>Base_X
</fort> ... **P**	</district> ... **P**	</base> ... **S**
<address>District_Y	<basin>Basin_Z	<waterSource>Basin_Z
</address> ... **P**	</basin> ... **P**	</waterSource> ... **S**
</show>	</watermap>	</infrastructure>

Table 1. Undesired Inference from Public Data

A possible ontology for this attack unifies the <waterSource> with <basin>, <fort> with <base> and <address> with <district> tags. Using this correlation, the attackers gain access to secret information (association between the Base_X and its water source in Basin_Z), without any access to the critical infrastructure database. Note, that the complexity of this attack is reduced by the simplicity of the ontology and the uniform access to online resources.

3. ONTOLOGY GUIDED XML SECURITY ENGINE

The motivation for the design of Oxsegin was to assist security officers and database administrators to securely update XML databases by identifying possible security violations from illegal inferences. Oxsegin uses a probabilistic inference engine with varying precision levels. Oxsegin indicates the possibility of unwanted inferences where the correlated data from the test files (publicly available data) matches the reference file (protected, confidential data). If unwanted inference is detected appropriate countermeasures must be performed, e.g., withhold some of the test files or execute non-IT measures.

The security engine has four main components: the Probabilistic Inference Module - PIM, the User Defined Inference Parameters Module - UDIPM, the Ontology Module and the XML Database Access Module. The Input and Feedback Module - IFM is not incorporated in the Oxsegin architecture. The IFM functionality is to supply the reference and test XML set, the inference parameters and to decide the appropriate actions if a security violation is detected. The response policy on detected security violations is outside of the scope of this paper.

PIM computes possible security violation pointers between the reference document and the set of test documents. Intuitively, a security violation pointer indicates tags from the corresponding reference and test DTD files that might constitute unwanted inferences. For each security violation pointer, PIM computes an associated confidence level coefficient that reflects the likelihood of security violation involving the set of tags. UDIPM allows the security officer to define different inference processing parameters that will control the complexity of inference analysis. The inference uses the semantic formalism and concept hierarchy supplied by the Ontology module.

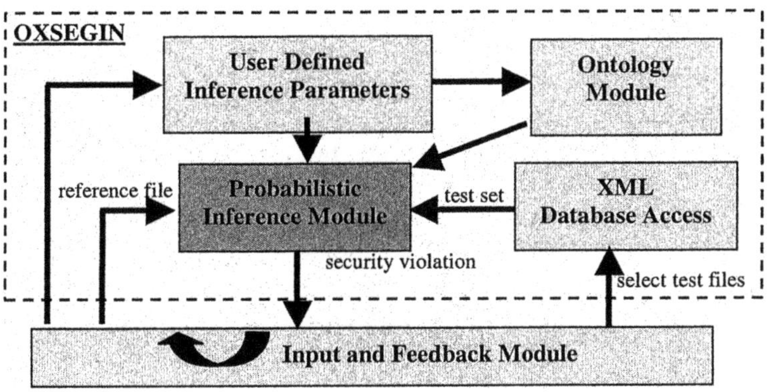

Figure 1. Replicated Information under Different Classification

The XML Database Access module represents a gateway to a collection of XML documents. The XML database can be the local, public document repository or files accessed via HTTP within a given web domain. As a result, Oxsegin can be used to securely publish documents over the web. In this case the reference DTD is the protected document and the test DTD is the set of all documents from the public domain.

3.1. Probabilistic Inference

PIM uses a set of procedures to identify security violations employing the ontology module to guide the inference process. Section 4 describes in full details the Correlated Inference Algorithm. The The input from the ontology module is used to abstract the concepts represented by the tags within the DTD files. A security violation pointer SVP is assigned to every unwanted inference. The confidence level coefficient CLC is computed for each SVP, based on the weights of the concepts in the ontology, the relative position of the tags in the DTD files, and the relative position of the concepts in the ontology class hierarchy.

Definition 1 *(Security Violation Pointer) Security Violation Pointer (SVP) is a set of tags* $T = \{t_1, \ldots, t_N\}$ *that represent a possible security violation via unwanted inference.*

Definition 2 *(Confidence Level Coefficient) The Confidence Level Coefficient (CLC) of an SVP is the likelihood of the inference involving the tags of the SVP.*

Within a DTD, we distinguish between syntactically identical tags at structurally different locations. We define all tags as a pairs, containing the tag's name and the tag's path information from the root node of the DTD. For clarity, in the following we omit the path information unless it is needed to differentiate between the tags.

To formalize ontologies we adapt the use of Frame Logic [13] as the conceptual modeling language. We assume that the security officer assigns a weight to each concept in the ontology class hierarchy to differentiate between less and more specific concepts from the perspective of the protected sensitive information. The more specific a concept is, the larger the weight assigned to it. The root of the ontology class-hierarchy has a minimal weight since it is the least specific concept. Concepts that are relevant to the given knowledge domain and the specific security requirements usually carry larger weights. After the security officer assigns the weights for each concept, the system computes the normalized weights for each concept. Normalized weights reflect the likelihood of the same syntactic forms to represent the same semantic concepts.

Definition 3 *(Ontological Abstraction Level) Given the concept C from ontology O, the Ontological Abstraction Level of C, denoted as OAL(C), is n if C is located at depth n in the corresponding ontology class hierarchy. The root concept* C_R *of the class-hierarchy has* $OAL(C_R)=0$.

Definition 4 *(Base Ontological Abstraction Level) The Base Ontological Abstraction Level of a tag t, denoted as BOAL(t), is the OAL of the concept C contained within the tag t.*

Definition 5 *(Abstracting a concept N steps) A concept C from an ontology O is abstracted N steps when it is replaced N times by its immediate parents in the corresponding ontology class-hierarchy.*

Definition 6 *(Container and Data Tags) A container tag is an XML tag that holds only structural information in the form of other XML tags and has no tag attributes. A data tags is an XML tag that contains at least one unit of information. A data tag may contain data and container tags.*

4. CORRELATED INFERENCE

In this section we propose an inference procedure that detects undesired inference attacks within a particular knowledge or semantic domain. The Correlated Inference Algorithm detects ontology-based attacks similar to the one described in Section 2. The procedure checks a reference DTD structure (corresponding to the classified information) against a set of test DTD structures (corresponding to the publicly available information) by abstracting tags using the ontology.

The main data structure used by the Correlated Inference Algorithm is an Inference Association Graph (IAG). Intuitively, IAG represents the associations among tags of an XML DTD structure. The nodes of an IAG correspond to the XML data tags and the edges represent associations between the tags. Figure 2 represents the IAG corresponding to the XML files in Table 1.

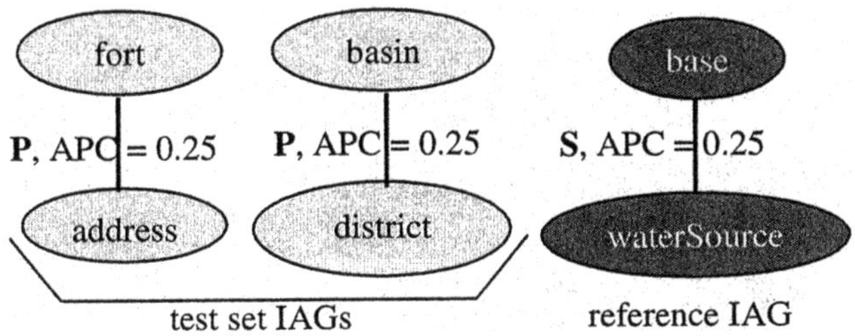

Figure 2. Inference Association Graphs IAGs

Each association has an attached Association Probability Coefficient (APC) that reflects the likelihood the corresponding nodes represent related concepts. In addition, associations can be classified according to the security policy of the organization. A security violation pointer identifies associations of different IAGs where two or more associations exist among the same tags but they have different security classifications. Such associations represent cases where users can derive information in one set of documents while they are disallowed to access the same information in a different set of documents.

Definition 7 *(XML Association) For any two nodes n_1 and n_2 in the DTD and their immediate parent P with security label L_P , P defines an XML association between n_1 and n_2. The association has a corresponding security label L_P and P represents the association source.*

Definition 8 *(Association Probability Coefficient) Association Probability Coefficient, denoted as APC, corresponding to an association be-*

tween tags n_1 and n_2 with an association source P, represents the probability that P is used to semantically correlate tags n_1 and n_2.

Definition 9 *(Inference Association Graph) The Inference Association Graph of an XML DTD structure, denoted by IAG=(V, E), is a graph with nodes V (data tags of the XML) and edges E (associations among the tags). Each edge is labeled with a pair (L_P, APC_P), representing the security label and probability coefficient of the association source tag.*

Definition 10 *(Document Structure Level DSL(t)) Given a tag T from a DTD tree D, the document structure level of T in D, denoted as DSL(T), is the maximum depth of the sub-tree rooted at T. All the leaves $l_1, l_2, \ldots, l_k$ in the DTD have $DSL(l_i) = 0$.*

Algorithm 1: Build IAG
Input: DTD
Output: IAG

BEGIN
  FOR ALL data tags T_l in DTD DO
    Create a corresponding node V_l
  FOR ALL tags T_i in DTD DO
    FOR ALL V_j, V_k such that T_i is the nearest parent of both tags T_j, T_k, corresponding to nodes V_j and V_k, respectively AND $\text{Depth}(T_j)\text{-Dept}(T_i) < \text{MaxDepth}$, $\text{Depth}(T_k)\text{-Dept}(T_i) < \text{MaxDepth}$ DO
      Create the edge e between (V_j, V_k)
      Label e with (L_{T_i}, APC_{ijk})
END

Note, that it is always possible to find an XML association between any two tags in a DTD structure since the root tag is the parent for all tags in the DTD tree. However, this type of remote association is rarely relevant. In general, it is reasonable to assume that APCs decrease with the distance between the associated elements and the source. Algorithm 1. gives the procedure to build the IAG. To reduce the complexity of the inference process, the algorithm limits the number of tags considered for XML associations. Associations are considered only if the relative difference between the tags and the association source in the DTD tree is less than MaxDepth (set accordingly to the specifics of the XML data).

$$APC_{ijk} = \frac{1}{1 + Depth(T_j) - Depth(T_i)} * \frac{1}{1 + Depth(T_k) - Depth(T_i)} * \frac{1}{1 + |Depth(T_j) - Depth(T_k)|} * \frac{1}{DSL(T_j) + 1} * \frac{1}{DSL(T_k) + 1}$$

$\frac{1}{1+Depth(T_j)-Depth(T_i)}$ and $\frac{1}{1+Depth(T_k)-Depth(T_i)}$ coefficients in the definition of APC_{ijk} quantify the relative depth difference in the DTD tree between the associated tags and the source of the association. APC decreases with the distance between the tags and the association source. $\frac{1}{1+|Depth(T_j)-Depth(T_k)|}$ coefficient quantifies the relative depth difference between the associated tags. Tags at the same depth have a corresponding APC larger than tags at different depth in the DTD tree. $\frac{1}{DSL(T_j)+1}$ and $\frac{1}{DSL(T_k)+1}$ coefficients quantify the structural complexity of the associated tags. Tags that represent the root of larger sub-trees are more likely to be container tags, and this reduces the relevance of any association involving them.

Object[ ].	OAL=0 WGT=1	P=1/50
waterSource :: Object	OAL=1 WGT=15	P=15/50
basin :: waterSource	OAL=2 WGT=1	P=1/50
place :: Object	OAL=1 WGT=15	P=15/50
district :: place	OAL=2 WGT=1	P=1/50
address :: place	OAL=2 WGT=1	P=1/50
base :: Object	OAL=1 WGT=15	P=15/50
fort :: base	OAL=2 WGT=1	P=1/50

Table 2. Ontology represented with Frame Logic statements

After building the IAG for each XML DTD structure in the test set, the ontology is used to integrate them into a single structure - the test set IAG. The Frame Logic statements in Table 2. represent the ontology associated with the knowledge domain of the XML DTD structure in Table 1. Each concept is shown with the associated ontology abstraction level OAL, weight WGT, and normalized weight P. If the DTD structures in the test set belong to the same knowledge domain, abstracting the tag names may create pairs of duplicated nodes among different IAGs. Merging the duplicated nodes connects the test set IAGs. Each node in the IAG has an attached Concept Abstraction Level coefficient (CAL). Intuitively, CAL reflects the likelihood that the new concept is an abstract representation of the tag that is replaced. For the initial concepts in the DTD structure, CAL=1. Then for each abstraction, CAL is modified using the probability of the new concept in the ontology.

Definition 11 *(Concept Abstraction Level) Concept abstraction level (CAL) is the likelihood that the concept from the ontology hierarchy is* *an abstract representation of the initial XML tag name. For repeated replacements, CAL is the probability the present concept is an abstract representation of the original tag name.*

Given the tree structure of the XML documents as well as the ontology hierarchy, all tags would eventually collapse into a single node if abstracted to the root of the ontology. To prevent this from happening, the Correlated Inference Algorithm has a set of restrictions on the abstraction process and the tags that it uses. The concepts are only abstracted within two predefined OAL limits: MaxOAL and MinOAL. MaxOAL is usually set to the depth of the ontology hierarchy tree while the MinOAL is set according to the specifics of the ontology. Usually, MinOAL is the average ontology depth of the concepts targeted by the inference attacks and is set by the security officer based on a particular knowledge domain. The second restriction on the abstraction process is based on the targeted tags. Tags located towards the root of the XML document are usually container tags, mostly used for structuring the document and rarely involved in semantic correlations. The security officer assigns a maximum level MaxDSL in the XML structure to consider tags in the abstraction process (DSL the document structure level).

Integrating the test set IAGs simulate the natural human brain inference process in three distinct stages. In the first stage the concepts associated with XML tags are abstracted, unifying same notions originally under different syntactic forms. In the second stage, by eliminating the duplicated nodes and collapsing the multi-structure IAGs, the system simulates the inference link between multiple files with related data. In the third stage the system performs a transitive correlation to simulate linking XML tags through similar abstract concepts. The transitive correlation relates two tags through an XML association (IAG edge) with a common third tag. Since the targeted inference is usually between multiple DTD structures, it follows naturally to perform the transitive correlation after duplicated node reduction. Algorithm 2. gives the formal description of the Correlated Inference Algorithm.

Each edge added in the transitive correlation of the test set IAG represents a possible illegal inference. The Correlated Inference Algorithm checks all these edges against the reference IAG to identify security violation pointers. The test for security violation pointers is performed on edges, since the edges represent valid XML associations. Each edge added to the test set IAG by the transitive correlation is compared to all edges in the reference IAG. The system places a security violation pointer (SVP) on pairs of edges between similar nodes if the reference edge security label dominates the test set edge security label. Intuitively this means that an association from the reference DTD structure

Algorithm 2: Correlated Inference
Input: Test set IAGs and Reference IAGs
Output: Security Violation Pointers (SVP)

MAIN
Check security violation for all existing edges of test and reference IAGs
FOR all edges use **Procedure 2** to identify SVPs
Abstract tags in test IAGs to create new associations
Let S be the set of all tag pairs (T_i, T_j)$\in$ test set IAGs
FOR ALL pairs (T_i, T_j) in S
  Use **Procedure 1** to abstract T_i and T_j to the nearest concept c such that $c = T_i^l = T_j^k$
  IF $T_i^l = T_j^k$ THEN
    Merge nodes T_i and T_j:
    Remove T_j; direct all edges to T_i, CAL_{T_i}=min[CAL_{T_i};CAL_{T_j}]
    Create edges through transitive correlation:
      FOR ALL tags T_h and T_k with an edge to T_i DO
        Let security label L=max[$L_{e(T_i,T_h)}$;$L_{e'(T_i,T_k)}$]
        Let APC=$APC_{e(T_i,T_h)}$*$APC_{e'(T_i,T_k)}$
        Connect T_h and T_k by e_n with label (L,APC)
Check security violations due to newly created edges
FOR all new edges use **Procedure 2** to identify SVPs
Check data-level matches of SVPs
FOR $\forall$ SVP_i such that CLC_i>DSTcoef DO
  Perform data search on associated tags
  IF data-level match found THEN
    CLC_i=1
END(MAIN)

Procedure 1: Abstract tag T
Input: Ontology class hierarchy H, tag T
Output: (Abtracted T)= T^n
Let $c, c_1, \ldots, c_n$ concepts$\in H$, $c = T$, c_i immediate parent of c_{i-1}
T^0=T, $n < MinOAL$
FOR i=1 TO n DO
  $T^i = c_i$
  CAL_{T^i}=$CAL_{T^{i-1}}$*P(c_i)
END(Procedure 1)

Procedure 2: Edge test for SVP
Input: edges $e = (n_1, n_2)$, $e' = (n'_1, n'_2)$ with security classifications L_e, $L_{e'}$
Output: SVP and CLC or nothing
Abstract tags of nodes n_1 and n_2 of e and n'_1 and n'_2 of e'
  IF $e \equiv_H e'$ ($n_1^k = n_1'^l$ AND $n_2^x = n_2'^y$) and $L_e \neq L_{e'}$, say $L_e \succ L_{e'}$ THEN
    CAL_{avrg},CAL_{max},CAL_{min}=(average,max,min) CAL for e, e' nodes
    CLC=CAL_{avrg}*APC_e*$APC_{e'}$*(1-|CAL_{max}-CAL_{min}|)
    Place SVP on e and e' nodes with CLC
END(Procedure 2)

is classified at a higher security level than an association among the test DTD structures discovered by the transitive correlation procedure. The edges are matched for a security violation employing again the ontology hierarchy to abstract concepts for each tested edge. Each SVP has a confidence level coefficient CLC computed based on the APC of the edge and the CAL of the nodes. The last coefficient in computing CLC, $1 - |CAL_{max} - CAL_{min}|$ quantifies the relative difference between the maximum and minimum level of abstraction for the concepts in the XML associations. Concepts on the same level of abstraction in the ontology hierarchy have a higher associated CLC.

Figure 3 shows the reference IAG and the integrated test set IAG corresponding to the IAGs in Figure 2 and the XML files in Table 1. The tag <fort> was abstracted to <base> and the tag <basin> was abstracted to <waterSource>. Both tags <address> and <district> were abstracted to <base> inducing a transitive correlation between <base> and <waterSource>. The new XML transitive association between <base> and <waterSource> is classified public according to the Correlated Inference Algorithm. This triggers a security violation between the test set and the reference IAG where the same association is classified secret.

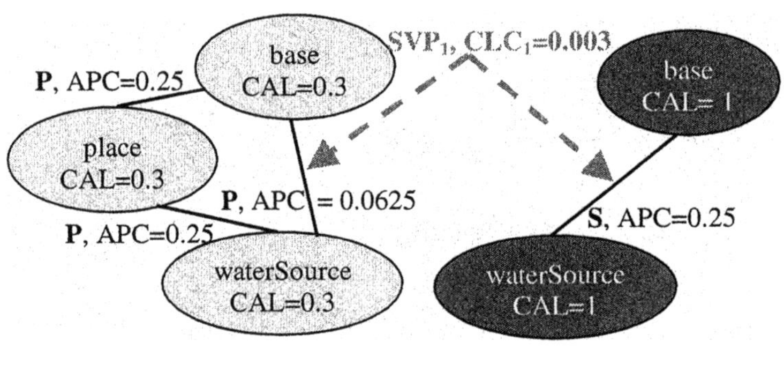

Figure 3. Unified Inference Association Graph

If the CLC corresponding to a particular SVP is above the Data Search Threshold coefficient (DSTcoef), the system provides low-level data granularity search. If data items associated with the reference and test set XML DTD structures match, the associated CLC is set to 1, the maximum confidence level. The low-level data search provides maximum security but also maximum processing complexity. High-level detection may produce false positive security violation pointers with high confidence coefficients. Data granularity search decreases the amount of false positives but does not guaranty to eliminate all of them. The

Correlated Inference Algorithm runs the analysis for security violation pointers on the DTD structure level. This represents an advantage for large XML documents databases where usually more than one document corresponds to any given DTD file. Operating at the DTD level is similar to high-level security detection with reasonable accuracy under reasonable computational complexity. For more accurate detection the procedure uses specialized data granularity search to identify security violations with maximum confidence level.

5. CONCLUSION

This paper presents a new method to prevent inference attacks in large XML databases. We show how ontologies can be used to implement automated attacks on large XML databases and develop methods and techniques to detect such attacks. Although ontological inferences have been studied from the perspective of providing interoperation, the security impacts of these new technologies have not been investigated and there are no tools to prevent these threats.

To the authors' best knowledge, Oxsegin is the first proposal to provide a semantically enhanced XML security framework. This paper adds a new component to the security engine to prevent inference attacks based on correlated data. The Correlated Inference Algorithm computes security violation pointers and their associated confidence level probability. The procedure can be tuned to run at different complexity levels to enhance the efficiency of the model. The main contribution of our model is to be able to handle large amount of semi-structured data that is infeasible by using human experts only.

References

[1] S. Abiteboul, D. Quass, J. McHugh, J.Widom, and J. Wiener. (1997). *The Lorel query language for semi-structured data.* Journal of Digital Libraries. Volume 1

[2] B. Amann, I. Fundulaki, and M.Scholl, et at. (2001). *Mapping XML Fragments to Community Web Ontologies.* Proceedings Fourth International Workshop on the Web and Databases

[3] E. Bertino, S. Castano, E. Ferrari, M.Mesiti. (2000). *Specifying and Enforcing Access Control Policies for XML Document Sources.* WWW Journal, Baltzer Science Publishers, Vol.3, N.3.

[4] E. Damiani, S. De Capitani di Vimercati, S. Paraboschi, and P. Samarati. (2000). *XML Access Control Systems: A Component-Based Approach.* In Proc. IFIP WG11.3 Working Conference on Database Security, The Netherlands.

[5] P. Devanbu, M. Gertz et al. (2001). *Flexible authentication of XML documents.* ACM Conference on Computer and Communications Security.

[6] F. Dridi and G. Neumann. (1998). *Towards access control for logical document structure.* In Proc. of the Ninth International Workshop of Database and Expert Systems Applications, pages 322–327, Vienna, Austria.

[7] M. Erdman, S.Decker. Ontology-aware XML Queries. http://www.aifb.uni-karlsruhe.de/ mer/Pubs/semantic-xql.webdb00.pdf

[8] M. Erdman and R. Studer. (to appear). *How to Structure and Access XML Documents with Ontologies.* Data and Knowledge Engineering, Special Issue on Intelligent Information Integration

[9] M. Erdman and R. Studer. (1999). *Ontologies as Conceptual Model for XML Documents.* Proc. of the 12-th Workshop for Knowledge, Acquisition, Modeling and Management. Banff, Canada.

[10] A. Gabillon and E. Bruno. (2001). *Regulating Access to XML Documents.* In Proc. IFIP WG11.3 Working Conference on Database Security.

[11] T.R. Gruber. (1993). *A Translation Approach to Portable Ontology Specifications.* Knowledge Acquisition. Vol.6, no.2, pp199-221

[12] S. Jajodia and C. Meadows. (1995). *Inference problems in multilevel secure database management systems.* In Information Security: An integrated collection of essays, pages 570-584, IEEE Computer Society Press, Los Alamitos, C.A.

[13] M. Kifer, Georg Lausen, James Wu. (1995). *Logical Foundations of Object Oriented and Frame Based Languages.* Journal of ACM, vol. 42, p. 741-843

[14] M. Kudo and S. Hada. (2000). *XML Document Security based on Provisional Authorizations.* In Proc. of the 7th ACM conference on Computer and Communications Security, Athens Greece, November.

[15] T. Lee and J. Hendler(2001). *The Semantic Web.* Scientific American.

[16] OIL. *Ontology Inference Layer.* http://www.ontoknowledge.org/oil/

[17] J. Robie, J. Lapp, and D. Schach. (1998). *XML Query Language (XQL).* Proceedings of the W3C Query Language Workshop (QL-98), Boston.

[18] W3C. (2001). *XML Encryption Requirements.* W3C Working Draft, http://www.w3.org/TR/2001/WD-xml-encryption-req-20011018

ANTI-TAMPER DATABASES:
Querying Encrypted Databases

Gultekin Ozsoyoglu[#], David A. Singer[+], Sun S. Chung[#]
[#]EECS Department, [+]Math Department, Case Western Reserve University, Cleveland, OH 44106, (gxo3, das5, ssc7)@po.cwru.edu

Abstract A way to prevent, delay, limit, or contain the compromise of the protected data in a database is to encrypt the data and the database schema, and yet allow queries and transactions over the encrypted data. Clearly, there is a compromise between the degree of security provided by encryption and the efficient querying of the database. In this paper, we investigate the capabilities and limitations of encrypting the database in relational databases, and yet allowing, to the extent possible, efficient SQL querying of the encrypted database.

We concentrate on integer-valued attributes, and investigate a family of open-form and closed-form homomorphism encryption/decryption functions, the associated query transformation problems, inference control issues, and how to handle overflow and precision errors.

Key words: querying encrypted database, encryption algorithm, homomorphism encryption/decryption functions

1. INTRODUCTION

Mobile computing and powerful laptops allow databases with sensitive data to travel everywhere. Laptops can be physically retrieved by malicious users who can employ techniques that were not previously thought of, such as disk scans, compromising the data by bypassing the database management system software or database user authentication processes. Or, when databases are provided as a service [3, 4], the service provider may not be trustworthy, and the data needs to be protected from the database service provider. These examples illustrate the need to

- Encrypt data in a database since compromise will occur with the traditional ways of securing databases such as access controls [17, 13], multilevel secure database architectures [5, 11, 7], database integrity lock architectures [7], or statistical database inference controls [1].
- Allow, as much as possible, standard DBMS functionality, such as querying and query optimization, over encrypted data.

In this paper, we consider a database environment where (a) the database contains sensitive data available only to its legitimate users, and (b) the database can be captured by the adversary physically, and a compromise threat exists. We believe that a good way to prevent, delay, or contain the compromise of the protected data in a database is to encrypt the database, and yet allow queries over the encrypted data. This paper considers attribute (field)-level encryption for relational databases. We give an example.

Example 1. Consider a relational employee database with the relation EMPLOYEE (Id, Salary) where Id and Salary are integer-valued employee id and employee salary attributes. Assume that f() and g(), functions from integers to integers with inverses $f^{-1}()$ and $g^{-1}()$ respectively, are used to encrypt employee salaries and employee ids, and the relation EMPLOYEE and the attribute names Id and Salary are encrypted as the characters R, A, and B. Then the SQL query Q(DB) over the database DB Q(DB):

```
SELECT EMPLOYEE.Id FROM EMPLOYEE
        WHERE Salary=a
```

returns the employees with salary a. Q(DB) is rewritten into the SQL query $Q_E(DB_E)$ over the encrypted database DB_E as follows.

$Q_E(DB_E)$: SELECT R.A FROM R WHERE B=f(a)

Then, $Q_E(DB_E)$ is submitted to the DBMS, to be executed against the database DB_E. Assume that the output $O(Q_E(DB_E))$ of the query $Q_E(DB_E)$ is a single tuple with value y. Then the value y is decrypted as $g^{-1}(y)$, and returned as the output O(DB) of the query Q(DB).

We refer to the process of transforming the SQL query Q(DB) of the original database into the SQL query $Q_E(DB_E)$ of the encrypted database as the *query rewriting process.*

In this paper, we investigate techniques for encrypting a database, and the accompanying techniques to query the encrypted database, which we refer to as the *anti-tamper database,* and explore the tradeoffs among (a) the security of the database, and (b) the query expressive power and query processing. The site (computer) in which the anti-tamper database resides is called as the *anti-tamper site.*

Consider a database DB, and the set S of SQL queries Q on DB that correspond to the set of safe relational calculus [16] queries[1]. Let DB_E be the encrypted database DB (i.e., f(x)=y, for all $x \in DB$, $y \in DB_E$) with the transformed set S_E of SQL queries $Q_E(DB_E)$ on the database DB_E. For encrypting the database DB using the encryption function f(), we choose an encryption function f() that is a *group homomorphism from DB onto DB_E with respect to* S [12], i.e., for any query Q in S, we have $Q(DB) = f^{-1}(Q_E(f(DB)))$. This means that (a) SQL queries in S can be completely evaluated solely using a single query Q_E on the anti-tamper database DB_E, and, (b) with the exception of decrypting the output of $Q_E(DB_E)$) (possibly, at another "secure" site), there is no extra query processing burden on evaluating $Q_E(DB_E)$.

We make the following assumptions about the anti-tamper database:

- The encrypting of the original database is transparent and unknown to the legitimate users of the database. (no extra query specification/transformation burden on the legitimate users)
- The general encryption mechanism is made available to the public, including the adversary. However, certain parameters of the encryption mechanism (e.g., private keys) are kept secret so as to make the protected information in the database secure.
- The commercial DBMS that hosts the data does not know that the data in its database is encrypted. Commercial DBMSs are complex proprietary software systems, any security technique that is deployable without modifying the DBMS is more desirable over ones that require changes to the DBMS.

2. COMPUTING ARCHITECTURE

We employ the following *computing architecture* for our environment. Let the original database DB be encrypted into the *encrypted (anti-tamper) database* DB_E. Now, if DB_E directly becomes available to the adversary, its contents are devoid of semantics and, therefore not directly usable by the adversary. We employ an intermediary software agent, called the (Encryption/Decryption) *Agent*, which we assume to be secure. That is, the adversary cannot capture the Agent software code, and reverse-engineer its

[1] Thus, a query Q in S has a *Where* clause with conjunctions and/or disjunctions of predicates p, and existential and universal quantifiers. The predicate p either (a) specifies that a variable does/does not range over an attribute of a relation, or (b) specifies "$x\theta z$" where x is a variable, z is a variable or a constant, and $\theta \in \{<, >, =, \neq, \leq, \geq\}$. Q has a finite output and finite evaluation time.

encryption/decryption algorithms. We consider two alternative architectures:

- The agent resides at a site different than the site of the anti-tamper database DB_E, and has significant computational power and storage space. We refer to this site as a *secure site*, and to the Agent as a *secure-site Agent*. There may also be a secure DBMS at the secure site. We refer to this DBMS as $DBMS_{Agent}$.
- The agent resides at the site of the anti-tamper database, and has little computational power. We refer to this Agent as the *anti-tamper-site Agent*.

For both architectures, user queries are processed as follows:

a. The user forms a query Q(DB) against the original database DB, and submits it to the Agent.
b. The Agent rewrites the original query Q(DB) into either
   i) A single query $Q_E(DB_E)$ over the encrypted DB or
   ii) A set $\{Q_{Ei}(DB_E) | 1 \leq i \leq k\}$ of k different, k>1, queries,

and submits $Q_E(DB_E)$ or the query set $\{Q_{Ei}(DB_E)\}$, respectively, to the DBMS of the anti-tamper database, referred to as $DBMS_E$.

c. The $DBMS_E$ processes the query $Q_E(DB_E)$ or the query set $\{Q_{Ei}(DB_E)\}$, and returns the output $O(Q_E(DB_E))$ or the output set $\{O(Q_{Ei}(DB_E))\}$, respectively, to the Agent.
d. In the case of a single output $O(Q_E(DB_E))$, the Agent decrypts $O(Q_E(DB_E))$ into O(Q(DB)), the legitimate output of the original query Q against the original database DB, and returns it to the user. In the case of the multiple output set $\{O(Q_{Ei}(DB_E))\}$, the Agent decrypts each output $O(Q_E(DB_E))$, performs, if necessary, additional computations with the decrypted output set to obtain and return the answer O(Q(DB)) to the user.

Note that the *user site* in this architecture can be the secure site, the anti-tamper site, or yet a third (secure) site. If the user site is the third site, we assume that there is a secure communication channel between the Agent site and the user site. If the user and the Agent are both at the anti-tamper site then the decrypted output of a query returned to the user can be compromised (until it is destroyed by the user) if captured by the adversary.

3. ORDER- AND DISTANCE-PRESERVING, OPEN-FORM ENCRYPTION

In this paper, we concentrate only on the primitive data type *integer*. Next, we illustrate with examples the issues with the data type *integer*.

Def'n (*Order-Preserving Encryption*). Consider attribute V of relation R, and the encryption function f() for V values. The encryption function f() is order-preserving if when a > b for any two V values a and b in the original database DB then f(a) > f(b) in the anti-tamper database DB_E.

In other words, the encryption of attribute V retains the ordering in V. Arithmetic comparison operators <, >, ≥, and ≤ (but, not = and ≠) of primitive data types (e.g., integers) depend on the total ordering of attribute values.

Integer attributes can also participate in arbitrary arithmetic expressions of SQL queries. Let us consider one of the simplest arithmetic expressions, namely, arithmetic difference.

Def'n (*Difference-Preserving Encryption*). Given an attribute V with nonnegative integer or real values, and an encryption function f(), f() is *difference-preserving* if, for any two attribute V values a and b where (a – b) = k, we have f(a) – f(b) = r * k, where r is a constant.

In general, an encryption function f(x) that is difference-preserving for integers (and reals) has to be affine, i.e., f(x) = Ax+C, where C is a constant and A=r if x is a scalar.

When we employ an open-form encryption function, the system uses an *encryption algorithm,* which is more than computing a closed-form function, to encrypt original database DB into DB_E. Since DB_E creation is a one-time (database creation-time) task, employing a more time consuming encryption algorithm is acceptable. For decrypting query outputs as well as for intermediate processing, the agent also needs to execute a *decryption algorithm.*

Consider an integer-valued attribute V with values X, to be encrypted using open form order-preserving encryption. Let us assume that the encryption function f(X) and its inverse are in the form of E(K,X) and D(K,Y), respectively, where K is the secret key. We would like to define a family of functions Y=E (K,X), X=D(K,Y), where X,Y, and K are nonnegative integers:

1. K is the secret key. Given K, E and D should be efficiently computable.
2. For all X, Y, K, we have D (K, E (K,X))=X.
3. It should be hard(see 3.2 Inference Control) to find X from Y or Y from X in the absence of knowledge of K, even assuming complete knowledge of the functions E and D.
4. If X < X' then E (K,X) < E(K,X') for any K. (Order-preservation)

Assume that the domain for our function E_K, is the integers from 1 to N, and the range is the integers from 1 to M. For fixed K, let $y_n = E_K(n)$ for $1 \leq n \leq N$. Define a new sequence z_n by $z_1 = y_1 - 1$, $z_{n+1} = y_{n+1} - y_n - 1$. In other words, the z_i's are the differences (minus 1) between successive values of the encryption function $E_K(n)$. Then condition 4 above is equivalent to the statement $z_n \geq 0$ for all n.

If we have any order-preserving function we can define the corresponding sequence z_n; and the converse is also true: given a sequence $z_1, z_2, \dots, z_n$ of nonnegative integers, there is a uniquely determined order-preserving function for which z_i's are the differences. Furthermore, we have the algorithms in figure 1 for computing the encryption function $E_K(n)$ *and its inverse* $D_K(y_n)$.

Encryption:

$E_K(1) := 1 + z_1$; $E_K(n+1) := E_K(n) + 1 + z_{n+1}$;

Decryption:

Input: Y **Output:** $D_K(Y)$

```
begin
  i:= 0;  W := Y;
  while W > i do begin i := i + 1;  W := W – z_i
  endwhile;
  if W = i then return D_K(Y) := i else output ``Failure";
end.
```

Figure1. Encryption and decryption algorithms for order-preserving, integer-to-integer encryption

Our goal is to construct a family of functions indexed by a key K, which contains as little information as possible. One way to achieve this is to generate a pseudorandom sequence z_i using an initial seed K, and then use the algorithms in figure 1 to define the encryption and decryption functions. There are a large number of well-known algorithms [8] for generating pseudorandom integers efficiently which have known security properties.

To minimize information leakage of the proposed order-preserving encryption algorithm, one can optimize the encryption algorithm by altering the distribution of the z_i. For example, it might be better if each z_i is uniformly chosen from an interval depending on the sum of the previous z_i. Figure 2 lists such an algorithm.

1) *Generate a sequence of random integers y_i in the range* [1, M]. Assume that we have a family of pseudorandom functions R[K,n]=xn, where K is the secret key and n=1,2,3,... Typically this generates a stream of random bits, which can then be used to produce random integers[9]. There are a large number of pseudorandom number generators with useful security properties. See, for example, M. Blum and S. Micali [2] for an early example. Here, the key serves as the initiator of the sequence.
2) *Define z_i by the rules*:
   (a) $S_1 := z_1 := y_1$;
   (b) for $k \geq 1$, define A_k, z_{k+1} as $A_k =: M - S_k$; $z_{k+1} =: \text{Int}\,[y_{k+1} * A_k / M]$;
   (c) Define S_{k+1} as $S_k + z_{k+1}$

The encryption function is then defined by $f(k)=S_k$.

Figure 2. Encryption function f() with uniformly distributed and expanding z_i's

3.1 A Class of Queries with Simple Query Transformation and Same-Cost Query Processing

For the class of SQL queries equivalent to safe relational calculus queries, there is a very straightforward transformation from Q(DB) to $Q_E(DB_E)$:

Query Transformation Rule: Replace each constant c in Q(DB) with f(c) to obtain $Q_E(DB_E)$.

The query Q of example 1 illustrates the use of the Query Transformation Rule.

Theorem 1 below states that f() as defined in figure 2 is a group homomorphism from DB to DB_E with respect to the set of SQL queries equivalent to safe relational calculus queries. Moreover, the cost of evaluating a transformed query over the encrypted database is the same as the cost of evaluating the original query over the original database.

Theorem 1. Let DB be a relational database, f() be an encryption function as defined in Figure 2, DB_E be the encrypted database obtained from DB using f(), and O(Q(DB)) be the output of query Q on database DB. Then for any SQL query Q(DB) that is expressible in safe relational calculus, the corresponding single SQL query $Q_E(DB_E)$ obtained using the Query Transformation Rule is such that applying $f^{-1}(y)$ to each encrypted value y in $O(Q_E(DB_E))$ produces O(Q(DB)).

Proof: See the Technical Report [10].

Remark 1. Given any relational DBMS M, the query evaluation cost of Q(DB) on M is equal to the query evaluation cost of $Q_E(DB_E)$ on M.

Proof. Follows from the integer-to-integer, order-preserving transformations of each attribute.

Theorem 1 and Remark 1 are highly practical since (a) the class of safe relational calculus queries is a reasonably large class, (b) transformation from Q to Q_E is straightforward and not costly, and (c) all things being equal between DB and DB_E except encrypted values, processing Q and Q_E take the same amount of time. Nevertheless, Theorem 1 fails for SQL queries with arithmetic expressions and/or aggregate functions, as well as for SQL queries with object-relational features such as derived or complex types (as opposed to primitive types integers, reals, and strings). We give an example.

Example 2. Assume that the relation EMPLOYEE and the attribute name Salary are encrypted as characters R and B, and the attribute Salary is encrypted using an order-preserving encryption function f(). Then, the SQL query

SELECT AVG (EMPLOYEE.Salary) FROM EMPLOYEE WHERE Salary > 100,000

will need the evaluation of two queries:

$Q_{E1}(DB_E)$: SELECT SUM(R.B) FROM R WHERE B > f(100,000),

$Q_{E2}(DB_E)$: SELECT COUNT(R.B) FROM R WHERE B > f(100,000)

And, the Agent will compute the answer as a function of the responses O_1 and O_2 to Q_{E1}, Q_{E2} respectively, and f(). The answer is given by $f^{-1}(O_1/O_2)$. This formula works because the special form of f() preserves arithmetic means.

We make three observations. First, the query rewriting approach of Example 2 will fail if f() is not additive, i.e., f(a + b) = f(a) + f(b). That is, for any x and y values in the Salary attribute, the additivity property guarantees that $f^{-1}(f(x) + f(y)) = f^{-1}(f(x + y)) = (x + y)$. Second, open-form encryption functions by definition do not satisfy the additivity property. Third, when the aggregate operations are used in nested SQL queries (with correlated variables), the issue of rewriting the query becomes even more difficult.

Example 3. Consider the query in example 2. Now, assume that we have used an "instance-based" encryption; i.e., for each salary value a, there is a distinct f(a) value, not expressible in a closed form and maintained in a secondary data structure at the Agent. In this case, the query rewriting scenario of example 2 fails, and we are forced to return *all* of the salary values in the desired range as

$Q_{E3}(DB_E)$: SELECT R.B FROM R WHERE B > f(100,000)

with O_3 as the output. Then the Agent will need to (i) decrypt and sum up all of the values in the output O_3 into X, and (ii) compute the output of the query as X/O_2. This scenario will incur heavy time delays since DB_E salary values have to be shipped to the Agent, and the Agent needs to perform (possibly, a disk-based) addition, independent of the database query optimization process.

Thus, one important goal in query rewriting is to have minimal performance degradation in transforming and evaluating the expected set of queries of the original database DB.

3.2 Inference Control

Let V be an integer-valued attribute and Domain of V, Dom(V) be a set of integers in [1, N]. Let the encrypted domain E(Dom(V)) be a set of integers between the range [1, M], where M >> N. Let the attribute V values be represented by v_i, $1 \leq i \leq n$, which are encrypted to y_i's with an encryption function $f(v_i)$. v_i, y_i are monotonically increasing, that is $v_i < v_j$ when $i < j$, and $y_i < y_j$. We define the adversary's Knowledge Space (KS) as the set of two-tuples (v_i, y_i) i.e., for $(v_i, y_i) \in KS$, the adversary knows in advance that $y_i = f(v_i)$. And, the adversary may or may not know that v_i's range is [1, N], and y_i's range is [1, M].

We now briefly investigate the compromise risk; i.e., given KS, how much the adversary can infer about the values v_i. More precisely, when $|KS| = k$, we want to know the probability that an unknown (v_i, y_i) pair is revealed to the adversary. The system is said to be *compromised* when (v_i, y_i) is revealed to the adversary with a probability above the threshold τ.

Let v_{guess} denote a guess by the adversary for v_r. Let $P(v_{guess}=v_r| KS)$, (v_r, y_r) is not in KS, denote the probability that the adversary learns $f^{-1}(y_r)=v_r$ given KS. Then, we select the system-defined parameters so that $P(v_{guess}=v_r) < \tau$ for all r.

When the adversary (a) does not know any v_i, that is, KS = { }, and (b) knows that the domain range of V is [1, N], and the encrypted domain range is [1, M] then the probability that n unknown v_r values are revealed from n distinct y_r values is equivalent to the probability of guessing n numbers over the range [1, N]. Choosing y_1, the adversary guesses v_1 over [1, N] by $v_{guess.}$ Then the possible range of v_1 is [1, N-n+1] and $P(v_{guess}=v_1) = 1/(N\text{-}n +1)$. Similarly, with KS = {(v_1, y_1)}, the possible range for v_2 is [v_1+1, N-n+2] and $P(v_{guess}=v_2 \mid KS=\{(v_1, y_1)\}) = 1/(N\text{-}n\text{-}v_1+2)$. Generalizing, we have $P(v_{guess}=v_{k+1} \mid KS=\{(v_1, y_1), (v_2, y_2), \ldots, (v_k, y_k)\}) = 1/(N\text{-}n\text{-}v_k +k+1)$. Note that the uncertainty bound for each value depends on the previously compromised value and the next compromised value. Furthermore, if the adversary does not know the size of the encrypted domain M, (s)he can use the largest encrypted value y_n as the upper bound for M. Finally, the worst case is the case where v_i values in KS are evenly distributed over the domain range.

To distinguish the known values in KS from the original data instances v_i of V, we denote KS = {(s_1, t_1), (s_2, t_2), …, (s_k, t_k)}, where t_i (= y_i) is the encrypted value of s_i (= v_i), and $s_i < s_j$ when $i < j$. For any two consecutive elements s_j and s_{j+1} of KS, we denote by S a set of v_j values between s_j and s_{j+1}, and by T the set of encrypted y_i values between t_j and t_{j+1}. Assuming v_i values in S are equally likely (i.e., uniformly distributed) to be anywhere between s_j and s_{j+1}, we can compute the compromise probability as follows. Let v_{guess} denote the adversary's guess for v_r=s_j+1 in S. Then $P(v_{quess}=v_r) = 1/ s_{j+1}\text{-} s_j \text{-} |S|$. That is, once the values s_j and s_{j+1} are known by the adversary, the corresponding range between t_j and t_{j+1} is of no significance for the uncertainty range of v_r. Similarly, when $v_r = s_1 -1$ then $P(v_{guess}=v_r) = 1/s_1$ – (no. of encrypted values less than t_1). And, when $v_r = s_k +1$ then $P(v_{guess}=v_r)$= $1/ N - s_k$ – (no. of encrypted values after t_k). Combining the three cases for all v_r values, compromise occurs when $\max_{vr} \{P(v_{guess}=v_r \mid KS)\} > \tau$.

It is possible to have domain values with different distributions. Let R be a range between any two known values s_j, s_{j+1}in KS, and having |T| unknown values distributed over R with a hypergeometric distribution. Assume that the adversary guesses m values from R. If we let random variable *X* denote the number of correctly guessed values then *X*=k means the adversary got exactly k values correct. So, the probability of *X*=k would be:

$$P(X=k) = \binom{|T|}{k}\binom{|R|-|T|}{m-k} \Big/ \binom{|R|}{m}$$

By the definition of hypergeometric distribution, $E(X) = m|T|/R$ gives the expected number of compromised values.

4. ORDER-PRESERVING CLOSED-FORM ENCRYPTION AND DECRYPTION

The advantage of closed-form decryption is speed, whereas open-form decryption may be costly--even when the decryption requests are sorted and batched. On the minus side, inferring the closed-form of the decryption function for an attribute amounts to compromising all values of the attribute unless one-way encryption functions are used to protect the key K.

Closed-form encryption for integer-valued attributes has the disadvantage that, because a single closed-form function is employed for encryption, controlling the magnitude of the encrypted values becomes difficult, leading to overflow problems. One can employ a variety of techniques to control the sizes of encrypted values; here we discuss one approach: encrypting a single integer value into a set of integers.

We would like to find *encryption functions* whose closed-form inverses exist, are cheap to compute, and "lossless". We say that an encryption algorithm E is *lossless* for an attribute V when there exists a decryption algorithm D such that, for any value x , $1 \le x \le N$, $D(E(x)) = x$.

When the attribute value x is encrypted using a function, say, $E(x) = C_1x + C_0$, we refer to the constants C_0 and C_1 as the key K. We assume that users are informed of the encryption function, but not the key. We call the number of such constants C_i as the *degree of security*. Our goal in this section is to come up with an encryption algorithm E such that, given the desired degree of security n, the algorithm E locates a "lossless" encryption function E() with the degree of security of n.

4.1 Single Encryption Function and its Inverse for Decryption

One encryption approach is to use a single polynomial function f(x) as the encryption function E. Obviously, in this case, the degree of security is the number of constants employed by the function f(x). Therefore, given n as the degree of security, the goal is to find an n degree polynomial that has an inverse function in closed form:

$$F(x) = C_nX^n + C_{n-1}X^{n-1} + \ldots + C_1X + C_0$$

Remark 2. Let f be a continuous function on the closed interval $[x_1, x_2]$ and assume that f is strictly increasing. Let $f(x_1) = y_1$ and $f(x_2) = y_2$. Then the inverse function is defined on the closed interval $[y_1, y_2]$.

Thus, to check whether the function has the inverse function or not, we can compute dev(f(x)) = 0. If there exists at most one solution for dev(f(x)) = 0 , then the inverse function of the polynomial exists for all x. If there exists more than one solution, we find the largest k such that dev(f(k)) = 0; and the inverse function exists for $x \geq k$ (by Remark 2). The problem with this approach is that in general, the closed form of the inverse function of an arbitrary polynomial function may not exist even if the inverse itself exists. Therefore, next we introduce the approach of multiple encryption functions.

4.2 Multiple Encryption Functions and an Inverse

Instead of finding the inverse of a single n degree polynomial for a requested n degree of security, we now apply n 'simple' functions iteratively where each function has its closed form inverse. Some examples of simple polynomials with well-defined inverse functions are listed below.

$f_1(x) = C_0\, x + C_1$ $\quad f_2(x) = C_2\, x^2 + C_3$ $\quad f_3(x) = C_6\, x^3 + C_7$

Given n as the desired level of security, our goal is to find a sequence of functions f_i, $1 \leq i \leq k$, from the above list as a sequence of encryption functions with, altogether, n constants C_i (as the key K) so that applying the inverses of each function in the sequence in reverse order constitutes the decryption. The encryption algorithm is applied as the sequence f_i of functions in such a way that the output of $f_i(x)$ becomes the input of $f_{i+1}(x)$ for $1 \leq i \leq k-1$.

Example 4. Let $f_1(x) = C_0\, x + C_1,\ f_2(x) = C_2\, x^2 + C_3, f_3(x) = C_6\, x^3 + C_7$

$E(x) = f_3(f_2(f_1(x))) = C_6 (C_2 (C_0 x + C_1)^2 + C_3)^3 + C_7$

Note that each function f_i is *monotone*; that is, for $x_1 > x_2$, $f(x_1) > f(x_2)$.

4.3 Nonlossy multiple encryption functions

There are two types of errors that may occur and may make the encryption lossy when applying a sequence f_i, $1 \leq i \leq k$, of functions as encryption/decryption functions, namely, *overflow errors* (integers) and *precision (round-off) errors* (reals)[6].

When multiple functions are applied iteratively to encrypt attribute values of integer domain, the magnitude of the encrypted value rapidly increases even when we restrict the degree of each polynomial to either 1 or 2. Since computer arithmetic uses limited (e.g. 32-bit or 64-bit) number of bits to store a number, an attempt to store an integer of large magnitude greater than $2^{31} - 1$ for 32-bit arithmetic and greater than $2^{63} - 1$ for 64-bit will produce an integer overflow [15].

Therefore, to reduce the magnitude of encrypted values, one may apply the log function $f_{log}(x) = log_2 x + C$ where C is a security constant. In this section, we investigate the use of the log function during encryption. Note that the log function's input and output need to be real values.

Assume that the floating-point representation has a base B and a precision p (i.e., the number of bits to keep the fractional part of a real number). $\pm b_0 . b_1 b_2 b_3 ... b_{p-1} * B^e$ represents the number $\pm (b_0 + b_1 B^{-1} + ... + b_{p-1} B^{-(p-1)})B^e$, $(0 \leq b_j < B)$, where b_i is called the significant bits and has p digits, and e is the exponent [9]. With B = 2, 24 bits are used for significant bits for 32 bit arithmetic, 53 bits are used for 64-bit arithmetic [15].

When the encryption computations convert the domain of an attribute from integer to real (e.g., in the case of applying $f_{log}(x) = log_2 x$) or even when the domain of an attribute is real, information loss occurs if significant bits overflow (i.e., the precision error or round-off error occurs).

When the log function $f_{log}()$ is applied in the encryption function sequence, in order to avoid precision errors, we define the precision range for x with $f(x) = log_2 x$ by locating when f(x) loses its precision, i.e., we find x and x+1 where $y_n = log(x)$, $y_{n+1} = log(x + 1)$ and $y_n = y_{n+1}$.

Table 1. Precision Limits of log_2 (x) for 32-bit and 64-bit number representations

	32 Bit	64 Bit
X	757283_{10}	$2.02967093951847 * 10^{14}{}_{10}$
x+1	757284_{10}	$2.02967093951848 * 10^{14}{}_{10}$
Log(x) = Log(x+1)	19.530474_{10}	47.528239_{10}

From Table 1, after the application of $log_2(x)$ where x is a 32-bit or 64-bit number, the maximum value of $Int(log_2(x))$ avoiding precision errors is 19 or 47, respectively. To avoid an early overflow error for attributes with large domain values, the function f_{log} ( ) is always applied first.

We propose the following techniques to control and avoid overflow and precision errors during the encryption process. (See [11] for the detail.)

- After the application of each log function, We maintain an "encrypted-value vector" V_E such that we 1) store $C * Fract(f_{i,log}( )) = e_i$ into the encrypted-value vector V_E., (2) provide $w_i = (Int (f_{i,log} ( )) + C')$ as an input to the function $f_{i+1,1}$ ( ), where Int(r) and Fract(r) denote functions that return the integer part of r, and the fractional 24 bits of r as an integer, respectively, and C, C' are constants, and (3)repeat steps (1) and (2) above after application of each $f_{i,log}()$.

- After applying f_{i-1} (f_{i-2} (x)), let $z_i = f_{i-1,2}$ ($f_{i-2,1}$ (x)) for $z_i < 2^{31}$ for 32-bit arithmetic. Before converting z_i into a real number in order to apply the log function $f_{i,log}$, we split 32-bit integer z_i into $Left_i$ which indicates the leftmost 19 bits of 32 bit integer z_i and $Right_i$ which indicates the rightmost 13 bits of z_i. Then a different function sequence is applied to each part separately.

Finally, we propose an encryption function sequence $E(x) = f_{k,log}(f_{k-1,2}(f_{k-2,1}(\ldots(f_{7,log}(f_{6,2}(f_{5,1}(f_{4,log}(f_{3,2}(f_{2,1}(f_{1,log} (x))))))))\ldots)))$, where subscripts are used to number the functions and the function type (linear, quadratic or log). The subscript k of the function $f_{k,log}$ () in E(x) uniquely specifies the encryption function sequence. We refer to the subscript value k as the *index* of the encryption function sequence E.

4.4 Generating and Encryption Function Sequence with Desired Degree of Security

By applying the results of the previous section, the relationship between the encryption function sequence index k and the desired degree of security d can be defined as

$$d = a * ((k/3) * 7) + b$$

where a is 0 if $k < 3$ and a=1 if $k \geq 3$; and b is 0, 4, or 6 if (k mod 3) is 0, 1, or 2, respectively. Therefore, given the desired degree of security by the user, the system can generate the corresponding encryption function sequence E(x) in a straightforward manner.

Thus, we have proposed an encryption function sequence E(x) as an alternative closed form encryption function. The degree of security of E(x) is the number of constants C_i (coefficients) employed by the function sequence, and the set of C_i in E(x) constitute the secret key K in the encryption.

5. CONCLUSIONS

In this paper, we have proposed the first steps of an approach to securing databases: encrypt the database, and yet allow query processing over the encrypted database.

Much work remains to be done. Our approach needs to be extended to handle SQL queries with arithmetic expressions and aggregate functions as well as complex SQL queries with nested subqueries[14]. We have discussed only the encryption of integer-valued attributes; encrypting and querying attributes of other primitive/complex data types is another research direction.

6. REFERENCES

[1] Nabil R. Adam, John C. Wortmann: Security-Control Methods for Statistical Databases: A Comparative Study. ACM Computing Surveys 21(4): 515-556 (1989)

[2] Blum, M., Micali, S., "How to Generate Cryptographically Strong Sequences of Pseudo-Random Bits", SIAM Journal on Computing, 13 (1984), 850-864.

[3] Hakan Hacigumus, Balakrishna R. Iyer, Sharad Mehrotra: Providing Database as a Service. IEEE ICDE 2002

[4] Hakan Hacigumus, Balakrishna R. Iyer, Chen Li, Sharad Mehrotra: Executing SQL over encrypted data in the database-service-provider model. ACM SIGMOD Conference 2002: 216-227

[5] Sushil Jajodia, Vijayalakshmi Atluri, Thomas F. Keefe, Catherine D. McCollum, Ravi Mukkamala: Multilevel Security Transaction Processing. Journal of Computer Security 9(3): 165-195 (2001)

[6] Melvin J. Maron. Numerical Analysis – A Practical Approach, 1985 Macmillan Publishing Co., Inc.

[7] Multi-level secure database management schemes: software review, CMU Software Engineering Institute, available at http://www.sei.cmu.edu/str/descriptions/mlsdms_body.html

[8] Menezes, A.J, van Oorschot, P.C. and Vanstone, S.A., Handbook of Applied Cryptography, CRC Press, Boca Raton, 1997, page 239.

[9] Goldberg, D., "What Every Computer Scientist Should Know About Floating Point Arithmetic", ACM Computing Surveys, 1991, available at http://citeseer.nj.nec.com/goldberg91what.html

[10] Ozsoyoglu, G., Singer, D., Chung, S., "Querying Encrypted Databases", Tech. Report, EECS, CWRU.

[11] Xiaolei Qian, Teresa F. Lunt: A Semantic Framework of the Multilevel Secure Relational Model. IEEE TKDE 9(2): 292-301 (1997)

[12] R. L. Rivest, L. Adleman and M.L. Dertouzos, On data banks and privacy homomorphisms, in R. A. DeMillo et al., eds., Foundations of Secure Computation, Academic Press, New York, 1978, 169-179.

[13] Database Management Systems, R. Ramakrishnan, J. Gehrke, McGraw-Hill, 2000.

[14] Eisengerg, A., Melton, J., "Sql: 1999, formerly known as sql 3", ACM SIGMOD Record, 28(1), 131-138, 1999.

[15] Richard Startz. 8087/80287/80387 – Applications and Programming with Intel's Math Coprocessors. 1988 Brandy Books, a division of Simon & Schuster, Inc.

[16] Ullman, J.D., "Principles of Database and Knowledge-Base Systems", Vol 1., Computer Science Press, 1989.

[17] Duminda Wijesekera, Sushil Jajodia: Policy algebras for access control: the propositional case. ACM Conference on Computer and Communications Security 2001: 38-47

IV

AUTHORIZATION AND ACCESS CONTROL IN DISTRIBUTED SYSTEMS

ADMINISTRATION RIGHTS IN THE SDSD-SYSTEM

Joachim Biskup
University of Dortmund
44221 Dortmund
Germany
biskup@ls6.cs.uni-dortmund.de

Thomas Leineweber
University of Dortmund
Germany
Thomas.Leineweber@uni-dortmund.de

Jörg Parthe
University of Dortmund
Germany
parthe@ls6.cs.uni-dortmund.de

Abstract The SDSD-system offers state-dependent access control in distributed object systems. The system enforces protocols which declare sets of activity sequences as allowed, thereby forbidding any occurence of an activity outside the context of an allowed sequence. In this paper we conceptually extend the SDSD-system by introducing discretionary administration rights for controlling the activities of declaring, binding and starting SDSD-protocols. Additionally, we introduce second level administration rights for controlling the grant and revoke activities concerning administration rights. Exploiting the powerful potentials of the SDSD-system, the new concepts are implemented by special administration protocols. Administration protocols are enforced with the same techniques already used for application protocols concerning the functionality of the underlying object system. In this environment recursive revocation is shown to be feasible.

Keywords: Security, distributed object system, administration of access rights, access control, state-dependent access rights, revoking rights, recursive revocation

1. Introduction

Access control is a fundamental mechanism for enforcing security requirements in computing systems. Conceptually, and highly simplified, *access control* comprises two phases. In the first phase, one or several security administrators are *declaring access rights*, each of which state that some user is allowed to perform some action on some object. In the second phase, each user request is intercepted by a *monitor* that decides on the basis of the declared access rights whether or not the request actually shall be executed. In implementations, usually these phases are interwoven, and participants of the computing system can act both as administrator and as user. The basic approach of access control has been refined in various ways in order to deal with more specific aspects. In this paper we deal with the following aspects: state-dependent access rights, monitoring for distributed systems, and constraining the administration of access rights by access control in turn.

Concerning the first two aspects, we rely on our previous work [1, 5, 2] about the design of *state-dependent* access control and its enforcement in *distributed object systems* and the corresponding implementation by the *SDSD-system* (for *S*tate-*D*ependent *S*ecurity *D*ecisions). Varying the basic approach, access rights are no longer statically granted until an explicit revocation. Rather, in a conceptually first phase an administrator declares so-called *protocols* in order to specify which kinds of *activity sequences* of the distributed object system are considered to be allowed for formal participants. After instantiating a protocol by binding actual participants to the formal participants and starting a concrete instance of such an activity sequence, the distributed monitoring system assigns and withdraws *dynamic access rights* on a short term basis for just a single activity, thereby enforcing that only allowed sequences can actually occur.

For example, an administrator for an insurance company can allow activity sequences of the following form (which informally circumscribes a formal protocol presented in Figure 2 of [2]): each such sequence starts by drafting a contract, followed by a careful inspection with an acceptance decision; dependent on this decision: either the contract is confirmed and subsequently either it becomes valid based on a timely payment or it is rejected based on a missed payment deadline; or the contract is immediately rejected. While enforcing state-dependent access control, for instance the activity "contract rejection" cannot occur as an isolated event, rather it is dynamically enabled only just after the pertinent event of "missed deadline" or "negative inspection", respectively, and after an actual execution, the activity "contract rejection" is immediately blocked again.

The present paper aims at extending the SDSD-system with respect to the third aspect mentioned above, namely, how in turn to *control the administration* of allowed activity sequences. More specifically, we first address the most urgent problem: *How to allow participants of the system to act as administrator who can declare protocols, bind actual participants to an instantiated protocol and start a concrete activity sequence?* We even go one level further and address the immediate follow-up problem: *How to allow participants to allow other participants to act as administrator?* Additionally, we also consider the revocation problem for both levels: *How to revoke allowances to act as administrator or to grant such allowances, respectively?*

In terms of our example, we deal with the problem how one or more "administrators" are dynamically introduced and controlled, and how a protocol of the sketched kind is coming into existence and exploited in a controlled fashion. Abstractly speaking, we investigate the problem of *administration rights* within the framework of state-dependent access control in distributed object systems. This problem has been studied before within different frameworks, including theoretical studies on deciding the possibility of the proliferation of a right (showing undecidability in general [8] and decidability of special cases like the take-grant model [10]), mechanisms for dynamic rights amplification in systems like UNIX (by the suid-flag) [6] or Hydra [17], a variety of revocation options as in Oracle [11, 12] or role-based administration of roles [16, 4].

Though our solutions are original for our framework, as discussed in detail in Section 6, they are based on an established paradigm, namely, to smoothly integrate the control of the administration with the control of the primary functionality. Furthermore, we follow the well-known paradigm of discretionary access control. More specifically, the contributions of this paper can be summarized as follows: (1) By re-examining our SDSD-system, we identify *fundamental administration tasks*, namely protocol *declaration*, protocol (instance) *binding*, and protocol (instance) *starting* (Section 2). (2) Based on the literature, we set up a conceptual design with discretionary *administration rights* as first level rights for the fundamental administration tasks and corresponding *second level rights* for controlling those of the first level. This design also includes the notion of *ownership* and control of *revocations* (Section 3). (3) Exploiting the powerful potentials of the SDSD-system, we implement the design by defining appropriate *administration protocols* for the SDSD-system, which are then shown to enforce the conceptual administration rights by the (slightly extended) mechanisms of the SDSD-system (Section 4). Some details of the implementation are demonstrated by considering the "GrantGrant right" as an example (Section 5). (4) We sketch that even *recursive revocation* can be integrated into the extended SDSD-system. (5) The implementation is available as a *prototype*, implemented in JAVA and CORBA.

On first sight, our contributions seem technically specific for the SDSD-system. However, we emphasize that – independently of the specific control system under consideration – the administration of rights always does not only have static implications, but also dynamic ones.

2. The SDSD-System

The SDSD-system has been presented in [2] and its theoretical foundation in [1, 5]. Here, we will give only a short overview of the system. The SDSD-system realizes a state-dependent access control in a distributed object system. The monitored objects communicate via a *CORBA Object Request Broker*. Every monitored object (also called *functional object*) is wrapped by its own *security object*. The functional object and its security object form a so-called *(actual) participant*. A method call is permitted if an appropriate dynamic right is present. These rights are automatically granted and revoked by the system dependent on the current state and based on *allowed activity sequences*. The building components of these allowed activity sequences are triples consisting of an *activator*, an *executor* and an *action*. Such a triple, named *step*, expresses that the participant which acts as the executor performs an action (i. e. a method call on his functional object) on behalf of the participant which acts as the activator.

The specification of the allowed activity sequences is done with a so-called *protocol*. A formal definition of the language for protocols is given in [3]. The core of a protocol is a regular expression on steps. A step specifies a building component of an activity sequence and accordingly comprises an identifier for the activator, an identifier for the executor and an action (step rule). The latter is specified by an action identifier (first action rule) possibly followed by appropriate parameters (second action rule and param rules). Though desirable in any protocol, parameters have not been generally supported in the prototype, but they are needed and actually implemented for the specific types of protocols introduced in Section 4. The identifiers used to determine activator and executor of a step have to be declared in the remainder of the protocol and are the so-called *formal participants*. These are placeholders for the actual participants, who act as activator and as executor, and have to be bound before a concrete activity sequence is monitored.

When a new activity sequence should be started in the context of monitoring an application, several administration activities additionally have to take place. Some of them are under the control of the users of the application, others are done by the system, transparently for the users. Figure 1 gives an overview of the main activities and the order of their execution. The gray arrows and boxes show the functionality of the basic SDSD-system. The black arrows and the white boxes show the extensions introduced in Section 3 (et. seqq.).

First, some user has to specify the allowed activity sequences by declaring an *application protocol*. Next, the protocol has to be instantiated and bound. Therefore, another or the same user as before performs the binding activity. Thereby, he assigns actual participants to the formal participants considering the type constraints listed in the application protocol. As result of this activ-

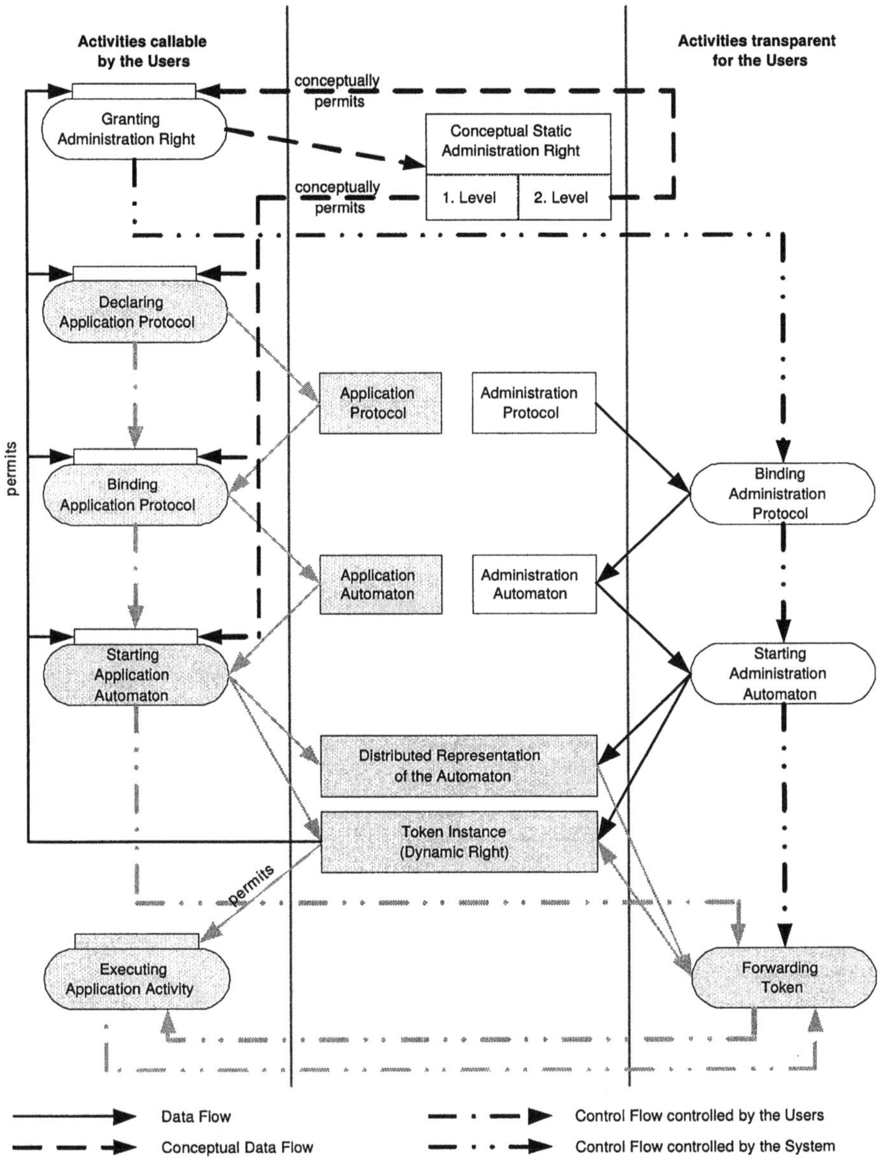

Figure 1. Overview of the main administration activities (declaring, binding, starting and granting) and the order of their execution. The functionality of the basic SDSD-system is represented by the gray arrows and the gray boxes, the proposed extensions are represented by the black arrows and the white boxes.

ity, a *finite automaton* is generated, which accepts exactly those sequences of steps (respectively the corresponding activity sequences) that are specified by the regular expression of the protocol. In the remainder this finite automaton is called *application automaton.* A declared application protocol can be instantiated and bound several times. After generating an application automaton, it has to be started. Therefore, some user performs the starting activity, which has two effects. First, a distributed representation of the application automaton is created and sent to the participants which are involved in that automaton. Second a *virtual security token* "is created".

Abstractly seeing, this token dynamically permits the execution of an application activity. Therefore, it is automatically forwarded to the participant who acts as the activator of the step which shall be executed next. The selection is taken by using the distributed representation of the automaton and is described at the end of this section. During the forwarding process the token is slightly changed, accordingly, in Figure 1 it is called token instance. After completion of an application activity the token is appropriately modified and forwarded again according to an activity sequence specified in the application automaton. In some sense, this token represents a *dynamic right,* since it is revoked immediately after single usage. After forwarding the token, the execution of a next application activity is permitted and so on. When the automaton reaches a final state the sequence is finished, thus the token and the distributed representation of the automaton are deleted.

The token and the process of forwarding it from one participant to another – as described above – are an abstract explanation of the actually used access control mechanism. Technically seeing, the security objects of the participants negotiate which application activity is permitted next by interchanging predefined messages. At first, the executor of the last executed step (called *last executor*) sends *offer* messages to the activators of possible next steps (according to the application automaton). If the functional object of an activator wants to execute the action belonging to the step, the activator answers with a *get* message. The last executor replies to one of the get messages he receives with a *put* message. This behaviour corresponds to forwarding the token in our abstract explanation. The receiving activator sends an *invoke* message to the executor of the belonging step. The invoked executor executes the action according to the step description. Thus, this step (respectively this application activity) is completed. Then the invoked executor sends – as the new last executor – new offer messages and so on.

All messages are interlinked by sequence numbers (this, among others, changes the token). Furthermore, messages as well as the application automatons are cryptographically signed and locally logged by the security objects to detect security violations.

3. Considered Problem and Approach

The SDSD-prototype, as reported in [2], only monitors the application activities but not the additional administration activities which might be crucial for achieving overall security: (1) Declaring Application Protocol, (2) Binding Application Protocol and (3) Starting Application Automaton. In Figure 1 this situation is indicated by showing a (gray) "monitoring box" on top of "Executing Application Activity" but not on top of the listed administration activities of the basic SDSD-system (the gray rounded boxes). In this paper we investigate in depth the problem of how the listed administration activities can be monitored by an extended SDSD-system, too. In terms of Figure 1, we will provide (the white) "monitoring boxes" for the administration activities such that application activities and administration activities are homogeneously supervised within the new SDSD-system.

We reconstruct the SDSD-system in a way, that the system offers so-called *administration operations,* which are used within the administration activities to accomplish the administration tasks. These operations are: (1) declare (a new application protocol), (2) undeclare (an application protocol), (3) bind (participants to an application automaton), (4) remove (a bound, but not yet started application automaton), and (5) start (an already bound application automaton).

As shown in Figure 1, the execution of an administration activity is monitored by the system (indicated by the boxes above the corresponding activity symbols; undeclaration and removal are not shown there). On a conceptual layer, these administration activities are permitted by first level static administration rights. These administration rights are granted and revoked – discretionarily – by the participants, sometimes directly with the aid of one of the two additional administration operations (1) grant (an administration right) and (2) revoke (an administration right, more exact: revoke a grant), or sometimes as a side effect of one of the other administration operations. The holder of an administration right is able to use it until the grantor revokes the originating grant as an explicit action by calling the revoke operation. Calling the grant or the revoke operation (revoke is not shown in Figure 1) is an administration activity itself, thus it is also monitored by the system. Conceptually seeing, their execution is permitted by a second level static administration right.

The set of administration right types is shown in Table 1. The *GrantGrant* right permits the execution of the administration activity grant, whereby the GrantGrant right, the GrantDeclare and the Declare right can be granted to any other participant of the system. The holder of the GrantGrant right is also allowed to revoke the grants caused by himself. The *GrantDeclare* right is a limited version of the GrantGrant right, i. e. granting a right and revoking a grant is restricted to the Declare right. A participant needs the *Declare* right to declare new application protocols or undeclare application protocols that he

Right	*Abbreviation*	*Permits*
GrantGrant	gg	granting gg, gd, d, resp. revoking corresponding grants caused by the holder of gg
GrantDeclare	gd	granting d, resp. revoking corresponding grants caused by the holder of gd
Declare	d	declaring new protocols resp. undeclaring protocols caused by the holder of d
Own	`o[Protocol prot]`	granting `b[prot]`, `s[prot, Automaton aut]`, `s[prot]`, resp. revoking corresponding grants
Bind	`b[Protocol prot]`	instantiating protocol `prot` (incl. binding) resp. revoking corresponding not yet started instances caused by the holder of `b[prot]`
Start	`s[Protocol prot]`	starting automatons that are instances of protocol `prot`
Start(Instance)	`s[Protocol prot, Automaton aut]`	starting automaton `aut` that is instance of protocol `prot`

Table 1. Summary of the administration right types.

has previously declared. The declarant of a protocol becomes the owner of it, i. e., he gets automatically the *Own* right. The owner of a protocol is allowed to grant all rights w. r. t. the protocol, namely, the *Bind* right and the two different types of the *Start* right and to revoke corresponding grants. The Bind right is necessary to instantiate an application protocol, i. e., to generate an application automaton and bind participants to this automaton. The first type of the Start right is solely referring to a protocol `prot`. The holder of this right is allowed to start any automaton that is an instance of `prot`. The other type of the Start right is additionally referring to a specific automaton instance `aut`, i. e., only this automaton instance can be started. Both types do not permit the abortion of any automaton, no matter who has started it. In contrast, the holder of the Bind right is allowed to remove automatons that he has previously bound. But if such an automaton is already started, its removal is forbidden.

4. Implementation

In Section 3 we have introduced conceptual static administration rights, which conceptually permit the execution of administration activities. These conceptual rights are different in kind from the dynamic rights (token) described in Section 2. The administration rights are explicitly granted and revoked by executing an appropriate administration activity. Furthermore, they can be repeatedly used (considering resource restrictions). In contrast, the dynamic rights are automatically assigned and withdrawn by the system. The withdrawal occurs directly after single usage.

To overcome these differences, we introduce a set of specialized protocols, called *administration protocols*. As shown in the right part of Figure 1, when a participant grants an administration right to another participant (or to himself), an appropriate administration protocol is chosen and bound (both within the binding administration protocol activity). The *administration automaton* generated in that process has two purposes: (1) It permits the grantee (holder) to execute all administration activities that are allowed by the granted administration right (e. g. grant an administration right to a participant on his own). (2) It permits the grantor to execute the activity "revoke the granted right, represented by this automaton". (Actually, as shown in Section 5, a special participant is allowed to end the automaton on behalf of the grantor.)

Next, this administration automaton is started. Analogously to starting an application automaton, a distributed representation of the automaton and a token (instance) are created. From this stage forth, the access control of administration activities is enforced almost in the same manner as the control of application activities. Only the selection which activator gets the put message is taken differently, namely on the basis of assigned priorities. As shown in Figure 1, binding an administration protocol and starting an administration automaton is not monitored by the system, since these activities are only initiated and executed by the system itself.

Apart from the participants mentioned in Section 2 (in the following called *functional participants*), other so-called *special participants* participate in administration automatons. These participants provide the operations that are used to carry out the administration tasks. There are three different types of special participants: *ProtocolManager*, *ProtocolStarter* and *GrantManager*. Participants of the first type, for simplification also called ProtocolManager (ProtocolStarter and GrantManager, respectively), offer the operations for declaring (`declare`) and undeclaring (`undeclare`) application protocols. Operations for instantiating application protocols (`bind`) as well as starting (`start`) and removing (`remove`) application automatons are provided by the ProtocolStarters. GrantManagers offer the operations for granting (`grant`) administration rights and revoking (`revoke`) corresponding grants. Furthermore, they gather the information on behalf of the functional participants, which administration rights those got, by whom and at what time. Each functional participant has exactly one GrantManager assigned to him. But one GrantManager can be assigned to several functional participants. Special participants do not have a functional object but only the (normally wrapping) security object. They do not need any user interaction. Thus, they can be settled on any host, particularly on especially secured hosts. Due to this property, they can be protected against malicious changing, therefore they are trustworthy participants. This trustworthiness is necessary, because crucial security checks have to be done in the context of the administration activities.

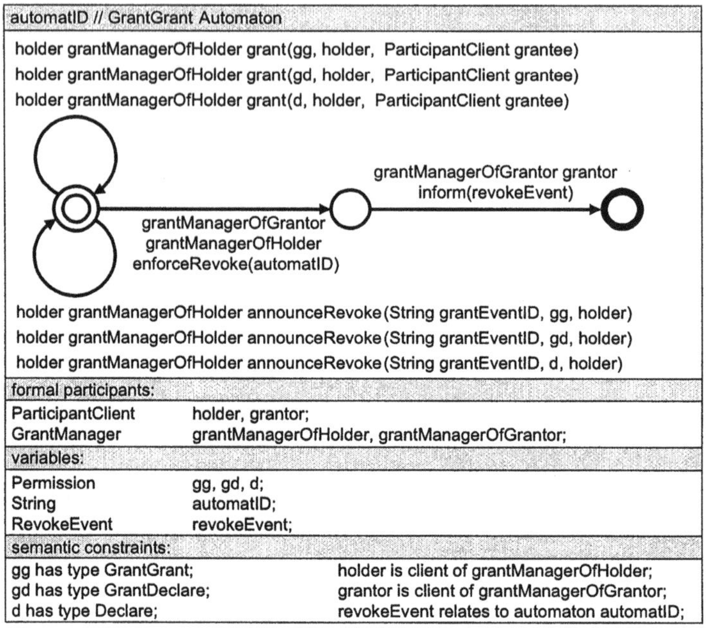

Figure 2. Automaton for the GrantGrant administration protocol

5. Some Details for Granting the GrantGrant Right

Granting a right is done by invoking the grant operation on a GrantManager. During the execution of the grant operation an appropriate administration protocol is bound to get an administration automaton. This administration automaton is then started. In this section we show some details of the GrantGrant right. The other rights introduced in Section 3 are treated similarly, as described in [13].

The administration protocol for the GrantGrant right is shown as an automaton in Figure 2. At this stage, the description of the protocol contains some additional information, which will be used during the process of creating the administration automaton and binding participants to the automaton. This information consists of (1) a list of the formal participants, (2) a list of variables and (3) a set of semantic constraints. The list of the formal participants specifies the types of the participants, who have to be bound to the automaton. In the case of the GrantGrant automaton these are (i) the `grantor`, (ii) the GrantManager that is assigned to the `grantor` (`grantManagerOfGrantor`), (iii) the grantee called `holder` and (iv) his GrantManager (`grantManagerOfHolder`). The "assigned to" relations are guaranteed by testing the two `is client of` semantic constraints. In contrast to general practice, separation of duties is not enforced in the case of binding an administration automaton. This is necessary in the case of granting a right to oneself, when the grantor and the grantee are identical. The list of variables defines variables to which values (resp. objects) have to be assigned during the binding process. Inter alia, these are three objects gg, gd and d, one for every right that can be granted by holding the GrantGrant right. The `has type` semantic constraints guarantee that every object has the correct type according to its name as specified in Table 1. The variable `automatID` records the unique identifier for this automaton. The variable `revokeEvent` is used during the revocation of a right.

After binding, the GrantGrant automaton is started, i. e. execution of a first step is offered to the eligible participants. The `holder` receives six offer messages (see Section 2 for an explanation) to execute a step, one for each step in which the `holder` can act as the activator. Three offer messages apply to the steps with the parameterized action `grant`, and three to the steps with the parameterized action `announceRevoke`. The `grantManagerOfGrantor` gets one offer for the step with the parameterized action `enforceRevoke`. He accepts this offer only if his client, i. e. the `grantor`, has instructed him to revoke the grant that has led to this automaton. If he accepts, the `enforceRevoke` step has the highest priority so that it will be the next step in this automaton.

By choosing one of the three offered `grant` steps the `holder` is able to grant the GrantGrant, the GrantDeclare or the Declare right to any functional participant. The `grant` operation offered by the GrantManager of the `holder` expects three arguments. In each case the first two are already set to values that are determined during the binding process. Considering the preceding type information (`ParticipantClient` is the common supertype of all functional participants) the argument for the last parameter `grantee` can be freely chosen.

By predetermining some values during the binding process, the `holder` is restricted to choose the parameters for the grant operation suitably according to the description of the right he holds. In the present case the first parameter states the right that could be granted. With the aid of the second one, the invoked GrantManager is informed about the fact that the passed `holder` will be the grantor of the grant activity that should be performed under the GrantGrant right held by the `holder`. As result of granting the right, the invoked GrantManager generates and starts a new administration automaton. In that second automaton the grantee of the grant acts as the `holder` and the grantor of the grant (the `holder` in the first automaton) as the `grantor`.

If in the first automaton the `holder` wants to revoke a grant that he has previously caused, he invokes one of the three `announceRevoke` steps, depending on the granted right. The only argument that has to be handed over by the holder is a value for the parameter `grantEventID`. The invoked GrantManager of the holder expects an identifier of an automaton that was caused by the grant of a right. The `holder` gets such identifiers as a return value of the `grant` operation. The other two already set arguments ensure that the `holder` is just able to revoke automatons that are caused by his grants.

The name of the operation `announceRevoke` expresses the fact that at this point the GrantManager (of the `holder` in the first automaton) is merely charged with the revocation. The actual enforcement is done in another automaton, because revoking a grant means to end the automaton that resulted from this grant. Therefore the GrantManager keeps the necessary information in his internal attributes and waits for an offer to execute the `enforceRevoke` step in the automaton, that should be ended. Normally, he has already got such an offer, since this step, resp. its edge, begins at the initial state of the automaton. If the `holder` of the second automaton (who is the `grantee` in the `grant` step of the first automaton) is accepting his offer, i.e. he executes a `grant` or an `announceRevoke` step, the offer for the `enforceRevoke` step has been invalidated. But after completion of the `grant` or `announceRevoke` activity, the automaton will be transferred to the initial state and inter alia an offer for the `enforceRevoke` step will be sent again. When the `enforceRevoke` operation is executed, the GrantManager gets to know that the `holder` of the second automaton (who is assigned to the GrantManager) will lose a right soon. Thus, the GrantManager examines within this operation, whether further revocations have to be recursively done. Further details of the revocation are presented in [3], which also contains a concrete example for using the GrantGrant right.

6. Related and Further Work

The idea to administrate an access control system like the SDSD-system with the help of itself is very appealing, but there are not many systems with this property. Mostly, a further higher level access control system is used to administrate a basic access control system. In [7] the access control system is explicitly decomposed into an enforcement manager and a policy manager. In contrast, in the SDSD-system, the administration of the policy is done with the help of the system itself.

A widely known self-administrable access control system is Role-Based Access Control (RBAC, [14]). The administrative layer is ARBAC97 [15] respectively ARBAC99 [16] (Administrative Role-Based Access Control). It is based on and used for a decentralized administration of Role-Based Access Control systems. The administration system is partitioned into different components. In ARBAC these components are for user-role assignments, permission-role assignments and role-role assignments. These components consist of administration concepts to create, modify and remove those assignments. In the SDSD-system, there are similar assignments, but as a difference, the activities leading to these assignments are controlled. Another model for self-administration of RBAC is SARBAC (Scoped Administration of Role-Based Access Control,

[4]). It is also uses RBAC for the control of a RBAC-system, but is somewhat different to handle.

An example for a system with dynamic internal administration of rights is Hydra [17]. It assigns rights to runtime objects (of the Hydra type `local namespace`) based on rights of the originating static object and based on rights of the calling object. The UNIX operation system has also the concept of dynamic rights amplification by the suid- and the guid-flag [6]. It allows the owner of a program to give other users additional rights when executing this program. These additional rights are limited to the rights the owner of the program already has. But if the owner of the program wants that a second user shall grant rights on the program to a third user, the ownership of the program has to be transferred to the second user.

The separation into the different administration activities Declare, Bind and Start has its similarities in Workflow Management Systems [9]. There, the administration tasks involved in the creation of a new workflow are the specification of a workflow process definition itself and the creation and the start of a workflow process instance. The declaration of a SDSD-protocol corresponds to the specification of a new workflow process definition, and the process of binding and starting corresponds to the creation and start of a workflow process instance. In contrast to the Workflow Reference Model, our model explicitly distinguishes between the two tasks of creating and starting a new process instance.

Some further work has also to be done: It may be feasible to provide the system with the ability to transfer the ownership of declared protocols to another participant or to separate the ownership of a protocol from the right to grant the Bind or the Start right by introducing some additional administration rights.

Our current prototype supports only one ProtocolStarter, one ProtocolManager, one place to store the declared application protocols (Protocol Repository) and one place of the not yet started application automatons (Protocol Instance Repository). A policy for the visibility aspects has to be specified and an appropriate mechanism has to be developed to overcome this limitation. Furthermore, it is desirable that the system supports the abortion of an already started automaton. As a first idea, the protocol definition language can be expanded to mark states of the automaton (maybe called checkpoints) at which it can be aborted in a safe manner. Another important administration activity which is not yet included in our system is the introduction of new participants into the SDSD-system. This activity also might be controlled by another administration right.

References

[1] Joachim Biskup and Christian Eckert. About the enforcement of state dependent security specifications. In T. F. Keefe and C. E. Landwehr, editors, *Database Security VII*, pages

3–17. North-Holland, 1994.

[2] Joachim Biskup and Thomas Leineweber. State-dependent security decisions for distributed object-systems. In M. S. Olivier and D. L. Spooner, editors, *Database and Application Security XV*, pages 105–118. Kluwer, 2002.

[3] Joachim Biskup, Thomas Leineweber, and Jörg Parthe. Administration Rights in the SDSD-System. Technical report, University of Dortmund, 2003. Link at `ls6-www.cs.uni-dortmund.de/issi/publications/2003.html`.

[4] Jason Crampton. *Authorization and Antichains*. PhD thesis, University of London, February 2002.

[5] Christian Eckert. *Zustandsabhï¿½gige Sicherheitsspezifikationen und ihre Durchsetzung*. Berichte aus der Informatik. Shaker Verlag, 1997.

[6] S. Garfinkel and G. Spafford. *Practical UNIX and Internet Security*. O'Reilly, 1996.

[7] Robert Grimm and Brian N. Bershad. Separating access control policy, enforcement, and functionality in extensible systems. *ACM Trans. on Computer Systems*, 19(1):36–70, 2001.

[8] Michael A. Harrison, Walter L. Ruzzo, and Jeffrey D. Ullman. Protection in operating systems. *Communications of the ACM*, 19(8):461–471, 1976.

[9] D. Hollingsworth. The workflow reference model. Document No. TC00-1003, 1995. Issue 1.1.

[10] R. J. Lipton and L. Snyder. A linear time algorithm for deciding subject security. *Journal of the ACM*, 24(3):455–464, 1977.

[11] Oracle Corp. *Oracle9i Database Administrator's Guide*, 2002. Part No. A96521-01.

[12] Oracle Corp. *Oracle9i SQL Reference*, 2002. Part No. A96540-01.

[13] Jörg Parthe. Deklaration und Ausführung neuer Handlungsabfolgen fr zustandsabhängige Handlungsrechte. Diploma thesis, Universität Dortmund. `ls6-www.cs.uni-dortmund.de/~parthe/downloads/par02.pdf`, 2002.

[14] R. S. Sandhu, E. J. Coyne, H. L. Feinstein, and C. E. Youman. Role-based access control models. *IEEE Computer*, 29(2):38–47, February 1996.

[15] Ravi Sandhu, Venkata Bhamidipati, and Qamar Munawer. The ARBAC97 model for role-based administration of roles. *ACM Trans. on Information and System Security*, 2(1):105–135, 1999.

[16] Ravi Sandhu and Qamar Munawer. The ARBAC99 model for administration of roles. In *15th Annual Computer Security Applications Conference*, pages 229–240, December 1999.

[17] W. A. Wulf, R. Levin, and S. P. Harbison. *Hydra/C.mmp: An Experimental Computer System*. McGraw-Hill Book Company, 1981.

SECURE AUTHORISATION FOR WEB SERVICES

Sarath Indrakanti Vijay Varadharajan Michael Hitchens
Information and Networked Systems Security Research, Division of ICS
Macquarie University, Australia.
{sindraka, vijay, michaelh}@ics.mq.edu.au

Rajat Kumar
Microsoft Pty., Australia
rajk@microsoft.com

Abstract: In this paper, we investigate the authorisation service provided by Microsoft® .NET MyServices [1]. We propose modifications and extensions to eXtensible Markup Language (XML) [2] based data structures' schemas to support a range of commonly used access policies in commercial systems. We have developed the modified access evaluation algorithms that take the proposed extensions into account. The extensions proposed in this paper have been used in the specification and analysis of a practical application involving access control to electronic patient records in hospitals.

Key words: Web Services, Security, Access Control and Authorisation.

1. MICROSOFT .NET MYSERVICES

Microsoft .NET MyServices [1] is the name for a set of XML message interfaces delivered as part of the Microsoft .NET initiative. It is a platform for building user-centric Internet applications. It provides a private, secure "digital safe deposit box" where users can place their personal data. This digital storage box serves as the single, central location where users can store, update, and control all of their personal data. .NET MyServices aims to provide a fine granularity of control to the user (owner of the data) once the information is placed in the digital safe deposit box. The user may choose to share that information with friends, family, groups with which they have an association, and businesses. Additionally, users can sign up to receive alerts on a number of desktop and mobile devices. .NET MyServices is implemented as a set of web services that utilise industry standards including XML and SOAP.

These services can use .NET Passport [10] to authenticate users and .NET Alerts to notify users of important events through a wide range of client devices and to gain access to key pieces of data. .NET MyServices aims to provide ownership and control of personal data to individual users.

2. AUTHORISATION SERVICE

In .NET MyServices, the following items are used in the design of the authorisation system.

The definition of a role in terms of the permissions that it has on different objects is specified using a role-template. A role-template defines the set of methods allowed by the role-template and the Scope visible to each method. A role-template has a name (e.g. rt1)

The mapping between the role-template and the user is defined by the function "Role". Then the users have a list of roles that are authorised to access the content in documents associated with those users. This is defined in role-list, which describes what information to share, who to share with and how to share it.

A role-map describes what information is to be shared and how that sharing is to occur. It defines for each role (from the role-list), what the allowable methods are, and what scope of data is visible while using this method. The role-map is the same for all instances of a particular service, and is authored by the implementer of the service. Hence the objective of the role-map is to simplify the security authorisation layer as it appears to the end user. It does this by specifying the fixed set of access patterns that occur on a given service.

For schema and examples of role-list and role-map documents, please refer to [3].

3. PROPOSED EXTENSIONS TO AUTHORISATION SERVICE

We propose extensions to the existing authorisation system in .NET MyServices thereby enabling it to support the following range of access control policies - Conditions and Actions based access policies, Role based access policies, Static and Dynamic separation of duty, Delegation, Chinese-wall policy and Joint action based policies. In each case, we will first describe the access policy requirements to be supported by the web service, discuss the existing limitations and propose extensions to data structures and schemas and specify the authorisation service. In describing our extensions to the authorisation service, we will use the term "provider" to denote an entity that owns the content document (or web service data) and the term "user" to denote an entity that accesses the provider's document. Due to space limitations, we have not discussed extensions to implement Chinese-Wall policy, Delegation policy and 'limited number of accesses' policy in this paper. They can be found in [4] along with a detailed description of our extended authorisation model.

Through out this paper, when we use the element 'role' in role-list schema skeleton extensions, we implicitly mean that it is a role, a delegated-role or a dynamic-role. Delegated-role and dynamic-role are defined in the sections to follow.

For simplicity, we only show the schema skeleton for 'role' element. The same applies to both methodRef and jointMethodRef elements in role elements in the role-list document. For simplicity, we only show the schema skeleton for methodRef element. Every .Net MyServices provider has a content document that actually stores his/her data and an access control list (ACL) document that stores authorisation information. We suggest every provider provisioned for a .NET MyService should also be provisioned a log document along with the content document and ACL (role-list) for auditing purposes. We will not be discussing the auditing aspects in this paper.

To begin with, we propose a small modification to the role-map schema that helps to identify uniquely a method-scope pair in the role-template. This is achieved by including an "id" attribute. This new attribute is introduced so that this pair can be referred to in a role element in a provider's role-list document. We will see later that this minor extension will be useful in the specification of fine-grained access control policies. An example with this minor extension (in bold) is shown in figure 1.

```
<roleMap>
      <hs:scope ... />
      <hs:roleTemplate name="rt0">
         <hs:method name="query" scopeRef="1" id = "1"/>
         <hs:method name="insert" scopeRef="1" id = "2"/>
      </hs:roleTemplate>
</roleMap>
```

Figure 1. Role-map extension with preliminary extension

We are now in a position to consider the extensions to schemas and data structures that would enable us to support the range of access control policies mentioned above.

3.1.1 Conditions and Actions

The existing authorisation service in .NET MyServices does not have the ability to specify conditions to methods when performing access control checks. Each role-template provides access to a number of methods on various scopes to a user. To further restrict access on each of those methods based on arbitrary conditions, we introduce a new element *methodRef*. This construct enables us to associate conditions and actions with a method. A method can have a condition and one or more actions associated with it. The modified schema skeleton for role-list document is shown in figure 2. The elements and attributes introduced to support Conditions and Actions based policies are described below.

```
<hs:roleList ... >1..1
    <hs:scope ... />
    <hs:role ... >0..unbounded .....
        <hs:subject .. />
        <hs:methodRef idRef = "..." >0..unbounded
            <hs:condition operation = "...">0..1 {any}
                <hs:predicate name = "...">0..unbounded
                    <hs:parameter name= "..." value = "...">0..unbounded {any}
                    </hs:parameter>
                </hs:predicate>
                <hs:condition operation = "..."/>0..unbounded
            </hs:condition>
            <hs: action id = "..." type = "...">0..unbounded
                <hs:predicate name = "...">0..unbounded
                    <hs:parameter name= "..." value = "...">0..unbounded {any}
                    </hs:parameter>
                </hs:predicate>
            </hs:action>
        </hs:methodRef>
        <hs:expiresAt>0..1</hs:expiresAt>
            {any}
    </hs:role>
</hs:roleList>
```

Figure 2. Modified schema skeleton for role-list document

/roleList/role/methodRef element refers to the ID of the method for this role in its role-template. Multiple method IDs can be referenced here. For instance, methodRef = "1,2". In this case the conditions and actions are performed for the methods with id 1 and 2. */methodRef/@idRef* attribute gives the reference to the method id in the role template referred to by this role.

/roleList/role/methodRef/condition element is a Boolean formula. If the formula evaluates to true then the access is granted. In general, the condition expression can involve several predicates involving standard logic operators such as 'and', 'or' and 'not'. Defining a condition element within another condition element can specify recursion. Each predicate may have one or more parameters.

A parameter can be specified in three ways: (a) as a string in its 'value' attribute (b) as a list of arbitrary elements and (c) as a single 'function' element. If a value attribute is specified, all the child nodes are ignored even though they are specified. Also, if some elements other than 'function' elements are specified, every 'function' element is ignored even though it is specified. Consider an example of a predicate: compareStr(s1,s2,s3) is a predicate where s1 is 'eq'(equal) or 'neq' (not equal) and s2 and s3 are two strings to be compared. This predicate compares two strings according to the operator. Consider an example of a function: getDate() is a function, which takes no parameters, and it returns a text node representing the current date.

/roleList/role/methodRef/action specifies actions that need to be performed when an access request is made to the method(s) through methodRef. Each action has an ID so that it can be uniquely referenced (using Xpath). The type attribute is used to define whether the action is only performed when the access is granted (on_access) or is always performed whether or not access is granted (always). The predicates in

action expressions are similar to those defined in conditions except that there should be at least one predicate element.

3.1.2 Role Hierarchy

One of the advantages of the role-based (RBAC) [5][9] approach is that it can model the privileges in an organisation more effectively. A simplistic view of an organisation structure is a hierarchical ordering of responsibilities, with the senior positions encompassing all the privileges of the junior positions, with some extra privileges. Such a role hierarchy can be achieved by providing hierarchy in role template definition. At present, most of the services in .NET MyServices use only about 3-5 role templates and there is no hierarchy. We propose the following extensions to .NET MyServices authorisation service to enable role based access control and role hierarchy. Each service should define a dynamic role-map at the user level. The role-map should be static at the web service level but the provider should be able to change it when needed. Therefore, every provider should have his/her own role-map along with the web service role-map. Let us call the provider's role-map the provider-role-map (XML document name = providerRoleMap). New scopes can now be defined in this provider-role-map instead of in the provider's role-list. We also remove all scope definitions from the role-list for a provider and move them to the provider-role-map for consistency. Role-templates' ID in provider-role-map should be anything other than rT0, rT1, rT2, rT3 and rT99 as these are the default role-template IDs. Every method in the default web service role-map and provider-role-map should have an ID number attribute to uniquely identify the method.

When a provider is provisioned to a service, the provider has his or her own provider-role-map document along with the content, system, log and acl (role-list) documents. The XML Schema skeleton for providerRoleMap is shown in figure 3.

The schemas for scope, role-template and their child elements and their attributes are the same as for those defined for the web service role-map. Other elements and attributes introduced to implement role hierarchy policy are described below.

```
<hs:providerRoleMap changeNumber="..." id="..." creator="..."
    xmlns:hs="http://schemas.microsoft.com/hs/2001/10/core">1..1
  <hs:scope id="...">0..unbounded
    <hs:name xml:lang="..." dir="...">0..unbounded</hs:name>
    <hs:shape base="...">1..1
      <hs:include select="...">0..unbounded</hs:include>
      <hs:exclude select="...">0..unbounded</hs:exclude>
    </hs:shape>
  </hs:scope>
  <hs:roleTemplate name="...">0..unbounded
    <hs:fullDescription xml:lang="..." dir="...">0..1</hs:fullDescription>
    <hs:includeRT name = "..."</hs:includeRT>0..unbounded
    <hs:method name="..." scopeRef="..." id =
          "...">0..unbounded</hs:method>
    <hs:override rtName="..." idRef = "..."
                  methodName = "..." scopeRef="..." />0..unbounded
    </hs:override>
  </hs:roleTemplate>
</hs:providerRoleMap>
```

Figure 3. Provider-role-map schema skeleton

providerRoleMap/roleTemplate/includeRT element is used to specify hierarchy. A role-template can inherit another role-template's privileges with this element. See figure 4. */includeRT/@name* attribute is used to refer to the role-template whose privileges can be inherited.

providerRoleMap/roleTemplate/override element is used to override either a scope or method name in a method element in a role-template. This can be used to implement role hierarchy as shown in scenarios below. */override/@rtName* attribute refers to the role-template (that is inherited) in which the overriding has to be done. If the mentioned role-template is not inherited with an includeRT element, override element is ignored. */override/@idRef* attribute is provided to refer to the method element (using its ID) from the inherited role-template that is to be overridden. */override/@methodName* is an optional attribute. It is to be used only when the method in the inherited role-template is to be overridden. */override/@scopeRef* is an optional attribute. It is to be used only when the scope in the inherited role-template is to be overridden.

Note that the role templates inherited can either be the default role templates from the web service role-map or from provider-role-map. To achieve role hierarchy, a suitable new role-template (with needed hierarchy definition) in the provider-role-map is created. Then it is to be referred in the suitable role element(s) in provider's role-list. For illustration purposes, a few scenarios are shown in figure 4. Role-templates rt10, rt20 and rt30 are defined. rt30 inherits privileges from both rt10 and rt20. Method with ID '4' from rt10 is overridden in rt30 to 'create'. 'insert' method's scope from rt20 is overridden to 2 in rt30.

```
<hs:roleTemplate name="rt10">
  <hs:method name="query" scopeRef ="1" id = "1"/>
  <hs:method name="insert" scopeRef="3" id = "2"/>
  <hs:method name="replace" scopeRef="3" id = "3"/>
  <hs:method name="delete" scopeRef="3" id = "4"/>
</hs:roleTemplate>
<hs:roleTemplate name="rt20">
  <hs:method name="query" scopeRef ="5" id = "1"/>
  <hs:method name="insert" scopeRef="5" id = "2"/>
</hs:roleTemplate>
<hs:roleTemplate name="rt30">
  <hs:includeRT name = "rt10">
  <hs:includeRT name = "rt20">
  <hs:override rtName="rt10" idRef= "4"
                  methodName = "create" />
   <hs:override rtName = "rt20" idRef = "2" scopeRef ="2" />
  <hs:method name="query" scopeRef="4" id = "1"/>
  <hs:method name="insert" scopeRef="4" id = "2"/>
  <hs:method name="replace" scopeRef="4" id = "3"/>
</hs:roleTemplate>
```

Figure 4. Role-template example with role hierarchy policy

3.1.3 Dynamic Separation of duty

Dynamic separation of duty [6] can only be determined during system operation. This is whereby a user having chosen a specific action or role at run time is not authorised to perform another action or assume another role. To begin with, the user is allowed to perform either of the actions or assume either of the roles. We achieve dynamic separation of duty by adding a new element called 'dynamicRole' to the schema of role-list. The modified schema skeleton for role-list document is shown in figure 5.

Extensions to the role-list schema are described below:

/roleList/dynamicRole element is introduced to support dynamic separation of duty policies. Most of the child elements and attributes for this element are exactly the same as for 'role' element. Therefore, only the new added elements and attributes are described here. */dynamicRole/RT* - A minimum of 2 (or more) RT elements should be used in each dynamicRole element. This element encapsulates both role-template and the scope on which it is used along with the conditions and actions on the methods. The user with a dynamic-role has access to any of the role-templates and on any of the scopes provided by the dynamic-role. The role-template - scope pairs are mutually exclusive. Once the user accesses a role-template on a scope (through a RT element), s/he is not allowed to access any other privileges provided by his/her other RT elements. */dynamicRole/RT/scopeRef* element stores the scope to which the user has access with the role-template in this RT element. */dynamicRole/RT/roleTemplateRef* element stores reference to one of the role-templates' ID to which the user has access.

/roleList/dynamicRole/usedRT/ element is used to store information to enable dynamic separation of duty. */usedRT/idRef* element stores the ID reference to one of the RT elements (in this dynamic-role). Until the first time the user accesses any of the privileges in his/her RT elements, this is a null element. Once the user accesses

privileges provided by any of the RT elements, the ID of that RT element is written here by the authorisation service.

```
<hs:roleList ... >1..1
  <hs:scope ... />
  <hs:role ... />
  <hs:dynamicRole scopeRef="..." roleTemplateRef="..." ....>0..unbounded
   .......
    <hs:subject ... />
    <hs:RT id = "...">2..unbounded
      <hs:scopeRef>0..1</hs:scopeRef>
       <hs:roleTemplateRef>1..1</hs:roleTemplateRef>
      <hs:methodRef idRef = "..." >0..unbounded
          <hs:condition operation = "...">0..1            ...
   </hs:condition>
       <hs:action id = "..." type = "...">0..unbounded .....
   </hs:action>
        </hs:methodRef>
    </hs:RT>
    <usedRT>1..1
      <idRef>1..1</idRef>
    </usedRT>
    <hs:expiresAt>0..1</hs:expiresAt>
    {any}
  </hs:dynamicRole>
</hs:roleList>
```

Figure 5. Modified schema skeleton for role-list document

All the methods in every RT element in a dynamicRole element implement at least the 'checkAccess' predicate, which does the following:

When the user accesses one of the role-templates (provided by the RT elements) on the scope allowed for the first time, it sets the idRef element in usedRT to the RT's ID.

Next time a user with dynamicRole element tries to access a scope with a role-template provided by any other RT elements, access is denied. Access to RT with ID stored in usedRT element is only allowed.

3.1.4 Joint Action Based Policies

Joint action based policies [7] are used in situations where trust in individuals needs to be dispersed. Often this arises because individuals are trusted according to their expertise, which in turn maps the concept of trust to a specific set of actions. In delegation, there is a partial or complete granting of privileges, whereas in joint actions agents may acquire privileges, by working together in tandem, which none posses in isolation.

Consider the following example. A patient is admitted to the hospital if both the patient and a doctor agree. That is, the policy is that the doctor and patient jointly need to agree for the action "admission of the patient to the hospital" to be authorised. Modified XML schema skeletons for provider-role-map and role-list documents are shown in figures 6 and 7 below.

Schema extensions to provider-role-map document are as follows: *providerRoleMap/roleTemplate/jointMethod* element is added to a role-template. It defines a joint method and its quorum number. Its name, scopeRef and id attribute schemas are the same as method element's schema. They are not redefined here. */jointMethod/quorum* element gives the authorisation system the quorum number for this joint method. Quorum is the minimum number of users that have access to this joint method via the same role-template and call the joint method for it to be performed. Till the quorum is reached, a temporary flag is set in their role element as defined below.

```
<hs:providerRoleMap ... >1..1
  <hs:scope ... />
  <hs:CWP_sets ... />
  <hs:roleTemplate name="...">0..unbounded
    <hs:fullDescription xml:lang="..." dir="...">0..1</hs:fullDescription>
    <hs:includeRT name = "..."</hs:includeRT>0..unbounded
    <hs:method name="..." scopeRef="..." id =
                  "...">0..unbounded</hs:method>
    <hs:override rtName="..." methodName = "..."
                                    scopeRef="..." id = "..."/>0..unbounded
    <hs:jointMethod name = "..." scopeRef = "..." id = "...">0..unbounded
     <hs:quorum>1..1</hs:quorum>
    </hs:jointMethod>
  </hs:roleTemplate>
</hs:providerRoleMap>
```

Figure 6. Modified schema skeleton for provider-role-map document

Schema extensions to role-list document are as follows: */roleList/role/jointMethodRef*: There are as many jointMethodRef elements in a role element as there are joint-methods in the role-template it is referring to. It is similar to a methodRef element expect that it has a boolean flag element. All other elements are exactly the same as those defined in methodRef schema. */jointMethodRef/@idRef attribute* refers to the joint method's ID and is used to refer to the joint-method in this role's role-template.
/roleList/role/jointMethodRef/condition/flag element is used to store if joint access request is made. */condition/flag/reducedScope* is an optional element. It may so happen that a user should gain authorisation only to perform a joint action on a further reduced scope than that permitted by her role-template. This scope element solves such purpose. Its shape element's schema is the same as shape element's schema for scope element in role-map. */condition/flag/value* element is by default set to false. When the request for the joint-method comes in from the user (with this role element), this element is set to true. Until the quorum is reached only the flag in the joint-method elements in different users' role elements is set to true. Once the quorum is reached, the actual action is performed on the content document of the provider.

```
<hs:roleList ...>1..1
    <hs:scope .../>
    <hs:role ... >0..unbounded ....
     <hs:subject .../>
    <hs:jointMethodRef idRef = "..." >0..unbounded
      <hs:condition operation = "...">0..1
        <hs:flag>1..1
          <hs:reducedScope>0..1
      <hs:shape base="...">1..1
            <hs:include select="...">0..unboundedd</hs:include>
            <hs:exclude select="...">0..unboundedd</hs:exclude>
       </hs:shape>
          </hs:reducedScope>
          <hs:value>1..1</hs:value>
          <hs:flag/>
          <hs:predicate name ..../>1..unbounded
          <hs:condition operation = "...">0..unbounded </hs:condition>
          <hs:action.../>0..unbounded
    </hs:jointMethodRef>
    <hs:methodRef ... />0..unbounded
    <hs:expiresAt>0..1</hs:expiresAt>
    {any}
  </hs:role>
</hs:roleList>
```

Figure 7. Modified schema skeleton for role-list document

A new predicate 'checkQuorum' is defined for all services that need to implement joint action based policy. Every jointMethodRef element in a role element must at least call this predicate in its condition. 'checkQuorum' predicate does the following:

- Whenever a call to a joint method is made, it checks the number of flags that are set to true in the role elements that have access to this joint method via the same role-template the caller has access to.
- If the number of flags set to true is more than or equal to the quorum number mentioned in the joint method definition in the role-template, then the actual change is made to the content document. Or else the flag in the caller's jointMethodRef element is set to true.

4. AUTHORISATION EVALUATION

The .NET MyServices authorization algorithm is redefined here to into account of the extensions proposed to the authorisation service as follows. Please see [1] for original authorisation algorithm.

The user, application and platform identities as well as the credential type are determined from the incoming message. The matching role from the provider's role-list document is then located. If a matching role or dynamic-role is not found, then the request fails with an authorisation fault. If a matching role is found and if it contains an expiresAt element, then the role is checked to see if it has expired. If not, then the role-template that is referenced by the role is found from the role-map or provider-role-map. This template is checked to see if the method requested is allowed. Using the scope from the role-map or provider-role-map (referenced by role-template), combined with the optional scope referenced by the role, the node set that is visible to this message is determined.

If a matching dynamic-role is found, and if it contains an expiresAt element, then the dynamic-role is checked to see if it has expired. If not, the idRef element's value of usedRT in the dynamic-role element is checked. If the idRef element's value is null, the role-template and scope referenced by first RT element are located from the role-map or provider-role-map that is referenced by the dynamic-role. This template is then used to determine whether the method or joint-method requested is allowed. The scope is used to determine if the operation requested is within that scope. If either the method is not allowed or the operation is not within the scope, then the role-template and scope referenced by second RT element are located. Then whether the method or joint-method requested is allowed by the template or not is determined as well as whether the operation requested is within that scope for all other RT elements. If none of the role-templates and scopes allows access to that requested method on the requested scope, then the message fails with an authorisation fault. The usedRT's idRef element is set to the value of the 'id' attribute of the RT element that contains role-templates and scopes with privileges requested in the message. If usedRT's idRef element's value refers to an RT element's ID, and if either the method is not allowed by the role-template in the RT element or if the operation requested is not within the scope allowed, the message fails with an authorisation fault. Using the scope from the role-map or provider-role-map, combined with the optional scope referenced by the RT element in the dynamic-role, the node set visible to this message is computed.

If the method requested is a normal method, all conditions are evaluated and if any one returns false, then a fail message is sent. All the actions with 'type' set to "always", are performed. All the actions with 'type' set to "on-access" are only preformed if condition is true. If the method requested is a joint-method then there exists at least one predicate (checkQuorum) in the condition element. The condition is evaluated. If it returns false, the message fails with an authorisation fault. If not, all the actions with 'type' set to "always", are performed. All the actions with 'type' set to "on-access" are only performed, if condition is true. The requested operation is then performed ensuring that the user has no access to information outside the scope computed above.

5. PRACTICAL APPLICATION

We have applied the proposed extensions to the authorisation service by developing an access control system for electronic patient records. In this section, we only briefly describe some of the various access policies mentioned above in Section 4 that have been specified in this system. For a detailed description of the system and the authorisation policy specification, refer to [4].

In our demonstration, we assume that an electronic Patient Record System (PRS) is used by several hospitals in a metropolitan city. Hence each hospital is the provider and patients are users. A patient record is stored as a XML document. In this paper, we will not describe the structure of the patient record. We are currently preparing a separate paper on this complete system.

Examples of the role hierarchy policies specified in this system - A Receptionist Rose can create a patient's name in a blank medical record. A Nurse Nancy can read a patient's general information and has Receptionist privileges. A Doctor Alice can read entire medical record. Doctor also has Nurse and Receptionist privileges. A Doctor in charge Bob can not only read but also write to record and informed consent sections. However, he can only write once into the informed consent section. He also has Doctor's privileges. This scenario is achieved by introducing new role-templates and then creating the required role hierarchies using these templates as described above in Section 4.

We have specified both static and dynamic separation of duty policies. In the static case, for instance in the role hierarchy example above, the duties of a nurse, doctor and doctor in charge are statically separated by creating role-template elements for them in the provider-role-map and then referring to them (or directly referring to the default role-template elements from the role-map) in the role-list for the provider – in this case all the hospitals. In the case of dynamic separation of duty, we have policies such as doctors Doug and Lee can write a report after a medical procedure or certify it but not both. That is, one doctor should not be able to both write a report and certify it. Depending on the action taken by a doctor, access is controlled in a dynamic fashion.

In terms of the Chinese-wall policy, the PRS has patients grouped into hospital name and department categories as shown below.

Set A: Departments (Cancer research, Cardiology, Neurology)

Set B: Hospitals (ABC Hospital, PQR Hospital, XYZ Hospital)

An example in our system occurs when a hospital implements Chinese-wall policy on trainee doctors when they access the patient records. Trainee doctors may do research by accessing patients records from only one of the departments from Set A and from only one of the hospitals in Set B. Once a trainee doctor (Tom) accesses a document from a category say Cardiology from Set A, he is not allowed to access any other category from that set. Similarly if Tom accesses a record from ABC Hospital, he is not allowed to access patient records from any other hospital from Set B. Note that here we have patient records from multiple hospitals.

Our system has different examples of the delegation policy. A simple one occurs when a doctor Alice delegates part of her privileges to her personal assistant Patricia. Note that this is a case of partial permanent delegation. This is achieved by adding a delegated-role to the appropriate provider's role list. An example of a joint action policy in our system is as follows: A discharge medical report can only be certified by two doctors jointly, for instance, the duty doctor in the hospital and the patient's surgeon. Once again this is achieved using the constructs specified in Section 5 involving role-templates and role elements and a Boolean flag.

6. CONCLUDING REMARKS

In this paper, we have considered the authorisation model in .NET MyServices and discussed the limitations of the authorisation service in terms of the policies that can be supported. Then we proposed new extensions to the XML data structures' schemas that could help to support the specification of a range of commonly used access policies in commercial systems. In particular, we have provided new extensions for supporting conditional authorisation, role hierarchy, dynamic separation of duty, Chinese-wall policy, joint action based policies and limited number of accesses to objects. We have developed the modified access evaluation algorithms that take the proposed extensions into account. We have then discussed the application of the modified authorisation service to an electronic Patient Record System. We are also currently investigating the extensions proposed in this paper to extend the XACL [8] and creating a distributed authorisation service for XML Web Services.

7. ACKNOWLEDGEMENTS

Vijay Varadharajan would like to thank Australian Research Council and Microsoft Pty. Australia for their support.

REFERENCES

[1] Microsoft .NET MyServices Specification 2001, Microsoft Press

[2] T. Bray et al. 'Extensible Markup Language (XML) 1.0' (Second Edition), World Wide Web Consortium (W3C), http://www.w3.org/TR/REC-xml (October, 2000)

[3] The .NET Security Service, Chapter 7, pp. 141-157, .NET MyServices Specification, MS Press, 2001.

[4] S. Indrakanti: 'Authorisation Service in .NET MyServices', Technical Report, Dept. of Computing, Division of ICS, Macquarie University, Dec.2002.

[5] R. Sandhu et al, 'Role based access control models', IEEE Computer, 1996, pp. 38-47

[6] R. Simon and M. Zurko: 'Separation of duty in role-based environments.' Proceedings of the 10th computer security foundations workshop, Rockport, MA, USA, 1997, IEEE CS Press, pp. 183-194.

[7] V. Varadharajan and P. Allen: 'Joint Action based Authorisation Schemes', ACM 30, *Oper. Syst. Rev.*, 1996, 3, pp. 32-45

[8] M. Kudo and S. Hada: 'XML Document Security based on Provisional Authorisation', Proceedings of the ACM Conference on Computer and Communications Security (CCS), Nov 2000, Greece.

[9] M. Hitchens and V. Varadharajan: 'Design and specification of role based access control policies'. IEE Proceedings - Software, Vol.147, No.4, August 2000, pp.117-129

[10] Microsoft .NET Passport Web Site, http://www.passport.net

A DECENTRALIZED APPROACH FOR CONTROLLED SHARING OF RESOURCES IN VIRTUAL COMMUNITIES

E. Bertino
Dipartimento di Informatica e Comunicazione
Universitá degli Studi di Milano
bertino@dico.unimi.it

E. Ferrari[1], A.C. Squicciarini[2],
[1] *Dipartimento di Scienze Chimiche, Fisiche e Matematiche*
Universita' degli Studi dell'Insubria, Como
[2] *Dipartimento di Informatica e Comunicazione*
Universitá degli Studi di Milano
elena.ferrari@uninsubria.it; squiccia@dico.unimi.it

Abstract A Virtual Community is a composition of heterogeneous and independently designed subsystems, focusing on large-scale resource sharing. One of the key aspects of virtual community management, is how to enforce a controlled and selective sharing of resources in such a dynamic and decentralized environment. The traditional way is to have all the access requests mediated by a trusted third-party. However, this approach has the drawback that the third party can become a bottleneck for the whole system. By contrast, in this paper we propose a decentralized approach to virtual community management that relies on a controlled sharing of rights and duties among community members. In the paper, besides dealing with community policy specification we provide a framework able to manage all the phases of the the community life.

Keywords: Virtual communities, decentralized systems, selective and controlled resource sharing, policy specification.

1. Introduction

A Virtual Community is a composition of heterogeneous and independently designed subsystems, focusing on large-scale resource sharing, innovative applications and in some cases high performance computation. The sharing that we refer to is the direct access to computers, software, and data emerging in fields like science, industry and engineering. Several open issues need to be addressed, such as how to manage access policies to coordinate resource sharing, how to establish a community, how to ensure that member communities respect community policies and so on. Protocols to define how to establish sharing relationships between participants must also be enforced: each member entering into a community has to agree on what it is permitted to do and also what it is obliged to do. Resource sharing must be carefully controlled, with resource providers and controllers defining clearly and carefully what is shared, who is allowed to share and the conditions under which the sharing occurs. Resource sharing is therefore conditional, each provider has to define and publish the conditions under which it makes its resources available. Such conditions (or policies) must always be consistent with the community policies, regulating the whole organization. Further, once resource sharing is defined, the member is obliged to give access to its services according to the stated rules. Since the need to set up a collaborative sharing of resources is fundamental to many diverse disciplines and activities, our work focuses on suggesting a broad class of strategies to establish an efficient virtual organization. The goal of our work is thus to define an overall architectural framework for a collaborative environment, characterized by a flexible and dynamic structure where participants share resources in an efficient and decentralized way. The principle we apply to address decentralized control is based on the concept of *sharing* rights and duties among all members of the community. In particular, we introduce the concept of *witness*, that is, a community member that can act as a trusted third party monitoring the exchange of resources between two parties. Different from other proposals [4, 6] the witness can dynamically change and is not empowered to control all community issues, thus it cannot become a bottleneck for the whole system. Decentralization of responsabilities is obtained through the use of administrative credentials. Indeed, in addition to the witness, we also introduce the concept of *community guard*, that is, a member responsible of accepting or refusing the joining of new members. Due to lack of space, in the paper we mainly focus on the basic components needed for enforcing a controlled sharing of resources in a virtual community. Related work (e.g., [4]) mainly focus on how to manage decentralized policies for heterogeneous resources that are not under a centralized control. However, none of them addresses issues as members entitlements, delegation of entitlements, violation detection, and sanctioning mechanisms [5]. By contrast in this paper we deal with some of these aspects and devise strategies to setup communities in an effective and decentralized way. The remainder of this paper is organized as follows. Next section presents the basic elements of a virtual community. In particular, Section 2.3 presents the policy language we have developed to encode community and local policies. Section 3 deals with processes underlying a community. Finally, Section 4 concludes the paper.

2. Basic Elements of a Collaborative Environment

Formally, a collaborative environment *CE* can be modelled as a tuple $\langle S, \mathcal{AC}, R, NS \rangle$, where S is the set of **subjects** belonging to the community, R the set of shared **resources**, and $\mathcal{AC}$ represents the set of **administrative credential types** defined throughout the community. Finally, *NS* is the **normative state**, that is, the set of policies, directions and rules regulating the community. We assume that our framework supports a key-management infrastructure such as VersaKey [7], where each subject is actually identified by its public key certificate. Moreover, each subject is qualified by means of credentials. Credentials are digitally signed certificates issued by trusted third party authorities stating properties and attributes of their owners. In what follows, we illustrate the basic building blocks of a virtual community.

2.1. Administrative credentials

Subjects of a *CE* can act as service providers as well as service consumers, and also, under certain conditions detailed in the following sections, community controllers. To regulate the assignment of roles across the community, the community also relies on a set of pre-defined administrative credentials $\mathcal{AC}$ that correspond to specific roles that need to be played by one or more community members for the correct functioning of the community. The number of subjects to which each administrative credential is assigned can vary from 1 to k, where k denotes the whole population, on the basis of the rules defined in the normative state. Unlike traditional credentials, administrative credentials are issued by the community itself when the subject subscribes to the organization. Both conventional and administrative credentials are expressed using an XML based language [2]. The administrative credential types we refer to are the following:

Resource provider. It is the credential assigned to all the subjects sharing their resources across the community. A resource provider can either directly manage disclosure and access to its resources, or delegate this task to one or more resource managers, by issuing administrative credentials.

Resource Manager. It is the credential assigned to all the subjects entitled to manage a resource by a resource provider. Resources managed by a resource manager can belong either to the community or to a third party that delegates resource administration. The corresponding credential will specify the name of the subject, a link to the profile of the resource it manages, and the owner of the resource who delegates the resource management.

*Witness.*This credential type is assigned to subjects entitled to monitor that a specific resource request by a subject to a service provider has been correctly processed according with both local and community policies. A witness must then be able to detect possible community laws violation as they occur in the processes it witnesses. Witnesses can also be in charge of exercising additional functions, for instance, they may also randomly control sharing processes that they do not directly witness.

Community guard. It denotes the members empowered to accept or refuse the joining of new members. A community guard has the task of eventually issuing administrative credentials to the applicants. Moreover, it is in charge of checking compatibility of applicant local policies with community laws and, under certain circumstances, certifying the validity of local policies.

The above set of administrative credential types can be extended when needed. Each subject may possess one or more administrative credentials. The set of members possessing a specific administrative credential can share a special key to exercise administrative functions. Once the member receives one of the administrative credentials and the corresponding key, it is authorized to execute all the associated functions. The whole description of rights and duties associated with each administrative credential is formalized into a set of XML documents published in the community repository. In the following given a subject $s \in S$ and an administrative credential type $ac \in \mathcal{AC}$ we denote by $belong(s, ac)$ the fact that s is associated with a credential of type ac.

2.2. Community resources

The key element characterizing a community is the set of resources shared by its members. Resources typically have different enquiry mechanisms and capabilities that vary according with resource characteristics.

Since different policies can be adopted to regulate each type of resource we first need to provide a taxonomy of resource types. However, because of the rapidly growing number of collaborative applications and the rapid evolution of distributed systems the adopted resource characterization, borrowed from [3], is partial and open to update. The set CR of resource types we refer to consists of the following elements: CR={*Computational Resources, Storage Resources, Network resources, Code Resources, Catalogs*}. To make policy specification easier we assume that each resource is univocally identified and has a set of characterizing properties that can be exploited in the specification of policies. For instance, a storage resource can be characterized by space availability, disk bandwidth, the types of data that can store, the mechanisms used for file transfer and backup. Like for subjects, resource properties are collected into credentials associated with the resources themselves. Resource credentials are issued by community guards when the corresponding resource is included into the set R of resources shared across the community, and they are stored at resource providers site. In the following, when no further specification is added, with the term credential we refer to subject credential, whereas we use the term resource credential to refer to a credential associated with a resource. Resources may either belong to community members or to the community itself. Resources belonging to specific members are called *local* resources, whereas resource belonging to the community are called *community* resources. Local resources are under the owner control, however their administration can be eventually delegated to other members via administrative credentials.

Example 1 *Suppose that a University has established a collaboration with a research center and a laboratory to cooperate on a common research project. Suppose moreover that the project is sponsored by EU and that the consortium has bought hardware and/or software instruments with EU funds. Such resources are an example of community resources. Moreover, suppose that the participating laboratory makes available its server for storing community data. The server is then an example of local resource.*

Resources can be further classified into *on-duty* and *on-choice* resources, depending on whether the corresponding providers are obliged to share the resource or can deliberately choose to share them. When a community resource is added one or more members are chosen to act as providers, and therefore they are in charge of administering the resource. All community resources are on-duty, since they must be granted to community members and can not be released for use on discretion of their managers. By contrast, local resources can be either on-duty or on-choice, depending on the statute in force and on member availability.

2.3. Virtual community policies

Sharing resources across a virtual community must be regulated by both *community* and *local* policies. Local policies are basically expressed in term of properties and capabilities that requesters have to possess in order to obtain resources. Such capabilities are stated as conditions against the requester credentials. Community policies are access control policies regulating access to resources belonging to the community itself. Besides local and community policies, sharing of resources is also regulated by *community directions*, which are high-level instructions defining minimal conditions that resource providers have to satisfy while granting local and community resources within the community. Both community policies and directions are part of the normative state of the community, as explained in Section 2.4. Directions can be of two different kinds, *positive* or *negative*. Positive directions quantify the resources that must be shared, specifying who must be granted the access and, eventually, the frequency or the direction validity. By contrast, negative directions are used to specify denials such as services not permitted across the community or subjects that must not be allowed to receive some resources. Since directions only give some general instructions, resource providers are allowed to enforce more specific policies as long as they do not conflict with any community direction. A community direction can be formally defined as follows.

Definition 1 (Community direction). *Let $CE = \langle S, \mathcal{AC}, R, NS \rangle$ be a virtual community, and let CR be the set of resource types characterizing R. A community direction* **cd** *is a tuple of the form:*
$\langle typeR, resq, temp, credset, sign \rangle$ where:
- $typeR \in CR$ denotes the type of resources to which the direction refers to;
- $resq$ (resource quantification) specifies the set of conditions that providers of resources of type $typeR$ must satisfy;
- $temp$ is a temporal expression denoting a time interval or a periodic expression, specified according to the formalism proposed in [1];
- $credset$ is a set of credentials identifying the subjects to which the direction refers to;
- $sign \in \{positive, negative\}$ specifies whether the direction is negative or positive.

Resq is expressed as a set of conditions against resource properties specifying the features of the resource that has to be granted. Such conditions are expressions of the form "*property_name op a*", where *property_name* is a resource property (contained in the corresponding profile), *op* is a comparison operator, and *a* is a constant or an expression compatible with the property value. Note that it is not required to constraint all the elements of a resource credentials. Properties that are not constrained can be autonomously regulated by local policies of resource providers. The *Credset* component is a set of credential type names denoting credentials needed by subjects in order to be able to access the resource under the specified conditions. Finally, the time interval component defines the period the direction has to be enforced, and/or the frequency (e.g., every Monday) the resource must be available for sharing. *Credset* and *temp* are optional elements. When they are not specified they can be locally regulated by resource providers.

Example 2 *Suppose that a university grants both students and professors 10 gb of disk storage during the academic year. Moreover, suppose that students are not allowed to store file containing gif images and can not use fast internet providers during week-ends. The corresponding directions are formalized as follows:*

- $\langle$`diskStorage`, `size` $=$ 10gb, [1/1/2003, 1/1/2004], {`students`, `teachers`}, `positive`$\rangle$
- $\langle$`diskStorage`, `datatype` $=$ `gif`, [1/1/2003, 11/1/2004], {`students`}, `negative`$\rangle$,
- $\langle$`Network`, `bandwidth` $=$ 256 Kb, [Saturday, Sunday], {`students`}, `negative`$\rangle$,

The second and the third directions are examples of negative directions constraining resources available for students.

We assume that community directions are enforced for all community providers. However, Definition 1 can be easily extended to keep track of the service providers to which the direction refers to. We assume that community directions are always consistent, that is, it is not possible that community directions are in conflict among themselves. This means that we assume that consistency of directions is checked each time a new direction is added or an update occurs to an existing direction.
Policies regulating disclosure of resources can be either *strong* or *weak*. *Strong* policies regulate disclosure of on-duty resources, that the members are obliged to share. Strong policies are digitally signed by a community member entitled to perform such a task (typically a guard or a community founder), which signs them when the corresponding resource is added to the list of on-duty resources and the corresponding resource credential is issued.

Example 3 *Referring to Example 2, consider a mass storage provider obliged to share 10 gb of its hard disk. Since the sharing of resource is a condition for membership, the corresponding policies will be strong and local.*

Each time a *strong* policy for a local resource is entered or needs to be modified, it must be validated by the signature either of a guard or of a community founder,which checks its consistency with the community directions. Updates can be executed on provider initiative or to comply with new community directions. Referring to Example 2, if the direction changes asking for 15 gb of disk storage, all the corresponding policies that conflict with this new direction have to be updated by the providers and validated by one administrator entitled to sign strong policies. Similarly, community strong policies are updated upon proposal by one of the managers of the resource, but the updates need to be validated by the whole set of managers.
Weak policies are local policies defined by providers for governing on-choice resources. Such policies govern disclosure of resources that the provider is not obliged to grant. Providers can autonomously update weak policies without asking for any validation by community administrators. They only have to inform the other members whether an update to the policies occurs broadcasting a message to the rest of the community. In case of a not correct enforcing of weak policies, sanctions will be lighter than in case of no correct enforcing of strong policies.

Example 4 *Suppose that the server of Example 3 makes available 25 gb of its hard disk. The 15 gb offered in addition to the 10 gb that the server is obliged to grant are regulated by local weak policies.*

Policies are formally defined as follows.

Definition 2 (Policy). *Let* $CE = \langle S, \mathcal{AC}, R, NS \rangle$ *be a virtual community. A policy* **p** *for* CE *is a tuple of the form:*
$\langle r, rescond, subjcond, grade, time, type \rangle$, *where:*
- $r \in R$ *denotes a resource ID;*
- $rescond$ *is a list of conditions on resource credentials, specifying the features of the granted resource;*
- $subjcond$ *is a list of credentials and/or credential properties, stating credentials and conditions against them that must be satisfied in order to obtain access to* r*;*
- $time$ *denotes the validity period of the policy;*
- $grade \in \{strong, weak\}$ *specifies whether the policy refers to an on-duty, or on-choice resource;*

- *type* $\in \{local, community\}$ *denotes whether resource r belongs to a member or to the community itself.*

The component *rescond* of a policy specifies the resource actually shared, constraining the properties of the released resource or the features of the service granted. Since each resource is identified by a credential the list of properties consists of the attribute and tag names contained in the corresponding XML credential. The component *subjcond* specifies the subject credentials and conditions on them that requesters need to possess in order to obtain r. Such conditions are expressions of the form "*attribute_name op a*", where *attribute_name* is an attribute name, *op* is a comparison operator, and a represents a constant or an expression compatible with the attribute value. The last two components of a policy specification specify the grade and the type of policy and must be always specified. By contrast, components *time* and *subjcond* can be omitted from the policy specification. If the *subjcond* component is omitted it means that the resource may be granted to all the community members, whereas if *time* is not specified, it means that there are no temporal constraints for granting the resource.

Example 5 *With respect to the community direction of Example 2, suppose that a storage provider makes available 15gb of its disk storage, identified by code DS1, for teachers and 10 gb for students. The corresponding policies are the following:*
1) $\langle$`DS1, size` $=$ `10 gb disk,` $\{$`students, teachers(grade` $=$ `full)`$\}$`, strong, local`$\rangle$; *2)* $\langle$`DS1, size` $=$ `5 gb disk, teachers(grade` $=$ `full, dep` $=$ `biology), weak, local`$\rangle$.
The first is an example of strong policy since it regulates the portion of disk storage the server is obliged to grant. By contrast, the second policy is an example of weak policy. The policy states that only full professors of the biology department can access the 5 gb of memory in addition to the amount granted by the previous policy.

Community directions and policies therefore work together to grant a correct functioning of the whole community. Directions have higher priority than local policies and therefore in case of conflict they take the precedence. For instance, a community direction can oblige network providers to provide a fast connection every day from 8 a.m. to 10 p.m. Each storage provider is empowered to autonomously define under which conditions it grants the service but it should assure the continuity of the service during the specified hours. Intuitively, a policy is in conflict with one or more directions when its enforcement can cause a violation of the direction. More precisely, a policy and a direction may conflict when:

• The policy forbids a resource access to a member which is entitled to access it by a positive direction.

• The policy allows some of the accesses permitted by a positive direction to a member, but the conditions specified in the policy are more restrictive than those stated in the corresponding positive direction.

• The policy allows resource accesses that are explicitly prevented by a negative direction.

Example 6 *With respect to Example 2 consider the following policies: 1.* ⟨`PROV1`, `bandwidth` = `256Kb`, {`students`}, [`Monday-Saturday`], `strong`, `local`⟩; *2.* ⟨`DS1`, `8 gb disk`, {`students`}, `strong`, `local`⟩.
Suppose that the first policy is specified by an internet provider, stating that it grants fast connection to students from Monday to Saturday. This policy conflicts with the last negative direction of Example 2 which denies the access on Saturday. Moreover, suppose that the storage provider of Example 5, updates the first policy reducing the disk storage availability from 10 to 8 gb. The resulting policy will be in conflict with the first positive direction of Example 2 but not with the negative one, which forbids storing gif files.

When a conflict is detected, the provider is obliged to rewrite the conflicting policy. If it refuses to comply with this obligation it is consequently sanctioned, usually with the revoking of the provider credential for the involved resources. Note that since weak policies do not correspond to providers obligations they can never be in conflict with any positive direction. Finally, community policies community directions, typically when a positive direction is updated influencing the validity of the community policy. Community policies also may need to be updated in order to be correctly enforced. As discussed earlier, in order to be modified such kind of policies need to be validated not only by a single community manager, but by all the managers administering the same resource.

2.4. Normative state of the community

Previous work [5] introduced the concept of normative state as a set of access permissions of community members, and their obligations to provide access to their services. We extend such concept defining the normative state as a set of information about the community structure, regulating not only resource management but also policy enforcement. More precisely, the normative state contains community directions as well as policies regulating access to community resources. Additionally, it includes all those kinds of information that help the members to actively participate to community life. Such information concern aspects like the management of the community, sanctioning mechanisms and violation punishments. The normative state can be divided into three sections corresponding to three different kinds of information concerning respectively resource sharing, management structure and enforcement mechanisms.

Resource sharing. The core of such section is the collection of community directions (described in Section 2.3) giving instructions concerning policy specifications for the shared resources. Community policies are also included, regulating access to those resources belonging to the entire community. Moreover, this section collects summary information on the resources shared within the community. More precisely it contains an entry for each shared resource specifying the owner, the type of resource and whether the resource is governed either by strong or weak policies (i.e., the member is obliged or not to share the resource). Finally, for each resource the section also lists the member entitled to manage (e.g. Resource manager) and control accesses to the resource itself.

Management information. This section collects information defining how authorities and responsibilities are, or can be, distributed within the organization. For what concerns how authorities are distributed this section keeps track of the administrative credentials assigned to each subject. Moreover it specifies rights and duties associated with each administrative credential type and the criteria to assign administrative functions to each member. To this purpose, several approaches can be adopted. A possible approach is constraining the ratios of members that must be authorized to exercise administrative function to the whole population. Another criteria might require that each member must be associated with at least one administrative credential, or establish the minimum percentage of members that must be assigned to each administrative credential. The specified constraints impacts the degree of decentralization enforced within the community. Intuitively, the more members are authorized to exercise administrative functions the more decentralized will be the resulting community.

Sanctioning mechanisms and violation detection. The last section of the Normative state defines how to detect and manage cases when members fail, or do not comply with community laws. More precisely, such section contains a classification of the possible violations with the related sanctioning mechanisms, and a description of the devised mechanisms and protocols to detect the violations.Unlike the description of the devised mechanisms, which are expected to be standardized for all the communities, the classification of illegal actions strictly depends on the reference scenario and the type of environment considered.

3. Community management

To explain how we realize a decentralized system enforcing a controlled and selective sharing of resources we now briefly detail the management process underlying a community. The steps we focus on are *community setup*, that is, how a community is started, *new member association*, that is, how new members can subscribe to a community, and, finally the process of leaving the community, that is, *leave of a member.*

- **Community setup** Several issues have to be addressed in order to setup a new community. First, a community is said to be established when the minimal conditions to correctly execute sharing of resources hold. Operatively, community founders have to publish a first version of the normative state, defining the set of administrative credentials and choosing the founders that will receive such administrative credentials. Moreover, resource credentials specifying resource properties must be issued to the resource managers for each resource of the set R of shared resources. The first issue facing community founders is then to decide key aspects of the normative state that better fit the community goals. In order to define a framework that is as adaptable and flexible as possible we do not define a unique type of community. Indeed, our framework supports the definition of several community types, regulated in different ways, and can be properly customized according to specific community requirements and needs.

- **New members association** One controversial issue about how to join a community regards the entities with whom the requesters have to interact. In centralized systems such task is performed by a specific entity which has the control of the whole community. To avoid centralized approaches where reliability of the whole community is entrusted to a single entity in our framework this role is played by a set of members referred as *community guards* (or guards, for short) whose specific task is to perform the joining phase. This phase is actually carried out as an interaction between the applicant and a guard. The aim is to verify requester properties in order to accept or refuse the subscription. Moreover, community guards eventually sign local strong policies of the applicant, in order to certify policies consistency with community directions. A guard can also assign administrative credentials, on the basis of evaluation of applicant competences and capabilities. The phase starts when a requester contacts a subject of the community to join it. If the receiver is not a community guard the request is forwarded to a member having the *community guard* credential.

- **Leaving the community** There are two different ways to leave the community: voluntary leave or forced leave. According to the first, a member announces that it is leaving forwarding a leaving message to all community members. The remaining members update the normative state, and delete on cascade all information about the leaving member. Moreover, if the leaving member was either a community administrator or a resource provider, it is deleted from the corresponding lists, and all the administrative credentials it owns are revoked. The second way is the heaviest form of sanctioning provided by the community and consists of banning. As well as for voluntary leaving, to exclude a member all information concerning it must be deleted from the normative state. Note that if the member was an administrator and the community makes use of a community public key for signing administrative credentials a new key must be sent out according with the adopted key management system [7]. The remaining participants can then use the new key for exercising administrative functions, but not the member which just left.

4. Conclusions

In this paper we have presented a flexible framework for managing virtual communities whose goal is resource sharing based on selective and flexible policies. In the paper we have mainly focused on the language to specify policies and directions, and on the steps to deal with the various phases of the community life. The work presented in this paper is part of an on going research project. We are currently working on XML policy specification and on web services for policy management. Also, we are developing mechanisms to check local policy correctness against community policies. Finally, another interesting area to explore concern protocols and strategies to share resources among community members in a flexible a decentralized manner.

References

[1] E. Bertino, C.Bettini, E.Ferrari, and P.Samarati. An Access Control Model supporting Periodicity Constraints and Temporal Reasoning. *ACM Transactions on Database Systems,* vol 23, n. 3, pp. 231–285, September 1998.

[2] E. Bertino, E. Ferrari, A. Squicciarini $\mathcal{X}$-TNL: An XML-Based language for Trust Negotiation. *Proceedings of the 4th International Workshop on Policies for Distributed Systems and Networks*, Como, Italy, June 2003.

[3] I. Foster, C. Kesselman, S.Tuecke. The anatomy of Grid-Enabling Scalable Virtual Organizations. *International Journal of Supercomputer Applications*, 15(3), 2001

[4] L.Pearlman, V. Welch, I.Foster A Community Authorisation for Service Group Collaboration *Proceedings of the 3rd International Workshop on Policies for Distributed Systems and Networks* page 50-59, Monterey California, USA, June 2002. IEEE.

[5] B. Sadighi Firozabadi, M. Sergot. Contractual Access Control. *To appear in the proceeding of Security Protocols, 10th International Workshop*, Cambridge, UK, 2002.

[6] B. Sadighi, M. Sergot, O. Bandman. Using Authority Certificates to Create Management Structures, April 2001. *Proceedings of the 9th International Workshop on Security Protocols*, Cambridge, UK.

[7] M. Waldvogel, G. Caronni, D. Sun et. al. The VersaKey Framework: Versatile Group Key Management Department of Computer Engineering, ETH Zurich. Technical Report TIK-57, 1998.

[8] World Wide Web Consortium. Extensible Markup Language (XML) 1.0, 1998. Available at `http://www.w3.org/XML`

SUPPORTING DELEGATION IN SECURE WORKFLOW MANAGEMENT SYSTEMS

Vijayalakshmi Atluri[1], Elisa Bertino [2], Elena Ferrari[3]
and Pietro Mazzoleni[2]

[1] MSIS Department and CIMIC, Rutgers University, atluri@cimic.rutgers.edu
[2] DiCo Department, University of Milan, bertino,mazzoleni@dsi.unimi.it
[3] SSCCFFMM Department, University of Insubria, Italy, Elena.Ferrari@uninsubria.it

Abstract Workflow systems are today used in numerous business application domains including office automation, finance and banking, as well as in scientific application domains, for automating their day-to-day applications, Often, organizations establish a set of security policies that regulate how the business process and resources should be managed. For reasons of ease in management, these security policies are expressed in terms of *roles*. In addition to simple authorization rules specifying which subject/role can execute a task in a workflow, many business processes require support for more complex authorization constraints, such as *separation of duties*. In this paper, we present an approach that supports *delegation* and assign users to roles in such a way that no constraints are violated. In particular, we introduce the notion of *delegation consistency* and propose algorithms to assign tasks to users such that they guarantee delegation consistency.

Keywords: Access control, Workflow Systems, Delegation

1. Introduction

Workflow management aims at modeling and controlling the execution of business processes involving a combination of manual and automated activities in an organization. Workflow systems are today used in numerous business application domains including office automation, finance and banking, as well as in scientific application domains such as in spatial processes and DNA sequencing, for automating their day-to-day applications. A *workflow* is defined as a set of coordinated activities that achieves a common business objective [1]. An activity, or a *task*, is a logic step or description of a piece of work that contributes toward the accomplishment of a process [7, 5]. Tasks that build up the workflow are usually related and dependent upon one another, which in turn are specified by *task dependencies.* A *workflow management system* (WFMS) is a system that supports process specification, enactment, monitoring, coordination and administration of workflow process through the execution of software, whose order of execution is based on the workflow logic [1].

The desired security to ensure the secrecy, correctness and integrity are adhered to a business process and are specified through a set of security policies, which are commonly used to define constraints that regulate how the business process and resources should be managed. For reasons of ease in management, often these security policies are expressed in terms of *roles.* In addition to simple authorization rules specifying which subject/role can execute a task in a workflow, many business processes require support for more complex authorization constraints, such as *separation of duties* (SOD) [4, 8].

In [2], Bertino et al. present a language to express these different types of authorization constraints as clauses in a logic program, and propose solutions to verify the consistency of the constraint specification and to assign users and roles to tasks of the workflow in a such a way that no constraints are violated. In this paper, we extend the work presented in [2] to support *delegation* in secure workflow systems. The basic idea behind delegation is that an active entity in a system, called *delegator* delegates authority to another active entity, called *delegatee*, to carry out some functions on behalf of the former. In the context of workflow systems, delegation amounts to transfer of duties of executing a task within a workflow. We call this task the *delegated task.*

In case of delegation, one must ensure that no authorization constraints are violated due to the delegation activity. We illustrate the problem of the inconsistencies due to the interplay between authorization constraints and delegation by considering a simple example.

Example 1 *Let W be a workflow, which represents the process of reviewing a paper for a conference, consisting of three tasks* $\{T_1, T_2, T_3\}$

Assume T_1 *refers to submitting a paper,* T_2 *refers to preparing three reviews, and* T_3 *refers to collecting the reviews and making the final decision to accept or reject the paper. The obvious dynamic separation of duties constraints in this example include: (1) Though anyone among the set of reviewers may be a reviewer, for any given paper, the three reviewers have to be different individuals, and (2) an author cannot be the reviewer for his own paper. Now suppose that a user, John, wishes to delegate the duty assigned to him to one of his colleagues (Jane). Such a delegation is legitimate and may prove valuable as Jane may have better expertise on the topic of the paper. However, if the delegation is entertained without taking the authorization constraints into account, a violation of the constraint may arise. A violation occurs if John is assigned to review a paper coauthored by Jane, and he further wishes to delegate it to Jane.*

This paper is organized as follows. Section 2 reviews the workflow model and the authorization rules proposed in [2]. Section 3 presents our workflow delegation model. Section 4 provides an overview of the different phases of our approach, that are delegation consistency analysis phase, planning phase, and runtime phase which are further described into Section 5,6, and 7 respectively. Section 8 concludes the paper and outlines future work.

2. Authorization Constraints in Workflow

2.1. The Workflow model

As in most WFMSs, we assume that a workflow consists of several tasks to be executed sequentially.

Each task is associated with one or more roles, which are the only ones authorized to execute the task. In the remainder of this paper, U, $\mathcal{R}$ and $\mathcal{T}$ denote the set of users, the set of roles, and the set of tasks in a given workflow, respectively. Additionally, U_i denotes the set of users authorized to play role R_i. We refer to the association of roles with tasks in a workflow as *workflow role specification*, formally defined as follows.

Definition 1 *(***Workflow Role Specification***) A workflow role specification W is a list of task role specifications* $[\texttt{TRS}_1, \texttt{TRS}_2, \ldots, \texttt{TRS}_n]$*, where each* $\texttt{TRS}_i$ *is a triple (T_i, RS_i, act_i) where $T_i \in \mathcal{T}$ is a task, $RS_i \subseteq \mathcal{R}$ is the set of roles authorized to execute T_i and $act_i \in \Gamma$ is the number of possible activations of task T_i.*

In the following, we use the term workflow and workflow role specification as synonyms. A workflow may have several workflow instances. We assume that each instance inherits the same workflow role specification from the workflow from which it is generated.

2.2. Constraint language

Authorization constraints, used to express security policy, are defined as clauses in a normal logic program [6]. Such language is not intended as the end-user language for expressing constraints but it is internally used by the system to make it easy for analyzing and enforcing constraints. However, a visual programming environment can be developed on top of this language along the lines of the system discussed in [3]. In [2], authors present a constraint language semantics to formalize specific information about the workflow. Such semantics is built upon sets of predicate symbols denoted as *specification*(SP), *execution* (EP), *planning* (PP) and *comparison* (CP) predicates. Constraints are expressed as rules of a logic program. An authorization rule *ar* is an expression of the form: $H \leftarrow A_1, \ldots, A_n$, *not* $B_1, \ldots,$ *not* B_m, $n, m \geq 0$, where H, $A_1, \ldots, A_n$ and $B_1, \ldots, B_m$ are atoms and *not* denotes negation by failure [6]. H is the rule *head*, whereas $A_1, \ldots, A_n$, not $B_1, \ldots,$ B_m is the rule *body*.

For instance, the rule $ar_1 = \texttt{cannot\_do}_u(U_i, \texttt{T}_2) \leftarrow \texttt{execute}_u(U_i, \texttt{T}_2, k)$, states that if user U_i has been assigned more than k times for executing task T_2, it cannot be assigned any longer for T_2.

We call *Authorization Constraint-Base* of a workflow W $(ACB(W))$, the set of rules specifying all the authorization constraints associated with W. Given $ACB(W)$ for a workflow W, it is possible to compute the set of roles/users that must be prevented/obliged to execute a task T_i. In the rest of the paper, we denote as *Denied_Roles*(T_i), *Denied_Users*(T_i), *Obliged_Roles*(T_i), *Obliged_Users*(T_i) these sets.

3. The Workflow Delegation Model

3.1. Delegation Predicates

In this section, we formally introduce the *delegation predicates*, $\mathcal{DP}$, as the set of predicates used to specify the different types of task delegations in a workflow. We categorize them into the following two types - *delegation predicates* ($\mathcal{BP}$) *and volunteer delegation predicates* ($\mathcal{VP}$) where $\mathcal{DP} = \mathcal{BP} \cup \mathcal{VP}$.

Delegation Predicates: The predicates belonging to $\mathcal{BP}$ contain delegation predicates as well as the predicates for rejecting delegation. They comprise *delegate_tu*(U_i, T_k, U_j), by which a user U_i delegates to user U_j all the instances of task T_k assigned to him/her by the WFMS, *delegate_tu*(U_i, T_k) by which U_i expresses the intention to delegate T_k without specifying the delegatee user, *reject_del_t*(U_i, T_k) by which U_i rejects instances of T_k delegated to him/her by any other user and finally *reject_del_tu*(U_i, T_k, U_j) rejecting only T_k delegated to U_i from U_j.

Moreover, $\mathcal{BP}$ contains two additional predicates: *delegate_ru*(R_i, T_k, U_j) and *delegate_rr*(R_i, T_k, R_j) that , differently from the others, cannot be specified by any workflow user, but are reserved to the workflow administrator. These predicates specify that the instances of task T_k assigned to users belonging to role R_i are redirected to user U_j or any users belonging to role R_j. Those predicates allow the administrator to temporarily change the possible task instance assigned to a role without modifying the basic authorizations.

Volunteer Predicates: Similar to the delegation predicates, it is possible to define *volunteer* predicates, $\mathcal{VP}$.
Volunteer predicate, $volunteer\_t(U_i, T_k, n)$ allows a user (U_j) to nominate himself for the execution of a certain number (n) of instances of a task (T_k) that have been delegated by another user, perhaps based on certain incentives he/she may receive due to such an activity. We provide this capability because we believe that it is not realistic for a user to nominate himself only for tasks delegated by a specific user. To make this specification more realistic, we enhance the semantics of the language with a parameter that allows the user to set a maximum limit on the number of delegated tasks he wishes to volunteer for.

3.2. Delegation Rules

We use the formalism introduced in section 2 and the delegation predicates $(\mathcal{DP})$ to define delegation rules. Formally:

Definition 2 (**Delegation Rule**) *A delegation rule is of the form* $dr : H \leftarrow L_1, \ldots, L_n$, *where* H *is a delegation predicate and* L_i, $i = 1 \ldots n$ *is either an execution or a delegation literal.*

Given a delegation rule dr, in the following we will use Delegator(dr), Delegatee(dr) and Task(dr) to refer to the *Delegator User*, the *Delegatee User* and the *Delegated Task* of the delegation predicates in the left hand side of dr, respectively.

Definition 3 (**Constraint-Base**) *Let* W *be a workflow. The Delegation Constraint-Base associated with* W *(written* $DCB(W)$*) is the set of delegation rules. The constraint base of* W*, denoted as* $\mathcal{CB}(\mathcal{W}) = ACB(W) \cup DCB(W)$.

4. Overview of our Approach

In this section, we provide a roadmap of the methodology adopted in this paper to support the issue of delegation in secure workflow systems so that no authorization constraints are violated. Specifically, we address the problem of assigning roles and users to tasks of a workflow such that both authorization and delegation rules are satisfied. Our methodology is organized according to three phases, as shown in Figure 1.

1 *Static Analysis Phase:* In this phase, we analyze the consistency of the delegations. The consistency analysis is in turn organized done in two levels, internal and external. The internal analysis is to determine if there are inconsistencies in the delegation rule base (i.e., $DCB(W)$) itself. External analysis is to determine if the del-

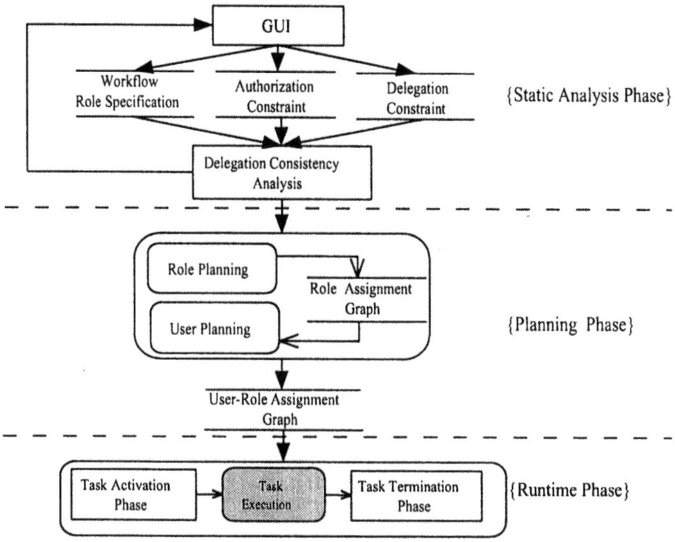

Figure 1. Phases in constraints authorization analysis and enforcement

egation rules can be enforced without causing any inconsistencies when authorization rules are also enforced.

2 *Planning Phase:* The goal of this phase is to generate role and user assignments to tasks before the workflow execution. Note that while much of the role-task assignment can be done during this phase, a complete user-task assignment cannot be done prior start executing the workflow. This phase comprises of two sub-phases: (i) The *Role Planning Phase*, in which we employ an exhaustive algorithm to generate a *Role Assignment Graph* (*RAG(W)*) representing all possible role assignments for each task in the workflow. (ii) The *User Planning Phase*, in which we employ a heuristic approach that plans assignments of users based on *RAG(W)* and authorization rules in $ACB(W)$. We denote the graph generated as a result of this process by *User Role Assignment Graph, (URAG(W))*.

3 *Runtime Phase:* The goal of this phase is to select an authorized user according to the rules in $\mathcal{CB}(\mathcal{W})$. In the sub-phase, referred to as *Task Activation Phase*, the delegation rules are enforced and the inconsistencies among rules are resolved. Then, the task can be executed by the assigned user. The runtime phase, which is executed for each task of the workflow, is terminated with the *Task Termination phase*, which prunes *URAG(W)* with the results

of the task execution and prepares the system for subsequent task assignments.

5. Delegation Consistency Checking

In Section 3, we have defined delegation as a set of logic constraints. Here, we develop the formalism to help verify the consistency of these rules with respect to the overall workflow specification. This analysis is carried out statically as well as during the runtime. The *Static Analysis*, addressed in this section, aims at resolving conflicts that arise independently from a specific instance of the workflow. This check can be done statically in the sense that it does not depend on the execution history of the workflow. The analysis conducted during the runtime phase identifies and resolves inconsistencies arising for a particular assignment of users to tasks in a workflow. We address this runtime evaluation part in Section 7.

Intuitively, $\mathcal{CB}(\mathcal{W})$ is said to be *statically consistent* with respect to delegation, if all the delegation rules do not result in violation of any authorization constraints. The first type of static inconsistency arises when there is a cycle in the specification of delegations. A *delegation cycle* occurs when users' intentions to delegate a task creates an infinite loop. Although it is not an inconsistency in its strictest sense, it is important to identify such condition as well because it effects the feasibility of executing a workflow.

In addition to identifying cycles in delegation rules, the static analysis check aims at evaluating inconsistencies that arise among delegation and authorization constraints in the workflow. For example, assume the rules $cannot\_do_u(John, T_1) \leftarrow$ and $delegate\_tu(Jane, T_1, John) \leftarrow$ belong to the model of a $\mathcal{CB}(\mathcal{W})$. In this case, an inconsistency can be statically discovered since John cannot be delegated for T_1 under any circumstances given that he is not allowed to execute T_1. In order to verify the consistency among the delegation rules and the authorization rules, i.e., in $\mathcal{CB}(\mathcal{W})$, the following concepts are introduced. These define the set of possible users that can delegate, volunteer or being delegated for a given task T_i:

- *Delegator_Users*(T_i) $= \bigcup \{u_j \mid \mathtt{delegate\_}t(u_j, T_i) \in \mathcal{CB}(\mathcal{W})$ OR $\mathtt{delegate\_}tu(u_j, T_i, u_i) \in \mathcal{CB}(W)\}$ *Delegator_Users*(T_i) represents the set of users who wish to delegate the execution of T_i according to the rules in $\mathcal{CB}(\mathcal{W})$;

- *Delegatee_Users*(T_i) $= \bigcup\{u_j \mid delegate\_tu\ (u_i, T_i, u_j) \in \mathcal{CB}(\mathcal{W})\}$ *Delegatee_Users*(T_i) represents the set of users who have T_i delegated by some other users according to the rules in $\mathcal{CB}(\mathcal{W})$;

- $Volunteer\_Users(T_i) = \bigcup\{u_j \mid volunteer\_tu\ (u_j, T_i, u_i) \in \mathcal{CB}(\mathcal{W})\}$
  $Volunteer\_Users(T_i)$ represents the set of users who volunteer themselves for the execution of instances of T_i, according to the rules in $\mathcal{CB}(\mathcal{W})$;

It is important to ensure that users who cannot execute a task are not allowed to delegate, being delegated and volunteer for the execution of the task. Furthermore, it is necessary to verify that users who are supposed to execute a task should not delegate it to some other user. The above requirements are formalized in the following definition.

Definition 4 (Delegation Consistency)
We say that $\mathcal{CB}(\mathcal{W})$ is consistent with respect to delegation if and only if the following is verified: $\forall T_i \in W$,

- *If* Obliged_Users$(T_i) \neq \emptyset$, *then*
  (Delegator_Users(T_i) $\cap$ Delegatee_Users(T_i)) - Obliged_Users(T_i) $= \emptyset$;

- *If* Denied_Users$(T_i) = \emptyset$, *then*
  Denied_Users(T_i) $\cap$ Delegatee_Users$(T_i) = \emptyset$; *and*

- Denied_Users(T_i) $\cap$ Volunteer_Users$(T_i) = \emptyset$.

6. Planning phase

The *planning phase* generates the set of possible roles and user assignments to the workflow tasks so that all the authorization constraints are satisfied. This phase is performed statically, i.e. before the workflow execution starts, and aims at both providing an initial plan and reducing, as much as possible, the number of operations to be accomplished by the system at runtime. Planning is accomplished in two subphases: *role planning phase* and *user planning phase.*

6.1. Role Planning phase

Our approach to identify role assignments for a given workflow W is similar to the solution proposed in [2]. It begins with the assumption that the number of roles associated with a task is not large. Therefore, an exhaustive approach is taken where all the possible combinations of roles assigned to the tasks are evaluated against the authorization constraints. To keep role planning feasible, we assume all the task activations be executed by the same role. However, at runtime we relax this assumption by letting different task activations assigned to different users. The result of this phase is the *Role Assignment Graph, $RAG(W)$*, defined as follows:

Definition 5 *(Role Assignment Graph)*
Let $W = [\texttt{TRS}_1, \texttt{TRS}_2, \ldots, \texttt{TRS}_n]$ *be a workflow role specification with* $\texttt{TRS}_i = (T_i, (RS_i, \succ_i), act_i)$, $i = 1, \ldots, n$. *The Role Assignment Graph of* W *(RAG(W)) is a labeled graph* $G = (V, E)$ *defined as follows:*

- **Vertices.** *There is a vertex labeled* (T_i, R_j), $T_i \in \texttt{TRS}_i, R_j \in RS_i$ *only if the assignment of role* R_j *to task* T_i *does not violate the authorization constraints. A vertex labeled* (T_i, R_j) *thus states that role* R_j *can be assigned to task* T_i *during the workflow execution.*

- **Edges.** *There exists an arc connecting* (T_i, R_j) *to* (T_h, R_k) *only if assigning task* T_i *to a user belonging to role* R_j *and assigning task* T_h *to user belonging to* R_k *for the same workflow instance do not violate any constraints.*

RAG(W) contains a path $\{(T_1, R_1) \ldots (T_n, R_n)\}$ if and only if the assignments of R_i to T_i, $i = 1 \ldots n$ do not violate any workflow constraint.

Example 2 *Consider a workflow* W *with three tasks* $T = (T_1, T_2, T_3)$ *that can be executed by users belonging to roles* $\{R_a, R_b, R_c\}$*, respectively. Suppose* $\mathcal{CB}(\mathcal{W})$ *contains the following rules:*
$ar_1 = cannot\_do_r(R_c, T_1) \leftarrow$,
$ar_2 = cannot\_do_r(R_a, T_3) \leftarrow execute_r(R_a, T_1, 1)$,
$ar_3 = cannot\_do_r(R_c, T_2) \leftarrow$, *and*
$ar_4 = cannot\_do_r(R_b, T_3) \leftarrow execute_r(R_b, T_2, 1)$ RAG(W) *generated according to Definition 5 is as shown in Figure 2. The selected nodes and paths are all the ones consistent with respect to the rules in* $\mathcal{CB}(\mathcal{W})$. *For instance, there is no edge between* (T_2, R_b) *and* (T_3, R_b) *in* RAG(W) *since it conflicts with rule* ar_4.

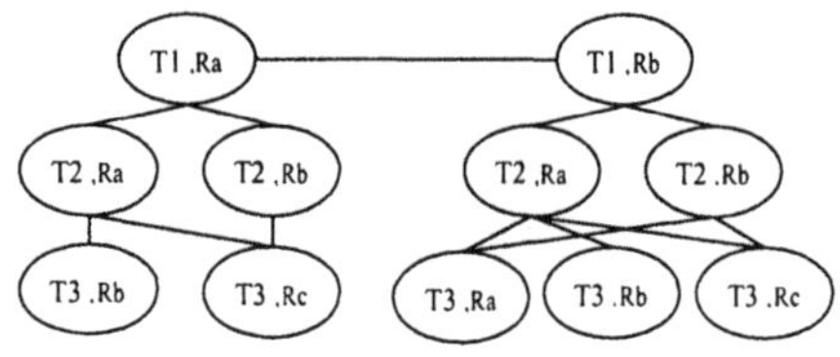

Figure 2. the *RAG(W)* generated for the workflow in to Example 2

6.2. User Planning Phase

In a workflow, it is quite common that the number of users is much larger than the number of roles. Specifically, the number of users assigned to a role significantly increases as we traverse from higher level roles to lower level roles in the role hierarchy. The exhaustive strategy described in Section 6.1, can no longer be applied to user planning since the number of possible users assigned to a task can be very high. Therefore, we chose to execute user planning completely at runtime. However, even though we do not do user planning in advance, we statically enhance *RAG(W)* with more information to speed up the runtime phase. To accomplish this, we introduce *User-Role Assignment Graph, URAG(W).* Essentially, *URAG(W)* is an enhanced and sometimes instantiated version of *RAG(W)* with information concerning which users belonging to a given role must or must not be assigned for the execution of a task. Briefly, in this phase, we evaluate rules which are not influenced by the workflow execution so they can be verified in advance, and if it is the case that a user belonging to a role R_j must execute a task T_k, then each node (T_k, R_j) in *RAG(W)* is updated with such information. We denote the node representing such users with '+'. Analogously, each node in *RAG(W)* is complemented with information about the set of users that must be prevented from executing that task, according to the constraints specified by the static rules. We denote the node representing such users with '-'. Formally, *URAG(W)* can be defined as follows:

Definition 6 *(***User-Role Assignment Graph***) Let* RAG(W) *be a Role Assignment Graph for a workflow* $W = [\mathtt{TRS}_1, \mathtt{TRS}_2, \ldots, \mathtt{TRS}_n]$*, where each* $\mathtt{TRS}_i = (T_i, (RS_i, \succ_i), act_i)$*,* $i = 1, \ldots, n$*. Let* $CB_S(W)$ *be the set of static rules belonging to* $\mathcal{CB}(\mathcal{W})$*. The* User-Role Assignment Graph *of W,* URAG(W)*, is a labeled graph* $G = (V, E)$ *defined as follows:*

- **Vertices.**
  There exists a vertex labeled $v_k = (T_i, R_j, users, value)$ *for each* $(T_i, R_j) \in RAG(W)$ *where* users *and* value *are defined as follows:*
  - *If* $Auth_{User} = \{u | must\_execute_u(u, T_i) \leftarrow belong(u, R_j) \in CB_S(W)\} \neq \emptyset$ *then* $users := Auth_{User}$*,* $value = +$*; Otherwise*
  - *If* $Auth_{User} = \{u | cannot\_do_u(u, T_i) \leftarrow belong(u, R_j) \in CB_S(W)\} \neq \emptyset$*, then* $users := Auth_{User}$*, and* $value = -$*;*
  - *If cases 1 and 2 do not hold, then* $users = \emptyset$*, and* $value = -$*.*

- **Edges.**
  There exists an arc from $v_m = (T_i, R_j, users(v_m), value(v_m))$ *to* $v_n = (T_h, R_k, users(v_n), value(v_n))$ *only if there exists an arc from* (T_i, R_j) *to* (T_h, R_k) *in* RAG(W).

Example 3 *Consider the workflow of Example 2, and assume that* $\mathcal{CB}(\mathcal{W})$ *contains the static rules*

$r_1 = ((must\_execute_u(u_i, T_2) \leftarrow belong(u_i, R_A), u_i = \{John, Jane\})$, *and* $r_2 = ((cannot\_do_u(u_i, T_3) \leftarrow belong(u_j, R_C), u_j = \{Bob, Bill\})$ *in the model. The resulting* URAG(W), *generated according to Definition 6, is presented in Figure 3.*

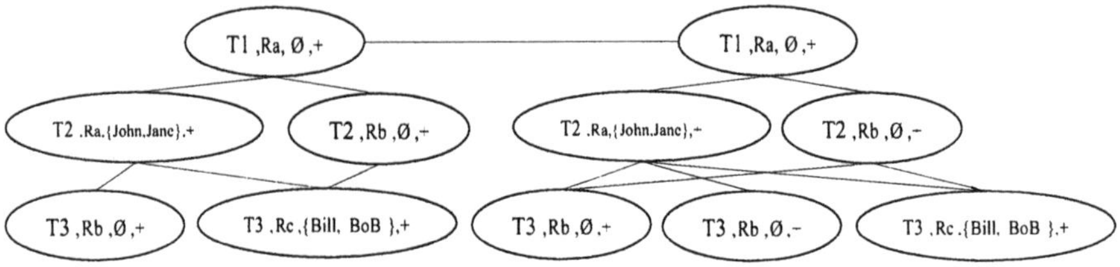

Figure 3. The *URAG(W)* for Example 3

7. Runtime Phase

The runtime phase is executed upon task activation and termination. It consists of two phases: the *Task activation phase* executed before the actual execution of the task to define users assigned for carrying out the activities, and the *Task termination phase*, executed after the termination of the task to update the workflow with the task's execution results and to prepare *URAG(W)* for subsequent task assignments.

Task activation phase: The check in this phase entails verifying several conditions in order to identify the user authorized to execute a task T_j. In this phase a user (or several users in case of multiple task execution) is assigned to task T_j. First, this phase identifies a candidate role among the ones authorized to execute T_j. We call n_{ass} the node and $Role(n_{ass})$ its referred node. Second, from $Role(n_{ass})$ the system selects a possible candidate user (u_{ass}). Two cases are possible here: if $value(n_{ass}) = +$, then u_{ass} has to be selected from $users(n_{ass})$; if $value(n_{ass}) = -$; otherwise u_{ass} needs to be picked from all the users belonging to $Role(n_{ass})$ except from the ones in $users(n_{ass})$. Finally, before sending T_i to u_{ass} for execution, the system needs to verify that no inconsistencies arise between u_{ass} and rules in $\mathcal{CB}(\mathcal{W})$ having the same task in the head and in one of the execution literals of the body (such as example $cannot\_do_u(Bob, T_i) \leftarrow execute_u(Bob, T_i)$). Those constraints, defined as *Recursive* rules in the following, cannot be evaluated before or after the process of assigning tasks to user in a workflow.
To evaluate a rule in $Recursive(T_i)$, we use an hypothetical reasoner. For example, to determine whether the execution of the task T_i by user u_j would violate $Recursive(T_i)$, we insert into $\mathcal{CB}(\mathcal{W})$ the rules, called *Assignment Hypotheses*, $\mathtt{execute}_u(u_j, T_i, k) \leftarrow$ and $\mathtt{success}(T_i, k) \leftarrow$.

There rules allow evaluation of $Recursive(T_i)$. If successful, the candidate user is entitled to execute T_i and the hypotheses can be removed from $\mathcal{CB}(\mathcal{W})$. Otherwise, u_j is not authorized to execute T_i and the process continues selecting another user among the ones available.

Task Termination phase: This is performed after task execution. During this phase, information about the user who has executed the task is inserted into $\mathcal{CB}(\mathcal{W})$. Rules
$\mathtt{execute}_r(Role(n_{ass}), T_j, k) \leftarrow$ and $\mathtt{execute}_u(u_{ass}, T_j, k) \leftarrow$ are added to $\mathcal{CB}(\mathcal{W})$ and used by the system to update nodes in *URAG(W)* upon the evaluation of $Simple(T_j)$ using the same methodologies presented in section 6.2.

Delegation Rule Application. The peculiarity of delegation rules, which are a special case of recursive rules as described before, is that these rules can only be evaluated after a user has been actually assigned for the execution of a task. In other words, until the assignment process is finished where a user u_i assigned for T_j, u_i's (*Delegator*) intention to delegate T_j to some other user u_k (*Delegatee*) cannot take place. The reason why the system should be prevented from applying delegation in advance, is to eliminate the possibility of overcoming the authorization system by delegating a task to an unauthorized user.

Different assumptions can be made in case of role-delegation since they are defined only by the workflow administrator. To improve the performance of the assignment process, their evaluation is applied as soon as a Delegator Role is selected by the system as a candidate for executing the task.

The process of evaluating user delegation rules, is applied as soon as a user has been successfully assigned for executing a task. It starts with a check as to whether a delegating rule exists in the model which formalizes the user intentions to delegate the task. If such rule exists, the system first identifies a delegatee user and then verifies that the delegation does not violate any recursive rules. To determine a delegatee user, we provide three progressive solutions. First we look at the user specified in the delegating rule. If delegatee is not in the rule or the user is not authorized for the task, we examine the volunteer users. Finally, if the model does not contain any volunteer user, we extend the search to all the users authorized for the task.

8. Conclusions and Future Research

In this paper, we have presented an approach that provides support for delegation in workflow systems in such a way that no authorization constraints are violated while entertaining delegation.

Currently, we are working on several extensions to this work, which are briefly explained below. We are currently extending our work to include several types of conditions that specify under which circumstances a delegation can occur (such as time related and workload related situations). In fact, while this paper proposes a solution where delegation is considered for all the instances of a given task, we are aware that in reality a person might wish to nominate someone for a work under certain circumstances. However, even if we did not present this here, our approach is carved in such a way that it can be easily extended to address these different types of conditions. Additionally, we plan on extending the our approach to verify if a given task can be delegated or not and when the right to delegate can be transmitted to another user.

We intend to introduce the concept of *Delegation Access Control* associated with a task that is independent from the workflow. This will enable delegation to be enforced over several workflows, including inter-organizational processes, in a decentralized manner.

References

[1] Workflow reference model. Technical report, Workflow Management Coalition, Brussels, 1994.

[2] Elisa Bertino, Elena Ferrari, and Vijayalakshmi Atluri. An Approach for the Specification and Enforcement of Authorization Constraints in Workflow Management Systems. *ACM Transactions on Information Systems Security*, 2(1), February 1999.

[3] S.K. Chang, G. Polese, R. Thomas, and S. Das. A Visual Language for Authorization Modeling. In *Proc. of the IEEE Symposium on Visual Languages (VL97)*, 1997.

[4] David D. Clark and David R. Wilson. A comparison of commercial and military computer security policies. In *Proc. IEEE Symposium on Security and Privacy*, pages 184–194, Oakland, California, April 1987.

[5] Dimitrios Georgakopoulos, Mark Hornick, and Amit Sheth. An Overview of Workflow Management: From Process Modeling to Workflow Automation Infrastructure. *Distributed and Parallel Databases*, pages 119–153, 1995.

[6] J.W. Lloyd. *Foundations of Logic Programming*. Springer-Verlag, 1984.

[7] Marek Rusinkiewicz and Amit Sheth. Specification and Execution of Transactional Workflows. In W. Kim, editor, *Modern Database Systems: The Object Model, Interoperability, and Beyond*. Addison-Wesley, 1994.

[8] R. Sandhu. Separation of Duties in Computerized Information Systems. In *Database Security IV: Status and Prospects*, pages 179–189, 1991.

V

SECURITY TECHNOLOGIES FOR THE INTERNET

MODIFYING LDAP TO SUPPORT PKI

D.W.Chadwick, E. Ball, M.V. Sahalayev
University of Salford

Abstract: One of the impediments to a successful roll out of public key infrastructures (PKIs), is that Lightweight Directory Access Protocol (LDAP) directories do not fully support PKIs. In particular, it is not possible to search for X.509 attributes (certificates or CRLs) that match user defined criteria. This paper describes the various approaches that have been suggested for enabling users to search for X.509 attributes, namely component matching and attribute extraction. The implementation of attribute extraction in the OpenLDAP product is then described.

Key words: X.509, public key certificates, attribute certificates, CRLs, PKI, LDAP, Search

1. INTRODUCTION

The Lightweight Directory Access Protocol (LDAP) [1] was originally conceived as a simplified version of the X.500 Directory Access Protocol (DAP) [4]. X.500 was designed to be a general purpose repository for storing (mainly communications related) attributes of entities, including security attributes such as public key certificates (PKCs) and certificate revocation lists (CRLs). However, during the simplification process of designing LDAP, many features of the DAP were lost, including the ability to fully support public key infrastructures (PKIs). In particular, whilst X.500 DAP could support the searching for and retrieval of public key certificates based on their contents, LDAP could not. For example, a Search such as find the encryption public key (i.e. keyUsage extension is set to keyEncipherment) for the user whose email address (i.e. the SubjectAltName rfc822Name) is A.B.Person@someUni.ac.uk, cannot be supported by LDAP. LDAP is unable to perform this search because it does not know how to carry assertion values in the protocol. Worse still, the original LDAPv2 did not have a correct way of encoding public key certificates or CRLs for storage or retrieval.

The original LDAP protocol was based on encoding fields of the DAP ASN.1 [9] protocol as ASCII strings [2] for carrying over TCP/IP. However, only selected fields from the DAP were chosen for encoding in LDAP. (This is why LDAP is called Lightweight.). DAP on the other hand uses the Basic Encoding Rules (BER) [10] for encoding its protocol elements for transfer, so it is not necessary to specify how any particular field is encoded. BER automatically specifies this for all fields Thus X.500 DAP automatically knows how to encode and transfer public key certificates and their assertion values that are defined in X.509 [8], since they are specified in ASN.1. X.500 DAP inherently knows the structure, contents and transfer encodings of all current and future PKI attributes and extensions that are or may be defined in X.509 (as long as they continue to be defined in ASN.1).

Additions to version 3 of LDAP [7] rectified many of the shortcomings of the original LDAP, and allowed LDAP servers to correctly store and retrieve X.509 attributes, but searching for them was still impossible. This is because the X.509 attributes are simply transferred and stored as binary blobs by LDAPv3, with the server having no knowledge about their structure and contents. Further, no string encodings were specified for the assertion values, so that it still remains impossible to Search for X.509 attributes containing specific fields. A fuller description of the limitations of LDAP when used to support PKIs is given in [11].

Since LDAP has become the primary way of accessing X.500 based directories, and is supported by all the major vendors, e.g. Microsoft, Netscape, IBM, Novell etc., this lack of support for PKIs is a serious impediment to the roll out of PKIs. Indeed, the US Federal PKI pilot reported that the lack of a fully functional inter-operating X.500 directory was one of the inhibitors of PKI rollout [12]. Similarly, the final report [13] of the recently completed EC PKI Challenge project (see http://www.eema.org/pki-challenge) states that PKIs are being held back by the lack of support for them in related technologies such as LDAP/X.500 directories and S/MIME clients. Consequently, the authors set out to rectify the primary deficiency in LDAP, i.e. its inability to Search for X.509 related attributes, by firstly defining a standard LDAP schema for the X.509 attributes, and secondly implementing this schema and its associated matching rules in the OpenLDAP product (see http://www.openldap.org). The schema will allow LDAP servers to know the structure and contents of the X.509 attributes, and will allow assertion values in Search filters to identify specific fields in the attributes. This paper describes the results of this research.

1.1 String Matching

The first approach was to follow the traditional LDAP route. This takes the existing X.500 matching rules and defines how all the ASN.1 type fields of the X.509 attribute value assertions can be carried as ASCII strings in the LDAP protocol [14]. For example, the notBefore Validity time of a PKC might be transferred in a certificate assertion value as yyyymmddhhmmssZ, and might follow the third $ separator character (where preceding $ separated strings might hold the certificate serial number, the issuer's name, and the subject key identifier). Where there is a CHOICE in the equivalent ASN.1 type, for example as in the GeneralNames construct, keywords are defined and these precede the value, so that it is obvious which option has been chosen, e.g. dns myorg.com or ip 123.4.5.6. An extension to the LDAP standard schema would define which ASN.1 type fields of assertion values are to be encoded for transmission in the LDAP protocol (part of the simplification of LDAP is that not every field in the DAP assertion need be transferred). The individual ASN.1 fields of an X.509 attribute value assertion can then be passed as ASCII strings in matching rule assertion values in the LDAP protocol, by LDAP clients wishing to search for X.509 attributes containing particular field values.

When an X.509 attribute e.g. a PKC, is passed to an LDAP server, it should parse the attribute, pull out the individual ASN.1 values, and store these in its indexes, in the same way that it might store and index email address attribute values. The LDAP server will need to have a lookup table, or equivalent, that knows the X.509 matching rules and the order of occurrence of each field in the assertion values presented by the user, so that it can compare them to the correct indexes that it is storing.

Whilst this approach is relatively easy to understand, and follows the traditional LDAP method, it lacks the ability to automatically cater for new ASN.1 type fields, new certificate extensions and new matching rules. The problem is that the string encoding of each field in the assertion values, and any new keywords, are specific to each X.509 syntax. As new X.509 attributes, and new certificate and CRL extensions are defined along with their new matching rules, new LDAP string encodings (and possibly new keywords) will need to be defined for each new assertion value. Consequently new Internet standards will need to be written (or existing ones updated) each time this happens. It would be better if a more automated approach could be defined.

2. COMPONENT MATCHING

An improvement on the original approach was first suggested by Legg, who produced an Internet Draft called Component Matching [15]. This took a more fundamental approach to the problem. Instead of defining LDAP string encodings for complex ASN.1 types, it defined UTF8 string encodings at the lowest level of ASN.1 granularity - the built-in types. Thus string encodings were defined for each ASN.1 built-in type such as INTEGER, BOOLEAN, OCTET STRING, SEQUENCE, CHOICE etc. The encoding of more complex ASN.1 types would then be built up automatically from their component parts. (This part of the document was subsequently released as a separate Internet Draft called the Generic String Encoding Rules for ASN.1 Types, and this is now a standards track RFC [16].) Legg also defined how string assertions could be specified about the components of ASN.1 values, through a ComponentAssertion construct. This defines how each component can be referenced, as well as specifying the assertion value and the matching rule to be used when performing the comparison. Referencing components can be via an identifier, or by its position, for example, a user can assert if the nth value in a SEQUENCE OF INTEGER is greater than or equal to some assertion value.

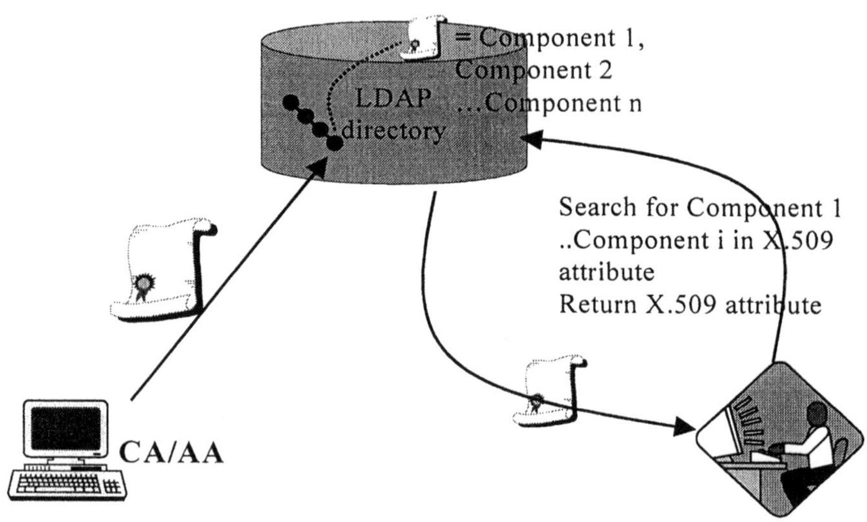

Figure 1. Component Matching

Working with Legg, we produced two Internet Drafts, one for public key certificates [17], the other for attribute certificates [21], describing how the generic string encoding rules can be applied to the assertion values for the X.509 attribute matching rules defined in [14]. We then started to implement this using the open source code of OpenLDAP.

This implementation proved difficult for a number of reasons. Firstly it meant that all existing LDAP clients would need to be modified to support LDAP extensible matching rules, and the generic string encoding rules, so that individual components within an X.509 attribute could be specified by the client and passed to the server. Secondly all existing servers would need to be modified to support the new matching rules, and the generic string encoding rules for assertion values. The matching process is complex. Incoming X.509 attributes have to be parsed, their individual fields have to be located within the DER[1] byte stream, and pointers to the bytes stored in the indexes of the LDAP database, along with their corresponding keywords taken from the definition of their assertion values. When a client sends an assertion value (as an ASCII string), the server has to match the presented keyword against the correct index, then use the associated pointer to pull the value out of the ASN.1 DER byte stream, covert it into an ASCII string, and then compare this with the presented ASCII value using the appropriate matching rule (e.g. equality match or substring match). This continual conversion from ASCII strings to DER bytes and back again is not very efficient, but is unavoidable since LDAP is based on ASCII strings and X.509 attributes are based on DER bytes.

3. ATTRIBUTE EXTRACTION

Other researchers in Germany were also working on the same problem of how to search for X.509 attributes in LDAP directories. Klasen and Gietz were dubious about the approach of Chadwick and Legg. Although it was elegant and easily extensible, they did not believe that all the LDAP suppliers would implement this mechanism in their products. In fact Legg had already implemented component matching in the LDAP server product of his company whilst the Internet Draft was being refined. But this had been made much easier by the fact that their back end database was based on X.500 rather than on LDAP, so every field of every attribute was stored and processed in its DER format by the database. This meant that no conversion had to take place when the server received X.509 attributes for storage, and

[1] DER (the Distinguished Encoding Rules) is a subset of BER

when clients presented LDAP string assertion values, these were converted in their DER equivalents, and passed to the back end database.

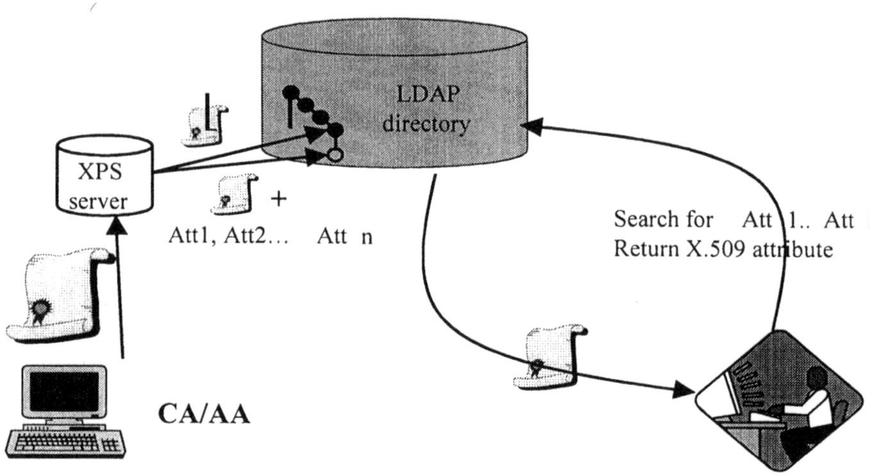

Figure 2. Attribute Extraction

Klasen and Gietz proposed an alternative solution, based on the work-around that PKI administrators are taking today. This is to extract a field from an X.509 attribute and store it as a simple, searchable attribute, in the same entry in the LDAP database. For example, in order to support S/MIME, the PKI administrator extracts the user's email address from the Subject Alt Name field of the public key certificate, and stores this in an email address attribute in the user's LDAP entry. The sending user then searches the LDAP directory for the needed email address, and asks the LDAP server to return the public key certificate attribute from the entry matching the email address. The assumption is that no-one will have tampered with the LDAP directory, and that the email address attribute and the subject alt name field in the certificate will be identical.

Klasen and Gietz extended this model, by defining a set of ~30 attributes for public key certificates, where each attribute holds a field from a public key certificate [18]. For example, the x509keyUsage attribute holds the key usage field, whilst the x509authorityKeyIdentifier attribute holds the authority key identifier field (this is the identifier of the public key used to sign this certificate or CRL). If a front end X.509 attribute Parsing Server (XPS) is used to automatically parse X.509 attributes and extract the fields into these attributes, it means that existing LDAP servers will not need to be modified. No new matching rules or assertion values need to be defined, since the 30 new attributes use existing matching rules and assertion values.

The simplicity of this approach is that most existing (i.e. configurable) LDAP clients will not need to be modified either. They can use their existing assertion value creation code, and simply need to be configured with new attribute types to be used with it.

We decided to alter our modifications to OpenLDAP by adopting Klasen and Gietz's approach. We added XPS functionality to OpenLDAP, so that OpenLDAP can act as either a stand alone XPS server, or a combined XPS and LDAP server. We also wrote two new Internet Drafts to compliment [18], one that defines new LDAP attributes for CRLs [19], the other for attribute certificates [20].

4. XPS IMPLEMENTATION

4.1 The DIT Design

The conventional X.500 design is that X.509 certificates are typically held in the entry of the user, as a multi-valued userCertificate attribute, holding for example a certificate for digital signature verification, and a certificate for encryption. In the XPS design, each certificate is held in a separate subordinate entry of the existing user's entry. This certificate entry holds the set of attributes defined in [18] for public key certificates or in [20] for attribute certificates, along with the complete unmodified certificate. In addition, the XPS server has a configuration option that allows the certificates to be still held in the user's entry as a multi-valued attribute. This is useful for example if a client wishes to retrieve all the attributes of a particular user. The subordinate entries allow LDAP clients to search for fields of the certificate, by using the corresponding attributes and their assertion values. When the attribute(s) is(are) matched, the corresponding certificate in the same entry can be retrieved. The subordinate entries can be named in one of three ways, by using:

a) a combination of the certificate serial number and issuer name (which are guaranteed to be unique), as a multi-valued RDN, or
b) the certificate serial number and issuer name concatenated into a single string (to be used by those LDAP servers e.g. MS Active Directory) that do not support the standard LDAP feature of multi-valued RDNs, or
c) the serial number on its own (this is only suitable for LDAP servers that will only ever store certificates from a single CA)

The OpenLDAP XPS server has a configuration option allowing the administrator to choose the naming scheme most suitable for him.

CRLs are stored in a slightly different way to certificates. They are typically either stored in the CA's entry, or in any entry that is pointed to by the CRL Distribution Point extension in a certificate. When using the XPS server, each CRL is stored in a subordinate entry of the previous entry, but this time each CRL may create a subtree of entries. The immediately subordinate entry holds all the attributes defined in [19], except for the revocation time and CRL entry extensions (such as revocation reason). The latter are stored in subordinate entries of the former, there being one subordinate entry per revoked certificate. The reason that a subtree of entries had to be created, rather than a single subordinate entry, is that LDAP attributes are a set of values, rather than a sequence of values. Therefore it is not possible to relate multi-valued attributes together in any meaningful way. Since each revoked certificate has its own revocation time and set of extensions, it would not make sense to store a set of revocation times and revoked certificate serial numbers in two separate attributes of the same (subordinate) entry, and expect a client to be able to determine which certificate was revoked at which time. By placing each revoked certificate in a separate child entry, it is possible to search for certificates revoked at a certain time, or with a certain revocation reason etc.

4.2 Configuration Options

OpenLDAP has been modified so that it can be an X.509 attribute Parsing Server (XPS) and operate in either standalone mode, or as a front end to an existing LDAP server. Those sites that are already using OpenLDAP as their LDAP server, will typically operate in standalone mode, by upgrading to the appropriate OpenLDAP release. Those sites that use any other make of LDAP server, can simply place the OpenLDAP XPS server as a front end to their existing LDAP server as in Figure 2. The Certification Authority is then configured to talk to XPS rather than its existing LDAP server. XPS parses the incoming request, modifies it, and passes the resulting requests to the existing LDAP server.

The configuration file for the XPS server contains a number of options. Administrators can choose which X.509 attribute types are to be trapped and have their attributes extracted by XPS, which attributes are to be extracted from them and what these attributes should be named, whether these attributes should still be stored in their parent entries as well as the new subordinate ones, whether a CRL should be stored as a subtree of entries or not, what form of names to be used for the new subordinate entries, and finally where error and write-ahead logs should be stored. Write-ahead logs are needed because LDAP servers do not support transactions, therefore the XPS server has to store its set of intended updates in a WAL before actually applying them to the LDAP server. This will allow XPS to rollback the LDAP server should an error occur midway through the set of updates.

5. DISCUSSION AND CONCLUSION

The component matching approach is a more elegant solution, since the X.509 attributes are only stored once in the LDAP directory, and matching is performed directly on their contents. Attribute extraction on the other hand, doubles or trebles the storage requirements of the LDAP server, and matching is performed on the attributes associated with the X.509 attribute, rather than on the X.509 attribute itself. It would therefore be possible, especially if the LDAP server was hacked, for the attributes to no longer accurately reflect the contents of the associated X.509 attribute.

However, attribute extraction is somewhat easier to implement than component matching, especially on the client side. Furthermore, by using a stand alone XPS server, existing LDAP servers do not need to be modified. Given the past reluctance of LDAP vendors for more than 5 years to solve the problem of searching for PKI related attributes, we have some doubts if they are likely to implement component matching anytime soon. We therefore conclude that attribute extraction is the best pragmatic solution to quickly solving the current problem of PKI users who need to search for X.509 attributes in an LDAP directory.

ACKNOWLEDGEMENTS

This research was funded by the European academic community, in particular by TERENA, CESNET, SURFnet, UNINETT, RedIRIS and SWITCH.

REFERENCES

[1] W. Yeong, T. Howes, S. Kille. "X.500 Lightweight Directory Access Protocol." RFC 1487, July 1993.

[2] Howes, T., Kille, S., Yeong, W., Robbins, C. "The String Representation of Standard Attribute Syntaxes". RFC 1778, March 1995

[3] Wahl, M., Coulbeck, A., Howes, T., Kille, S. "Lightweight Directory Access Protocol (v3): Attribute Syntax Definitions". RFC 2252. December 1997.
[4] ISO 9594-3/ITU-T Rec. X.511(1988) The Directory: Abstract Service Definition
[5] Wahl, M., Howes, T., Kille, S. "Lightweight Directory Access Protocol (v3)", RFC 2251, Dec. 1997
[6] ITU, "Information Technology - Open Systems Interconnection - The Directory: Public-key and attribute certificate frameworks", ITU-T Recommendation X.509, March 2000.
[7] Wahl, M., Howes, T., Kille, S. "Lightweight Directory Access Protocol (v3)", RFC 2251, Dec. 1997
[8] ISO 9594-8/ITU-T Rec. X.509 (2001) The Directory: Authentication Framework
[9] ITU-T Recommendation X.680 (1997) | ISO/IEC 8824-1:1998, Information Technology - Abstract Syntax Notation One (ASN.1): Specification of Basic Notation
[10] ITU-T Recommendation X.690 (1997) | ISO/IEC 8825-1,2,3:1998 Information technology - ASN.1 encoding rules: Specification of Basic Encoding Rules (BER), Canonical Encoding Rules (CER) and Distinguished Encoding Rules (DER)
[11] D.W.Chadwick. "Deficiencies in LDAP when used to support a Public Key Infrastructure", Communications of the ACM, March 2003/Vol 46, No. 3 pp. 99-104.
[12] Electronic Messaging Association Challenge 2000 "Report of Federal Bridge Certification Authority Initiative and Demonstration" DRAFT 101500, August 2000 (Available from http://csrc.nist.gov/pki/documents/emareport_20001015.pdf)
[13] EEMA/ECAF PKI Challenge Project "D8.1 – Final Report", IST-2000-25012, March 2003
[14] D.W.Chadwick."Internet X.509 Public Key Infrastructure - Additional LDAP Schema for PKIs and PMIs". <draft-pkix-ldap-schema-00.txt>, July 2000
[15] S. Legg. "LDAP & X.500 Component Matching Rules", <draft-legg-ldapext-component-matching-11.txt>, June 2003
[16] Legg, S., "Generic String Encoding Rules (GSER) for ASN.1 Types", RFC 3641, October 2003.
[17] Chadwick, D.W., Legg, S."Internet X.509 Public Key Infrastructure - LDAP Schema and Syntaxes for PKIs ", <draft-ietf-pkix-ldap-pki-schema-00.txt>, June 2002.
[18] Klasen, N., Gietz, P. "An LDAPv3 Schema for X.509 Certificates",<draft-klasen-ldap-x509certificate-schema-03.txt>, July, 2003
[19] Chadwick, D.W., Sahalayev, M. V. "Internet X.509 Public Key Infrastructure - LDAP Schema for X.509 CRLs", <draft-ietf-pkix-ldap-crl-schema-01.txt>, June 2003
[20] Chadwick, D.W., Sahalayev, M. V. "Internet X.509 Public Key Infrastructure - LDAP Schema for X.509 Attribute Certificates", <draft-ietf-sahalayev-pkix-ldap-ac-schema-00.txt>, February 2003
[21] Chadwick, D.W., Legg, S."Internet X.509 Public Key Infrastructure - LDAP Schema and Syntaxes for PMIs", <draft-ietf-pkix-ldap-pmi-schema-00.txt>, June 2002.

ECPV: EFFICIENT CERTIFICATE PATH VALIDATION IN PUBLIC-KEY INFRASTRUCTURE

M. Halappanavar and R. Mukkamala
Department of Computer Science, Old Dominion University, Norfolk, VA, USA

Abstract In the current public-key infrastructure (PKI) schemes based on X.509, a relying party must validate a user's certificate as well as the existence of a path from its trust points to the CA of the certificate. The latter part is referred to as certificate path validation. In this paper, we suggest an efficient certificate path validation scheme (ECPV) that employs delegation with efficient computing at relying parties. In particular, in our scheme, a relying party is provided with certificate path validation trees (CPVTs) depending on its trust points and applicable trust policies. This information should enable a relying party to perform certificate path validation locally. The CPVAs can be deployed either as autonomous entities or in a federated mode. We discuss the two major components of ECPV: the data harvester and the data analyzer. Some of the concerns of security, trust, and performance are also discussed.

Keywords: Certificate Path Validation Authority (CPVA), certificate path validation trees (CPVT), delegated path discovery (DPD), delegated path validation (DPV), public-key Infrastructure (PKI), security and trust

1. INTRODUCTION

Digital certificates have emerged as a popular tool to provide authentication, privacy, integrity, non-repudiation and other security requirements in modern day transactions [1]. PKI provides a comprehensive infrastructure for issuing and managing public keys in the form of digital certificates to a set of users [1,10]. When two users want to communicate with one another in a secure manner, they will have to authenticate each other prior to the actual communication. This stranger-to-stranger communication is made possible by having a trusted third-party (TTP) in the form of Certification Authority (CA) whom both the parties trust. When a user or subject submits a certificate to a relying party (RP) for a service, the relying party would like to validate the user certificate prior to offering a service.

Typically, the validation of a certificate is done in three steps. In the first step, a relying party (RP) builds a chain of trust, also known as certificate chain, starting from the CA that has issued the user's certificate to the CA that RP trusts (also known as a trust point). This step is known as *certificate path discovery*. Generally, trust between CAs is established by issuing CA-CA cross-certificates. These certificates can also be revoked from time to time. Thus there is a need to confirm the validity of the links in the certificate chain built in step one. The second step conducts the validation, and is referred to as *certificate path validation*. (The logic for the validation process described above is described in RFC 2459 [9,10] and is based on various parameters specified in certificate policies.) In the third step, the validity of the issued certificate is itself verified with information provided by its CA. In this paper, we are interested in the first two steps of the validation process.

Recent research trends in public-key infrastructure favor delegation of authority for certificate path validation to trusted-severs and for path discovery to untrusted-servers. DPV (Delegated Path Validation) and DPD (Delegated Path Discovery) are examples of such protocols [9]. These protocols are still evolving and are described in Internet drafts [8,9]. Simple Certificate Validation Protocol (SCVP) is another delegation protocol that is conceptually similar to DPV and DPD [6].

In this paper, we propose an efficient certificate path validation (ECPV) scheme to overcome the weaknesses in the current path validation protocols. Our scheme is based on one or more certificate path validation authorities (CPVA) that upload RPs with a certificate path validation trees (CPVT). An RP, in turn, can use this locally available tree to validate certificate paths of user certificates. The trees shall be periodically updated by the CPVA. The CPVAs can be implemented either as an autonomous entity working in isolation or organized as a federation to share information.

The paper is organized as follows. In section 2, we discuss some of the issues in certificate path validation and current solutions. In section 3, we describe the proposed ECPV scheme for certificate path validation. A more detailed description of the CPVA module is provided in section 4. Two possible options for deployment are discussed in section 5. Section 6 reviews the security, trust, and performance aspects of the proposed scheme. Finally, section 7 summarizes the contributions of the paper and discusses plans for future work.

2. ISSUES IN CERTIFICATE PATH VALIDATION

As explained in section 1, certificate path validation involves the task of discovering a path and then verifying its validity. The path discovery is both computation and communication intensive, since it involves discovering a network of CAs that trust each other. Several factors contribute to the complexity. First, there are many possible trust topologies [5,8,9,11]. Strict hierarchical, multi-rooted hierarchical, mesh, bilateral cross-certification, and bridge topologies are a few example topologies. However, many of the present RP implementations make simple assumptions about the trust structure and are not capable of handling these complex trust relationships [11,14]. Changes in the trust hierarchies over time also necessitate changes in the relying party software, an impractical proposition.

Second is the trust policy issue. Each RP has an acceptable trust policy for the chain of CAs that it is trying to validate for a given certificate [3]. The policy would describe the minimum level of CA practices that it expects from each of the CAs on the path. Similarly, each CA also specifies, in its CA-CA certificate, the practices (policies) that it trusts other CAs to follow [1,2]. As a consequence of a wide variety of such policies, the task of RP becomes more complex during path discovery since it should only select those links that are compatible with its (RP's) own policy. Checking the policy compatibility is not a simple process [2,7,9].

Third, response time is also one of issues for certificate path validation. For example, an RP is very much interested in responding to its users as soon as possible with the service they requested. However, it cannot do so until the path validation and the subsequent certificate validation are complete.

Fourth, CA and repository availability is also an important concern to an RP. All of the CAs and the relevant certificate and revocation information repositories need to be available for an RP to discover and validate a path. If a trust path is long, with several CAs, there could be a problem in data collection as some entities along the path may not be accessible during validation [9,11,14]. In other words, even though a CA-CA certificate is valid, due to the inability to access a CA's data at the validation time, an RP may not be able to validate a certificate.

Finally, RP is concerned about the cost of validation. It would like to minimize this cost. When each RP undertakes the task of discovery and validation (i.e., if it is not delegated to a server), it is an expensive process. Substantial cost savings may not be realized if the entire process of validation is repeated for each certificate that the RP receives, even when delegated to a trusted validation server.

From the above discussion, it is clear that certificate validation is a complex process involving considerable amount of communication and computational resources.

3. ECPV: PROPOSED SCHEME FOR CERTIFICATE PATH VALIDATION

ECPV is based on the idea that it is much more efficient to provide a relying party with path validation information in the form of trees (CPVT) rather than to require the RP to request an external server for each certificate validation. Section 3.1 describes the CPVTs in greater detail.

3.1 Certificate Path Validation Trees (CPVT)

To explain the concept of CPVT, let us consider the example in Figure 1. Figure 1(a) describes a set of trust relationships between a set of CAs (CA1-CA9). Here, an arrow between one CA and the other (e.g., from CA1 to CA5) indicates that one CA has issued a cross-CA certificate to the other (e.g., CA1 issued a certificate to CA5). The arrow type indicates the similarity between the trust parameters, which could be established by policy mappings (e.g., CA1 policy OID_x maps to policy OID_y for CA5).
Suppose a relying party RP1 trusts CA1. In addition, it accepts input parameter set 1 for some type of requests and input parameter set 3 for other types of user requests. In this case, the intent is to build two trees for RP1 with CA1 as the root, one with IP set 1 and the other with IP set 3. Figures (1b) and (1c) are the required trees derived from Figure 1a. These are what we refer to as certificate path validation trees or CPVTs. For RP1 to accept a certificate issued by CAx under IP set 1, for example, it expects a path from CA1 to that CAx in the CPVT in Figure (1b). In this case, for example, only CA1, CA3, CA7, and CA9 meet the criteria. In fact, each directional edge in Figure 1 is associated with an expiration time (not shown in the figure), derived from the expiration time of the cross-CA certificate and the CRL (or ARL) issued by the parent CA. Thus, an edge in the network or CPVT is valid only if it has not expired at the time of its usage. The advantages of building the path from trust point, commonly referred to as building in *reverse direction*, are very well discussed in [7].

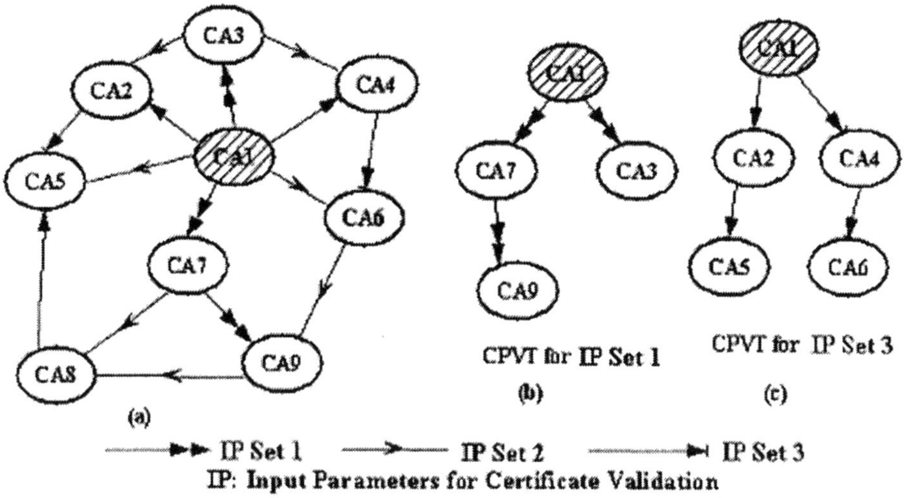

Figure 1. Illustration of Certificate Path Validation Trees (CPVT)

3.2 System architecture

The system architecture for ECPV is shown in Figure 2. The various components of the system are as follows:

(1) *CA Module*: The certification authority (CA), its registration authority (RA), the repository (REP), and OCSP responder together represent the CA module.

(2) *CPVA module*: The CPVA (Certificate Path Validation Authority) is the critical module that will perform the process of path discovery and verification. This module consists of harvester (HRV) and analyzer. CPVA is responsible for building the CPVTs and distributing them to the RP modules.

(3) *RP module*: The relying parties (RP) service the requests from subjects for certificate validation. The relying parties provide requisite information, including trust points and validation policies, to the CPVA module, which builds relevant CPVTs based on the input and download CPVTS to the RPs. RPs are the primary users of the infrastructure for validation of certificates.

(4) *Subject module*: Subjects or clients request service from the RPs and offer their certificates for validation. The subject's influence the system design and performance from their diversity and rate of requests.

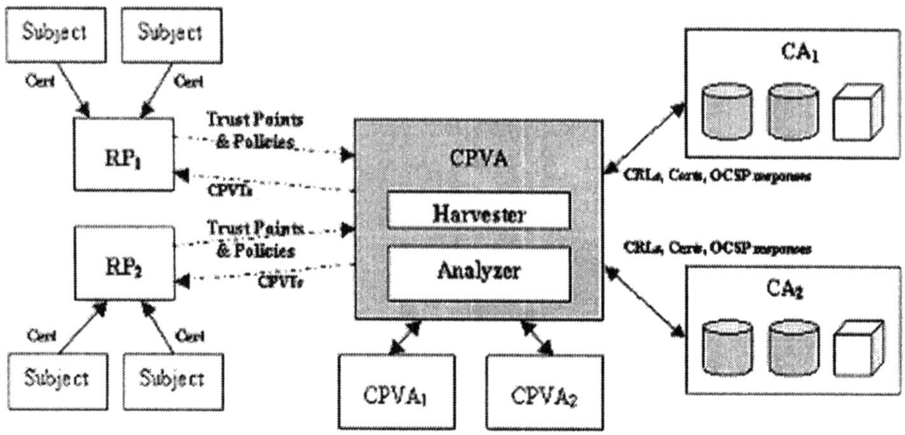

Figure 2. System Architecture

Another important aspect of our architecture is the interactions among the modules. Among all interactions in our system, the following three are relevant with respect to this paper: (i) the RP-CPVA interactions, (ii) CPVA-CA interactions, and (iii) CPVA-CPVA interactions. We summarize these three types of interactions in the form of scenario-like description of events starting from an RP submitting a request to the uploading of CPVTs to it.

1. Each relying party (RP) submits a set of input parameters with vital information like trust point CAs, policy constraints, name constraints, maximum path length, etc.
2. The CPVA consolidates the RP information and requests its harvester component to collect data a set of <trust point, input parameter set> pairs.
3. Harvester collects all the requisite information including CA certificates, CRLs, OCSP responses, etc. (In the federated scheme, a harvester may also collect CPVTs from other CPVAs).
4. The analyzer analyzes the collected data, and builds CPVTs based on the RPs' requests initially received. The analysis includes looking into the CRLs (also referred to as ARLs [1,10]) and the OCSP responses for validity of CA certificates. In addition, it needs to take a note of the validity of each response---how long is a published CRL applicable. Using this information, it builds CPVTs with trust points as the roots.
5. The CPVA uploads the appropriate trees to the respective RPs (i.e., each RP gets only the relevant CPVTs).
6. Since some edges of a CPVT may expire after the initial upload, the trees automatically get pruned at the RP while being used for certificate

verification. In addition, the CPVA also keeps track of the expirations and updates its trees with periodic data. The updated trees may be either automatically uploaded (in a push scheme) or requested by a RP (in a pull scheme).

4. THE CERTIFICATE PATH VALIDATION AUTHORITY (CPVA)

As shown in Figure 2, CPVA has two components: harvester and analyzer. While the claimed simplicity of RP software comes from the harvester's functionality, the benefits in performance are due to both the components. We now describe these components.

4.1 The harvester

The concept of harvester is adopted from the concept of data harvesting in digital libraries [14]. A harvester traverses the CA repositories and OCSP responders and collects all the requisite information like certificates, CRLs, and OCSP responses.

The repositories use multiple directory protocols like DAP, LDAP, FTP and HTTP, and also have directory chaining, directory referrals. This necessitates the harvester software to be complex and capable of communicating with different protocols. The components of the harvester, as follows:

- *Bulk Harvester:* The bulk harvester is activated for gathering of information at initialization as well as occasionally to refresh data.
- *Incremental Harvester:* The incremental harvester is executed frequently to keep the data current. It can be activated on events like certificate expiry, CRL expiry, addition of new CAs, etc.
- *The Scheduler:* The Scheduler components triggers the incremental harvester and the bulk harvester at appropriate times to keep the data up-to-date.
- *Data Normalizer:* Since the collected data during the harvesting can be in different formats, the data normalizer reformats the data into single format for easy processing by the data analyzer module.

4.2 The analyzer

Once the harvester has obtained all the relevant information, it is the responsibility of the analyzer to construct the CPVTs to upload to the relying parties. In addition, the analyzer is responsible for detecting any changes in the current CPVTs that it may have previously uploaded to RPs. For example, in a push model where the CPVA is responsible for updating the CPVTs at the RPs, the data analyzer should be able to upload the changes (or the new CPVTs) to the affected RPs. Since data analyzer is mainly responsible for constructing the CPVTs for the relying parties, the next task is to generate CPVTs from the mesh. There are several options in building the trees.

The analyzer has the following four components.

- *The Client Processor:* The Client processor consolidates the data received from the various RPs that the CPVA serves.
- *The CPVT Builder:* The builder performs the primary action of building the CPVTs based on the information obtained from the Harvester and other CPVAs. The Builder builds the trees for different trust points according to particular input parameter set.
- *Harvester Coordinator:* This component interacts with the harvester to specify the information that the harvester needs to collect and feed the Scheduler with appropriate times for re-harvesting the data.
- *Federation Coordinator:* As shall be discussed in section 5, the CPVA scheme can be deployed in autonomous mode or in a federated mode. When the federated model is used, the data analyzer will collect CPVTs from other CPVAs and use them to build the CPVTs.

5. DEPLOYMENT OPTIONS WITH ECPV

The ECPV scheme with CPVAs as primary components can be deployed in at least two ways: autonomous and federated. In the autonomous mode, the CPVA shall work in isolation to collect the data, to build the CPVTs, and serve only its clients. Certainly, this scheme is not highly scalable and does not offer high performance benefits in information processing. These disadvantages can be overcome by the federated mode of deployment where CPVAs would coordinate with another to build and to maintain the CPVTs in a highly scalable and distributed manner.

5.1 Autonomous harvesting

When RPs handle certificates from a few domains, and the number of CAs are limited, autonomous harvesting works very well. In this method, each CPVA module is independent (of other CPVAs). Its harvester is responsible for contacting the individual CAs/OCSP responders/directory repositories to obtain the needed certificates, revocation lists, and certificate status responses. CPVA module is responsible for several RP's (say in its domain). It is responsible for harvesting data from CAs related to requests from its RPs.

5.2 Federated harvesting

Once PKI technology becomes popular among the internet users, there would be thousands of CAs issuing certificates for their own specific domains. In other words, unlike a handful of CAs we currently have (e.g., Verisign, Entrust, etc.), there would be several autonomous ones issuing and managing certificates. In such an environment, it would not be possible for a single harvester to obtain information about all CAs, their CRLs, and the trust paths connecting them.

6. SECURITY, TRUST, AND PERFORMANCE ISSUES

As stated already, the primary impetus for our work is two-fold: to simplify the task of relying parties by delegating some of the data collection and processing work to CPVAs; and to arrive at a scheme that is efficient and scalable. These objectives are to be achieved without compromising the security and trust offered by the traditional certificate path validation schemes. In this section, we briefly discuss our scheme in the context of security, trust and performance.

6.1 Security and Trust Aspects of ECPV schemes

One of the primary concerns of a relying party in adopting the ECPV for path discovery and validation is of trust. In other words, why should a relying party trust that the information provided by CPVA is correct? This concern exists even with the current delegated path discovery and validation protocols [8,9]. But let us look at our schemes.

Under autonomous deployment, where the CPVA collects all the needed information (e.g., CRLs, expiration times, OCSP responses, etc.) by itself and prepares customized CPVTs for each relying party, the solution is simple. A CPVA signs the provided CPVT. Thus, there is a guarantee that an impostor process has not supplied incorrect results. This also ensures non-repudiation. In fact, to encourage more RPs to use its service, a CPVA may offer some kind of a guarantee as is done by Digital Signature Trust (http://www.digsigtrust.com) in the case of public-key certificates.

In addition, optionally, it provides all the information used to arrive at the CPVT. Since the information is itself signed by the providing entities (e.g., a CA digitally signs the CRL that it issues, and an OCSP responder signs its response), the evidence is self-explanatory and is trusted.

Under federated deployment, a CPVA that provides the CPVT to a relying party is not necessarily the one that directly contacted the corresponding CAs. Instead, it may have received either the raw information or part of the trees from other CPVAs. So it appears that the trust is somewhat weakened. However, if each CPVA signs its response (e.g., partial trees) or simply forwards the CA signed raw information to its requester, then the concern is mitigated. For example, if each CPVA, when it receives a signed partial CPVT from another CPVA, checks the signature, prepares a new CPVT (if it merged several partial CPVTs into one), and digitally signs it, then there would be no problem of trust. The idea of providing guarantees (as in Digital Signature Trust discussed above) by each CPVA further enhances the trust aspects of using the CPVA servers. If the RP does not trust the CPVA, it can receive all the supporting data along with the CPVT and verify, this process is considerably faster than RP having to perform the path discovery process all by itself.

6.2 Performance aspects of CPVA schemes

Let us consider CPVA and its impact on the relying parties. Clearly, a relying party is simplified due to the delegation of data collection and path construction to CPVA. This is similar to SCVP and DPD/DPV [8,9]. But CPVA significantly differs from other schemes in the information it provides to the RPs. While other schemes only provide the status information (yes/no/error/don't know) to an RP's request, CPVA empowers a relying party with validation trees that could be used by the RP to locally verify users' certificates. In other words, the response time, or latency, of an RP is greatly improved due to CPVA. In addition, by providing policy-specific CPVTs, an RP is able handle requests with varied values. For example, if a request is for a low-value service, it could use a CPVT of a weaker trust assurance. On the other hand, for a high valued transaction it could use a CPVT with a strong trust assurance. In summary, by caching the CPVTs, the performance of the RPs is greatly improved. In addition, the CPVA can handle much larger number of RPs since it receives requests from RPs less frequently.

Now let us look at the comparison between autonomous and federated schemes. Clearly, the load on CPVA is much larger in the autonomous scheme since its harvester is responsible for directly collecting data from all the required CAs. On the other hand, in federated mode, the load is distributed among several CPVAs. However, in this scheme, since the same request (and hence data) flows through several CPVAs, there is higher communication and processing overhead on the network and the intermediate CPVAs. But this scheme is highly scalable and has better performance than autonomous mode.

Both schemes can greatly benefit from caching at the RPs and at the CPVAs. Since CA's certificates often have longer life and are less likely to be revoked, the CPVTs tend to have much longer validity periods. This means that a CPVT once uploaded to an RP can be used for quite some time to validate subject's certificate paths. In addition, the incremental approach of updating the trees along with the push/pull methods used to distribute the changes greatly enhances the performance of the RPs as well as the overall system.

6.2.1 Costs and benefits

The performance of CPVA can best be quantified in terms of its costs and benefits when compared to traditional validation schemes.

The following benefits are claimed performance *advantages* of CPVA over traditional schemes:

- **Improved response time at RPs due to reduced time for certificate path validation**. This implies that RP's response to user's service requests is improved.
- **Improved system availability at RPs due to localized certificate path validation**. This implies that the user requests are much more likely to be validated and serviced.
- **Reduction in overall communication cost in the system due to harvesting at CPVA.** This is due to the harvesting of CA and cross-CA certificate data ahead of time and using this information to supply validation trees to the RPs.

However, these benefits are accrued at the following *costs*.

- **Cost of harvesting.** The harvester may collect more (bulk) information than needed. In addition, it needs to collect data to keep CPVA's validation trees up-to-date.

- **Cost of analysis.** The analyzer needs to analyze harvested data and build trees some of which may never be needed.

In summary, while the RPs benefit by receiving the validation trees for local certificate path validations, the system of CPVAs place additional communication and computing overhead on the system. In this section, we provide a back-of-the-envelope analysis to quantify the costs and benefits.

6.2.2 Key Parameters influencing CPVA Performance

While several parameters influence the performance of the proposed scheme, the following three *parameters* are the key factors.

- *Validity period and revocation of CA-CA certificates:* Each CA-cross certificate is valid for certain period of time. Unless its issuing CA revokes it, a cross certificate is valid until the specified expiration time. Whenever such a certificate expires or has been revoked, it results in the following costs for the CPVA:
    - Communication cost for the harvester to collect information to update the validation data.
    - Computation cost to select and rebuild the affected validation trees (if any).
    - Communication cost to send updated trees to the affected RPs

- *Rate of validation requests:* Rate of validation requests of RPs determines how effectively the validation trees are being used by the RPs. For example, when the rate of requests is high, it implies that the savings due to local validation trees at RPs is high, and, hence, it may offset the cost of building, maintaining, and uploading of these trees to RPs.

- *Maximum (trust) path length and topology:* Wider adoption of PKI will necessitate greater number of CAs, probably with complex CA-CA trust relationships. For medium to low security applications, larger (5-10) values for the maximum path length can be adopted to facilitate wider acceptance of certificates.

7. CONCLUSIONS AND FUTURE WORK

In this paper, we proposed an efficient certificate path validation scheme. In our scheme, a relying party receives a certificate path validation tree (CPVT) from the delegated server (CPVA). The tree is stored locally at the relying party. A relying party can now validate the path locally. The delegated server consists of a data harvester and a data analyzer. We proposed some implementation schemes for both these components. The local caching of CPVTs greatly reduces the overhead due to delegated server. At the same time, since a relying party is not responsible for collecting data from different CAs and OCSP responders on the internet, its software can still be simple. We have suggested several options for implementing the data harvester and the data analyzer. We have also shown that our scheme does not weaken the security and trust properties of delegation.

We are currently looking into further design options for implementing the CPVA. One of our objectives is to improve the efficiency of harvester and analyzer. We are also looking into extending the representation structures from trees (CPVT) to other data structures.

REFERENCES

[1] C. Adams and S. Lloyd, Understanding Public-key Infrastructure: Concepts, Standards, and Deployment Considerations. Macmillan Technical Publishing, 1999.

[2] R. Housley, W. Ford, W. Polk, and D. Solo, Internet X.509 Public Key Infrastructure Certificate and CRL Profile, RFC 2459, January 1999.

[3] S. Lloyd (Editor), CA-CA Interoperability, White paper, PKI Forum, March 2001. Available at (http://www.pkiforum.org/pdfs/ca-ca_interop.pdf)

[4] R. Moskowitz, "An Unlikely PKI Cavalry," Network Computing, Security Watch Column, Nov. 1999.

[5] A. Malpani, Bridge Validation Authority, White paper, Valicert, December 2001, Available at http://www.valicert.com/corporate/library/pdfs/Bridge_VA_Whitepaper.pdf

[6] Malpani and R. Housley, "Simple Certificate Validation Protocol (SCVP)," Internet Draft , March 2002.

[7] S. Chokhani and W. Ford, Internet X.509 Public Key Infrastructure Certificate Policy and Certification Practices Framework, RFC 2527, March 1999.

[8] D. Pinkas and R. Housley, "Delegated Path Validation and Delegated Path Discovery Protocol Requirements," Internet Draft, May 2002.

[9] D. Pinkas, "Delegated Path Validation and Delegated Path Discovery Protocols," Internet Draft, July 2001.

[10] P. Hesse, *Certification Path Development Software, Briefing to FPKITWG*, April 2000.

[11] M. Branchaud and J. Linn, *Extended Validation Models in PKI: Alternatives and Implications*, *Proc. 1st Annual PKI Research Workshop*, Bethesda, Maryland, USA, April 16, 2002, pages: 30-36.

[12] T. Cormen, C. Leiserson, and R. Rivest, *Introduction to Algorithms*, Prentice-Hall, December 2000.

[13] G. Coulouris, J. Dollimore, and T. Kindberg, *Distributed Systems: Concepts and Design,* Third Edition, Addison-Wesley, 2001.

[14] C. Bowman, P. Danzig and D. Hardy, *Harvest: A Scalable, Customizable Discovery and Access System*, Technical Report CU-CS-732-94, University of Colorado – Boulder.

[15] G. Coulouris, J. Dollimore and T. Kindberg, *Distributed Systems Concepts and Design*, Addison-Wesley Publishers Limited, Third Edition 2001.

SEMANTICS-AWARE PERIMETER PROTECTION

Marco Cremonini, Ernesto Damiani and Pierangela Samarati
Dipartimento di Tecnologie dell'Informazione
Università di Milano
26013 Crema - Italy
{cremonini,damiani,samarati}@dti.unimi.it

Abstract Web services security is becoming a critical concern for any organization adopting the XML-based Web services approach to application integration. While many access control techniques for Web services are becoming available, several issues still need to be solved in order to correctly split the burden of securing Web services between the perimetral and the service level. In this paper, a technique is presented able to make perimetral defences semantics-aware. Application-level *semantics-aware firewalls* enforce filtering rules directly on SOAP messages based on the nature of the services they request. Our semantics-aware firewalls rules are written using a flexible XML-based syntax that allows sharing metadata concepts with service level access control policies, supporting complex security policies that integrate perimetral defences with access control. Moreover, they can be quickly integrated into organizations' existing infrastructure, deployed rapidly and scaled as needed. Also, they integrate easily with existing infrastructure and can be operated by current staff, potentially achieving a low total cost of ownership with respect to service level solutions.

1. Introduction

It is widely acknowledged that open standards such as XML [3] and HTTP [9] offer reduced integration cost, boosting the potential for increasing organizations' capability to compete and succeed in today's global e-market. A well established trend toward a Web-centric scenario for both user-to-application and application-to-application interactions exploits Web services[1] flexibility, expressivity and standardization. As

[1]The term *Web services* describes Web application components build upon existing and emerging technology standards including XML, SOAP, WSDL and HTTP.

far as protocols are concerned, Web services growing success hints to a scenario where HTTP, with its secure variant HTTPS, is the only general-purpose application protocol used for a variety of services. The benefits of this evolution are clear:

- A simplified and homogeneous level 7 of the ISO/OSI stack with a single reference application protocol, i.e. HTTP, together with a standard remote method invocation technique, i.e. SOAP [2], overcomes the usual difficulties in integrating specialized services and proprietary platforms;

- a standard data interchange format, i.e. XML, makes integration of functions offered by heterogeneous systems much easier than it was in the past.

There is an additional claimed benefit of the Web-centric model, which has perhaps more to do with business than with technical reasons: tunnelling remote method invocations through HTTP connections, serves the goal of solving *firewall traversal* problems caused by the attitude of system administrators, and actually of most network security best practices, of blocking most application protocols at the corporate network perimeter. As a matter of fact, Web services firewall traversal capabilities introduce significant security risks, encouraging companies to selectively expose pieces of their enterprise applications. While a number of access control techniques for Web services are becoming available [7, 1], many researchers agree that the temptation to deal with Web services' security by access control alone should be resisted, because a number of security and operating issues are more effectively solved at perimetral level. In order to check SOAP traffic crossing organizations' perimeters, however, firewalls should become semantics-aware, at least to a degree. Commercial SOAP proxies are becoming available capable of performing sophisticated filtering of SOAP payload (to name but a few, Reactivity XML firewall, `http://www.reactivity.com`, and Quadrasis/Xtradyne SOAP Content Inspector, `http://www.quadrasis.com`, are examples of dedicated hardware appliances; Check Point Application Intelligence, `http://www.checkpoint.com`, instead, is the new SOAP proxy feature provided by the last release of market leader Firewall-1). However, the debate on their usage and impact is still at a preliminary stage: while enterprises have quickly come to realize the importance of securing XML, they are only beginning to understand the many operating issues and the corresponding costs involved in implementing XML security at the single service and at the perimetral level. In this paper, we introduce a new concept in application security, the *semantics-aware perimeter protection*, aimed at cost-effectively sharing with service-level access control the heavy protection burden that Web services applications require, reducing the risks associated with integrating heterogeneous applications that cross organizational boundaries. In our approach, semantics-aware firewalls are not just simple filters acting on XML payload: rather, they systematically monitor XML-based messages between business partners, customers and others, enforcing rules written in a highly expressive, XML based language. When it is computationally feasible, rules enforced by semantics-aware firewalls may refer to service properties smoothly integrating with service level access control policies. Like our approach to XML and SOAP access control [5, 6, 7], our semantics-aware firewalls cleanly separate Web services security from the business logic in each application. This allows administrators to independently define and audit multiple-level security policies. The paper is structured as follows: Section 2 presents some basic concepts, relevant to our approach, referred to: Web services, the SOAP protocol, perimeter protection and network firewalls. Section 3 presents our new concepts of semantics-aware perimeter protection. It clarifies the context, which problems are tackled, how SOAP headers should be customized for perimetral security, and highlights some performance and manageability requirements. Section 4 describes how semantic-aware filtering rules are modelled in our framework, specifies their syntax and semantics, and presents a case-study example of semantic-aware policy. Section 5 draws our conclusions and sketches our plans for future works.

2. Basic concepts

2.1. Web services in a nutshell

Web services are the last evolution of basic Remote Procedure Calls (RPCs) and are aimed at providing a new form of distributed computing environment for business-to-business and business-to-consumer applications. Aside implementation differences with respect to RPCs, Web services emphasizes the adoption of standard technologies: a standard definition mechanism, standard lookup services and standard transport definitions. The goal is to make remote systems fully interoperating.

For the purpose of this paper, we are expecially interested in SOAP [2, 12], which is the key technology for carrying out Web services interactions on the net. In the following we give a brief overview of SOAP features that are relevant within the scope of this paper. In particular, we focus on the *SOAP HTTP Binding* scenario [12], which is represented by applications exchanging SOAP messages via HTTP.

SOAP is a stateless, one-way message exchange paradigm that, if combined with features of the underlying application protocol, could be used to realize different interaction patterns like: the *response* message exchange pattern, which is provided by the use of the HTTP *GET* method in a HTTP request to return a SOAP message in the body of the HTTP response; the *request/response* pattern, which is the one followed by using the HTTP *POST* method for passing SOAP messages in the body of HTTP requests and response messages; and the *request/multiple responses*, which is not directly supported by HTTP but should be implemented at application level [12]. We are interested in the *request/response* exchange message pattern, because expecially well-suited for RPC-like interaction, as Web services are.

The general structure of a SOAP message consists of an XML document composed by an `Envelope` element that contains two sub-elements: an `Header` and a `Body`. A SOAP `Header` contains auxiliary information such as directives or contextual information related to the processing of the message. SOAP is exensible in an application-specific manner by customizing such auxiliary header's information. Within a SOAP `Header`, sub-elements called `Header Blocks` represents data logically grouped that can be used by intermediaries handling a SOAP message between a sender and an ultimate receiver.

2.2. Perimeter protection concepts

The goal of perimeter protection is to deploy security measures at the perimeter of a corporate network. The perimeter of a corporate network is represented by the access points to and from external networks, like the network segments connecting the company to the Internet, external routers facing the Internet Service Provider's network, dial-in modem pools, Virtual Private Networks, or Wireless LANs.

The underlying assumption that motivates security measures based on the notion of corporate's perimeter is that relying on host-based security only is not an effective strategy. If interaction between untrusted domains and application hosts are not mediated by any filtering component, then *all* application servers are exposed to the whole range of security threats, either based on application related features or network accesses. Securing and hardening all application servers to be resistant to direct Internet attacks has been proven to be extremely hard, too complex and expensive to maintain for representing a general solution. Here comes perimetral defense that uncouples possibly hostile environments from data or resources to be protected and inspects interaction either at network or application level.

Firewalls are the main and most popular perimeter protection systems. A firewall is a system or a group of systems that enforces an access control policy on network traffic as it passes through access points [4].

Firewalls are typically classified into three main classes: *static packet filtering*, *stateful firewalls*, and *proxies*.

3. Semantics-aware perimeter protection

Traversing firewalls is more a management than a technological problem, since every firewall technology lets system administrators make the screening provided by firewalls completely transparent at will, with respect to every communication protocol. In other words, every remote method invocation protocol could traverse firewalls provided that system administrators configure the perimetral policy accordingly. Unfortunately, many applications and protocols have been proven to be highly insecure or simply too complex to be effectively secured. This situation has brought most system administrators to prevent some application-level traffic from flowing through perimeter defences. From the network security's viewpoint the fact that traversing firewalls is usually severely restricted should be regarded as an useful feature and the right attitude of a savvy administrator rather than a problem. ¿From the standpoint of application service providers, vendors or developers of Internet application services and corporate managers willing to exploit the business possibilities of the Internet, the constraints imposed by firewalls impair full exploitation of business opportunities. While one might be tempted to remove this impairment by entirely leaving application security to service-level access control policies, this choice is likely to prove unwise in the long run. Indeed, an inherent danger of the widespread adoption of Web services would be neglecting the value of perimeter protection by assuming that Internet applications and users will attempt to directly interact with Web services, with no intermediate screening and active monitoring. This would make the services' interfaces open to exposure: if compromised (and all components direcly exposed to Internet connections should be considered at high risk), application policies might be subverted and critical assets, databases and systems, might be put to risk.[2]

[2]Also, lowering the importance of perimetral defences policy would leave definition and management of corporate security to application managers alone, another choice that may prove organizationally unwise.

3.1. The firewall traversal problem

The SOAP protocol lets interactive application traffic to be tunnelled through regular HTTP communications, which makes the usual association between service and application port for TCP and UDP communications no longer descriptive of the type of service carried out by a certain flow of packets (i.e. all SOAP-based services appear directed to servers responding at port 80, the conventional HTTP daemon). The net effect of this use of HTTP as a general-purpose application protocol for distributed computing is that conventional firewalls, screening network traffic mostly at level 2 and 3 of the TCP/IP stack, are no longer able to efficiently filter out packets. Firewalling SOAP network traffic needs content-based inspection capabilities and detailed knowledge of Web services and their semantics.

With SOAP, there is no longer a straight separation between the perimetral and the service level with respect to data used for enforcing security policies. Both must use same data, either in the SOAP header or body, and with similar enforcing mechanisms. This makes perimetral and service levels more strictly coupled than in the past and calls for a new comprehensive and integrated approach to corporate security by developing systems that allow managing a uniform corporate security policy and permit to enforce it at both the perimeter and the service level.

3.2. Using SOAP headers for perimeter protection policies

SOAP headers, used to hold metadata associated with the requestor, have already been used to carry security credentials. A first proposal exploiting SOAP's headers for enforcing access control was presented by Damiani et al. [7]. The authors represented all the information characterizing the subject of a request by means of a custom header included in each SOAP call. This usage of SOAP's headers has then gained acceptance and has been adopted in popular frameworks like the Microsoft WS-Security specification [1], which proposes a set of SOAP extensions that can be used to implement integrity and confidentiality in Web services.

Both [1] and [7] are based on the assumption that a requestor of a service declares the possession of some personal credentials to the server providing the requested Web services, which, in turn, authenticate the requestor and provide the permissions corresponding to a defined security policy. This design choice is coherent with the overall design principle of SOAP interactions and security model, where requestor credentials, stored in the *Header* part, are firstly used to prune an access control policy, and then each service request is matched at run-time against the set of permissions available for the given requestor. However, it does not match two basic requirements of a perimeter protection policy, namely:

- *Filter Granularity.* There exists a trade-off between communication performances and complexity of filtering techniques. Filtering operations at the corporate's perimeter should generally be coarse-grained and not requiring complex parsing activity;
- *Organization-wide Policy Management.* There exists a clear separation of duties between corporate system administrators and application administrators with respect to the definition and management of access control policies. Attributes to be matched against a perimeter protection policy should be corporate-wide and specify application classes instead of being related to single services and single requestors.

3.3. Performance and manageability requirements

¿From the performance point of view, SOAP-based screening at corporate borders could become a severe communication bottle-neck. A list of requirements that should be taken into account when dealing with performance issues follows:

- simplicity of screening mechanisms (e.g. string pattern matching or simple regular expression matching), with the option of making them more complex and refined only at will;
- heavy usage of cryptographic mechanisms could easily become the dominating factor of processor workloads with consequent degradation of routing capabilities of network traffic;
- complex parsing techniques of the SOAP Body and network latency due to communication with third-parties like Security Token Services, Authorization engines or Certification Authorities are possibly sources of severe degradation of performance and routing capabilities;
- in real-world situations, communication efficiency is one of the most critical assets for business and, in practice, always takes the precedence over security. Security measures that may cause network degradation, are likely to be simply ignored.

As far as manageability is concerned, some functional requirements may be identified. Namely, firewall rules' evaluation should exploit:

- Grouping of requestors by common properties like affiliation and business role;

- Classifications of Web service interfaces in a descriptive structure based on the functions they offfer or on their location.

This way, a perimeter protection component could firstly parse some requestor's general properties, like the organization, the business role or network parameters, which are not application-specific. This lets a network or security administrator to fully define the perimetral policy with a little knowledge of application details and manage it in a (semi)independend fashion with respect to most modifications that application managers will make.

Then, the Web services requested, or the functional class of services to which the one requested belongs to, should be taken into account. Using a superset of the actual requested service, according to a classification to be specified, may help in terms of ease of both definition of the policy by the security administrator (i.e. he/she does not need to know the actual service names and meanings) and management (i.e. the administration task is (semi)independent from changes in service names or creations).

We shall develop on this descrition in the next section.

4. Design and implementation guidelines

4.1. Model

The solution proposed here is based on the results of the work by Damiani et al. [7] that presents a solution for an *Authorization Filter* for SOAP messages. Our architecture of the semantic-aware perimeter protection component has three main logical parts: a set of filtering rules representing the security policy and a mechanism to enforce it; a classification of requestors based either on groups or roles; and a functional classification of Web services.

The data structure that maintains the rules is stored persistently in XML and it offers an interface that permits to get a decision about allowing or dropping a SOAP message. It also provides other administration interfaces, for modifying the rules and for synchronizing the requestors and Web services classifications according to a common ontology that should be corporate-wide shared, between semantic-aware perimeter level filters and service level authorization filters.

Requestors Classification. Requestors, as said, should be grouped ac-

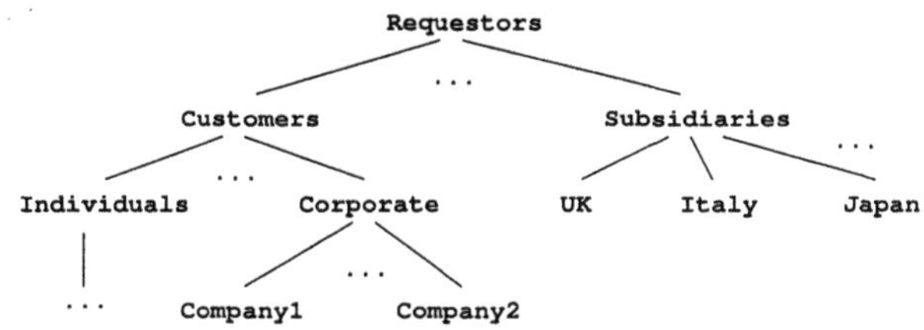

Figure 1. An example of requestor/organizational role classification

cording to some general and application-independent properties, based on business roles, affliations, etc. Figure 1 shows an example of requestor classification based on their organizational roles, such as *Customers* or *Subsidiaries*, *Individual* customers or *Corporate* customers and so on. Requestors classification represents the *subject* part of our authorization rules. Intuitively, more general groups (e.g. *Customers*) can be used for specifying broader rules (e.g. within an Internet banking context, "all customers could enjoy some services from the financial department"). More specific groups (e.g. *Company1*), instead, could be used for finer rules (e.g. "Company1 subscribed a trading on-line option, so Company1's requestors could enjoy the trading services of the financial department"). Individual requestors not falling in any group are treated as singleton groups.

Web services Classification. Web services, according to our proposal, should be classified into functional homogeneous categories and these categories, instead of single services, are used as authorization *objects*. This way, perimeter access control performs a filtering that is (semi)independent from specific services and based on corporate-wide criteria. In the example just mentioned describing the requestors classification (i.e. "Company1 subscribed a trading on-line option, so Company1's requestors could enjoy the trading services of the financial department"), we are ruling the access to a family of services called *Trading*, possibly grouping many actual services, like *PurchaseStock* and *ShowQuote*. Figure 2 gives an example of this Web services functional categorization.

4.2. Authorization syntax and semantics

Figure 3 presents the structure of authorization rules proposed by our model. Each rule is characterized by five attributes:

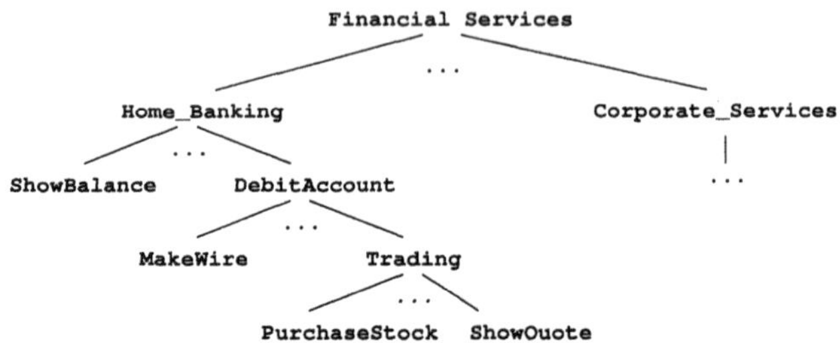

Figure 2. An example of service/functional category classification

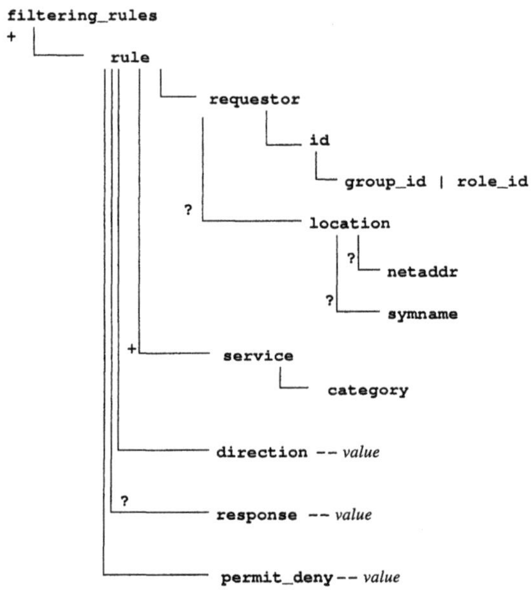

Figure 3. Filtering Rules structure

- *requestor*, the subject part of the rule, is a singleton (*id*) or a pair (*id*, *location*), where *id* could be a group or a role defined within a requestor classification, and *location* could be a range of IP addresses or a symbolic name. For convenience, the value *ANY* should be specified when each requestor's *id* must be matched;

- *service*, the object part of the rule, takes values from the Web services classification. For convenience, the value *ANY* should be specified when each service must be matched;

- *direction* has the value *IN* for rules applied to incoming messages and the value *OUT* for rules applied to outgoing messages. Incoming SOAP messages could be requests from an external requestor towards an internal, protected Web service, or responses of an external Web service to an internal requestor, the opposite holds for outgoing messages. If the rule must be applied in both directions, for convenience the value *BOTH* can be set;

- *response* takes the value *YES* when the rule applies to a SOAP response only; it takes the value *NO* when the rule applies to a SOAP request only; and it is left undeclared when the rule does not depend on this information;

- *permit_deny* has the value *PERMIT* for positive authorization and value *DENY* for negative authorization. A positive authorization states that, for requestors described by *requestor*, the categories to which the requested services specified in the SOAP Body belongs to, described by *service*, are available and the message can pass through. A negative authorization, instead, states that *requestor* is not authorized to require any Web service belonging to *service*, then the SOAP message must be dropped.

4.3. Example of semantic-aware firewalling

Following the classification examples of Figure 1 and Figure 2, Table 1 presents an example of semantic-aware firewalling. The policy we want to enforce is: *All customers have a home banking account providing for some basic services like the account balance. Debit operations and on-line trading need specific banking accounts. Only Company1 has an on-line trading subscription for its personnel connecting from subnet 140.121.5.* For this example, we assume that the message exchange pattern is in the *request/response* form. Accordingly, the policy defined in Table 1 is composed by the following rules, to be evaluated sequentially from Rule 1 to Rule 6:

Rule 1 specifies that incoming SOAP requests (`direction value = "IN"`; `response value = "NO"`) from personnel of Company1 (`group_id Company1`), or sub-groups of, connecting from subnet 140.121.5 (`netaddr 140.121.5.*`), and requested services of the Trading category (`category Trading`), or super-sets of, are permitted to pass through (`permit_deny value = "PERMIT"`).

Rule 2 specifies that outgoing responses (`direction value = "OUT"`; `response value = "YES"`) to incoming requests ruled by Rule 1 are permitted.

Table 1. Example of semantic-aware perimeter protection policy for some home banking services

1	<requestor> <id> <group_id> Company1 < /group_id> < /id> <location> <netaddr> 140.121.5.* < /netaddr> < /location> < /requestor> <service> <category> Trading < /category> < /service> <direction value = "IN" /> <response value = "NO" /> <permit_deny value = "PERMIT" />
2	<requestor> <id> <group_id> Company1 < /group_id> < /id> <location> <netaddr> 140.121.5.* < /netaddr> < /location> < /requestor> <service> <category> Trading < /category> < /service> <direction value = "OUT" /> <response value = "YES" /> <permit_deny value = "PERMIT" />
3	<requestor> <id> <group_id> Customers < /group_id> < /id> < /requestor> <service> <category> DebitAccount < /category> < /service> <direction value = "ANY" /> <permit_deny value = "DENY" />
4	<requestor> <id> <group_id> Customers < /group_id> < /id> < /requestor> <service> <category> Home_Banking < /category> < /service> <direction value = "IN" /> <response value = "NO" /> <permit_deny value = "PERMIT" />
5	<requestor> <id> <group_id> Customers < /group_id> < /id> < /requestor> <service> <category> Home_Banking < /category> < /service> <direction value = "OUT" /> <response value = "YES" /> <permit_deny value = "PERMIT" />
6	<requestor> ANY < /requestor> <service> ANY < /service> <direction value = "BOTH" /> <permit_deny value = "DENY" />

Rule 3 says that generic Customers, or super-groups of, cannot access services in the DebitAccount category or sub-sets of. Both requests or responses, either incoming or outgoing (`direction value = "ANY"`), are denied and hence dropped (`permit_deny value = "DENY"`).

Rule 4 says that incoming requests from generic Customers or sub-groups of, requesting services of the Home_Banking category, or super-sets of, are permitted to pass through;

Rule 5 specifies that outgoing responses to incoming requests ruled by Rule 4 are permitted.

Rule 6 is a *default rule* stating that if any of the previous does not applies, then we want to drop the messages.

5. Conclusion and Future Work

In this paper we gave a functional description of a semantics-aware firewall, a perimeter protection component matching a requestor's general properties and the functional class of requested Web services against a locally stored access control list.

The benefits of our approach are several

- the solution is scalable by designing filtering rules of increasing complexity (i.e. simpler and faster controls for direct Internet traffic for a first layer of filtering, possibly followed by more detailed controls for messages already screened);
- the solution can be customized according to the needs of specific businesses;
- untrusted requestors do not interact in an unfiltered fashion with Web services, which are highly critical components;

Moreover, the perimeter protection solution described can be smoothly integrated with the solution for fine-grained access control for SOAP Web services developed in [7] by some of the authors, composing this way an overall comprehensive approach to SOAP Web services security issues.

However, the solution proposed is not complete and many issues are still open. Other more complex message exchange patterns should be considered. Considering filtering techniques, we plan to extend our proposal to *stateful* semantic-aware firewalls by correlating messages exchanged according to HTTP and SOAP protocol semantics. Another important issue for our work is the full integration between this semantic-aware perimeter level and the fine-grained access control level, and the development of solutions for coordinating the two levels of security policies.

References

[1] Atkinson, B. and et al. Web services security (ws-security), April 2002. http://msdn.microsoft.com/ws/2002/04/Security.

[2] Box, D. and et al. *Simple Object Access Protocol (SOAP) 1.1.* World Wide Web Consortium (W3C), May 2000. http://www.w3.org/TR/SOAP.

[3] Bray, T.,Paoli, J., Sperberg-McQueen, C.M., and Maler, E. *Extensible Markup Language (XML) 1.0 (Second Edition).* World Wide Web Consortium (W3C), October 2000. http://www.w3.org/TR/REC-xml.

[4] Brenton, C. and Hunt, C. *Active Defense: A Comprehensive guide to network security.* Sybex, 2001.

[5] Damiani, E., De Capitani di Vimercati, S., Paraboschi, S. and Samarati, P. Controlling access to XML documents. *IEEE Internet Computing*, 5(6):18–28, November/December 2001.

[6] Damiani, E., De Capitani di Vimercati, S., Paraboschi, S. and Samarati, P. A fine-grained access control system for XML documents. *ACM Transactions on Information and System Security*, 5(2):169–202, May 2002.

[7] Damiani, E., De Capitani di Vimercati, S., Paraboschi, S. and Samarati, P. Securing SOAP e-services. *International Journal of Information Security (IJIS)*, 1(2):100–115, February 2002.

[8] Damiani, E., De Capitani di Vimercati and Samarati, P. Towards Securing XML Web Services. In *Proc. of the 2002 ACM Workshop on XML Security*, Washington, DC, USA, November 2002.

[9] Gettys, J., Mogul, J., Frystyk, H., Masinter, L., Leach, P. and Berners-Lee, T. Hypertext Transfer Protocol – HTTP/1.1, June 1999. http://www.ietf.org/rfc/rfc2616.txt.

[10] Graham, S. and et. al. *Building Web Services with Java: Making Sense of XML, SOAP, WSDL, and UDDI.* Sams Publishing, 2002.

[11] Kudo, M.and Hada, S. XML Document Security and e-Business applications. In *Proc. of the 7th ACM Conference on Computer and Communication Security*, Athens, Greece, November 2000.

[12] Mitra, N. *SOAP Version 1.2 Part 0: Primer.* World Wide Web Consortium (W3C), May 2002. http://www.w3.org/TR/soap12-part0/.

SYSTEMATIC DEVELOPMENT OF A FAMILY OF FAIR EXCHANGE PROTOCOLS

Paul D Ezhilchelvan and Santosh K Shrivastava
University of Newcastle, Newcastle upon Tyne, NE1 7RU, UK

Abstract: Exchange protocols play an important role in application areas such as e-commerce where protocol participants require mutual guarantees that a transaction involving exchange of items has taken place in a specific manner. A protocol is fair if no protocol participant can gain any advantage over an honest participant by misbehaving. This paper presents a family of fair exchange protocols for two participants under a variety of assumptions concerning participant misbehaviour, node reliability and message delays.

Keywords: Fair Exchange, Security, Digital Signatures, Crash tolerance, Distributed Systems, Trusted Third Party.

1. INTRODUCTION

Fair exchange protocols play an important role in application areas where protocol participants require mutual guarantees that an exchange of data items has taken place in a specific manner. An exchange is fair if a dishonest participant cannot gain any advantage over honest participants by misbehaving. Two-participant fair-exchange protocols that make use of a trusted third party have been studied extensively in the literature (e.g., [1, 5, 11]); these protocols maintain fairness even if the dishonest participant can tamper with the protocol execution in an unrestricted (malicious) manner. They however require that an honest participant's node execute the protocol correctly – suffering no failures. We call them non-fault-tolerant. A crash-tolerant fair exchange protocol, on the other hand, ensures no loss of fairness to an honest participant even if the participant's node crashes during the execution, provided it eventually recovers [4].

In this paper we develop a number of fair exchange protocols under a variety of assumptions concerning i) user misbehaviour, ii) node failures and iii) communication delays. The development is systematic: we begin by classifying dishonest participants into *restricted abusers* (they cannot tamper with the protocol execution in an arbitrary manner) and unrestricted or *malicious abusers*, and the communication model into *synchronous*, where a known bound on message delays exists, and *asynchronous*; we develop the first protocol under the most constrained set of assumptions: restricted abuser, synchronous communication and no fault tolerance. We then relax the restricted abuser assumption to malicious abuser and then the synchrony assumption into asynchrony. The resulting family of non-fault-tolerant protocols is then transformed into a family of crash-tolerant ones.

A major advantage of our approach is that it enables a reader to gain a deeper understanding of the impact of a given set of assumptions on the problem of fair exchange; it also highlights the relationships that exist between fairness, fault tolerance and communication delay assumptions. We first describe the problem and the underlying system models (section 2), and then develop a family of non-fault-tolerant protocols (section 3), followed by their crash-tolerant counterparts (section 4). Section 5 summarises the characteristics of the protocols developed and concludes the paper.

2. SYSTEM MODELS AND THE PROBLEM DESCRIPTION

We consider two mutually untrusting users, U_A and U_B, who have data items I_A and I_B respectively that are unknown to the other user prior to the exchange. User U_x, $X \in \{A, B\}$, intends to send I_x in return for receiving I_Y, where $Y \in \{A, B\}$ and $Y \neq X$. P_x denotes the process that executes an exchange protocol on behalf of user U_x on his node N_x.

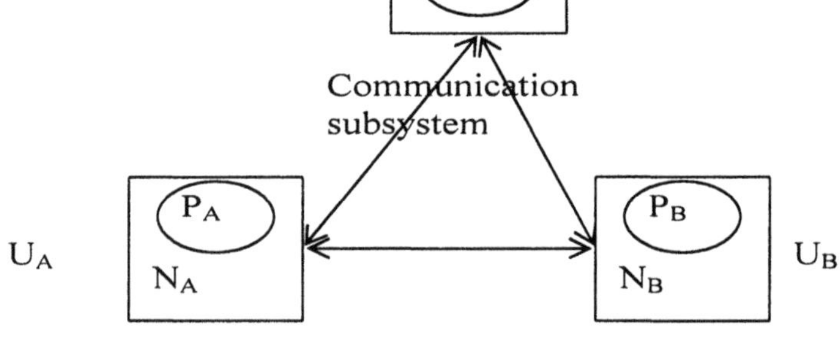

Figure 1. The Fair-Exchange System.

Our distributed exchange system (Figure 1) has a third node hosting the trusted third party (TTP) process. The exchange must preserve fairness as well as *non-repudiation*: a user gets irrefutable evidence of the actions performed by his process (to guard against the other user's false denial of the occurrence of an action or event).

2.1. Classifying User Misbehaviour

Generally, the problem of fair exchange is addressed in a context where a dishonest user, say U_B, *totally controls* the behaviour of P_B and tries to undermine every attempt to ensure fairness and non-repudiation. We term those dishonest users as *malicious abusers* and distinguish such users from a class of *restricted abusers*: a dishonest user is said to be a restricted abuser if he is unable to obtain the values of variables or procedures contained in a piece of (binary) code which his local process receives from the TTP and uses during protocol execution. Say, user U_B is a restricted abuser and the TTP gives P_B a piece of code Π_B that contains, say, some secret encryption keys. By our definition, U_B cannot obtain the keys in Π_B by visual inspection or through a trace analysis even after P_B has executed U_B. The definition does not however restrict the ability of U_B to delay, block, inspect, or tamper with any message which an execution of Π_B generates or is destined to receive.

One way to realise our notion of a restricted abuser is to have each P_X receive the TTP code Π_X via a secure channel and execute it in a tamper-proof part of the user node. We note here that there is much interest in developing tamper-proof computing subsystems by the industry led Trusted Computing Platform Alliance, TCPA [8]. Further, smartcards can be used to achieve such tamper-proof, computing subsystems for small, critical computations [2, 10]. Thus, developing fair-exchange protocols under the restricted abuser model is of practical interest, and also exposes the benefits that the model has to offer.

2.2. Classifying Node Behaviour

A fair-exchange protocol is fault-tolerant if it ensures that fairness is preserved to an honest participant despite the participant's node suffers failures of the assumed type. In other words, an honest user does not suffer loss of fairness when his node is unreliable. We consider two types of node behaviour:

Reliable: An honest user's node never fails.

Crash-recovery: An honest user's node fails by stopping to function (crash); it recovers within some finite (but unknown) time after a crash and may crash again after its recovery. An honest user's node has access to a stable store whose contents survive the node crash.

When a user node is regarded to be reliable, the cause of any node crash is attributed to the user who has misbehaved and is therefore not entitled to any fairness guarantee. This is the traditional view taken in the TTP-based protocols (e.g., [1, 5, 11]) which are therefore not fault-tolerant (see [4]). In line with the existing, non-fault-tolerant protocols, the TTP is assumed to be *reliable* and *secure* against intrusions and Trojan horses.

2.3. Classifying Communication Delays

Communication between correctly functioning processes is assumed to be resilient to network failures: a message loss is tolerated by retransmission and a message corruption is detected using encryption and reduced to a message loss. A network intruder is therefore assumed to be a restricted abuser: a message in transit is a black box to him; he cannot modify it and have it undetected at the destination. He can only delay a message from being accepted at a destination. We consider two types of network intrusion: intruder gives up delaying a given message transmission after a known period of time or after some unknown finite time, leading to two models: in the *synchronous* model, correct processes exchange messages with delays bounded by a known D; in the *asynchronous* model, D is finite but unknown.

2.4. Properties of a fair exchange Protocol

A user is *honest* if he makes no attempt to modify the behaviour of a protocol process except through the permitted operations.

Termination: Any execution of the protocol terminates for an honest user U_X. Termination for an honest U_X can be either a *normal* termination in which P_X delivers I_Y to U_X or an *exceptional* termination where P_X informs U_X that the exchange is unsuccessful.

No_Loss_Of_Fairness: If P_X of honest U_X terminates exceptionally, U_Y does not receive I_X.

Non-repudiation: when P_X delivers I_Y to honest U_X, it also provides irrefutable evidence against any false denial on I_Y having been sent by U_Y.

The above properties are met trivially if P_A and P_B terminate always exceptionally.

Non-Triviality: If U_A and U_B are honest, both are guaranteed to have normal termination.

Non-triviality is easy to guarantee for the synchronous, non-fault-tolerant case. When the fair-exchange protocol is deterministic (not probabilistic) in nature, honesty of both the users alone is not sufficient to guarantee non-triviality for the case of crash-recovery nodes and synchronous communication, as well for the case of asynchronous communication. The reasons for this inability are as follows. In crash-recovery model, the bound on the time taken by an honest user node to recover from a crash is unknown and a dishonest user may never allow his node to recover. So, a correctly functioning process (of an honest user or the TTP) that is waiting too long for a message from a user process cannot resolve whether the latter is honest and its message is unduly delayed due to a crash or is dishonest and is not going to transmit the expected message; similarly, in the asynchronous model, it cannot resolve whether the user process from whom a message is expected is honest and its message is still in transit or is dishonest and the message will not be transmitted at all. (Readers familiar with the FLP impossibility result [3] may find these arguments remarkably similar.) Therefore, meeting the termination property would mean that an execution of the protocol may have to terminate exceptionally even if both users are honest. Therefore, the necessary condition for ensuring non-triviality is that the honest users be willing to re-execute the protocol after every exceptional termination; the sufficient condition differs with the combination of assumptions and is stated below: there must be an execution in which

(i) user nodes do not crash, for the case of crash-recovery nodes and synchronous communication;

(ii) message delays do not increase, for the case of reliable nodes and asynchronous communication; and,

(i) and (ii), for the case of crash-recovery nodes and asynchronous communication.

2.5. Assumptions, Notations and the Exchange Preliminaries

In all our protocols, the TTP, assumed to be secure and reliable, is used to set-up the context for, and to initiate, the actual exchange. We make the following additional assumptions.

A1: Processing within correctly functioning nodes is synchronous: delays for task scheduling and processing are bounded by a known constant.

A2: The clocks of the TTP and the functioning nodes of honest users are synchronised to real-time within a known bound which, for simplicity, is assumed to be zero. A recovering node receives the current time from its user.

Notations

M: a message;

V_A (V_B): procedure to verify if I_A (I_B) satisfies its description Σ_A (Σ_B) advertised by U_A (U_B).

eK(M): encryption of M using key K;

$Sig_X(M)$: signature of P_X, $X \in \{A, B\}$, on M using the private key of U_X;

$Sig_{TTP}(M)$: TTP's signature on M. Signatures are both signer- and content-dependent, and are verifiable using the signer's public key.

L: a label that identifies a given exchange;

N: a large random number (*nonce*) generated securely by TTP to uniquely identify messages of a given execution of the protocol for a given exchange; and,

H: one-way and collision-resistant hash function: it is not feasible to compute from H(N), N nor another N' such that H(N) = H(N').

Π_x: contents of a message sent by the TTP to P_x to initate the exchange phase.

When a party $Z \in \{A, B, TTP\}$ sends a message M it also includes $Sig_Z(M)$ as the evidence of origin for M. A recipient accepts a received M only if the accompanying $Sig_Z(M)$ is found authentic. For brevity, we will not make the details of this verification explicit and a received message will only refer to a message received with an authentic evidence of origin; further the pair $\{M, Sig_Z(M)\}$ will simply be written as M which will be indicated by its significant fields.

Exchange Preliminaries

All our protocols are structured into two phases: the *start-up* phase followed by the *exchange phase* when the actual exchange of promised data items takes place. During the start-up phase, the following three steps are carried out:

Step 0.1: Each U_X approaches a trusted authority TA_X to generate a verification procedure V_X using which any party can verify if a data item I satisfies specification Σ_X. For example, if I_B is a piece of software S, U_B must approach a software licensing authority (trusted by U_A) who evaluates S against the specification Σ_B that U_B advertised. If satisfied, the authority computes an evidence of evaluation E_B = H(S); V_B is then generated as a program which contains E_B and evaluates the predicate E_B = H(I) when invoked to verify a data item I. Using the conventional notations, the step is:

$U_A \rightarrow TA_A$: (I_A, Σ_A);	$U_B \rightarrow TA_B$: (I_B, Σ_B);
$TA_A \rightarrow U_A$:{V_A, Σ_A, Sig_{TA_A}(V_A, Σ_A)};	$TA_B \rightarrow U_B$:{V_B, Σ_B, Sig_{TA_B}(V_B, Σ_B)};

Step 0.2: Users exchange their $\{V, \Sigma, Sig_{TA}(V, \Sigma)\}$, decide on the TTP and on a (future) time T_{EX} when the TTP should initiate the exchange phase.

Step 0.3: $U_A \rightarrow$ TTP: $(A, B, T_{EX}, \{V_A, \Sigma_A\}, \{V_B, \Sigma_B\}, rtt_{AB})$: similarly, $U_B \rightarrow$ TTP: $(A, B, T_{EX}, \{V_A, \Sigma_A\}, \{V_B, \Sigma_B\}, rtt_{BA})$. The last field rtt_{XY} is U_X's estimation of the round trip time between its node and N_Y.

Upon receiving messages sent in step 0.3, the TTP verifies whether all fields except the last one are identical. If so, the TTP decides on a unique L for the exchange if the exchange is new; generates a nonce N for the exchange phase and records N in a variable *active_run#*(L)= N. If the exchange is not new, it only generates a new nonce and records it in *active_run#*(L). It then sends Π_B to N_A and Π_B to N_B which include the parameters L and H(N) which are used to identify messages of a given execution. The nature and the complete contents of Π's sent by TTP depend on the exchange phase of the protocol for a chosen combination of various assumptions discussed earlier.

TTP Involvement

A protocol is said to keep TTP *offline* if it is possible for honest user processes to achieve normal termination without interacting with TTP after the exchange phase is initiated. Such a protocol is also called *optimistic* in the literature. If TTP is not off-line, it is said to be *on-line.*

A protocol is said to use a *state-keeping* TTP if it requires the TTP to respond to messages from user processes for an unspecified amount of time; the protocol is said to use a *state-relinquishing* TTP if it requires the TTP only for a specified duration after the exchange phase has been initiated. From cost point of view, TTP is preferred to be offline and state-relinquishing.

3. NON-FAULT-TOLERANT FAIR EXCHANGE PROTOCOLS

3.1. Restricted Abuser, Synchronous Communication (Protocol P1)

The TTP sends a code Π_A to P_A and Π_B to P_B. P_A and P_B perform the exchange phase of the protocol P1 by executing the code given to them. Embedded in Π_X are L, H(N), V_X, Δ, and keys K_A and K_B, each with TTP's evidence of origin. Δ is set to D (the known bound on message delays), K_A and K_B are symmetric and random session keys. When a dishonest U_X is only a restricted abuser, he cannot obtain K_A and K_B from Π_X nor undetectably modify V_X embedded within Π_X. However, U_X can delay, block, inspect, or tamper with any message P_X generates or is destined to receive while it executes Π_X.

On executing Π_A, P_A first verifies whether I_A (input by U_A) passes V_A embedded within Π_A. Only if I_A passes the verification, P_A continues the execution: it encrypts the verified I_A using K_A, forms a message M_A and encrypts M_A with K_B. The encrypted M_A, like all messages sent by P_A, contains a signature generated using the private key of U_A and is sent to P_B. (Any message without valid signature is ignored and hence assumed not 'received' by a destination.) P_B decrypts the received M_A, and if the contents are correct, it sends an acknowledgement $Ack_B(A)$ to P_A. P_B similarly sends M_B to, and expects to receive $Ack_A(B)$ from, P_A. The message exchange between P_A and P_B are depicted in Figure 2, where a process sending a message shown along an out-going arrow is conditional upon that process having received the messages shown along all incoming arrows. P_X, after receiving Π_X, starts executing both the rounds concurrently: send M_X and wait for $Ack_Y(X)$ while waiting for M_Y before $Ack_X(Y)$ can be sent; a timeout of 2Δ is used to avoid indefinite waiting.

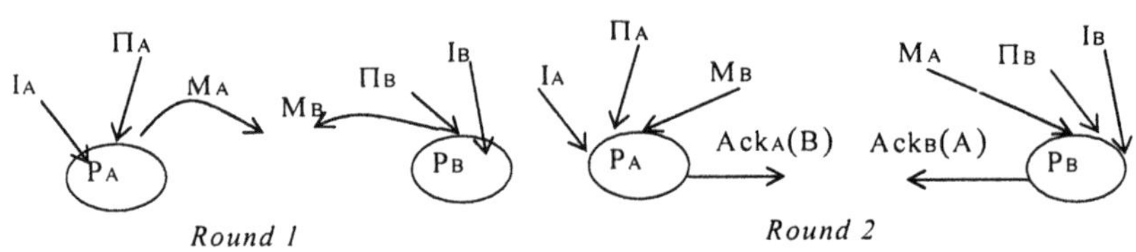

Figure 2. Protocol P1: Message exchange rounds between user processes.

Table 1 summarises the messages used and the intended direction of their flow. A message is indicated by its significant fields, the first three fields will be: the label L, the sender, and H(N). Note that the first and the third message fields uniquely refer to a given execution.

The condition on P_A (P_B) for computing I_B (I_A) from M_B (M_A) is: both M_B (M_A) and $Ack_B(A)$ ($Ack_A(B)$) must be received within 2Δ time after receiving Π_A (Π_B) from TTP. If P_A receives only M_B (within 2Δ time), it asks TTP to *resolve* the exchange by sending message Res_A that contains both M_A and the received M_B. If it receives neither M_B nor $Ack_B(A)$, it *requests* TTP to abort the exchange by sending message Req_A that contains only M_A. TTP, having initiated the exchange at its clock time T_{EX}, executes the following steps at $T_{EX} + 4\Delta$:

Step T1: if it has received Req from both processes or Res from at least one process, it sets variable *outcome* = *resolved* and resolves the exchange by sending $M_{TTP}(X)$ to both processes;

Step T2: if it has received Req from only one process, it sets *outcome* = *aborted* and aborts the exchange by sending $Abort_{TTP}(X)$ to both processes;

Step T3: if it has received no message, it sets variable *outcome* to *unknown*;

Step T4: it terminates (as a state-relinquishing TTP).

$\Phi_A = eK_A(I_A)$	$\Phi_B = eK_B(I_B)$
$M_A = eK_B(L, A, H(N), \Phi_A); A \rightarrow B$	$M_B = eK_A(L, B, H(N), \Phi_B); B \rightarrow A$
$Ack_A(B) = (L, A, H(N), H(M_B),$ *My_ack*); $A \rightarrow B$	$Ack_B(A) = (L, B, H(N), H(M_A),$ *My_ack*); $B \rightarrow A$
$Res_A = (L, A, H(N), M_A, M_B,$ *Resolve_request*); $A \rightarrow TTP$	$Res_B = (L, B, H(N), M_B, M_A,$ *Resolve_request*); $B \rightarrow TTP$
$Req_A = (L, A, H(N), M_A,$ *Abort_request*); $A \rightarrow TTP$	$Req_B = (L, B, H(N), M_B,$ *Abort_request*); $B \rightarrow TTP$
$M_{TTP}(A) = (L, TTP, H(N), M_B,$ *My_ack*); $TTP \rightarrow A$	$M_{TTP}(B) = (L, TTP, H(N), M_A,$ *My_ack*); $TTP \rightarrow B$
$Abort_{TTP}(A) = (L, TTP, H(N),$ *Abort_granted*, A); $TTP \rightarrow A$	$Abort_{TTP}(B) = (L, TTP, H(N),$ *Abort_granted*, B); $TTP \rightarrow B$

Table 1. Description of messages used in Protocol P1.

An honest P_A terminates normally by receiving either M_B and $Ack_B(A)$ or $M_{TTP}(A)$; exceptionally by receiving $Abort_{TTP}(A)$. The protocol keeps TTP off-line (step T3 above). The four properties of fair-exchange (Section 2.4) are met by P1 because: (i) dishonest user, say U_B, is a restricted abuser, so he cannot force P_B to deliver I_A against the protocol conditions nor can he obtain K_A and K_B from Π_B; (ii) an honest P_A sends $Ack_A(B)$ to P_B only if it receives M_B in a timely manner; (iii) any message that P_A sends to TTP reaches before $T_{EX}+4\Delta$; and, (iv) TTP's response, if any, is identical to both P_A and P_B.

3.2. Malicious Abuser, Synchronous Communication (P1.1)

1. P1.1 is the same as P1 except some messages of the exchange phase have different contents. This is because a dishonest user, say U_B, can obtain the keys K_A and K_B in the program Π_B supplied by TTP at the start of the exchange phase. The following changes are needed:

2. Π_A is a message containing all parameters as before except K_B: Π_A = (L, H(N), V_A, Δ, K_A); similarly, Π_B = (L, H(N), V_B, Δ, K_B). Further, TTP should not have used K_A and K_B before.
3. Π_A does not contain K_B means that P_A cannot encrypt M_A with K_B (see Table 1). Therefore M_A is (L, A, H(N), Φ_A) and M_B is (L, A, H(N), Φ_B).
4. P_A includes K_A in its $Ack_A(B)$ so that if P_B has both M_A and $Ack_A(B)$ it can terminate normally without having to contact TTP. So, $Ack_A(B)$ of Table 1 becomes (L, A, H(N), H(M_B), K_A) and $Ack_B(A)$ becomes (L, B, H(N), H(M_A), K_B).
5. Finally, $M_{TTP}(A)$ by which TTP instructs P_A to resolve the exchange, must contain K_B: $M_{TTP}(A)$ = (L, TTP, H(N), M_B, K_B). Also, $M_{TTP}(B)$ = (L, TTP, H(N), M_A, K_A).

Remark: *Dispute Resolution*: Non-repudiation guarantee ensures that when honest P_A terminates normally, it has evidence that P_B sent the item which P_A delivered to U_A. However, if U_B is dishonest, U_A might find I_B not passing the verification test V_B which it agreed with U_B in the start-up phase. Consider this scenario: malicious U_B obtains K_B from Π_B, generates M'_B with authentic evidence of origin but with $I'_B \neq I_B$, and transmits M'_B in place of M_B. Since Π_A does not contain K_B (see modification 1 above), P_A cannot check whether the I'_B in the received M'_B meets V_B at the end of the first round itself (see figure 2). Since M'_B is found to have authentic evidence of origin, it will send $Ack_A(B)$ that contains K_A, thus letting P_B terminate normally without ever contacting TTP. Only after being delivered of I'_B, U_A can find out that I'_B does not pass V_B and that U_B has been dishonest.

If U_B is a restricted abuser, the above scenario cannot arise: Π_B is tamper-proof relative to the abilities of U_B and therefore is can contain K_A using which P_B encrypts M_B in P1. Since U_B cannot obtain K_A, he cannot modify M_B to M'_B and make P_A accept M'_B. Thus, in P1, what U_A receives is guaranteed to be the expected one.

P1.1 only guarantees that P_A delivers to an honest U_A what a malicious U_B *actually* sent in exchange for I_A, not necessarily what U_B has pledged to send. The TTP can guarantee fairness to U_A in such a scenario, by contacting the trusted agent TA_B employed to generate V_B which U_A accepted. This corresponds to a weaker form of fairness enforcement in the hierarchy of [9]: fairness can only be guaranteed with the help of a trusted agent outside the fair-exchange system (figure 1) and without any cooperation from U_B. The issue of post-exchange dispute resolution is discussed and addressed in [6, 7] for malicious abusers. The protocols of [6, 7] make use of *inverse* and *compatible* keys to verify an encrypted item without decrypting it. Using these special types of encryption keys, P1.1 can also be modified to ensure that an honest user receives in a normal termination only the item he bargained for. The modification is simple and shown in [2]. It preserves the

2-round structure which is provably optimal [5]. The protocol of [6], like P1.1, keeps the TTP off-line but requires 4 rounds when both users are honest.

3.3. Restricted and Malicious Abusers, Asynchronous Communication (P1A and P1.1A)

Protocols P1 and P1.1 are not appropriate for the asynchronous model. This is not surprising as [5] shows that, in the non-fault-tolerant case, there cannot be an asynchronous protocol that works with a TTP that is off-line *and* state-relinquishing, and goes on to present a protocol with an off-line and state-keeping TTP. We here present protocols P1A and P1.1A with an on-line and state-relinquishing TTP, by deriving them from P1 and P1.1 respectively. The derivation is simple: in round 2 (see figure 2), P_X sends $Ack_X(Y)$ to TTP, not to P_Y; it then waits for either $M_{TTP}(X)$ or $Abort_{TTP}(X)$.

In the start-up phase, TTP should obtain round trip time (rtt) measurements with each P_X (as rtt_A and rtt_B) and estimate 2Δ = maximum$\{rtt_A, rtt_B, rtt_{AB}, rtt_{BA}\}$.

```
TTP:
  when (clock = T_EX) do {
    send Π_A to P_A; send Π_B to P_B; Set_of_M M_Bag_L = { };
    repeat {receive(M); deposit M in M_Bag_L;} until clock < T_EX+ 4Δ;
    if  (Ack_A(B)∈ M_Bag_L and Ack_B(A) ∈ M_Bag_L)
        then {send Ack_B(A) to P_A; send Ack_A(B) to P_B;} // resolved
        else {send Abort_TTP(A) to P_A; send Abort_TTP(B) to P_B;} } /* end do
```

Figure 3. Pseudo-code for TTP in protocols P1A and P1.1A.

If honest users re-execute the protocol for a given exchange after every exceptional termination, *non-triviality* is guaranteed if there exists an execution in which the message transfer delays between P_A, P_B and TTP do not exceed the Δ determined by TTP at the start of the exchange phase; i.e., if message transfer delays do not increase during an execution.

4. CRASH-TOLERANT PROTOCOLS

4.1. Restricted Abuser, Synchronous Communication (P2)

Two extensions are necessary for protocol P1 to be crash tolerant. *Pessimistic (synchronous) checkpointing*: P_X of an honest user logs every received message and check-points its state before the received message is processed. Thus, in fig. 2, an honest P_X must receive *and* log the messages of the incoming channels before it can send out a message. *State-keeping TTP*:

in step T4, the TTP does not terminate the execution, but continues to operate depending on the value of *outcome*: if *outcome* is *unknown*, the TTP executes steps T1 – T3 after a period of 4Δ time; otherwise, it responds to a message from P_X with $M_{TTP}(X)$ or $Abort_{TTP}(X)$, if *outcome* is *resolved* or *aborted* respectively. This modification permits a recovered P_X to terminate. Note that when TTP sets *outcome* to *resolved* or *aborted*, it is irreversible.

Impossibility of making P1 Crash-tolerant

Even with the use of pessimistic logging and state-keeping TTP, P1 cannot become crash-tolerant even if the dishonest user is a restricted abuser. Consider the following scenario. Let N_A crash during the second round shown in figure 2 and before P_A receives $Ack_B(A)$; that is, P_A has logged I_A, Π_A, sending of M_A, and M_B. Let dishonest U_B block all messages P_A sent to P_B but retains a copy of these incoming messages. P_B, having received no message from P_A within 2Δ time, will send Req_B for which TTP will respond by setting *outcome* = *aborted* and sending $Abort_{TTP}(B)$. Say U_B blocks $Abort_{TTP}(B)$ as well and crashes his node. The recovered P_A will find itself in having received only M_B and will send Res_A which, say, reaches TTP after *outcome* was set to *aborted*; TTP's response will be to send $Abort_{TTP}(A)$ to P_A. Let U_B re-boot N_B, delete Π_B from stable-store, and adjust the clock to make it appear as if the exchange phase is being executed for the first time. He replays the arrival of Π_B and of the blocked messages of P_A exactly at those instances when they arrived during the first execution. Since P_B 'receives' both M_A and $Ack_A(B)$, it delivers I_A to U_B.

Outline of Protocol P2

At the core of P1's inability to be crash tolerant is the fact that having both MA and $Ack_A(B)$ is a sufficient condition for P_B to deliver I_A without consulting TTP at all. To remedy this, we need to add one more round to protocol P1 which P_X executes after having executed the first two rounds (concurrently) and check-pointed its state. In the third round, shown in Figure 4, P_A sends a second acknowledgement $Ack^2{}_A(B)$ to P_B indicating the reception of $Ack_B(A)$ and M_B.

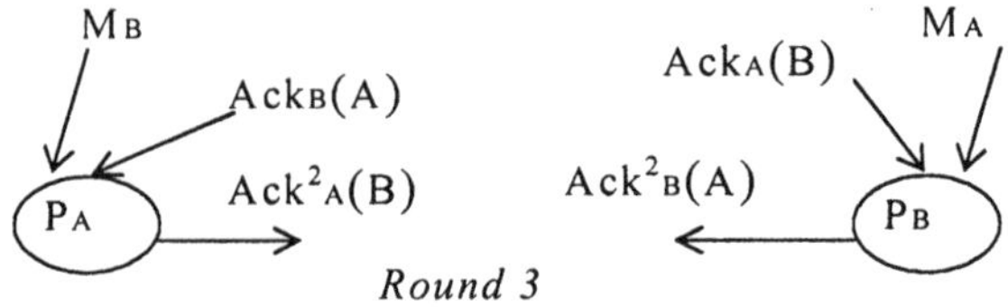

Figure 4. The additional message round in P2.

If P_A does not receive $Ack^2_B(A)$ within 2Δ time after it has sent $Ack^2_A(B)$, P_A appeals to TTP by sending $First\_Acks_A$ that contains both $Ack_A(B)$ and $Ack_B(A)$. TTP, after receiving $First\_Acks_A$, sends $Ack^2_{TTP}(A)$ to P_A only if it has not earlier received Req_A (which would have resulted in sending $Abort_{TTP}(B)$ to P_B). Thus, the condition for normal termination of P_A is: *received*($Ack^2_{ZA}(A)$), where $Z_A \in \{B, TTP\}$. By symmetry, the condition for normal termination of P_B is: *received*($Ack^2_{ZB}(B)$), where $Z_B \in \{A, TTP\}$. Three messages used in addition to those used in P1 are shown in Table 2.

$Ack^2_A(B)$=(L, A, H(N), $H(Ack_B(A))$, *My_ack²*); A→ B	$Ack^2_B(A)$=(L, B, H(N), $H(Ack_A(B))$, *My_ack²*); B → A
$First\_Acks_A$ = (L, A, H(N), $Ack_A(B)$, $Ack_B(A)$); A → TTP	$First\_Acks_B$ = (L, B, H(N), $Ack_B(A)$, $Ack_A(B)$); B → TTP
$Ack^2_{TTP}(A)$ = (L, TTP, H(N), $H(Ack_A(B))$, *My_ack²*); TTP → A	$Ack^2_{TTP}(B)$ = (L, TTP, H(N), $H(Ack_B(A))$, *My_ack²*); TTP → B

Table 2. Description of additional messages used in P2.

4.2. Malicious Abuser, Synchronous Communication (P2.1)

Protocol P2.1 is the same as P2, except that some of the messages used need to be changed:

1. Π_A, M_A, $M_{TTP}(A)$, Π_B, M_B, and $M_{TTP}(B)$ of Table 1 change as mentioned in Section 3.2. $Ack_A(B)$ and $Ack_B(A)$ remain exactly as shown in Table 1.
2. In Table 2, *My_ack* = K_B in $Ack^2_B(A)$ and in $Ack^2_{TTP}(A)$; similarly, *My_ack* = K_A in $Ack^2_A(B)$ and $Ack^2_{TTP}(B)$.

Remark: *Simple Extension to Asynchronous Communication model.* P2 and P2.1 work correctly in the asynchronous model if TTP computes Δ during the start-up phase as described for P1A and P1.1A.

4.3. Malicious and Restricted Abusers, Asynchronous Communication, on-line TTP (P2A and P2.1A)

These protocols are obtained by making P1A and P1.1A crash-tolerant by having process P_X pessimistically checkpoint its state (as in P2 and P2.1) before processing a received message and by making TTP state-keeping. The latter is done as follows: for any message received from P_X after $T_{EX} + 4\Delta$, TTP sends $Ack_Y(X)$ to P_X if both $Ack_A(B)$ and $Ack_B(A)$ have been received before $T_{EX} + 4\Delta$; otherwise it sends $Abort_{TTP}(X)$.

5. SUMMARY AND DISCUSSIONS

Table 3 summarises the protocols' characteristics using the following abbreviations:

- a dishonest user (DU) can be either a restricted abuser (RA) or a malicious abuser (MA),
- communication delay model (C) can be synchronous (S) or asynchronous (As),
- faults tolerated (FT) can be none (No) or crash (Cr), and
- the TTP can be either off-line (Off) or on-line (On), and either state-relinquishing (Sr) or state-keeping (Sk).

Protocol	**DU**	**C**	**FT**	**TTP**
P1	RA	S	No	Off/Sr
P1.1	MA	S	No	Off/Sr
P1A(P1.1A)	RA(MA)	As	No	On/Sr
P2	RA	S/As	Cr	Off/Sk
P2.1	MA	S/As	Cr	Off/Sk
P2A(P2.1A)	RA(MA)	As	Cr	On/Sk

Table 3. Characteristics of the Protocols Developed.

On-line TTP: state-relinquishing vs. state-keeping. Because of its simplicity, a non-fault-tolerant protocol with an on-line TTP is likely in practice, and a need may later arise to enhance the protocol to be crash-tolerant. Can an online-TTP protocol be made crash-tolerant simply through message logging, regardless of whether the delay model is synchronous or asynchronous? The answer depends on whether the non-fault-tolerant protocol keeps the TTP state-relinquishing or state-keeping. Our protocols P1A and P1.1A suggest that it is possible to design online-TTP protocols that keep the TTP state-relinquishing even with asynchronous delays. In making them crash-tolerant, we have to make the (on-line) TTP a state-keeping one (see P2A and P2.1A in Table 3). Thus, the answer to the above question is yes, provided the issue of state-relinquishing *vs.* state-keeping TTP is given due consideration.

Optimising the cost of message logging. The work by [4] proposes a logging-based approach to achieving crash-tolerant fair-exchange. It defines a point of no return for a user process, and claims that if the process would synchronously log all received messages before entering this point, then logging of other received messages can be done asynchronously. Their definition of point of no return suggests that there is only one such point for each process (Section 3.2 of [4]). We remark here that our protocol P2.1 without check-pointing and message logging is identical to the time-optimal protocol (scheme 3) of [5] which is asynchronous and non-fault-tolerant. Applying the approach of [4] to make this protocol crash-tolerant does *not* work: the point of no return for honest P_A turns out to be its sending M_A to P_B (see figure 2, round 1); suppose that N_A crashes in round 3 (see Fig. 4) after P_A has sent $Ack^2{}_A(B)$ but before $Ack_B(A)$ and M_B were to be logged by the asynchronous logging scheme; note that $Ack^2{}_A(B)$ contains K_A (see Section 4.2). Honest U_A suffers loss of fairness, even if U_B does not misbehave; to avoid loss of fairness, P_A must also log all received messages before sending $Ack^2{}_A(B)$. It appears that some protocols can have *multiple points* at which pessimistic logging is essential. Given that the number of messages received by a user process in a given execution is small, attempts to minimise the overhead of logging may not be worth the effort after all; further, every message received (and logged) may be useful later in any dispute resolution.

Acknowledgements

This work is funded by the UK EPSRC grant GR/N35953/01 (Information Co-ordination and Sharing in Virtual Enterprises) and by the European Union Project IST-2001-34069 *TAPAS* (Trusted and QoS-Aware Provision of Application Services). Our thanks are due also to the anonymous reviewers of the 17th IFIP Conference on Database and Applications Security.

6. REFERENCES

[1] N. Asokan, M. Schunter and M. Waidner. Asynchronous protocols for optimistic fair exchange. *IEEE Symposium on Research in Security and Privacy*, pp. 86-99, 1998.

[2] P. Ezhilchelvan and S. Shrivastava. Systematic Development of a Family of Fair Exchange Protocols (Full Paper). *Technical Report CS-TR-820*, School of Computing Science, University of Newcastle. December 2003.

[3] M.J. Fischer, N.A. Lynch, and M.S. Paterson, "Impossibility of Distributed Consensus with one faulty Process," *Journal of the ACM*, Vol. 32, No. 2, pp. 374-382, April 1985.

[4] P. Liu, P. Ning and S. Jajodia. Avoiding Loss of Fairness Owing to Process Crashes in Fair Data Exchange Protocols. *Inernational Conference on Dependable Systems and Network*. pp. 631-40, June 2000.

[5] B. Pfitzmann, M. Schunter and M. Waidner. *Optimal Efficiency of Optimistic Contract Signing*. Proc. *ACM Symp. on Principles of Distributed Computing*. New York, 1998.

[6] I. Ray and I. Ray. An Optimistic Fair Exchange E-commerce Protocol with Automated Dispute Resolution. *EC-Web* 2000, pp. 84-93.

[7] I. Ray, I. Ray, N. Narasimhamurthy: A Fair-exchange E-commerce Protocol with Automated Dispute Resolution. DBSec 2000, pp. 27-38.

[8] Trusted Computing Platform Alliance, http://www.trustedpc.org.

[9] H. Vogt, H. Pagnia, and F. C. Gartner. Modular fair exchange protocols for electronic commerce. *15th Annual Computer Security Applications Conference*, pp. 3-11, Dec. 1999.

[10] H. Vogt, H. Pagnia, and F. C. Gartner. Using Smart cards for Fair-Exchange. *WELCOM 2001*, LNCS 2232, Springer, pp. 101-113, 2001.

[11] J. Zhou and D. Gollmann. Evidence and non-repudiation. *Journal of Network and Computer Applications*, 20(3):267-281, July 1997.

VI

ACCESS CONTROL MODELS AND TECHNOLOGIES

HIGH-SPEED ACCESS CONTROL FOR XML DOCUMENTS

A Bitmap-based Approach

Jong P. Yoon

Center for Advanced Computer Studies, University of Louisiana, Lafayette, LA 70504-4330

Abstract: One of the important tasks of managing eXtensible Markup Language (XML) documents is to uniformly specify and securely maintain both target documents and authorization policies. However, since existing techniques decouple access authorization from query processing, the query processing time with access control is not satisfactorily fast. The access control requires the overhead in addition to the time required for query processing, and the powerful expression of authorization policies makes it impossible to accelerate the determination of access authorization. In this paper, we propose a bitmap-based access authorization technique for both fast and secure services of XML documents. The authorization policies are encoded into a bitmap index and further to be coupled an index of XML documents. User access requests are encoded into bitmap-masks. By applying bit-wise operations of a bitmap-mask to the authorization bitmap index, authorization can be determined significantly fast. The contribution of this paper includes 1) the dual goals achieved for fast and secure accesses to XML document collections, and 2) early propagation of subjects and objects in bitmap indexes.

Key words: High-speed access control, High-speed query processing, Bitmap-based Approach

1. INTRODUCTION

The eXtensible Markup Language (XML) is a de facto W3C standard for representing and exchanging information on the Internet. In recent years, documents in widely varied areas are increasingly represented in XML [1], and numerous query languages [6] (http://www.w3c.org) have been also proposed. XML documents that contain security-sensitive information need to require an authorization before being available for retrieval.

XML documents (*objects*) need to be available only for those user credentials (*subjects*) if they are authorized according to the authorization policies (*actions* and *permissions*). The determination methods for users access authorization can be represented as quadruple ⟨*subject, object, action, permission*⟩. The determination therefore is simply to match a bitmap mask (representing a user's request) with an authorization bitmap index (representing authorization policies) to obtain the quadruple ⟨*subject, object, action, permission*⟩. The determination for access authorization is conceptually simple, but it yet accelerates the query process time. Most methods we know for access authorization are not satisfactorily fast. It is partly because the access control requires the overhead in addition to the time required for query processing, and partly because the powerful expression of authorization policies makes it uneasy to make fast a determination. The propagation of subjects and objects is naturally to be evaluated at run time of authorization.

Consider the following examples that motivate our research.

Example 1.1: In database systems, an access authorization is first checked, and followed by query processing. Assume that a user <u01> requests to read the XML element <e_i>. What if the XML element <e_i> is not available in the database? Of course, in this case, no checking for access authorization is necessary. Unless acquiring an authorization, the user cannot know the absence of what is requested. However, if the database system put access authorization together with query processing in one framework, this problem can be avoided.

Example 1.2: Assume again that a user <u01> requests to read the XML element <e_i>, and an authorization policy authorizes <r02> to read <e_j>. If the user with the role <r02> requests <e_i>, the first determination on authorization is that <u01> cannot read the XML element <e_i>. However, if the authority of <r02> is propagated to <u01> (or subject propagation), and the access to <e_j> is propagated to <e_i> (or object propagation), then the determination becomes positive. Notice there are two types of propagation: subject propagation and object propagation. Such propagation, especially object propagation, is not efficiently considered at the time of access authorization.

In this paper, we propose a bitmap-based authorization technique for XML document access control. The authorization policies are encoded into bitmap indexes. User access requests are encoded into bitmap-masks. By applying bit-wise operations, authorization can be determined significantly fast.

The contribution of this paper includes 1) the dual goals achieved for fast and secure accesses to XML document collections, and 2) early propagation of subjects and objects in bitmap indexes.

This remainder of this paper is organized as follows: Section 2 describes related literatures. Section 3 reviews the preliminaries regarding XML and bitmap indexing techniques and the model of access control. Section 4 describes the technique of bitmap indexing. Early propagation of subjects and objects is discussed. Section 5 describes the access control method in the authorization bitmap index using bit-wise operations. Section 6 describes experimental evaluation. Finally, We conclude our work in Section 7.

2. RELATED WORK

In this section, we describe bitmap indexing techniques and access control techniques.

The collection of bitmaps in a bitmap index forms a 2-dimensional bit matrix [5]. In this paper, we apply the bitmap indexing techniques to security management. Bit-wise operations developed in the earlier work will also be generalized to the multi-dimensional bit matrix context.

Several access control policies are devised for controlling access to information and databases [8,10]. Proposed are the closed policy and the flexible open policy. When a system imposes a specific policy on users, the users can work on the confines imposed by the policy [4]. Multiple access control policies within a single system are enforced, derived, and resolved if any conflicts [10]. Specification of negative authorizations can be stated for accesses to be denied [3].

Numerous conflict resolution policies have been developed. Some of those policies are denial-take-precedence [3], most-specific-take precedence [7], most-specific policy together with the concept of strong and weak authorizations [3], and explicit-precedence policies [11].

3. PRELIMINARIES

In this section, we introduce XML documents briefly, and bitmap indexing for XML documents.

Each document (*d*) in an XML document collection *D* is represented in XML. So, *d* contains one or more words (*w*) that are associated with XML-element paths (*p*). For example, consider Figure 3.1. The XML-element path order/item/desc has a value food in the document, while order has "International purchase" in it. An XML-element path is a sequence of XML elements from the top to the node containing content using XPath [13]. A collection of XML documents is a set of the triplets $\langle d, p, w\rangle$.

Each such document $\langle d, p, w\rangle$ can be encoded into a bitmap. A bitmap is defined as a two-dimensional set of bits representing the existence of a pair (p, w) in *d*. An example of XML documents is Figure 3.1.

In addition, one of XML documents we consider in this section is an authorization policy. This paper does not aim to propose a new model for authorization policies, but employ the previous work by Damiani and et al [8] to represent authorization policies uniformly together with XML documents like order.xml. An authorization policy specifies the determination of user accesses (*subject*) to XML documents (*object*). Objects are XML documents. A credential of a subject is user id (uid) or role id (rid) accessed through a specific ip address. An authorization policy is a specification that *permits* positively (or grants) or negatively (or denies) an *action* of a *subject* on an *object*. Objects (or XML documents) are hierarchically organized, and broadly speaking they are widely distributed as stated by using XLink as shown in Figure 3.1. Similarly, subjects (or users and ip addresses) are hierarchically organized as shown in Figure 3.3, and somehow distributed.

```
<?xml version="1.0" ?>
<xml:xlink xlmns:xlink="http://.../xlink" />
<order>International purchase
  <item id="t1">gold apples
    <desc>food</desc>
    <quantity>5</quantity>
    <price>9.99</price>
  </item>
  <item id="t2">cd-player
    <desc>appliance</desc>
    <color>white</color>
    <quantity>2</quantity>
    <price>49.00</price>
  </item>
  <nego item_id="all" on="price">
    <offer>
      <price> <sum item_id="all" compute="*" arg1="quantity" arg2="price" /> </price>
      <term>Valid terms</term>
    </offer>
    <deal>false</deal>
  </nego>
  <delivery>2 Rex St., Lafayette, LA 70504
    <xlink:locator href="http://lafayette.la/map.jpg" />
    <xlink:arc from="remote" to="local" actuate="onRequest" /></delivery>
</order>
</xml>
```

Figure 3.1. Coder Example in XML

Figure 3.2 exemplifies an authorization policy file. Because of hierarchical organization of subjects and objects, XML elements, subject and object, specify the attribute propagation. There are three propagation direction: 1) no propagation, 2) downward propagation, and 3) upward propagation. Possible propagation of subjects is stated as the partial ordering in Figure 3.3. For example, the second authorization, a2, specifies a downward propagation of subject, user of rid. The same authority for the subject user can be effective for other users, u33, u15, u7, and u19, as shown in Figure 3.3. On the other hand, the fifth authorization, a5, specifies an upward propagation of object, order/delivery. The same access effect on the XML path, order/delivery, can be effective for its super element, order.

```
<authorization_list>
 <authorization aid="a1">
  <subject propagation="F"><uid>u21</uid> <uid>u33</uid></subject>
  <object propagation="F">order.xml/order/item order.xml/order/delivery</object>
  <action>read</action>
  <permission>granted</ permission>
 </authorization>
 <authorization aid="a2">
  <subject propagation="down"><rid>user</rid></subject>
  <object propagation="F">order.xml/order/item[2] order.xml/order/nego/offer[2]/price</object>
  <action>read write</action>
  < permission>granted</ permission>
 </authorization>
 <authorization aid="a3">
  <subject propagation="F"><uid>engineer</uid></subject>
  <object propagation="down">order.xml/order</object>
  <action activation="T">read write</action>
  < permission>granted</ permission>
 </authorization>
 <authorization aid="a4">
  <subject propagation="up"><rid>comp_staff</rid></subject>
  <object propagation="down">order.xml/order/item</object>
  <action>read</action>
  < permission excluded_by="ip" ip="33.129.20.edu">denied</ permission>
 </authorization>
 <authorization aid="a5">
  <subject propagation="F"><uid>sales</uid></subject>
  <object propagation="up">order.xml/order/delivery</object>
  <action>read</action>
  < permission>denied</ permission>
 </authorization>
 <authorization aid="a6">
  <subject propagation="down"><rid>comp_staff</rid></subject>
  <object propagation="down">order.xml/order/nego/offer</object>
  <action activation="T">write</action>
  < permission>denided</ permission>
 </authorization>
</authorization_list>
```

Figure 3.2. XML Authorization Policies

The access control model adapted from [8] in this paper makes use of authorization policies ⟨*s*, *o*, *a*, *m*⟩. Having a request ⟨*s*', *o*', *a*⟩ posed to XML document ⟨*d*, *p*, *w*⟩, the determination using the authorization policy is ⟨*s*', *o*', *a*, *m*⟩ if *s*' and *o*' are matched[1] with *s* and *o* respectively, where *m* denotes either grant or denial. If the permission is granted, the answer becomes ⟨*d*, *p*, *w*⟩ if *o* is matched with *p*. This paper describes the method of high-speed determining an authorization for an access to XML documents. Generating answers is not within the scope of this paper.

[1] By match we mean they are the same, or one is contained in another, by propagation of subject and object.

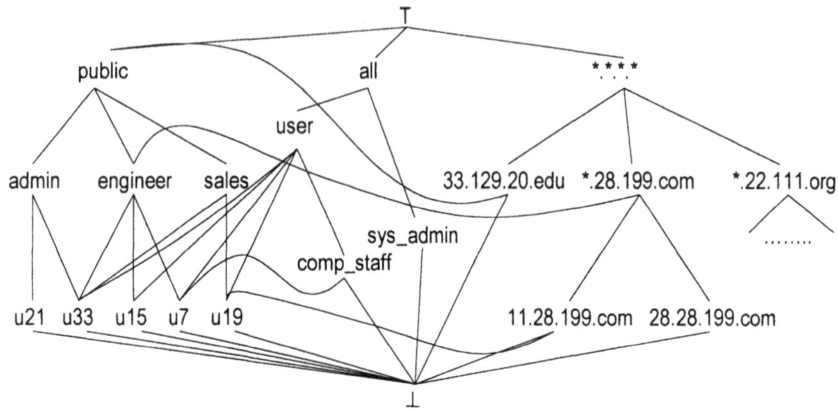

Figure 3.3. Partial Ordering of Subjects

4. BITMAP INDEXING

In this section, we propose the bitmap indexing technique that can speed up the determination process for access authorization and associate with query processing. Authorization policies are first encoded into a bitmap index. The bitmap index represents the existence of pairs (XML path, value) that are specified in the authorization policy file in Figure3.2. Consider a request posed to a collection of XML documents. A secured information system should have the both capabilities of query processing and security management. Depending upon equipping these capabilities, there may be three broad approaches:

Decoupled authorization. Having the two capabilities separately, a naïve approach is to obtain the determination from the security management by matching with the request. Once matched, the request is performed by the query processing and so applied to the XML document collection.

Tightly coupled authorization. The query processing and the security management are coupled tightly together. Once one capability is performed, the other capability can be achieved with paying no extra effort. This approach has drawbacks such as less flexibility in modification and inefficiency in extendibility.

Pipelined authorization. Outcome of security management is pipelined with query processing. Only appropriate documents authorized from the security management are further processed for query processing. This paper focuses on the pipelined but yet high-speed authorization.

The pipelined authorization is proposed to conduct the following steps: 1) Parsing an authorization policy file, 2) Encoding the information about the authorization policies into bitmaps, 3) Encoding the XML path of an XML document collection, 4) Early propagating both subjects and objects. What follows in the subsections includes our proposed methods of encoding and early propagation. We also assume that a collection of XML documents has been encoded into BitCube [14]. Briefly speaking, similar to the construction method of an authorization bitmap index, the BitCube is constructed for XML documents, setting 1's and 0's in bitmaps.

4.1 Encoding into Bitmaps

The following files are encoded into bitmaps: Authorization policy file, XML document collection, and user requests. User requests are encoded into bit-mask dynamically at run-time, while authorization policies and XML documents are once encoded into bitmap indexes at compile-time.

An authorization policy describes who (subject) has an authority (permission) of a specific action (action) on XML documents (objects). Among many XML elements and attributes as shown in Figure 3.2, minimum but yet useful information is considered. Such information is illustrated in Figure 4.1: (a) is a list of XML paths which is minimum but yet useful from Figure 3.2, and (b) is a list of values that are associated with the paths listed in (a). For example, the XML path, subject/uid has values, engineer, sales, u15, u19, u7, u21, and u33. Each pair (XML path, value) indicates a position of the bits in the bitmap index. The pair (subject/uid, engineer) = [0,2] indicates the first bit column of the bitmap index shown in Figure 4.1(c).

Similarly, a temporary XML bitmap index is created for the XML document order.xml shown in Figure 3.1 together with other two documents, order2.xml and order3.xml. By "temporary" bitmap index, we mean that this bitmap index is to be propagated to represent possible authorizations further. Possible authorizations are derived from the attribute descriptions, e.g., propagation attributes with values. The early propagation is discussed in the next subsection. Figure 4.2 (a) is a list of XML paths, each of which is a pointer to a bit column in the temporary XML bitmap index in (b).

4.2 Early Propagation

There are two early propagations considered in this section: 1) subject early propagation and 2) object early propagation. The authority for a specific object or subject can be propagated. The propagation of objects or subjects is characterized by the direction of propagations, or by the rate of propagations. The propagation attribute associated with subjects or objects can have values of false ("F"), upwards ("up") or downwards ("down"), each of which indicates the direction of propagation. In the following subsections, subject early propagation, object early propagation, and the degree of propagations will be discussed.

(subject/uid) = 0
(subject/rid) = 1
(subject/ip) = 2
(action/type) = 3
(object/href) = 4
(permission) = 5
(permission/excluded_by) = 6
(permission/ip) = 7

(a)

(comp_staff) = 0
(denied) = 1
(engineer) = 2
(granted) = 3
(read) = 4
(sales) = 5
(user) = 6
(u15) = 7
(u19) = 8
(u7) = 9
(u21) = 10
(u33) = 11
(write) = 12
(33.129.20.edu) = 13
(100.29.199.com) = 14
(*) = 15
(ip) = 16

(b)

	[0,2]	[0,5]	[0,7]	[0,8]	[0,9]	[0,10]	[0,11]	[1,0]	[1,6]	[2,13]	[2,14]	[3,4]	[3,12]	[4,15]	[5,1]	[5,3]	[6,16]	[7,13]
authorization1	0	0	0	0	0	1	1	0	0	0	0	1	0	1	0	1	0	0
authorization2	0	0	0	0	0	0	0	0	1	0	0	1	1	1	0	1	0	0
authorization3	1	0	0	0	0	0	0	0	0	0	0	1	1	1	0	1	0	0
authorization4	0	0	0	0	0	0	0	1	0	0	0	1	0	1	1	0	1	1
authorization5	0	1	0	0	0	0	0	0	0	0	0	1	0	1	1	0	0	0
authorization6	1	0	0	0	0	0	0	0	0	0	0	0	1	1	1	0	0	0

(c)

Figure 4.1. Authorization Bitmap Index

4.2.1 Early Propagation of Subject

The value for the propagation attribute in Figure 3.2 indicates the direction of propagation. The propagation is available along the partial ordering hierarchy in Figure 3.3. For example, the subject element of the first authorization policy has the propagation attribute value of "F," which means no propagation is allowed. But, in the second authorization policy, the subject element has the value "user" for the rid sub-element and the value "down" for the propagation attribute. What it means to be is to propagate the authority of rid user down to sub-subjects. The sub-subjects in the partial ordering hierarchy of Figure 3.3 are comp_staff, u15, u19, u7, and u33. The authority of user is propagated to comp_staff, u15, u19, u7, and u33, as well.

As the authorization policy file is parsed, this propagation information is obtained and exploited to early propagate in the authorization bitmap index. The initial bitmap index in Figure 4.1(c) is evolved to the bitmap index as shown in Figure 4.3. The bits for subject are early propagated.

(order) = 0
(order/item[1]) = 1
(order/item[1]/desc) = 2
(order/item[1]/color) = 3
(order/item[1]/quantity) = 4
(order/item[1]/price) = 5
(order/item[2]) = 6
(order/item[2]/desc) = 7
(order/item[2]/color) = 8
(order/item[2]/quantity) = 9
(order/item[2]/price) = 10
(order/nego/offer[1]/price) = 11
(order/nego/offer[1]/term[1]) = 12
(order/nego/offer[2]/price) = 13
(order/nego/offer[2]/term[1]) = 14
(order/nego/offer[2]/term[2]) = 15
(order/nego/deal) = 16
(order/delivery) = 17
(order/delivery/xlink:locator) = 18
(order/delivery/xlink:arc) = 19

(a)

	0	1	2	3	4	5	6	7	8	9	10	11	12	13	14	15	16	17	18	19
order.xml	1	1	1	0	1	1	1	1	1	1	1	1	1	0	0	0	1	1	1	1
order2.xml	0	0	1	1	1	1	1	0	0	0	0	1	0	1	1	1	1	0	0	0
order3.xml	0	1	1	1	1	1	0	0	0	0	0	1	0	0	0	0	0	0	0	0

(b)

Notice that actual files for order2.xml and order3.xml are omitted in this paper

Figure 4.2. A Temporary Bitmap Index for XML Documents

4.2.2 Early Propagation of Object

The authority on an object is propagated onto appropriate objects, but the temporary bitmap of XML documents is exploited to early propagate objects. The temporary bitmap index in Figure 4.2 represents the existence of pairs (XML path, value) in each document, but does not make the authorities "fully" available to any legal authorized users. Notice that the legally authorized users are obtained by the early propagation of subjects. To overcome this incomplete information, the early propagation of objects is developed.

The authorization on XML documents is burgeoning to serve in high-speed with secured XML documents. For example, an XML document in Figure 3.1 is encoded in the temporary bitmap index as shown in Figure 4.2.

	[0,2]	[0,5]	[0,7]	[0,8]	[0,9]	[0,10]	[0,11]	[1,0]	[1,6]	[2,13]	[2,14]	[3,4]	[3,12]	[4,15]	[5,1]	[5,3]	[6,16]	[7,13]
authorization1	0	0	0	0	0	1	1	0	0	0	0	1	0	1	0	1	0	0
authorization2	0	0	1	1	1	0	1	0	1	0	0	1	1	1	0	1	0	0
authorization3	1	0	0	0	0	0	0	0	0	0	0	1	1	1	0	1	0	0
authorization4	0	0	0	0	0	0	0	1	1	0	0	1	0	1	1	0	1	1
authorization5	0	1	0	0	0	0	0	0	0	0	0	1	0	1	1	0	0	0
authorization6	0	0	0	0	1	0	0	1	0	0	0	0	1	1	1	0	0	0

Figure 4.3. Authorization Bitmap Index after Subject Early Propagation

This temporary bitmap index is then propagated downward or upward according to the authorization policy. The authorization policy bitmap index is burgeoning into Figure 4.4. In the authorization bitmap on top of the figure, the first two rows in the bitmap index are pipelined with the temporary bitmap indexes on the bottom (thru the labels c1 and c2). Only the limited information but the one actually requested is available. For example, if the document order.xml is requested, only the bits, 1, 6, and 17, i.e., the content of order/item[1], order/item[2], and order/delivery are provided. However, by the third authorization policy, although order.xml/order is requested, because the propagation is allowed, the authority on that object can be propagated downward to all of its sub-elements. The third authorization, authorization3 is pipelined with the temporary bitmap index through the label c3. If order.xml/order is requested, then not only the content requested but also all propagated contents, order/item[1]/color, order/nego/offer[2]/price, order/nego/offer[2]/term[1], and order/nego/offer[2]/term[2] become available.

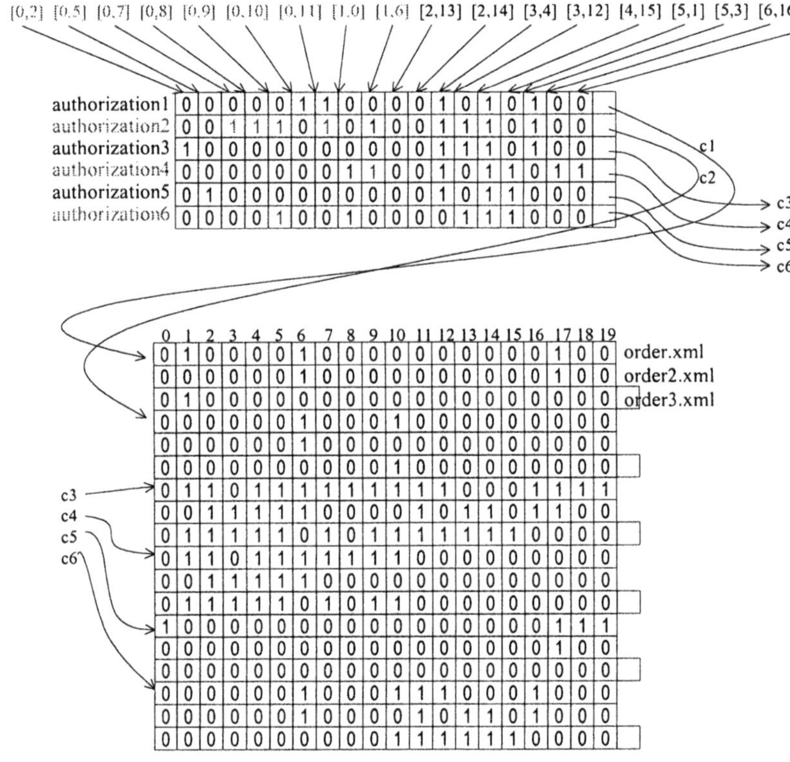

Figure 4.4. Burgeoning Example of Authorization Policy Bitmap Index

5. ACCESS CONTROL IN AUTHORIZATION BITMAP INDEX

One of the advantages exploiting a bitmap index is the significant improvement in operation evaluation and query processing. We consider bit-wise operations for a bitmap index. Bit-wise operations are AND, OR, and XOR. Consider a user request. A user request is encoded into a *bitmap mask*, q, using the same XML paths and values as the way encoding XML documents and authorization policies. Also, consider the burgeoned Authorization Policy Bitmap Index, α in short. Broadly speaking, the naïve approach for access control is as follows:

The bitmap mask is AND-ed with the authorization policy bitmap index. If the outcome is the same as the original bitmap mask, then the subject becomes authorized to access.

The bitmap mask is XOR-ed with each document in the BitCube. If the size of the outcome is 0, then the object can be accessible.

Having bit-wise operations with the Authorization Policy Bitmap Index, we discuss a pipelined processing for secure access control and for query answering. The burgeoned Authorization Policy Bitmap Index represents authorization policies together with corresponding document indexes, but not all the bits in the Authorization Policy Bitmap Index should be equally treated. The following subjection describes how differently to treat the bits.

5.1 Evaluation Scheme of Authorization Policy Bitmap Index

Consider Figure 5.1, which is simplified version of a burgeoned Authorization Policy Bitmap Index, α. There are six groups of bits, the bits for pid, uid, rid, action, permission, and object, and those bits are further grouped into five bit-regions, the region for (a), (b), (c), (d) and (e). Those six bit groups are classified based on the specification of authorization policies, while those five bit-regions are classified based on the evaluation of XML elements in authorization policies.

The bit-region (a) in Figure 5.1 is to check the general information about authorization policy, which can be used for conflict resolution, identification of policies, or query types. The evaluation of this region is an <u>exact match</u> based on the XOR operation: $|\alpha \text{ XOR } q| = 0$, where $|x|$ denotes the number of 1's in x.

The bit-region (b) in the figure is to check if a user is matched any one in uid or rid for its credential. That is, a query bitmap mask q is <u>contained in</u> the Authorization Policy Bitmap Index α. This containment is performed based on the AND operation: $(\alpha \text{ AND } q) = q$. Similarly, the bit-regions (c) and (e) can be performed. However, theses are evaluated separately and all evaluations should be satisfied before pipelining further.

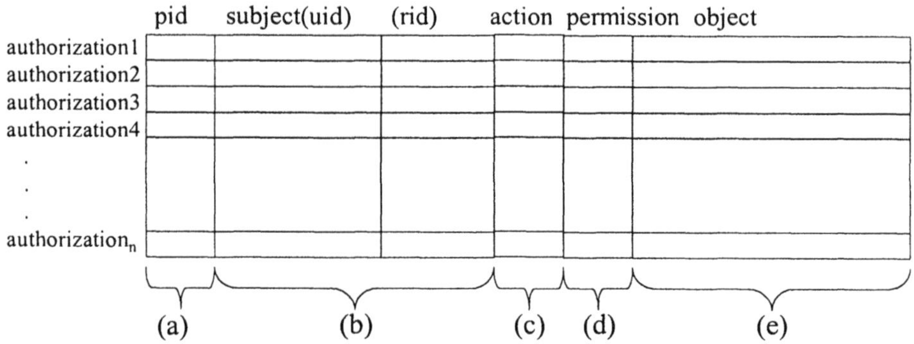

Figure 5.1. Bit-Region-based Evaluation

The bit-region (d) in the figure is to check the conditional determination of permission. Recall that permission is either granted or denied, and it can be conditionally by stating "excluded_by," e.g., ip address. For example, in the authorization a4 in Figure 3.3, from any ip address unless otherwise a credential user can access an object. If the bit for the excluded_by attribute is set to 1, then the rest bits of this region is evaluated by the XOR operation: $(\alpha \text{ XOR } q) = q$. If not, it is evaluated by the AND operation: $(\alpha \text{ AND } q) = q$.

The outcome of the evaluation of the bit-region (b), (c) and (e) is pipelined with the evaluation of the bit-region (d). If finally the bit-region (d) is successfully evaluated, then the BitCube is accessed to further comparison such as selection condition (*q2* in Figure 5.2).

Example 5.1: As an example, consider three requests in Figure 5.2. The request *q1* is encoded into the bitmap mask: 0 0 0 0 1 0 0 0 0 0 0 & 1 0 & 1 0 0 0 0 0 0 0 0 0 0 0 0 0 0 0 0 0 0 0, where & denotes the delimiter between the bit-group (b), (c) and (e). Of course, the bit-group (d) is not given by a request, but will be determined by an authorization. This mask is contained in the authorization2 of the Authorization Policy Bitmap Index in Figure 4.4. Thru the label c2, the outcome is pipelined to the burgeoned Index in Figure 4.4. However, none of these two authorization policies contain 1 0 0 0 0 0 0 0 0 0 0 0 0 0 0 0 0 0 0 0, meaning that the first bit for object /order is not available in any XML files labeled by c2. Therefore, nothing is returned. Although the request is allowed, no matches are returned.

Example 5.2: Consider the second request *q2*. The bitmap mask of q2 is 0 0 0 0 1 0 0 0 0 0 0 & 0 1 & 0 0 0 0 0 0 0 0 0 0 0 0 1 0 0 0 0 0 0 0 0. The authorization2 and authorization6 contain the user credential because both authorizations authorize for the write action. However, the evaluation of the bit-group (e) returns the objects of all three files. In those files, object requested is further evaluated for the comparison, say check for the word "Valid term," will be done in the BitCube.

Example 5.3: Again, in Figure 5.2, consider the request *q3*. Its bitmap mask is: 0 0 0 0 1 0 0 0 1 0 0 & 0 1 & 0 1 0 0 0 0 0 0 0 0 0 0 0 0 0 0 1 1 0 0. The credential of u7 is contained in the authorization2, authorization4, and authorization6. In this case, order.xml, order2.xml and order3.xml are partially accessed, but authorization4 allows more information than the other two. If there exists any type of conflicts, conflict resolutions should be considered. The conflict resolution is not within the scope of this paper either.

```
<access_req type="query">
  <object href="$p/order.xml/order" />
  <subject>
    <uid>u7</uid>
  </subject>
  <action type="read"/>
</access_req>
```

(q1) Uid u7 requests to read the items of orders

```
<access_req type="query">
  <object href="$p/order/nego/offer/term/[text()='Valid term]" />
  <subject>
    <uid>u7</uid>
  </subject>
  <action type="write"/>
</access_req>
```

(q2) Uid u7 requests to write on the documents whose negotiation term is valid.

```
<access_req type="query">
  <object href="$p/order.xml/order/item/[position()=1]" />
  <object href="$p/order.xml/order/item/*" />
  <subject ip="100.29.199.com">
    <uid>u7</uid>
    <rid>user</uid>
  </subject>
  <action type="read"/>
</access_req>
```

(q3) Uid u7 requests to read all the information about the first item of orders from the ip, 100.29.199.com.

Figure 5.2. Example of Requests

6. CONCLUSION

We proposed in this paper a new technique for secure but fast authorization for accesses to XML document collections. The techniques for encoding both authorization policies and XML documents, and pipelining them together in a bitmap index have been developed. The contribution of this paper includes 1) the dual goals achieved for fast and secure authorizations for accesses to XML document collections, and 2) early propagation of subjects and objects in bitmap indexes.

Our work can be applied to variously wide areas of information management. Pipelining manipulation of two semantically different information sources is possible. Bit-wise operations on bitmap indexes are useful to improve the evaluation of information processing.

Some of our future work includes 1) conflict resolution that can be performed in a bitmap index, and 2) incremental indexing that can be adaptive and scalable to the additions and deletions of XML documents.

REFERENCES

1. A. Arsanjani, B. Hailpern, J. Martin, P. Tarr, Web Services: romises and Compromises, ACM Queue, Vol. 1, No. 1, 2003, pages 48-58.
2. E. Bertino, P. Samarati, and S. Jajodia, Authorizations in Relational Database Management Systems, In Proc. Of the 1st ACM Conf. On Computer and Communications Security, pp. 130-139, 1993.
3. E. Bertino, S. Jajodia, and P. Samarati, A Flexible Authorization Mechanism for Relational Data Management Systems, ACM Transactions on Information Systems, Vol. 17, 1999, Pages 101-140.
4. S. Castano, M. Fugini, G. Martella, P. Samarati, *Database Security*, Addison-Wesley, Reading, 1995.
5. C. Chan and Y. Ioannidis, Bitmap Index Design and Evaluation, Proc. of Int'l ACM SIGMOD Conference, 1998, 355-366
6. A. Deutsch, M. Fernandez, A. Levy, D. Suciu, "XML-QL: A Query Language for XML," www.w3.org/TR/NOTE-xml-ql/, 1998.
7. D. Denning, T. Lunt, R. Schell, M. Heckman, W. Shockley: A Multilevel Relational Data Model. IEEE Symposium on Security and Privacy 1987: 220-234.
8. E. Damiani, S. Di Vimercati, S. Paragoschi, P. Samarati, A Fine-Grained Access Control System for XML Documents, ACM Transactions on Information and System Security, Vol. 5, 2002, Pages 169-202.
9. D. Ferraiolo, R. Sandhu, S. Gavrila, D. Kuhn, and R. Chandramouli, Proposed NIST Standard for Role-Based Access Control, ACM Transactions on Information and System Security, Vol. 4, 2001, Pages 224-274.
10. S. Jajodia, P. Samarati, M. Sapino, and V. Subrahmanian, Flexible Support for Multiple Access Control Policies, ACM Transactions on Databases Systems, Vol. 26, 2001, Pages 214-260.
11. H. Shen, and P. Dewan, Access Control for Collaborative Environments, In Proc. Of the ACM Conf. On Computer Supported Cooperative Work, pp. 51-58, 1992.
12. van den Akker, T., Snell, Q. Clement, M., The Guard Access Control Model: Set-based Access Control, Proc. Of the 6th ACM Symposium on Access Control Models and Technologies, pp. 75-84, 2001.
13. http://www.w3.org/TR/xpath
14. J. Yoon, V. Raghavan, V. Chakilam, and L. Kerschberg, "BitCube: A Three-Dimensional Bitmap Indexing for XML Documents", Journal of Intelligent Information Systems, pages 241-254, vol. 17, November, 2001.

CHINESE WALL SECURITY POLICY MODELS

Information Flows and Confining Trojan Horses

Tsau Young ('T. Y.')Lin
Department of Computer Science
San Jose State University
San Jose, California 95192
tylin@cs.sjsu.edu

Abstract In 1989, Brewer and Nash (BN) presented a fascinating idea, called Chinese wall security policy model, for commercial security. Their idea was based on the analysis of the notion, **C**onflict of **I**nterest binary **R**elation (CIR). Unfortunately, their formalization did not fully catch the appropriate properties of CIR. In this paper, we present a theory based on granulation that has captured the essence of BN's intuitive idea. The results are more than the Chinese wall models: Malicious Trojan horses in certain DAC Model (discretionary access control) can be controlled or confined.

Keywords: Simple Chinese Wall Security policy, Agressive(Strong) Chinese Wall Security policy, binary relation, conflict of interests, equivlaence relation.

1. Introduction

Recent developments, such as eCommerce and homeland security, have prompted us to re-visit the idea of Chinese Wall Security Policy (CWSP) model. "The Chinese wall policy combines commercial discretion with legally enforceable mandatory controls ..., perhaps, as significant to the financial world as Bell-LaPadula's policies are to the military." This is an assertion made by Brewer and Nash; see the abstract of [2]. We believe it is still valid.

In 1989, Brewer and Nash(BN) proposed a very intriguing commercial security model – called Chinese Wall Security Policy(**CWSP**) Model [2]. Intuitively, the essential idea was to build a family of impenetrable walls, called Chinese walls, among the dataset of competing companies.

No data that are in conflict can be stored in the same side of Chinese walls. BN's analysis of the security problem were fascinating and is still valid; the only unfortunate part is their mathematical model has not fully captured their analysis. It was based on

- The *incorrect assumption* that corporate data can be partitioned (decomposed) into mutually disjoin conflict of interest classes (CIR-classes); such a disjoint collection is called *a partition* in mathematics; see e.g., [3].
- Unfortunately, CIR-classes seldom disjoints; they do overlap, and hence Brewer and Nash theory does not held well.

In the same year at 1989 Aerospace Computer Security Application Conference, we reported BN's errors, and presented a modified model, called an aggressive Chinese Wall Security Policy model (**ACWSP**) [14]. In that paper, we did not bring out the essential strength of **ACWSP** model. A relatively inactive decade has passed; only few papers, which are, however, still based on the same erroneous assumptions, appeared. By refining the idea of **ACWSP**, in this paper, we have successfully captured the intuitive intention of BN "theory."

The theory that we are presenting is based on the development of a novel computing methodology. We observed that

- The collection of CIR-classes form a *binary granulation*, even though *not* a partition.

Intuitively a binary granulation is a collection of subsets, whose "core" or "centers" form a partition; see the main text below. In terms of binary granulation, we recapture the spirit of Chinese wall security policy (CWSP) model. The results are more than that; with mild assumptions, we can actually confine *malicious Trojan horses* on DAC model (Discretionary Access Control). Sensitive information will *not* flow into "enemy" hands, only flow among "friends."

2. An Analysis of Conflicts(CIR)

Before we launch on the new theory, we recall some analysis from [14]: **C**onflict of **I**nterests is a binary **R**elation (CIR) among corporations; it can be used to regulate the information flows among corporations.

2.1. Is CIR an equivalence Relation?

In BN-theory, CIR were assumed to be an equivalence relation **erroneously**, in other words, O were partitioned (decomposed) into mutually disjoint CIR-classes (conflict of interest classes) However, "conflict of interests," in normal daily usage, can not be transitive, at least not universally transitive.

Let us recall the example from [14]: The following two statements, at least, during the cold war period were valid.

USA was in cold war with USSR, and

USSR was in cold war with UK.

Could we conclude from these two assertions that

USA was in cold war with USSR.

This is rather absurd. Of course,in cold war with, is only an example, nevertheless, it does clearly indicate that CIR can not, in general, be transitive. So an equivalence relation, which is reflexive, symmetric and transitive, is not a proper mathematical model for CIR.

2.2. A Set of Axioms for Secure CIR

In this section, we re-visit the Aggressive Chinese Wall Security Policy(ACWSP) Model [14]. We recall (with some modifications) the axioms for the binary relation, $CIR \subseteq O \times O$:

CIR-1: CIR is symmetric.

CIR-2: CIR is anti-reflexive.

CIR-3: CIR is anti-transitive.

Some observations may be helpful: CIR-2 is necessary, since each company cannot conflict to itself. CIR-1 is always valid: If company A is in conflicts with B, B is certainly in conflicts with A. CIR-3 is imposed, because it implicitly required in BN's notion of Chinese walls (Section 3.1).

To stress its importancy, a new property will be explicitly listed as an "axiom", though it is implied by the others: Let E_{CIR} be the induced equivalence relation of CIR(See Section 3).

CIR-4: The granulation of CIR and partition of E_{CIR} are compatible, in the sense that each CIR-class (or in geometric term, CIR-neighborhood) is a union of E_{CIR} -equivalence classes. (See Proposition 2 of Section 3)

Intuitively, this is significantl; previously we have placed Chinese walls on the "boundaries" of CIR-classes in[14]. But each of these boundaries is "one-sided;" its complement is not an union of CIR-classes. But CIR-4 implies that that such boundaries are "two-sided;" Because the "interior and exterior" are both unions of E_{CIR}-equivalence classes.

CIR-5 (IAR): If we interpret CIR as "is an adversary of"-relation, then the complement is "is an ally of"-relation (IAR). IAR is an equivalence relation, by Corollary 4 of Section 4.

Theorem 2.2. If R is a symmetric and anti-reflexive and anti-transitive binary relation, its complement R' is an equivalence relation. In particular, IAR, as the the complement of CIR, is an equivalence relation.

Proof: Let $[X]_{IAR}$ be the IAR-equivalence class containing X. Then, we note that $[X]_{IAR} = [Y]_{IAR} \forall Y \in [X]_{IAR}$. Hence their complements are equal, so we have

Corollary $CIR_X = CIR_Y \forall Y \in [X]_{IAR}$. In other words, the information of any object in $[X]_{IAR}$ can flow freely among themselves

3. Chinese Wall Security Policies

BN proposed Chinese wall security policy to capture certain requirments in UK's financial sector. A decade later, we beleive their anlaysis is still useful and valid (but not their mathematical model). In this section, we will re-visit their requirements, namely, Chinese Wall Security Policy (CWSP).

3.1. Simple Chinese Wall Security Policy

We will continue on BN's notations: O is the set of all objects (corporate data), X, Y, and Z are objects in O.

1. **BN-Version** : "people are only allowed access to information which is not held to conflict with any other information that they already possess." See [2], Section "Simple Security", p. 207.

We will rephrese it mathemtically:

2. **SCWSP** *Simple Chinese Wall Security Policy* means

    There is no DIF from X to Y, if and only if $(X, Y) \in$ CIR,

    where DIF (direct information flows) means the agent y (who handles Y) *read* the data in Y(and may make a copy in Y).

In terms of DAC(Descretionary Acess Model)langauge, we should say x grants y a read-access right; and y read the data and make a copy in Y (making copy is permissible, even in strcit DAC model; see [23])
Please note the necessary-and-sufficient-condition type of statements. BN's rules allow an agent to read any two sets of data as long as they are not CIR. So we havw the dual of SCWSP:

3. Dual-SCWSP Dual-SCWSP is equivalent to CWSP, but opposite View:

There is DIF from X to Y, if and only if $(X, Y) \notin CIR$.

3.2. Agressive Chinese Wall Security Policy (ACWSP)

First, let us state a convention, some definitions and comments:

Convention : The symbol, CIR, always denotes a binary relation that satisfies the axioms.

Definition CIF (composite information flow) from X to Y is a sequence of DIFs (direct information flows), which starts from X and end at Y:

$$X = X_0 \longrightarrow X_1 \longrightarrow \ldots \longrightarrow X_n = Y,$$

where each "$\longrightarrow$" is a DIF.

Caution : We should stress here that simple security policy only regulate DIF's. Note that even if we are assured that there is no DIF from X to Y, it is conceivable some clever CIFs may send information, say from X, via Z, to Y. In other words, two *innocent* DIFs from $X \longrightarrow Z$ and $Z \longrightarrow Y$ could compose into a *malicious* CIF, $X \longrightarrow Z \longrightarrow Y$.

Such CIFs have been identified as Trojan horses. Confining the malicious Trojan horses is actually the essence of the main contribution of ACWSP-model.

ACWSP Agressive (Strong) Chinese Wall Security policy.

There is no CIF from X to Y, if and only if $(X, Y) \in$ CIR.

Chinese Wall Theorem. Under the assumption that CIR meets the axioms (anti-reflexive, symmetric, and anti-transitive),

ACWSP $\Longleftrightarrow$ SCWSP

Proof: First, let us note the following FACTs from Section **??**

FACT 1. CIR and IAR("is ally with") are complement to each other.

FACT 2. IAR is an equivalence relation.

We need some notations. Let X be an object (a company data) of O. Let

CIR_X (= $\{Y \mid (X,Y) \in$ CIR $\}$ be the CIR-class of X and

$[X]_{IAR}$ (= $\{Y \mid (X,Y) \in$ IAR $\}$), or simply $[X]$, IAR-equivalence class of X

Let X be an object (a company data) of O. Let

CIR_X (= $\{Y \mid (X,Y) \in$ CIR $\}$ be the CIR-class of X and

$[X]_{IAR}$ (= $\{Y \mid (X,Y) \in$ IAR $\}$), or simply $[X]$, IAR-equivalence class of X

To prove this theorem, we need to establish the following **Agressive(strong) Chinese wall security policy** for the given Simple CWSP:

$$\text{There is no CIF from } X \text{ to } Y \Longleftarrow (X,Y) \in \text{CIR}.$$

We will use indirect proof, so by assuming to the contrary, we have two conditions:

1. There is a sequence of DIFs (direct information flows)
$$X = X_0 \longrightarrow X_1 \longrightarrow \ldots \longrightarrow X_n = Y.$$
2. $Y \in CIR_X$.

Our task is to derive a contradiction; we will prove it by mathematical induction.

First, the initial assertion:

If $X = X_0 \longrightarrow X_1$ is a DIF, then $CIR_X = CIR_{X_1}$ and $[X]_{IAR} = [X_1]_{IAR}$

To prove this assertion, note that X_1, receiving information from X, cannot be in CIR_X. Hence, must be in its complement, that is,

$$X_1 \in [X]_{IAR}.$$

Since IAR an equivalence relation (FACT 2), we have

$$[X_1]_{IAR} = [X]_{IAR}.$$

By the fact that they are the complements, we have

$$CIR_X = CIR_{X_1}.$$

So the initial assertion is proved.

Next, we consider the induction case. The arguments are essentially the same. By induction assumption, we have

$$[X]_{IAR} = [X_j]_{IAR} \text{ and } CIR_X = CIR_{X_j}.$$

Next, consider the DIF, $X_j \longrightarrow X_{(j+1)}$.

Since $X_{(j+1)}$, receiving information from X_j, cannot be in CIR_{X_j}. By the FACT 2 again,

$$X_{j+1} \in [X_j]_{IAR} = [X]_{IAR}.$$

By the FACTs that IAR is an equivalence and CIR is its complement, we have

$$[X]_{IAR} = [X_{j+1}]_{IAR},$$

$$CIR_X = CIR_{X_{j+1}}.$$

This completes the induction proof. In particular

$$X_n = Y \in [X]_{IAR}.$$

This is contrary to one of the assumptions (Item 3.2). We have proved the strong Chinese wall security policy. That is, we have proved: SCWSP $\Longrightarrow$ ACWSP. The converse is obvious.

4. DAC Models and Trojan Horses

In this section, we take the DAC view on ACSWP model. If the agent x explicitly denies the read access to y, then we say

The information flow from X to Y is denied, or equivalently,

*N*o direct *I*nformation *F*low (NIF) from X to Y is permitted,

If the information flows between objects are regulated by NIF, we say O is a flow oriented explicitly denied DAC model. NIF defines a *B*inary relation (NIFR) among all objects.

Definition : A Composite Information Flow from X to Y is called a *malicious Trojan horse*, if NIF from X to Y is the given requirement.

Trojan Horse Theorem. If NIFR is anti-reflexive, symmetric and anti-transitive, then the following three assertions are equivalent

Malicious Trojan horses from X to Y may *not* occur

$\Longleftrightarrow$ DIF from X to Y may *not* occur

$\Longleftrightarrow$ $(X, Y) \in$ NIFR.

NIFR is a DAC form of CIR, so this theorem follows immediate from Chinese wall theorem.

5. Some New Views of ACWSP

The new observation on CIR gives a new insight to the CWSP-model. Here are the new views of theorems in [14] and [2].

THEOREM 1. Once a agent S_i has accessed an object O_j, the only other objects O_k accessible by S_i is inside the allied dataset of O_j, which is the outside of CIR_{O_j}.

THEOREM 2. The minimum number of agents which allow every object to be accessed by at least one agent is n, where n is the number of E_{CIR}-equivalence classes.

THEOREM 3. The flow of unsanitized information is confined to its allied dataset; sanitized information may, however, flow freely through the system.

6. Conclusions

The intuitive idea behind Brewer and Nash theory is useful for commercial security. By the new demands in eCommerce, as well as homeland security, we re-visited the BN-theory. In [19], we fuzzify the ACWSP model to make it more susceptible to uncertainty. In this paper, we refine ACWSP model by the new development of granular computing. The results are somewhat surprising, we can confine the malicious Trojan horses.

This paper realizes the BN's intend, however, it has more. From DAC's view, the results are just the beginning; it shows that information flows analysis on DAC is no longer a hopless subject. More analysis will be reported in near future.

Appendix: Granular Computing for CIR

Trojan horses in DAC model have been the weakest point of DAC model. Implicitly, BN's CWSP is designed to handle that. Unfortunately, their idea of using partition is a bit naive. This paper indicates that granulation seems a right notion. In next few sections, the new methodology will be explained.

1. Equivalence Relations and Partitions

A *partition* is a collection $\{N_j \mid j = 1, 2, \ldots\}$ of disjoint subsets whose union is V. This geometric notion defines naturally an algebraic notion, an equivalence relation, as follows:

$$E = \cup_j \{(p, u) \mid p \text{ and } u \text{ are in } N_j\}$$

This equivalence relation is reflexive, symmetric and transitive. N_j is called an equivalence class in mathematics. It also has been referred to as an elementary set, a block, a granule [24],[10],[21]. Conversely, an equivalence relation defines a partition; we skip the details.

Algebraically, a natural generalization of an equivalence relation is a binary relation. Geometrically, a "common" generalization of a partition is a covering. Unfortunately, a covering is not the geometric equivalence of a binary relation. The equivalent one is a more elaborate notion; see next subsection.

2. Binary Relations and Granulations

Let $R \subseteq V \times U$ be a binary relation. We will re-express R geometrically.

For each object $p \in V$, we associate a subset (binary set, neighborhood, or class) $N_p \subseteq U$ defined by

$$N_p = \{u \in U \mid (p, u) \in R\}$$

N_p consists of all elements v that are related to p by the binary relation R. Geometrically, N_p can be regarded as a neighborhood of p in the following sense: the points in N_p are "near to" or "related to" p via R. We will use binary neighborhood to remind us that algebraically, it is defined by a binary relation, while geometrically, it consists of points in proximity. Intuitively, N_p is the "nearest" neighborhood of p.

In BN-theory, CIR-classes are actually CIR-neighborhood. Just to be compatible with literature,we will use CIR-classes; readers should be cautioned that they are actually neighborhoods, not equivalence classes.

To help visualize the situation, we will use geometric language.

A binary granulation is an assignment that assigns to each object $p \in V$, a (possibly empty) subset $B_p \subseteq U$:

$$B : V \longrightarrow 2^U.$$

We will refer to the collection, $\{B_p \mid p \in V\}$, a binary neighborhood system and each B_p as a binary neighborhood of $p \in V$. They are called a basic neighborhood and a basic neighborhood system respectively in [16]. Though the subset B_p sounds arbitrary, it can be regarded as a binary neighborhood N_p of a binary relation, for all p. Formally, let us collect the comments into a

Proposition. Binary relation, binary granulation, and binary neighborhood system are equivalent.

In other words, given the map B (or the collection $\{B_p \subseteq U \mid p \in V\}$), there is a binary relation $R \subseteq V \times U$ such that $B_p = N_p$ and vice versa. So we will use the three terms interchangeably and denote all of them by B. The proof of the proposition is straight forward; we skip the details.

In application, a binary neighborhood at p

$$B_p = \{v \mid (p, v) \in B\}.$$

is often assigned a descriptive name, called elementary concept (or an attribute value in database community). The collection C of all those elementary concepts is called the concept space (or attribute domain). Formally, we define

A granular structure consists of 4-tuple

$$(V, U, B, C)$$

where V is called the object space, U is the data space (V and U could be the same set), B is a neighborhood system, and C is the concept space which consists of all the names of the fundamental neighborhoods of B. If B is a binary neighborhood system (binary relation), then the 4-tuple (V, U, B, C) is called a *binary granular structure.*

3. The Induced Partitions

In [17, 18], T. Y. Lin observed that the binary granulation relation,

$B : V \longrightarrow 2^U$

induced naturally a partition:

Consider the collection

$\{B^{-1}(w) \mid w \in 2^U\}$, called inverse image of w under B.

It is easy to verify that the collection forms a partition on V. We call it the induced partition of B, and denoted by E_B.

The equivalence class, $[p]_{E_B} = B^-1(B_p)$, or simply write as $[p]$, is called the *center* or *core* of B_p.

Proposition 1. The center $[p]$ consists of all those points that have the same binary neighborhood B_p ("same" in the sense of set theory).

Proposition 2. If $B \subseteq V \times V$ is a symmetric binary relation, and E_B is its induced equivalence relation, then each B-binary neighborhood is a union of E_B-equivalence classes.

Proof: Let B_p be the binary neighborhood of p. Let $x \in B_p$, and assume x and y are E_B-equivalence. By definition of equivalence in E_B, they have the same neighborhood, $B_x = B_y$. By the symmetry of B, $x \in B_p$ implies $p \in B_x = B_y$, and hence $y \in B_p$. In other words, both x and y are in B_p. Since y is arbitrary, this proves $[x] \subseteq B_p$, that is B_p contains the equivalence class $[x]$ of its member x. QED

This proposition is one of the main technical results that have a strong impact on Chinese Walls. The condition of symmetry in this proposition is needed: In the oringal version examples were given; for space consideration; we skip the examples.

4. The Complement of a Binary Relation

First some definitions

A symmetric binary relation B is a binary relation such that for every $(u, v) \in B$ implies $(v, u) \in B$.

A binary relation B is *anti-reflexive*, if B is non-empty and no pair (v, v) is in B.

That is, $B \cap \Delta = \emptyset$, where $\Delta = \{(v,v) \mid v \in V\}$ is the diagonal set.

A binary relation B is *anti-transitive*, if B is non-empty and if (u,v) belongs to B implies that for all w either (u,w) or (w,v) belongs to B.

$B' = V \times V \sim B$, which is the complement set of B, defines the complement binary relation (CBR).

Proposition 3. If B is symmetric, anti-reflexive and anti-symmetric, then the complement binary relation B' is an equivalence relation.

Proof: B is anti-reflexive, so the diagonal set is contained in the complement, that is, B' is reflexive. We will prove by indirect method: Assume to the contrary that (u,w) and (w,v) are in B' and its composition (u,v) were not (that is, $(u,v) \in B$). By anti-transitivity of B, we should either (u,w) and (w,v) belong to B; a contradiction. So the assumption $(u,v) \in B$ is incorrect; This leads to $(u,v) \in B'$); QED

Corollary 4. If B is symmetric, anti-reflexive and anti-transitive, then B' is the induced equivalence relation E_B.

Proof: Let $v \in V$ and B_v be its binary neighborhood. First we want to prove $B' \subseteq E_B$: That means we need to show that for any u, which is B'-equivalent to v, is E_B-equivalent to v, that is, $B_v = B_u$.

First, we will show $B_v \subseteq B_u$: Note that $(u,v) \in B'$, by assumption. Let p be a point in the B_v, that is, $(v,p) \in B$. Then, by anti-transitive and symmetry, (u,p) belong to B (otherwise, $(u,v) \in B$, which is absurd). That is, p is in the neighborhood of u. So we have proved that $B_v \subseteq B_u$.

Let $q \in B_u$ plays the role as p, by a similar arguments, We can show that $B_u \subseteq B_v$. So we have proved u and v have the same neighborhood, that is, $B_u = B_v$. This conclude the proof: $B' \subseteq E_B$.

Second, we will prove the reverse inclusion $E_B \subseteq B'$: Note that $(u,v) \in E_B$ implies $B_u = B_v$. Let p be a point in $B_u = B_v$, that is, both (u,p) and (p,v) belong to B. By anti-transitivity and symmetric, (u,v) belongs to B'. This proves the Corollary. QED

References

[1] Bell, D. 1987. Secure computer systems: A network interpretation. In Proceedings on 3rd Annual Computer Security Application Conference. 32–39.

[2] David D. C. Brewer and Michael J. Nash: "The Chinese Wall Security Policy" IEEE Symposium on Security and Privacy, Oakland, May, 1988, pp 206-214.

[3] Richard A. Brualdi, Introductory Combinatorics, Prentice Hall, 1992.

[4] W. Chu and Q. Chen Neighborhood and associative query answering, *Journal of Intelligent Information Systems*, **1**, 355-382, 1992.

[5] S. A. Demurjian and S. A. Hsiao "The Multimodel and Multilingual Database Systems-A Paradigm for the Studying of Database Systems, " IEEE Transaction on Software Engineering, 14, 8, (August 1988)

[6] Denning, D. E. 1976. A lattice model of secure information flow. Commun. ACM 19,2, 236–243.

[7] Hsiao, D.K., and Harary, F.,"A Formal System for Information Retrieval From Files," Communications of the ACM, 13, 2(February 1970). Corrigenda CACM 13,3 (March, 1970)

[8] Wong, E., and Chiang, T. C., "Canonical Structure in Attribute-Based File Organization," Communications of the ACM, Vol. 14, No. 9, September 1971.

[9] C. E. Landhehr, and C. L. Heitmeyer:Military Message Systems:Requirements and Security Model, NRL Memorandom Report 4925, Computer Science and Systemss Branch, Naval research Laboratory.

[10] T. T. Lee, "Algebraic Theory of Relational Databases," The Bell System Technical Journal Vol 62, No 10, December, 1983, pp.3159-3204

[11] T. Y. Lin, Neighborhood Systems and Relational Database. In: *Proceedings of 1988 ACM Sixteen Annual Computer Science Conference*, February 23-25, 1988, 725

[12] "A Generalized Information Flow Model and Role of System Security Officer", Database Security: Status and Prospects II, IFIP-Transaction, edited by C. E. Landwehr, North Holland, 1989, pp. 85-103.

[13] T. Y. Lin, Neighborhood Systems and Approximation in Database and Knowledge Base Systems, Proceedings of the Fourth International Symposium on Methodologies of Intelligent Systems , Poster Session, October 12- 15, pp. 75-86, 1989.

[14] T. Y. Lin, "Chinese Wall Security Policy–An Aggressive Model", Proceedings of the Fifth Aerospace Computer Security Application Conference, December 4-8, 1989, pp. 286-293.

[15] "Attribute Based Data Model and Polyinstantiation," Education and Society, IFIP-Transaction, ed. Aiken, 12th Computer World Congress, September 7-11, 1992, pp.472-478.

[16] T. Y. Lin, "Neighborhood Systems -A Qualitative Theory for Fuzzy and Rough Sets," Advances in Machine Intelligence and Soft Computing, Volume IV. Ed. Paul Wang, 1997, Duke University, North Carolina, 132-155. ISBN:0-9643454-3-3

[17] T. Y. Lin "Granular Computing on Binary Relations I: Data Mining and Neighborhood Systems." In: Rough Sets In Knowledge Discovery, A. Skoworn and L. Polkowski (eds), Physica-Verlag, 1998, 107-121

[18] T. Y. Lin "Granular Computing on Binary Relations II: Rough Set Representations and Belief Functions." In: Rough Sets In Knowledge Discovery, A. Skoworn and L. Polkowski (eds), Physica - Verlag, 1998, 121-140.

[19] T. Y. Lin "Chinese Wall Security Model and Conflict Analysis," the 24th IEEE Computer Society International Computer Software and Applications Conference (Compsac2000) Taipei, Taiwan, Oct 25-27, 2000

[20] T. Y. Lin "Feature Completion," Communication of IICM (Institute of Information and Computing Machinery, Taiwan) Vol 5, No. 2, May 2002, pp. 57-62. This is the proceeding for the workshop "Toward the Foundation on Data Mining" in PAKDD2002, May 6, 2002.

[21] T. Y. Lin "A Theory of Derived Attributes and Attribute Completion," Proceedings of IEEE International Conference on Data Mining, Maebashi, Japan, Dec 9-12, 2002.

[22] A, Motro: "Supportin Gaol Queries", in :Proceeding of the First Internatonal Conference on Expert Database Systems, L. Kerschber (eds)m April 1-4, 1986, pp. 85-96.

[23] S. Osborn, R. Sanghu and Q. Munawer,"Configuring RoleBased Access Control to Enforce Mandatory and Discretionary Access Control Policies," ACM Transaction on Information and Systems Security, Vol 3, No 2, May 2002, Pages 85-106.

[24] Z. Pawlak, Rough sets. International Journal of Information and Computer Science **11**, 1982, pp. 341-356.

[25] Z. Pawlak, "On Conflicts," Int J. of Man-Machine Studies, 21 pp. 127- 134, 1984

[26] Z. Pawlak, Analysis of Conflicts, Joint Conference of Information Science, Research Triangle Park, North Carolina, March 1-5, 1997, 350- 352.

[27] Polkowski, L., Skowron, A., and Zytkow, J., (1995),"Tolerance based rough sets." In: T.Y. Lin and A. Wildberger (eds.), Soft Computing: Rough Sets, Fuzzy Logic Neural Networks, Uncertainty Management, Knowledge Discovery, Simulation Councils, Inc. San Diego CA, 55–58.

[28] Sandhu, R. S. Latticebased enforcement of Chinese Walls. Computer & Security 11, 1992, 753–763.

[29] Sandhu, R. S. 1993. Latticebased access control models. IEEE Computer 26, 11, 9–19.

[30] Sandhu,R.S.,Coyne,E.J.,Feinstein,H.L.,and Youman, C. E. 1996. Rolebased access control models. IEEE Computer 29, 2 (Feb.), 38 – 47.

[31] Sandhu,R.AND Munawer, Q. 1998. How to do discretionary access control using roles. In Proceedings of the Third ACM Workshop on RoleBased Access Control (RBAC '98, Fairfax, VA, Oct. 22–23), C. Youman and T. Jaeger, Chairs. ACM Press, New York, NY, 47–54.

[32] W. Sierpinski and C. C, Kreiger, General Topology, University Toronto press, 1952

[33] T.C. Ting, "A User-Role Based Data Security Approach", in *Database Security: Status and Prospects*, C. Landwehr (ed.), North-Holland, 1988.

[34] Demurjian, S., and Ting, T.C., "Towards a Definitive Paradigm for Security in Object-Oriented Systems and Applications," J. of Computer Security, Vol. 5, No. 4, 1997.

[35] Liebrand, M., Ellis, H., Phillips, C., Demurjian, S., Ting, T.C., and Ellis, J., "Role Delegation for a Resource-Based Security Model," Data and Applications Security: Developments and Directions II, E. Gudes and S. Shenoi (eds.), Kluwer, 2003.

[36] Phillips, C., Demurjian, S., and Ting, T.C., "Towards Information Assurance in Dynamic Coalitions," Proc. of 2002 IEEE Info. Assurance Workshop, West Point, NY, June 2002.

[37] L.A. Zadeh, Fuzzy sets and information granularity, in: M. Gupta, R. Ragade, and R. Yager (Eds.), Advances in Fuzzy Set Theory and Applications, North-Holland, Amsterdam, 3-18, 1979.

[38] L. Zadeh, "Some Reflections on Information Granulation and its Centrality in Granular Computing, Computing with Words, the Computational Theory of Perceptions and Precisiated Natural Language." In: T. Y. Lin, Y.Y. Yao, L. Zadeh (eds), Data Mining, Rough Sets, and Granualr Computing T. Y. Lin, Y.Y. Yao, L. Zadeh (eds)

RBAC POLICY IMPLEMENTATION FOR SQL DATABASES

Steve Barker
King's College, U.K.

Paul Douglas
Westminster University, U.K.

Abstract We show how specifications of role-based access control (RBAC) and temporal role-based access control (TRBAC) policies in a logic language may be used in *practical* implementations of access control policies for protecting the information in SQL databases from unauthorized retrieval and update requests. Performance results for an implementation of a variety of RBAC policies for protecting an SQL databases and some optimization methods that may be used in implementations are described.

Keywords: RBAC, SQL, Internet Database.

1. Introduction

The protection of SQL databases from unauthorized access requests has long been recognized as being important. However, SQL standards and SQL products have hitherto included only limited options for expressing the protection requirements for the information contained in SQL databases.

In the SQL2 standard [11], the security-specific language features are restricted to simple GRANT and REVOKE statements. The GRANT-REVOKE model enables a *security administrator (SA)* to represent only a small subset of the access control policies that are needed in practice [4]. For instance, SQL does not enable conditional limitations on the use of a granted privilege to be specified [4]. Of course, views may also be used to help to control access to information, but combining views and GRANT-REVOKE statements complicates the expression of an access policy.

In the proposed SQL:1999 standard, language features for expressing RBAC policies are included. However, the proposals are again limited. For instance, SQL:1999 does not include features for representing temporal authorization policies. Although implementors of SQL database systems may offer more sophisticated options than those included in the SQL:1999 standard, current systems only provide limited options beyond the standard [23].

To augment the expressive power of access control languages, it is possible for a SA to use application programs written in some imperative language (e.g., C). However, the implementation of an access policy in a low-level, procedural language complicates the maintenance of an access policy and makes it difficult for SAs to reason about the consequences and effects of a policy specification.

The need for multipolicy specification using high-level specification languages with well-defined formal semantics has recently been recognised and a number of candidate proposals have been described in the literature [1, 7, 6, 15]. However, these proposals are theoretical in nature and performance measures for implementations of these models are usually missing (albeit [6] is an exception). The contribution of this paper is to describe some *practical* implementations of logic-based specifications of access requirements to protect SQL databases that are accessed over the internet. Another of our contributions is to show how practical implementations of our approach preserves the well-defined semantics upon which the specification of access control policies are based. Evidence for the practicability of our approach is provided in the form of a number of performance measures that we discuss in Section 5. A Java program is used to implement a system that integrates our access control subsystem with client applications and an SQL database. We choose to use Java because of its practical importance.

Recent work on protecting SQL databases has included [4], and [5]. In each of these proposals, SQL is used to implement access control policies for protecting the information in SQL databases, but without using any language-specific constructs for access policy formulation. The decision to use SQL to seamlessly protect SQL databases is a natural one and satisfies the attraction of requiring that a single language be used for implementing access control policies for protecting databases. However, SQL is a relatively low-level language (relative to logic languages), and SQL is not well-suited for proving properties of a policy specification [20]. As such, choosing SQL to formulate access policies for protecting SQL databases is not ideal. Moreover, in [4], the availability of an RDBMS that supports sophisticated *request modification* facilities [11] is assumed. Unfortunately, not all RDBMSs support the features that are required for the suggested approach, and the formal semantics, upon which the proposal is based, mixes operational and declarative features. In [5], the use of PL/SQL for implementing an access policy for protecting Oracle databases is described. The approach applies only to Oracle SQL databases. Moreover, the proposal involves transforming a formal policy specification from [2] into an equivalent PL/SQL form. However, no formal translation procedure is described. What is more, the implemented code is low-level and hence suffers from the same shortcomings exhibited if applications programs are used to implement access control policies (e.g., reasoning about the formal properties of a policy implementation is complicated).

The rest of the paper is organized thus. In Section 2, some basic notions in access control, RBAC, TRBAC and logic programming are described. In Section 3, the representation of RBAC and temporal RBAC (TRBAC) policies, by using *stratified logic programs* [22], is discussed. These policies are based on the $RBAC_{H2A}$ model that is informally defined in [26] and formally defined in [3]. Henceforth, we refer to the logic programs that implement $RBAC_{H2A}$ ($TRBAC_{H2A}$) policies as *RBAC* (*TRBAC*) programs. In Section 4, we describe our implementation of *RBAC*/*TRBAC* programs for protecting SQL databases from unauthorized access requests. In Section 5, we give some performance results for our approach. Finally, in Section 6, some conclusions are drawn and suggestions for further work are made.

2. Basic Concepts

The *RBAC* and *TRBAC* programs that we consider in the sequel are represented by using a finite set of *normal clauses* [21]. A normal clause takes the form:

$$H \leftarrow L_1, L_2, \ldots, L_m \qquad (m \geq 0).$$

The *head* of the clause, H, is an *atom* and $L_1, L_2, \ldots, L_m$ is a conjunction of *literals* that constitutes the *body* of the clause. The conjunction of literals $L_1, L_2, \ldots, L_m$ must be true (proven) in order for H to be true (proven). A literal is an atomic formula (a *positive literal*) or its negation (a *negative literal*); negation in this context is *negation as failure* [10], and the negation of the atom A is denoted by *not* A. A clause with an empty body is an *assertion* or a *fact*. In the sequel, we will be principally concerned with stratified programs.

An *RBAC* program S is defined on a domain of discourse that includes:

1 A set $\mathcal{U}$ of *users.*

2 A set $\mathcal{O}$ of *objects.*

3 A set $\mathcal{A}$ of *access privileges.*

4 A set $\mathcal{R}$ of *roles.*

The access privileges of interest to us in this paper are defined by the set:

$$\mathcal{A} = \{select, insert, delete, update\}.$$

The semantics of the access privileges in $\mathcal{A}$ are defined thus (where D is an arbitrary SQL database, ΔD is an updated state of D, and θ is a tuple):

- If a user u ($u \in \mathcal{U}$) has the privilege *select* on a set Θ of tuples ($\Theta \subseteq D$) and $D \models \theta$ then u is permitted to know that $\theta \in \Theta$ is true in D.
- If a user u ($u \in \mathcal{U}$) has the privilege *insert* on a set Θ of tuples ($\Theta \subseteq D$) then u is permitted to insert $\theta \in \Theta$ into D to generate $\Delta D = D \cup \theta$.
- If a user u ($u \in \mathcal{U}$) has the privilege *delete* on a set Θ of tuples ($\Theta \subseteq D$) then u is permitted to delete $\theta \in \Theta$ from D to generate $\Delta D = D - \theta$.
- If a user u ($u \in \mathcal{U}$) has the privilege *update* on a set Θ of tuples ($\Theta \subseteq D$) then u is permitted to change Θ to $\Delta\Theta$ and to generate $\Delta D = (D - \Theta) \cup \Delta\Theta$.

The $\mathcal{U}$, $\mathcal{O}$, $\mathcal{A}$ and $\mathcal{R}$ sets, comprise the (disjoint and finite) sets of user, object, access privilege and role identifiers that form part of the universe of discourse for an *RBAC* program. In this framework we have the following definitions.

Definition 1 *An authorization is a triple (u, a, o) that denotes that a user u ($u \in U$) has the a access privilege ($a \in A$) on the object o ($o \in O$).*

Definition 2 *If a is an access privilege and o is an object then a permission is a pair (a, o) that denotes that the a access privilege may be exercised on o.*

Definition 3 *A permission-role assignment is a triple (a, o, r) that denotes that the permission (a, o) is assigned to the role r.*

Definition 4 *A user-role assignment is a pair* (u, r) *that denotes that the user* u *is assigned to the role* r.

For *TRBAC* programs, in addition to elements from the sets $\mathcal{U}$, $\mathcal{O}$, $\mathcal{A}$ and $\mathcal{R}$, we require a set $\mathcal{T}$ of *time points.* We view time as a linearly ordered, discrete set of time points that are isomorphic to the natural numbers.

Definition 5 *A temporal authorization is a 4-tuple* (u, a, o, t) *that denotes that user* u *has the* a *access privilege on object* o *at time* t.

In this paper, we assume that a $(T)RBAC$ program defining a *closed policy* [8] is used to protect an SQL database. The implementation of various open policies or any number of hybrid (i.e., open/closed) policies for protecting D necessitates that only minor modifications be made to the approach that we describe (see [6]).

In the sequel, the constants that appear in clauses will be denoted by symbols that appear in the lower case; variables will be denoted by using upper case symbols. Moreover, we will use the constants u, o, a, r and t to denote a distinct, arbitrary user, object, access privilege, role and time, respectively. In clauses, we use the variables U, O, A, R and T to respectively denote a set of users, objects, access privileges, roles and times.

The result that follows is an immediate consequence of a $(T)RBAC$ program being a set of stratified clauses.

Proposition 1 *An* $(T)RBAC$ *program* S *has a unique 2-valued well-founded model that coincides with the perfect model of* S *[9].*

Corollary 1 $(T)RBAC$ *programs define a consistent and unambiguous set of authorizations.*

In our representation of $(T)RBAC$ programs, functions are only used to express structured terms and do not result in unbounded terms being generated during computation. Moreover, if a $(T)RBAC$ program is expressed by using built-in comparison or mathematical operators then we assume that a SA will express these definitions in a *safe* form [27] such that the arguments of a condition involving these operators are bound to constants prior to the evaluation of the condition.

3. Representing $(T)RBAC$ Programs

The $RBAC$ programs that we describe in this section are based on the specification of $RBAC$ as a normal clause program from [1]. In [1], a user U is specified as being assigned to a role R by a SA defining a 2-place $ura(U, R)$ predicate in an $RBAC$ program. For example, $ura(bob, r1) \leftarrow$ is used to record the assignment of the user Bob to the role $r1$. To record that the A access privilege on an object O is assigned to a role R, clause form definitions of a 3-place $pra(A, O, R)$ predicate are used. For example, $pra(insert, \rho(a, Y), r1) \leftarrow$ expresses that the role $r1$ is assigned the *insert* privilege on the binary relation ρ provided that the pairs (X, Y) inserted into ρ are such that $X = a$.

An $RBAC$ role hierarchy is represented by a partial order $(R, \geq)$ that defines a seniority ordering $\geq$ on a set of roles R. Role hierarchies are used to represent the idea that, unless constraints are imposed, "senior" roles inherit the permissions assigned to "junior" roles in an $RBAC$ role hierarchy. Hence, if $r_i \in R$, $r_j \in R$, and $r_i \geq r_j$ then r_i inherits the permissions assigned to r_j.

Following [1], an $RBAC$ role hierarchy is expressed in an $RBAC$ program by a set of clauses that define a 2-place *senior_to* predicate as the reflexive-transitive closure of an irreflexive-intransitive 2-place ds predicate that defines the set of pairs of roles (r_i, r_j) such that r_i is directly senior to role r_j in an $RBAC$ role hierarchy (i.e., r_i is senior to r_j and there is no role $r_k \in \mathcal{R}$ such that r_i is senior to r_k and r_k is senior to r_i).

In clause form logic, *senior_to* is defined in terms of ds thus (where '_' is an anonymous variable):

$$senior\_to(R1, R1) \leftarrow ds(R1, \_).$$
$$senior\_to(R1, R1) \leftarrow ds(\_, R1).$$
$$senior\_to(R1, R2) \leftarrow ds(R1, R2).$$
$$senior\_to(R1, R2) \leftarrow ds(R1, R3), senior\_to(R3, R2).$$

To represent that a user u is active in a role r at a time t, an $active(u, r)$ fact is appended to a $(T)RBAC$ program whenever u requests to be active in r and this request is allowed. The set of *active* facts in a $(T)RBAC$ program at an instance of time t is the set of roles that users have active at time t.

The set of authorization triples defined by an $RBAC$ program are expressed by the following clause:

$$\begin{aligned} permitted(U, A, O) \leftarrow\ & ura(U, R1), active(U, R1), \\ & senior\_to(R1, R2), pra(A, O, R2). \end{aligned}$$

The $permitted(U, A, O)$ clause expresses that a user U has the A access privilege on an object O if U is assigned to, and is active in, a role $R1$ that is senior to the role $R2$ in an $RBAC$ role hierarchy associated with the $RBAC$ program, and $R2$ is assigned the A access privilege on O.

Only minor modifications are required to extend $RBAC$ programs to $TRBAC$ programs. For a $TRBAC$ program S, the set of authorization triples defined by S may be expressed by the following clause:

$$permitted(U, A, O, T) \leftarrow time(T), ura(U, R1, T), active(U, R1), senior\_to(R1, R2), pra(A, O, R2, T).$$

The $permitted(U, A, O, T)$ clause expresses that a user U has the A access privilege on an object O at time T (extracted from the system clock using $time(T)$) if U is assigned to a role $R1$ at T, U is active in $R1$, $R1$ is senior to the role $R2$ in an $RBAC$ role hierarchy defined by the $TRBAC$ program, and $R2$ is assigned the A access privilege on O at T.

4. The Practical Implementation of $(T)RBAC$ Programs

In this section, we describe the practical implementation of $RBAC$ and $TRBAC$ programs for protecting SQL databases.

We have adopted a modular approach to developing the software that implements our proposal. There are three principal components in our implementation:

- The Main Program.
- The Security Module.
- The Database System.

The three components above are used with a client application. We refer to an implementation that is based on these components as a *composite system.* It follows that a composite system Σ is defined in terms of a 4-tuple $\Sigma = (\mathcal{M}, \mathcal{S}, \mathcal{D}, \mathcal{C})$ where: $\mathcal{M}$ denotes the main program; $\mathcal{S}$ denotes the security module; $\mathcal{D}$ denotes the database system; and $\mathcal{C}$ denotes a client application. The key features and issues relating to a composite system Σ are briefly outlined below.

The Main Program. The main program $\mathcal{M}$ is written in Java: Java is a suitable language for this type of application because of its comprehensive server programming support (using *Java Servlets* [18]) and its ability to communicate easily with a DBMS using JDBC [19]. In addition, it is easy to access applications written in a variety of other languages (through the *Java Native Interface (JNI)* [17] mechanism).

Java's support for distributed processing means that it will also be well-suited for future developments that we are considering for access control in a distributed DBMS environment.

The $\mathcal{M}$ module acts as a server program that receives access requests from a client application $\mathcal{C}$. The client application is written in HTML for display in a browser window. All user data will be entered via the browser, and all data will be returned to a browser; this is typically the case with e-commerce applications. The principal function of the $\mathcal{M}$ module is to call the $\mathcal{S}$ and $\mathcal{D}$ modules to respectively authorize an access request and to process the request with respect to an SQL database. In the case of a SELECT request involving a query Q on $\mathcal{D}$, the output produced by the $\mathcal{M}$ module is the set Θ of tuples that satisfies Q from $\mathcal{D} \cup \mathcal{S}$; Θ is the answer that is returned to $\mathcal{C}$ by $\mathcal{M}$. Alternatively, if the request for authorization is denied by $\mathcal{S}$, an error message indicating the denial of service is returned to $\mathcal{C}$ by $\mathcal{M}$ and no further action is taken; no request is passed to $\mathcal{D}$ and no DBMS activity occurs.

We have developed two alternative implementations of a session management system. We call these methods $M1$ and $M2$ where:

- $M1$ involves authorizing every database transaction individually, so the duration of a user session is precisely one transaction. This does involve a certain processing overhead, but gives a high level of security where the *RBAC* policy includes either temporal or *dynamic separation of duties* [26] constraints.

- $M2$ establishes a longer session that remains current until either the user terminates the session, or the session is terminated by the system (by, say, a timeout mechanism). The role allocation the user is given is recorded by an entry in a database table used purely for this purpose. The $M2$ method has the additional benefit of being easy to extend to include temporal constraints (i.e., constraints on access that are more sophisticated than a mere inactivity or length-of-session based timeout mechanism) and a dynamic separation of roles constraint. The latter option is straightforward to implement as our $\mathcal{S}$ module can directly consult the database table in which current role allocations are stored.

The Security Module. Within the $\mathcal{S}$ module, we use XSB [24] to implement the logic program that defines the access control applicable to an SQL database to be protected. XSB offers excellent performance that has been demonstrated to be far superior to that of traditional Prolog-based systems [25]. Calls to XSB from $\mathcal{M}$ are handled by the YAJXB [29] package. YAJXB makes use of Java's JNI mechanism to invoke methods in the C interface library package supplied by XSB. It also handles all of the data type conversions that are needed when passing data between C and Prolog-based applications. YAJXB effectively provides all the functionality of the C package within a Java environment.

Although we have used YAJXB in our implementation of composite systems, we note that a number of alternative options exist. Amongst the options that we considered for implementing composite systems were:

- Interprolog [14].
- One of the Java-based Prolog interpreters currently available (e.g., JavaLog [16]).
- a Sockets-based, direct communication approach [12].

Each of the above approaches has its own distinct drawbacks when compared with the approach that we adopted. Interprolog does work with XSB, so we could still take advantage of the latter's performance capabilities. However, Interprolog is primarily a Windows-based application. All of our development was done on a Sun Sparc/Solaris system; YAJXB, though primarily configured for Linux, compiles easily on Solaris. JavaLog was discounted because we felt that it did not offer sufficient performance for the types of implementations and volumes of data involved in practical applications of our approach. Finally, using sockets would give us a less flexible application because it would involve considerably more application-specific coding. Overall, we felt that the straightforwardness of the YAJXB interface makes it preferable to the Interprolog approach so far as interfacing with XSB is concerned. Moreover, XSB's highly developed status and excellent performance make it more desirable in this context than a Java/Prolog hybrid.

Once XSB has been successfully invoked by $\mathcal{S}$, XSB loads a program that contains the Prolog expression of an *RBAC* program (see above). This is used to determine whether the access requests made via the client application $\mathcal{C}$ are permitted (by $\mathcal{S}$) or not.

The C library allows the full functionality of XSB to be used. A variety of methods for passing Prolog-style goal clauses to XSB exists. However, we generally found that YAJXB's string method worked well. This method involves constructing a string σ in a Java String type variable, and using the *xsb_command_string* function (or similar) to pass σ to XSB. This approach allows any string that could be entered as a command when using XSB interactively to be passed to XSB by $\mathcal{S}$. YAJXB creates an interface object. The precise method of doing this is a call like

$$i = core.xsb\_command\_string(command.toString());$$

where the assignment, as one would expect, handles the returned error code. More sophisticated methods would allow for the return of data too; though this is not necessary where authorization is merely confirmed or denied.

The key technical results for query evaluation on SQL databases protected by using $\mathcal{D} \cup \mathcal{S}$ follow directly from the soundness and completeness results for SLG-resolution applicable to stratified theories. As $\mathcal{S}$ is a function-free stratified program and YAJXB only passes facts to XSB it follows that every authorized access request is provable by SLG-resolution and no unauthorized access is provable by (safe) SLG-resolution. These results extend to *TRBAC* programs.

Database System. Although $\mathcal{D}$, in a composite system, may be any SQL database, we have used Oracle in implementations of our system (because of its widespread use within industry). A composite system could easily be adapted to apply to a large number of existing Oracle applications. For the interface between $\mathcal{M}$ and $\mathcal{D}$, we have used JDBC [19]. JDBC is now a well-established technology and has the additional advantage that JDBC drivers exist for numerous DBMS packages. It follows that, with minimal modifications, a composite system could be used with any DBMS with which JDBC drivers may be used.

5. Performance Measures

In any system where data is accessed over the Internet, by far the biggest time overhead will be caused by communications costs. As our model does not introduce any additional traffic (i.e., the data sent by, and returned to, a remote user is the same as it would be if our authorization model were not used), this component of performance cost remains unchanged, and we do not therefore consider any specific time delay values. Similarly, the overheads associated with accessing the DBMS are unchanged, and we again do not consider any specific values.

The performance cost that we have added to a transaction is the one of calling the subsystem ($\mathcal{S}$) that we use to authorize access requests. Although the costs of using $\mathcal{S}$ are minimal when compared with communication costs, we have conducted various performance tests on an *RBAC* program that we use to protect SQL databases from unauthorized access requests. Our *RBAC* program includes a definition of a 53 role *RBAC* role hierarchy that has been represented by using a set of facts to represent all pairs of roles in the *senior_to* relation (a total of 312 *senior_to* facts). For our SQL tests, we have used the data from [5]. There is one user, one *ura* rule, 8 database objects (tables) containing a total of 432,261 tuples, and 720 *pra* rules. It is sufficient for test purposes to use one user to demonstrate a worst-case use of the access control information in an *RBAC* program. This worst case test involves assigning a user u to the unique top element in the *RBAC* role hierarchy, such that u has complete access to all of the tables used in the test queries. The permissions are assigned to the unique bottom element in the *RBAC* role hierarchy. Hence, our testing involves the maximum amount of multiple upward inheritance of permissions.

The experiments were performed using XSB Version 2.5 on a Sun Ultra 60 server (2 450MHz CPUs and 1GB RAM) running Solaris. Typically, the time taken to evaluate an authorization request is less than a hundredth of a second. Furthermore, where a user's request for data is not authorized, no database access takes place at all and no processing costs are incurred. A summary of our results for "fixed" costs is given in Table 1. By "fixed" we mean the fixed overheads of invoking XSB.

Operation	*Time (seconds)*
Start XSB	*0.07*
XSB loads and compiles RBAC program	*1.285*
XSB loads precompiled RBAC program	*0.01*

Table 1. Fixed Costs

The figures in Table 1 are averages: each operation was performed five times. On first load of the Prolog program (which in this case represents our *RBAC* policy), XSB compiles the code and stores the compiled version. Subsequently, if the program has not changed since the last compilation, XSB loads the compiled version, with a significant reduction in the load time.

The performance times that we give have been obtained using XSB's *statistics* package. XSB gives times for CPU usage in seconds, accurate to two decimal places.

Table 2 shows the results we obtained for a number of tests of access requests (averaged over ten runs). We performed worst case tests (see above) and, for comparison, best case tests (where there is no upward inheritance of permissions). For each, we tested with data that would give both possible outcomes for the requested database operation.

Case	*Outcome*	*Time (seconds)*
worst	*permitted*	*0.002*
worst	*denied*	*0.001*
best	*permitted*	*0.002*
best	*denied*	*0.0*

Table 2. Variable Costs

Given the magnitude of these figures, it is possible that measuring inaccuracies render the small differences between them difficult to evaluate. We confine ourselves to noting that the query execution time is minimal when compared with the time taken to start XSB and load the program. The total time required to authorize a database access request, if the RBAC program has not been updated since the last time it was compiled, is about a tenth of a second. This compares favourably with the results we obtained in [5], where a PL/SQL-based implementation of our *RBAC* model took 1.08 seconds.

In contrast to user queries on $\mathcal{D}$, it should be noted that a SA may evaluate administrative review queries with respect to an $RBAC_{H2A}$ program $\mathcal{S}$ directly. For example, to generate the set of users assigned to the role $r1$, in the process of performing a *user-role review* [26], a SA simply needs to use SLG-resolution to evaluate the goal clause $? - ura(U, r1)$ with respect to $\mathcal{S}$.

For completeness, we performed a number of such queries; the results are given in Table 3. We believe that the apparently identical times taken for almost all of the queries shows that the computation time was too small for XSB to accurately record.

Number of ura *facts*	*Number of Users assigned to role* r1	*Time (seconds)*
300	*1*	*0.01*
300	*6*	*0.01*
300	*40*	*0.01*
600	*6*	*0.01*
600	*65*	*0.04*

Table 3. Retrieval times for test database D.

6. Conclusions and Further Work

We have shown how the information in SQL databases may be protected from unauthorized access requests by using *RBAC* and *TRBAC* programs. The high-level formulation of an access policy as a logic program makes it relatively easy for a SA to express an access policy, to reason about its effects and to maintain it. Moreover, it is possible to use this specification of policy in an implementation of composite systems. We have demonstrated that the access policies that we use for protecting SQL databases may be efficiently implemented.

In future work, we intend to investigate how constraint checking on $\mathcal{S}$ may be incorporated into the approach that we have described here.

References

[1] Barker, S., Data Protection by Logic Programming, *1st International Conference on Computational Logic*, LNAI 1861, 1300-1313, Springer, 2000.

[2] Barker, S., $TRBAC^N$: A Temporal Authorization Model, *Proc. MMMANCS International Workshop on Network Security*, in V. Gorodetski, V. Skormin, and L. Popyak (Eds.), Lecture Notes in Computer Science 2052, Springer, 178-188, 2001.

[3] Barker, S., Protecting Deductive Databases from Unauthorized Retrieval and Update Requests, *Journal of Data and Knowledge Engineering*, Elsevier, 293-315, 2002.

[4] Barker, S., and Rosenthal, A., Flexible Security Policies in SQL, DBSec 2001, 187-199, 2001.

[5] Barker, S., Douglas, P. and Fanning, T., *Implementing RBAC Policies in PL/SQL*, DBSec 2002.

[6] Barker, S., and Stuckey, P., Flexible Access Control Policy Specification with Constraint Logic Programming, ACM Trans. on Information and System Security, 6, 4, 501-548, 2003.

[7] Bertino, E., Catania, B., Ferrari, E., and Perlasca, P., A System to Specify and Manage Multipolicy Access Control Models, *Proc. IEEE 3rd International Workshop on Policies for Distributed Systems and Networks (POLICY 2002)*, 116-127, 2002.

[8] Castano, S., Fugini, M., Martella, G., and Samarati, P., *Database Security*, Addison-Wesley, 1995.

[9] Chen, W., and Warren, D., A Goal-Oriented Approach to Computing the Well-Founded Semantics, *J. Logic Programming*, 17, 279-300, 1993.

[10] Clark, K., Negation as Failure, in H.Gallaire and J. Minker(Eds), *Logic and Databases*, Plenum, NY, 293-322, 1978.

[11] Date, C., *An Introduction to Database Systems (7th Edition)*, Addison-Wesley, 2000.

[12] Donahoo, M. and Calvert, K, *The Pocket Guide to TCP/IP Sockets*, Morgan Kaufmann, 2001.

[13] Ferraiolo, D., Gilbert, D., and Lynch, N., An Examination of Federal and Commercial Access Control Policy Needs, *Proc. 16th NIST-NSA National Computer Security Conference*, 107-116, 1993.

[14] InterProlog by Declarativa. www.declarativa.com/InterProlog/default.htm

[15] Jajodia, S., Samarati, P., Sapino, M., and Subrahmaninan, V., Flexible Support for Multiple Access Control Policies, ACM TODS,26, 2, 214-260, 2001.

[16] The ISISTAN Brainstorm Project: JavaLog. www.exa.unicen.edu.ar/~azunino/javalog.html

[17] Java Native Interface, *Sun Microsystems.* java.sun.com/products/

[18] Java Servlet Technology: Implementations and Specifications, *Sun Microsystems.* java.sun.com/products/jdk/1.2/docs/guide/jni

[19] The JDBC API, *Sun Microsystems.* java.sun.com/products/jdbc

[20] Libkin, L, The Expressive Power of SQL, *Proc. ICDT*, 1-21, 2001.

[21] LLoyd, J., *Foundations of Logic Programming*, Springer, 1987.

[22] Przymusinski, T., Perfect Model Semantics, *Proc. 5th ICLP*, MIT Press, 1081-1096, 1988.

[23] Ramaswarmy, C., and Sandhu, R., Role-Based Access Control Features in Commercial Database Management Systems, *Proc. 21st National Information Systems Security Conference*, 503-511, 1998.

[24] Sagonas, K., Swift, T., Warren, D., Freire, J., Rao, P., The XSB System, Version 2.0, Programmer's Manual, 1999.

[25] Sagonas, K., Swift, T. and Warren, D., XSB as an Efficient Deductive Database Engine , *ACM SIGMOD Proceedings*, p512, 1994.

[26] Sandhu, R., Ferraiolo, D., and Kuhn, R., The NIST Model for Role-Based Access Control: Towards a Unified Standard, *Proc. 4th ACM Workshop on Role-Based Access Control*, 47-61, 2000.

[27] Ullman, J., *Principles of Database and Knowledge-Base Systems: Volume 1*, Computer Science Press, 1990.

[28] Van Gelder, A., Ross, K., and Schlipf, J., The Well-Founded Semantics for General Logic Programs, *J. ACM*, 38(3), 620-650, 1991.

[29] Decker, S., YAJXB, www-db.stanford.edu/~stefan/rdf/yajxb

AN ADMINISTRATIVE MODEL FOR ROLE GRAPHS

He Wang and Sylvia L. Osborn *
Department of Computer Science, University of Western Ontario, Canada

Abstract For the role graph model, we have always assumed that the administration of the role graph and group graph is carried out by a single (centralized) administrator. This is not realistic in practise. In this paper, we present a decentralized administrative model for the role and group graphs. The model uses administrative domains, and administrative roles which are part of the role graph. A discussion of why domains cannot overlap is given, as well as a discussion of how users and privileges might be in more than one domain. Details of administrative privileges are given. We also present a detailed discussion comparing the new model to other administrative models for role-based access control.

Keywords: role-based access control, administration of access control

1. Introduction

The role graph model has been described in previous papers [6, 7], and is one version of role-based access control (RBAC). The model is described on three planes: the user plane on which users and groups can be modeled [9], the privileges plane on which implications among privileges can be modeled [3], and the role plane on which the role graph is built. The role graph represents role-role relationships by an acyclic, directed graph called the role graph. A tool has been developed which allows users to interact with algorithms for a role graph and a group graph, and to assign users/groups to roles [10].

Our previous papers have always assumed centralized administration of the role graph. This is not realistic in most applications of role-based access control. The motivation for using RBAC is that it helps with management of access control in an enterprise with many (i.e. thousands

---

*This research was supported by the Natural Sciences and Engineering Research Council of Canada.

of) users, roles and privileges. Such an environment is not manageable by one person. The purpose of this paper is to introduce decentralized administration for the role graph model.

Crampton and Loizou [1] and Sandhu et al. [12, 13, 8] have presented administrative models for RBAC. ARBAC97, presented in [13], discusses users, roles and privileges, how they interact, and how they can be managed. ARBAC02, in [8], modifies the user and permission aspects of their previous administrative model. Crampton and Loizou develop a concept called an administrative scope, which changes dynamically as the role hierarchy changes. Recently, others have also introduced administrative aspects to RBAC models [4, 2, 15]. We will give a more detailed discussion of these other models after introducing our own model.

The paper is organized as follows: Section 2 reviews the basic concepts of the role graph model. Section 3 introduces the administrative model. Section 4 gives descriptions of administrative operations on regular roles. Section 5 discusses operations on administrative domains and other administrative privileges, and includes a simple example showing how we get started. Section 6 contains a detailed comparison with other models. Conclusions are found in Section 7.

2. The Role Graph Model

In the role graph model [7], roles consist of a role name and a set of privileges, each of which is an (object, operation) pair. Roles are arranged in a role graph, with two distinguished roles: MaxRole and MinRole. MaxRole represents all the privileges in the role graph and need not be assigned to any user or group. MinRole represents the least privileges assigned to anyone in the system. We distinguish between *direct privileges* which are those directly assigned to a role, and *effective privileges* which consist of the direct privileges and those inherited from junior roles. The effective privilege set represents all privileges available to any user assigned to a role. Role r_i *is-junior* to role r_j if effective(r_i) $\subset$ effective(r_j). Role graphs have the following properties:

- there is a single MaxRole,
- there is a single MinRole,
- the graphs are acyclic,
- there is a path from MinRole to every role r_i,
- there is a path from every role r_i to MaxRole,
- for any two roles r_i and r_j, if effective(r_i) $\subset$ effective(r_j), then there must be a path from r_i to r_j,
- by convention we draw the graphs with MaxRole at the top, MinRole

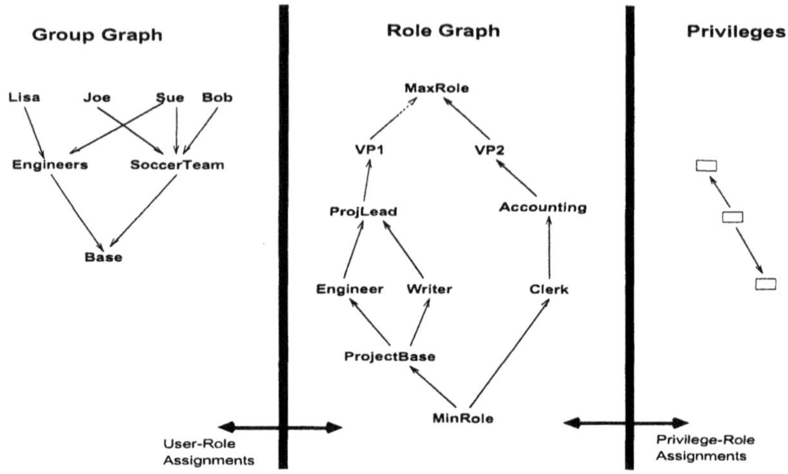

Figure 1. The Three-Plane Model

at the bottom, and junior roles lower on the page than their seniors.
- we remove transitive edges from the display to make the graph less cluttered.

The Group Graph model allows one to create sets of users, say to represent committees or people assigned to a project, who may not have the same job title. To simplify the model, each individual user is regarded as a group of cardinality 1. The edges in the group graph are determined by the subset relationship between two groups. By convention we draw the group graph with the Base group which contains all users at the bottom, and the groups representing individual user groups at the top.

Conceptually, we view the model on three planes, as shown in Figure 1. The structure of the group graph is developed on the left plane, the role graph is developed in the middle plane, and the privileges are represented in the right hand plane. Privileges are assigned to roles by operations on the role graph. We assume that if there are implications among privileges, all implied privileges are included when a privilege is assigned to a role [3]. Users are assigned to roles by considering the interaction between the group graph and the role graph. Other operations are available on role graphs to insert/delete roles, insert/delete edges and add/remove privileges from a role. Any of these role graph operations may alter the "shape" of the role graph when the role graph properties above are restored. As well, all of the operations abort and leave the role graph unchanged if a cycle would be created.

3. The Administrative Model

The operations already available in the role graph model were motivated by considering what might be useful to an administrator when trying to design the access control for a complex system. The structure of the administrative model presented here has been motivated by considering a large corporate environment and the hierarchical management style that is likely to exist in such an environment. We would like the administration to be captured by administrative roles, which are a (special) part of the role graph. Special privileges will be developed to allow the administrative roles to carry out their administrative operations. The administrative model needs to be aware of the algorithms already available for manipulating role graphs, and possibly put constraints on the extent to which a given security administrator may make changes to the role graph. At the same time, the role graph properties must also be maintained whenever an administrative role alters the role graph.

People in the business world usually draw a hierarchical organization structure called an organization chart or reports-to graph, which can also be called a supervision hierarchy [5]. The root node of this tree is the president or CEO; the lowest nodes are positions in departments or branches. This hierarchical structure is not the same as an RBAC role inheritance structure or role graph, because the higher level positions may have fewer privileges than the lower level positions. For example, the president of the company may only have privileges to carry out some very high level operations, and may not be permitted to look at all the details of all the data under control of the RBAC system.

In a typical company, access control is administered in a decentralized way by a group of administrators, security officers and other employees [11]. At the top, there is a CEO or CFO in charge of all security issues of the company. Under the CEO or CFO is an SSO (System Security Officer) whose responsibility is the creation and enforcement of the company security policy. Depending on the complexity of the company, there might be department security officers (DSOs) or branch security officers (BSOs). They represent the local security administrators for possibly decentralized parts of the company. Our administrative model must be able to describe such a decentralized management of access control.

Our administrative model is built on the idea of an administrative domain. Administrative domains (or admin domains) have some relationship to Crampton and Loizou's administrative scope and Sandhu's role range, but they have some important differences. The basis of our model is still the role graph, and the administrative roles will also be part of the role graph. The main idea is to divide the role graph into

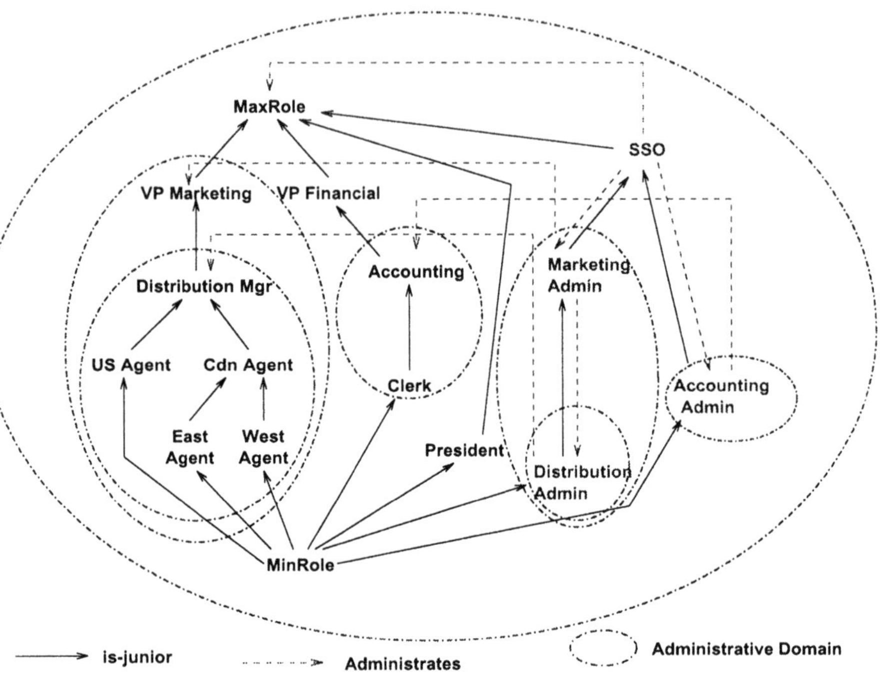

Figure 2. Role Graph with Administrative Domains

administrative domains in which operations can be carried out to alter the role graph, or users and privileges can be assigned to roles. We also need a way to relate administrators to the portion of the role graph that they are going to administrate.

An *Administrative Domain* is a set of roles which contains a top-most role d called the *domain identifier* or domain ID, and all roles in the role graph s such that s is-junior d, except for MinRole. In the role graph in Figure 2, several administrative domains are shown. As well, there are administrative roles: SSO, Marketing Admin, Distribution Admin and Accounting Admin. Edges showing the relationship between administrative roles and administrative domains are also shown in the Figure. This is a many-to-many relationship; for example the SSO administrates several domains in the example. The Distribution domain in the example is administrated by several administrative roles: Distribution Admin, and indirectly by Marketing Admin and SSO.

The model also includes a single highest admin domain called the *default domain*, which includes MaxRole and MinRole. The administrative role assigned to administrate this domain should be the highest administrative role in the company. This is the only administrator who can make changes to MinRole. In previous presentations of the Role Graph Model, this highest administrative role was assumed but not shown, and this was the only admin domain present. Thus this administrative model is consistent with the original Role Graph Model.

Consider the intersection I of two administrative domains, $I = D_1 \cap D_2$. If I is non-empty, then if $I = D_1$ or $I = D_2$, we say the domains are *nested.* If I is non-empty and not equal to D_1 or D_2, we say we have an *overlap. We do not allow administrative domains to overlap.* The reason for this is the following. Suppose, looking at Figure 2, there is a role X which comes between MinRole and West Agent, and between MinRole and Clerk. By the definition of administrative domains, this role would be in the accounting, marketing and distribution domains. The administrators of any of these domains could add or delete privileges to/from X. Thus these administrators could make changes to the role graph which would affect domains of which they are not the administrator. Thus, overlapping domains are not allowed. If there is some basic set of privileges which all domains need, they can be added to MinRole. The case where only some domains need a common privilege is discussed below.

Just as we do not want roles that exist in more than one domain, we also do not want edges that go from one domain to another. This can arise if privileges are allowed to be in more than one domain, which we *would* like to allow. There is always some data which may need to be shared between domains. For example, if each admin domain represents a branch of a large bank, the information about the bank's savings account customers should be available in every branch. Having such shared data means that there is probably some basic privilege like (customer data, read) which represents the sharing of the data. Creating a role with only this one privilege in domain D_1, would cause an edge to any role in domain D_2 which contains this same privilege. Having an edge from a role r_1 in domain D_1 to a role r_2 in domain D_2 means that if another privilege is added to role r_1, the role graph structure and algorithms will cause this privilege to be inherited by r_2, which again means that the administrator of D_1 is making changes that affect D_2.

There are several ways to deal with these shared privileges. One way is to put them all in MinRole. This may not always be feasible since they would also be inherited by every other domain. A second way, currently being implemented in a prototype [14], is to extend the model for privileges so that each privilege also has a domain ID. Privileges must have the same domain ID as the domain of any role they become part of. We can still equate the privileges by looking at the object name and access mode.

The third way to deal with shared privileges is to not have a domain ID attached to each privilege, but to check after each operation on the role graph if any edges have been created which cross domain boundaries, and if this is so, abort the operation (just as the current role graph algorithms abort any operation if a cycle would be created). If the security administrators are careful to always put these shared privileges into roles with some privilege unique to the domain, then edges between domains should never result.

Administrative domains also include users and groups from the group graph (not shown in Figure 2). We want it to be possible for a user to work in different domains (an employee might work at different branches of a bank on different days of the week), so that overlapping of the users in different domains is allowed. In the current prototype, each user has one or more domain IDs associated with it.

4. Administrative Operations on Regular Roles

Administrative roles, like other roles, have privileges. Since they are just roles, these privileges could be anything. However, in keeping with the desire to keep the model intuitive to people running real companies, these privileges should be restricted to being administrative privileges. Algorithms for these operations have been presented and implemented for a role graph with centralized administration [7, 10]. They have to be modified in order to enforce the concept of administrative domains. We have to add constraints to the role graph operations so that the operations permitted do not alter parts of the role graph outside of an administrative role's administrative domain. Note that modifying the group memberships or group-role assignments does not alter the role graph, but modifying privilege-role assignments can alter the role graph quite significantly.

Here is a list of the operations needed and how they must be modified to maintain the desired properties of administrative domains.

Add a privilege to a role: If an arbitrary privilege is added to a role, it will, by the inheritance caused by the is-junior relationships, be inherited all the way up to MaxRole. This is an example of where a local operation can affect parts of the graph outside of an administrative domain. We solve this problem by having an administrator of an enclosing domain (there is always one such domain, the default domain) add/remove privileges from the domain identifier, i.e. the top role in each domain, as direct privileges if necessary. Then the domain administrator is constrained to choosing from the domain ID's privileges when adding a privilege to a lower role in the domain. Such a privilege addition does not alter the effective privileges of the domain ID, and thus does not affect roles outside of the administrative domain. By adding a privilege to a role like West Agent (a privilege already available in Distribution Mgr) in Figure 2, it becomes a direct privilege of West Agent, and an effective privilege of role Cdn Agent. The domain administrator is prevented from adding privileges to the domain ID (since this must be done by a more senior administrator).

If the third technique for handling overlapping privileges is being used, then this operation, and all the other operations in this list, must be rejected if edges between domains result.

Delete a privilege from a role: By the same arguments as just given, privileges may be deleted from an arbitrary role in a domain, but they will remain in the direct privilege set of the domain ID. Only an administrator of an enclosing domain may delete privileges from the domain ID.

Add a role: There are two role addition algorithms given in [7]. The first one gives a role name, set of direct privileges, set of proposed immediate juniors, and proposed immediate senior roles. The constraints that need to be imposed now are that the privileges must all be in the effective privilege set of the domain ID, and the proposed juniors and seniors must all be roles in the domain or MinRole.

The second role addition algorithm gives the new role name, and proposed effective privileges. The role graph algorithm figures out its juniors and seniors. The constraint needed now is that the proposed effective privileges must all be in the effective privilege set of the domain ID. In the absence of privileges shared among domains, any juniors or seniors that the algorithm detects will all be within the specified domain.

Delete a role: The current algorithm gives the user the choice of keeping the privileges in the deleted role's seniors, or removing the privileges from the graph. In the administrative version, even if the privileges are removed from seniors, they must remain in the domain ID.

Insert an edge: Inserting edges can make privileges be inherited by roles where they did not previously exist. To avoid making changes outside of the administrative domain, inserted edges must involve two roles from the administrative domain being altered. This can include the domain ID.

Delete an edge: For similar reasons, deleted edges must have both roles from the administrative domain being altered.

Assign a user or group to a role: Both the role and the user or group must be in the same domain.

Remove a user or group from a role: Both the role and the user or group must be in the same domain.

These operations together with a domain ID become privileges that can be assigned to the appropriate administrative roles.

5. Operations on Administrative Domains

In addition to the above privileges which can be assigned to administrative roles, we need operations to create, destroy etc. whole domains. Important to these operations is a test of whether or not two domains overlap. We now discuss the details of these operations.

Create a new domain given r, its domain ID: This operation may be executed by an administrative role of an administrative domain D which contains r such that r is not the domain ID of D. To create the domain, we need to perform a depth-first traversal to all juniors of r, except for MinRole, and then check that the resulting domain does not overlap any existing domain.

Delete a domain given r, its domain ID: This operation may be executed by an administrative role of an administrative domain which contains r such that r is not the domain ID. All record of this domain must be removed, including any administrative privileges on it held by administrative roles.

Assign an administrative role to an administrative domain: This operation deals with how the "Administrates" edges appear in the graph. Administrative roles can form an (administrative) domain by themselves, or as in the figure, can be the domain ID of another administrative domain (by the definition of administrative domain, Marketing Admin and Distribution Admin in Figure 2 form an administrative domain). In order to assign, for example, the Distribution Admin administrative role to the administrative domain whose ID is Distribution Mgr, the role responsible must be in an administrative position with respect to both the admin role and the domain. So, in this example, this could be performed by Marketing Admin or SSO. In general, then, this operation can be performed by an administrative role which administrates both the domain and the admin role in the operation. The topmost admin role (SSO in the example) has to be able to assign itself as administrator of junior admin roles. This is also consistent since SSO administrates the default domain, which includes itself.

Assign an administrative privilege to an administrative role: This operation also can be performed by an admin role which administrates both the domain and the admin role involved. It may be that not all the possible administrative privileges listed in the previous section should be assigned to every administrative role. Thus, for example, we could build admin roles which can only assign users/groups to roles but cannot alter the role graph (to represent the Human Resources Department, for example).

Remove an administrative privilege from an administrative role: Constraints for this operation are as above. Every admin domain has the default admin domain's administrator as an administrator.

5.1. Other Administrative Privileges

In addition to the operations above on domains, there are some other admin privileges required. Initially, the system starts with the graph in Figure 3a. The initial admin role, SSO, needs the ability to create other admin roles, which it has by virtue of being the administrator of the default domain. In general, admin roles can also have the ability to create other admin roles as their own children. This privilege would not be granted to all admin roles. All of the admin privileges are granted at the discretion of an admin role, so the SSO could create a Human Resources (HR) admin role, which could create users, and assign them to domains, whereupon the administrators of those domains can assign them to roles in the domains. The HR admin role could create other admin roles as its children, and give them the privilege to create users, or other admin roles which are their children. Some of these administrative privileges are, then:

Create a Child Administrative Role: An admin role with this privilege can create sub-admin roles as its own children. The parent role has administrative rights over the newly created child role.

Assign the Create Child Privilege to an Administrative Role: This is also covered by the assign an admin privilege to an admin role operation above.

Create a User with Domain ID: The admin role must be an administrator of the Domain given.

Create a Group in the Group Graph with Domain ID: The admin role must be an administrator of the domain. All users in the group must be in the domain.

Add a domain ID to a user: The user may have additional domain IDs assigned. The admin role performing this must have an admin relationship with the user and the new domain.

Remove a domain ID from a user: The admin role performing this must have an admin relationship with the user and the domain.

5.2. Building up the Example

The system would start with the graph in Figure 3a. The SSO can add regular roles and admin roles, giving the second graph in Figure 3b.

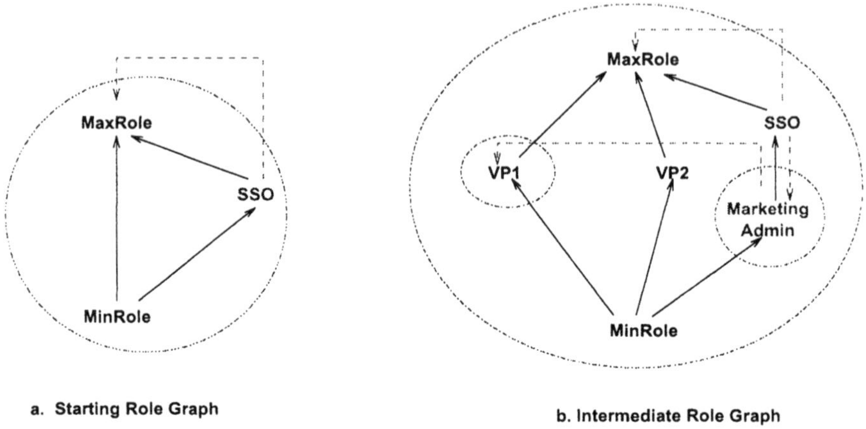

Figure 3. Building the Role Graph

From this graph, either Marketing Admin or SSO can create Distribution Mgr with the appropriate privileges, and the Distribution Admin admin role. SSO can also create the Accounting role and the Accounting Admin role. From this the graph in Figure 2 can be created.

6. Comparison with Other Models

We will begin by comparing our model with that of Sandhu [13, 8]. There are of course many similarities between these two RBAC models. Our role graph corresponds to the role hierarchy in RBAC96 and all subsequent versions of their model, our groups correspond to the groups in RRA97 which are roles with users but no permissions assigned, and our privileges correspond to abilities in RRA97. In fact, abilities model the implications among privileges [3], in that they form a bundle of privileges which should be assigned together to roles. Our algorithm in for following privilege implications gives the detail of how to put together their abilities [3]. Our group graphs provide more detail about how the groups are related. Nowhere, in the Sandhu papers, is there a discussion of anything equivalent to restoring the role graph properties. There is no explicit mention of adding a permission to a role, although deleting a permission is mentioned. Both adding and deleting permissions can cause the effective privileges of two roles higher in the graph to become identical, in which case a cycle in the graph would be created. No mention of how to deal with this is made in the Sandhu papers.

When it comes to the administrative model, URA97 [12, 13], in order to control user-role assignment, uses the idea of prerequisite roles. Clearly some way of constraining which users can be assigned is needed, but we feel it is not necessarily best modeled by being already in a role. This is replaced in ARBAC02 by the idea of a user pool, which is populated by the Human Resources department. Our idea of requiring that the user be labeled by the appropriate domain ID is meant to model the real-world situation of the user reporting to some manager. It can also correspond to the formation of user groups in our group graph model. The domain ID labeling of users is very similar to ARBAC02's user pool.

For permission-role assignments, PRA97 [12, 13] uses prerequisite roles, which are replaced by permission pools in ARBAC02 [8]. Our idea is to have the usable privileges be those defined as effective privileges in the domain ID role. We give very good motivation for this in discussing how it works together with the algorithms in the role graph model. The effective privileges of the domain ID can be regarded as a permission pool.

In general, in ARBAC97 [12, 13], administrative roles are given control over a role range, which informally has a single top and a single bottom node. We see no good motivation for having a single bottom to a role range. In a business environment, managers are given control over segments of the company. These segments may have subsegments, but the senior manager can usually have control over the finest details, which might also be in the control of a junior manager. Thus, our domains, have a bottom which stops just above MinRole; we feel this more realistically models what happens in real companies. Our discussion of the administrative operations shows no problems with this "open bottom" model when taking into account the role graph algorithms and properties.

Crampton and Loizou's model has a notion of an administrative scope for administrative operations [1]. Again, informally, this scope has a single bottom. The scope also changes dynamically to conform to a mathematical definition. We feel that our administrative domains, which do not necessarily have a single bottom, describe more realistically what happens in real companies. Moreover, the extent of the administrative domain should be the choice of the designer of the administrative model, and not a mathematical accident.

The Enterprise RBAC Model [4] uses the term scopes to refer to collections of objects and administrative permissions. Scopes are arranged in a DAG. Administrative permissions apply to a scope and all its subscopes, or can be restricted to the one scope node, or can be excluded for a scope. To some extent, this corresponds to not necessarily assigning all possible admin privileges to every admin role in our model. There is no discussion of the problems of overlapping scopes.

In [15], Wedde and Lischka describe a model for cooperative, distributed administration of an RBAC system. Their model is built on the idea of authorization spheres, which in turn consist units composed of subjects and objects. Units are arranged in a hierarchy which is different from the role hierarchy. Authorization spheres do not overlap, although no motivation is given for this.

In the role control center model of Ferraiolo et al., [2], administration is defined with respect to views. Views in turn are defined in terms of all seniors of a set of principles. In our terminology, views could have a single bottom and open top. Views are allowed to overlap. This this model is quite different from ours.

7. Conclusions

We have introduced an administrative model for the role graph model, which consists of administrative domains and administrative roles. There are several innovations in this new model.

The administrative model clarifies the relationships between administrative roles and regular roles. The regular roles are contained in administrative domain that is managed by an administrative role. An administrative role can manage its child administrative roles. We also show the administrative relations between the admin roles.

The administrative model described here supports decentralized administration. Our previous model assumed the administration is centralized, but large enterprises require decentralized control over access to data.

The model also fine tunes the role graph by adding new definitions, properties, rules and algorithms. In addition to the admin domain definition, we introduced the definition of administrative roles. Domains cannot overlap in the role plane but can overlap in the user/group plane and privilege plane. The problem of domain overlap is examined in detail; solutions for solving the problem caused by overlapping privileges are discussed. Required modifications of old algorithms are described. New algorithms that manage domain and administrative roles are also discussed.

We also compared our new model with other models in the literature. Our definition of administrative domain uses a "single top, open bottom" approach. We believe this approach is successful because it closely matches business management models. Our administrative model was designed based on a detailed analysis of business management. It should be easily understood by administrators and managers in the business world.

References

[1] Jason Crampton and George Loizou. Administrative scope and role hierarchy operations. In *Proc. 7th ACM SACMAT*, pages 145–154, 2002.

[2] D.F. Ferraiolo, G-J. Ahn, R. Chandramouli, and S.I. Gavrila. The role control center: Features and case studies. In *Proc. 8th ACM SACMAT*, pages 12–20, 2003.

[3] Cecilia M. Ionita and Sylvia L. Osborn. Privilege administration for the role graph model. In *Proc. IFIP WG11.3 Working Conference on Database Security*, July 2002.

[4] A. Kern, A. Schaad, and J. Moffett. An administration concept for the enterprise role-based access control model. In *Proc. 8th ACM SACMAT*, pages 3–11, 2003.

[5] Jonathan D. Moffett and Emil C. Lupu. The uses of role hierarchies in access control. In *Proceedings of the Fourth ACM Workshop on Role-based Access Control*, pages 153–160, 1999.

[6] M. Nyanchama and S. L. Osborn. Access rights administration in role-based security systems. In J. Biskup, M. Morgenstern, and C. E. Landwehr, editors, *Database Security, VIII, Status and Prospects WG11.3 Working Conference on Database Security*, pages 37–56. North-Holland, 1994.

[7] M. Nyanchama and S. L. Osborn. The role graph model and conflict of interest. *ACM TISSEC*, 2(1):3–33, 1999.

[8] Sejong Oh and Ravi Sandhu. A model of role administration using organization structure. In *Proc. 7th ACM SACMAT*, pages 155–162, 2002.

[9] S. Osborn and Y. Guo. Modeling users in role-based access control. In *Fifth ACM Workshop on Role-Based Access Control*, pages 31–38, Berlin, Germany, July 2000.

[10] Sylvia L. Osborn, Yan Han, and Jun Liu. A methodology for managing roles in legacy systems. In *Proc. 8th ACM SACMAT*, 2003.

[11] Thomas R. Peltier. *Information Security Policies, Procedures, and Standards: Guidelines for Effective Information Security Management.* Auerbach Publications, 2001.

[12] R. Sandhu and V. Bhamidipati. Role-based administration of user-role assignment: The URA97 model and its oracle implementation. In *Proceedings of IFIP WG 11.3 Eleventh Annual Working Conference on Database Security*, pages 239–254, Aug. 1997.

[13] R. Sandhu, V. Bhamidipati, and Q Munawer. The ARBAC97 model for role-based administration of roles. *ACM Trans. on Information and Systems Security*, 2(1):105–135, Feb. 1999.

[14] He Wang. Role graph administration in an enterprise environment. Master's thesis, Dept. of Computer Science, The University of Western Ontario, 2003.

[15] H.F. Wedde and M. Lischka. Cooperative role-based administration. In *Proc. 8th ACM SACMAT*, pages 21–32, 2003.

SAFETY AND LIVENESS FOR AN RBAC/ MAC SECURITY MODEL

C. Phillips, S. Demurjian, and T.C. Ting
Department of Electrical Engineering and Computer Science, U.S. Military Academy and Department of Computer Science and Engineering, University of Connecticut
charles.phillips@usma.edu and [steve, ting]@engr.uconn.edu

Abstract Our role-based/mandatory access control (RBAC/MAC) security model and enforcement framework for inter-operating legacy, COTS, GOTS, databases, servers, etc., limits: who (user/user role) can invoke which methods (based on value and MAC level) of artifact APIs at what times, and who (user) can delegate which responsibility (user role) at what times. In this chapter, we focus on assurance for the timeframe of access (of a user to a role, of a role to a method, etc.) and the attainment of the *Simple Security Property* (i.e., a subject cannot read information for which it is not cleared) and *Simple Integrity Property* (i.e., a subject is limited to writing information at its own level and lower), which together can be used to support *safety* and *liveness.*

Keywords: Security Assurance, Simple Security, Simple Integrity, Safety, Liveness.

1. Introduction

As agencies continue to assemble software artifacts (i.e., legacy, COTs, GOTS, databases, clients, servers, etc.), into interoperating applications, security assurance is critical [1, 6, 10, 11]. In the area of mandatory access control (MAC), assurance-related properties are: *Simple Security Property*, a subject can read information at the same or lower clearance level [3]; *Strict *-Property*, a subject can only write information at exactly the level for which it is cleared [12]; *Liberal *-Property*, a subject with a low clearance level can write to an object with the same or higher clearance level [3, 12]; and *Simple Integrity Property*, a subject can write information at its own level and lower [5]. In addition, assurance must focus on application behavior with respect to its defined and realized security policy, to attain *safety* (nothing bad will happen to a subject or object during execution) [8] and *liveness* (all good things can happen to a subject or object during execution) [2].

In this chapter, we explore assurance for our role-based/mandatory access control (RBAC/MAC) security model and enforcement framework for interacting software artifacts [9, 13, 14]. Our approach focuses on which methods of APIs can be invoked based on the security classification level of a role, the security clearance level of the user, and the values (parameters), time, and classification level of the method. Assurance guarantees are provided to insure that: a user (with one lifetime) playing a role (with another lifetime) can invoke a method (yet another lifetime) at the current time; the method invocation does not violate MAC domination (*Simple Security* for read-only and read-write methods, and *Simple Integrity* for read-write methods); and, a degree of *safety* (nothing bads happens when a user invokes a method) and *liveness* (all good things happen when a user invokes a method) is attained.

In the remainder of this chapter, Section 2 defines our RBAC/MAC security model. Section 3 focuses on the formal proofs of the security assurance guarantees for the available timeframe of method invocation and satisfaction of Simple Security and Simple Integrity Properties, leading to the attainment of safety and liveness. Section 4 concludes the chapter.

2. A RBAC/MAC Security Model

This section reviews the security model [13, 14] with delegation [9].

Def. 1: A *lifetime, LT,* is a time interval with start time (st) and end time (et), [st, et], et > st, and st/et is of the form (mo., day, year, hr., min., sec.). Concepts of LTs X and Y are: $X \triangleright Y$ means $Y.st \geq X.st$ and $Y.et \leq X.et$; $X \triangleleft Y \equiv Y \triangleright X$; If $ST = max\{X.st, Y.st\}$ and $ET = min\{X.et, Y.et\}$, then $Y \cap X$ is $\emptyset$ if $ET \leq ST$ or [ST, ET] if $ET > ST$; and $LT = [ct, \infty]$ is current time (ct) onward.

Def. 2: MAC concepts are: *Sensitivity levels*, $SLEVEL = \{U, C, S, T\}$ with unclassified (U), confidential (C), secret (S), and top secret (T) forming a hierarchy: $U < C < S < T$; *clearance (CLR)*, the SLEVEL given to users; and, *classification (CLS)*, the SLEVEL given to roles, methods, etc.

For assurance, LTs can guarantee that definition and access to privileges will always satisfy time limits. MAC will be used to guarantee the Simple Security and Integrity Properties [3, 5].

Defs. 3 to 6 are for a distributed application of resources, services, and methods, with LTs and CLSs.

Def. 3: A *distributed application, DAPPL,* is composed of a set of *software resources* (e.g., a legacy, COTS, DB, etc.), $R = \{R_i | i = 1..m\}$, each composed of *services*, $S_i = \{S_{ij} | j = 1..n_i\}$, each composed of *methods*, $M_{ij} = \{M_{ijk} | k = 1..q_{ij}\}$.

Def. 4: Each *method* $M_{ijk} = [M_{ijk}^{Name}, M_{ijk}^{LT}, M_{ijk}^{CLS}, M_{ijk}^{Params}]$ for $i = 1..m, j = 1..n_i, k = 1..q_{ij}$, of S_{ij} of R_i has name M_{ijk}^{Name}, LT M_{ijk}^{LT} (default [ct, ∞]), $M_{ijk}^{CLS} \in SLEVEL$ (default U), and M_{ijk}^{Params} parameters.

Def. 5: Each *service* $S_{ij} = [S_{ij}^{Name}, S_{ij}^{LT}, S_{ij}^{CLS}]$ for $i = 1..m, j = 1..n_i$, of R_i has name S_{ij}^{Name}, LT $S_{ij}^{LT} = [min\{M_{ijk}^{LT.st}\}, max\{M_{ijk}^{LT.et}\}]$ $\forall k = 1..q_{ij}$, and $S_{ij}^{CLS} = min\{M_{ijk}^{CLS} | k = 1..q_{ij}\}$.

Def. 6: Each *resource* $R_i = [R_i^{Name}, R_i^{LT}, R_i^{CLS}]$ for $i = 1..m$, has name R_i^{Name}, LT $R_i^{LT} = [min\{S_{ij}^{LT.st}\}, max\{S_{ij}^{LT.et}\}]$ $\forall j = 1..n_i$, and $R_i^{CLS} = min\{S_{ij}^{CLS} | j = 1..n_i\}$.

For assurance, we guarantee the dependencies that exist among the LTs (resource LT spans its services' LTs; service LT spans its resources' LT), and the minimality of CLS (resource CLS is minimum of its services' CLS; service CLS is the minimum of its methods' CLS). For examples, we use the U.S. Global Command and Control System (GCCS), with Figure 1 containing Joint and Component services with (CLSs).

Defs. 7 to 18 involve the privilege specification process for user roles against resources, services, and methods.

Def. 7: A *user role* $UR = [UR^{Name}, UR^{LT}, UR^{CLS}]$, represents a set of responsibilities, and has name UR^{Name}, LT UR^{LT} (default [ct, ∞]), and $UR^{CLS} \in SLEVEL$ (default U).

Def. 8: *A user-role list,* $URL = \{UR_i | i = 1..r\}$, has the r roles (Def. 7) for DAPPL.

For assurance, URs have specific LTs, used to check the "when" of access (i.e., can a user invoke a method at current time) and CLSs to check the "if" of access (i.e., does a UR's CLS dominate a method's CLS). For privileges, URs can be granted access to methods which have CLSs at or below the role's CLS (see Figure 2).

Def. 9: A *user,* $U = [U^{UserId}, U^{LT}, U^{CLR}]$ is an entity accessing a client, and has a unique U^{UserId}, LT L^{LT} (default [ct,∞]), and $U^{CLR} \in SLEVEL$ (default U).

Def. 10: A *user list,* $UL = \{U_i | i = 1..u\}$, has the u users (Def. 9) for DAPPL.

For assurance, users have specific LTs for checking the "when" of access (i.e., can a user play a role at current time) and CLRs for checking the "if" of access (i.e., does a user's CLR dominate a UR's CLS). Representative users for GCCS are shown in Figure 2.

Def. 11: A *signature constraint, SC,* is a boolean expression on M_{ijk}^{Params}, for $i = 1..m, j = 1..n, k = 1..g_{ij}$, to limit values.

```
(S) Joint Service     (S)  Weather (Token);
                      (S)  VideoTeleconference (Token, fromOrg, toOrg);
                      (S)  JointOperationsPlannning (Token, CrisisNum);
                      (S)  CrisisPicture (Token, CrisisNum, Grid1, Grid2);
                      (S)  TransportationFlow (Token);
                      (S)  LogisitcsPlanningTool (Token,  CrisisNum);
                      (S)  DefenseMessageSystem (Token);
                      (T)  NATOMessageSystem (Token);
(S) Component Service (S)  ArmyBattleCmdSys (Token, CrisisNum);
                      (S)  AirForceBattleManagementSys (Token, CrisisNum);
                      (S)  MarineCombatOpnsSys (Token, CrisisNum);
                      (S)  NavyCommandSystem (Token, CrisisNum);
```

Figure 1. GCCS Joint and Component Services and their Methods.

```
Roles: [CDR_CR1, [01dec02,01dec03], T]      [JPlanCR1, [01dec02, 01jun03], S]
       [JPlanCR2, [01jul01,01sep03], C]     [ArmyLogCR1, [10dec02,01mar03], S]
       [ArmyLogCR2, [01jul03,01aug03], C]
Users: General DoBest:    [DoBest, [ct, infinity], T]
       Colonel DoGood:    [DoGood, [01dec02,01jun03], T]b
       Major DoRight:     [DoRight, [01dec02,01jan03], S]
       Major CanDoRight: [CanDoRight, [01jan03,01feb03, T]
URAs:  [JPlanCR1, CrisisPicture, [ct, infinity],true]
       [JPlanCR1, ArmyBattleCmdSys, [10dec02,16feb03], true]
       [ArmyLogCR1, CrisisPicture, [10dec02,16feb03], Grid1<NA20 AND Grid2<NC40]
       [ArmyLogCR2, LogPlanningTool, [10dec02,16feb03], CrisisNum=CR1]
```

Figure 2. Sample Users, User-Roles, and User-Role Authorizations.

Def. 12: A *time constraint, TC,* is a LT (default [ct,∞]), and is utilized as follows: LTs of UR and method constrain the method assignment; LTs of UR, method, and user, constrain the method invocation; LTs of UR and user constrain the user authorization to the role; LTs constrain the time span of a delegation.

Def. 13: A *mandatory access control constraint, MACC,* is the *domination* of the SLEVEL of one entity over another, e.g., U's CLR $\geq$ UR's CLS or UR's CLS $\geq$ M's CLS.

For assurance, we provide guarantees that a user playing a role can invoke a method limited by parameter values (SC - Def. 11), method availability (TC - Def. 12), and the Simple Security and Integrity Properties applied by a user against a role invoking a method (Def. 13).

The next set of definitions is for authorizations of method(s) to user role(s) and of user role(s) to user(s), to bring together all of the concepts.

Def. 14: A *user-role authorization,* $URA = [UR, M, TC, SC]$, means UR (Def. 7) authorized to invoke M (Def. 4) within time TC (Def. 12 - default $[ct, \infty]$), limited by values SC (Def. 11 - default true). Figure 2 has URAs for JPlanCR1, ArmyLogCR1, and ArmyLogCR2.

Def. 15a: A $r \times q$ *UR authorization matrix, URAM,* where $q = \sum_{i=1..m, j=1..n_i} q_{ij}$, is:

$$URAM(UR_i, M_j) = \begin{cases} 1 & UR_i \text{ is authorized to invoke } M_j \\ 0 & otherwise \end{cases}$$

Def. 15b: A *valid user-role authorization list*, $VURAL = \{VURA_i \, \forall \, i = 1..v\}$, $v \leq r \times q$, has all *valid URAs* (Def. 15a).

Def. 16: A *user authorization*, $UA = [U, UR, TC]$, means U (Def. 9) is authorized to play UR (Def. 7) for time TC (Def. 12 - default $[ct, \infty]$) for when the role is available to U.

Def. 17a: An $r \times u$ *user authorization matrix, UAM*, is:

$$UAM(UR_i, U_j) = \begin{cases} 1 & U_j \text{ is authorized to } UR_i \\ 0 & otherwise \end{cases}$$

Def. 17b: A *valid user authorization list*, $VUAL = \{VUA_i | i = 1..w\}$, $w \leq r \times u$, has all *valid UAs, VUAs* (Def. 17a).

Def. 18: A *client, C,* is an authorized user U, identified by *client token* C = [U, UR, IP-Address, Client-Creation-Time].

For assurance, a valid URA (Defs. 14, 15a and 15b) can only be created if all required checks of a UR's capabilities against a M's characteristics are satisfied (i.e., TC and MACC checks), and the VURA then sets the criteria (UR, M, TC, SC) under which the invocation can occur. A corresponding set of guarantees also holds for a VUA.

The remaining set of definitions are for *role delegation* [9].

Def. 19: A *delegatable* $UR \in URL$, DUR, is eligible for delegation.

Def. 20: The *delegatable UR vector, DURV,* $\forall$ r *URs* $\in URL$ is:

$$DURV(UR_i) = \begin{cases} 1 & UR_i \text{ is a } DUR \\ 0 & UR_i \text{ is not a } DUR \end{cases}$$

Def. 21: An *original user*, $OU \in UL$, of a UR is authorized to the UR via the security policy ($\exists$ a VUA for the OU/UR, i.e., UAM(UR,OU) = 1), and not by a delegation.

Def. 22: A *delegated user*, $DU \in UL$, is a user U that can be delegated a UR by an OU/DU (there is not a VUA for the DU/UR, i.e., $UAM(UR, DU) \neq 1$)), where DU is not an OU for the same UR.

Def. 23: The $r \times u$ *user delegation/authorization matrix, UDAM,* is:

$$UDAM(UR_i, U_j) = \begin{cases} 2 & UR_i \text{ is a DU of } UR_i \\ 1 & U_j \text{ is an OU of } UR_i \\ 0 & UR_j \text{ is not authorized to } DU_i \end{cases}$$

For assurance, there must be guarantees on the capabilities of an OU with respect to the a DU to insure that LTs/TCs and CLS/CLR are consistent; the delegation is defined and checked at runtime.

Def. 24: *Delegation authority, DA,* is given to OU for delegation of a DUR to another user.

Def. 25: *Pass-on delegation authority, PODA,* is authority given to an OU/DU to pass on DA for a DUR to another OU/DU.

Def. 26: The $r \times u$ *delegation authority matrix, DAM,* is:

$$DAM(UR_i, U_j) = \begin{cases} 2 & U_j \text{ has DA and PODA for } UR_i \\ 1 & U_j \text{ has only DA for } UR_i \\ 0 & UR_j \text{ has neither DA nor PODA for } UR_i \end{cases}$$

Initially DAM has all 0 entries.

For assurance, there must be DA and PODA guarantees; DA allows an OU/DU to delegate, and PODA, allows an OU/DU to pass on that delegation authority to another DU, which is a dangerous privilege.

3. Towards Assurance Guarantees

Security assurance is critical in our model to allow the consistency of URs, CLR/CLS levels, LTs, role delegations, user authorizations, etc., to be verified when the security policy is defined, changed, and executed. Towards that end: Section 3.1 examines assurance guarantees on the *available time* of access for a method invocation; Section 3.2 details the attainment of the *Simple Security* and *Simple Integrity* Properties for method invocations; leading to Section 3.3 which explores *safety* and *liveness.* Overall, we have been influenced by others [4, 5, 8, 12, 15].

3.1. Time-Based Guarantees

To begin, we introduce *available time, AT*, which represents the maximum amount of time derived from various intersections of LTs and TCs of the authorizations for URs, OU, DU, and users, as given in Section 2. For example, $URA = [UR, M, TC, SC]$ involves LTs (for UR and M) and a TC, which must overlap to be a VURA. Formally, let $\Sigma^{LT} = \cap_{all i}\Sigma_i^{LT}$, where each Σ_i^{LT} represents a LT or a TC, using intersection for LTs/TCs as given in Def. 1. Then, any time t is in the maximum available time, AT, or $t \in \cap\Sigma_i^{LT} \forall\, i \Leftrightarrow t \in \Sigma^{LT}$. To assist in the proofs, we define:

Def. 1a: Let $Compare(X, Y)$ be a function that returns the overlap of LTs X and Y. $Compare(X, Y) = \{Y$ if $X \triangleright Y$; X if $Y \triangleright X$; $\emptyset$ if $Y \cap X = \emptyset$; $Y \cap X$ otherwise$\}$.

Using Def. 1a, we offer lemmas for the ATs for URAs (Def. 14), URs (Def. 7), UAs (Def. 16), DUs (Def. 22) and Users (Def. 9).

Lemma 1: If $URA_i = [UR, M, TC, SC]$ is a VURA, then $URA_i^{AT} = M^{LT} \cap UR^{LT} \cap TC$.
Proof:

1 By Defs. 14 and 15a, $URA_i = [UR, M, TC, SC]$ as a VURA means $URAM(UR, M) = 1$. By Def. 7, $UR = [UR^{Name}, UR^{LT}, UR^{CLS}]$. Set $URA_i^{AT} = UR^{LT}$.

2 By Def. 4, $M = [M^{Name}, M^{LT}, M^{CLS}, M^{Params}]$. Apply Def. 1a with $URA_i^{AT} = Compare(URA_i^{AT}, M^{LT})$.

3 By Def. 12, a TC is a LT. In $URA_i = [UR, M, TC, SC]$, TC constrains when UR authorized to M. Apply Def. 1a with $URA_i^{AT} = Compare(URA_i^{AT}, TC)$.

4 If $URA_i^{AT} \cap ct = \emptyset$, then $URA_i^{AT} = \emptyset$ and proof completes.

5 Otherwise, $URA_i^{AT} = M^{LT} \cap UR^{LT} \cap TC$ since it is equivalent to $URA_i^{AT} = URA_i^{AT} \cap TC$ (by steps 2 and 3 of the proof and substituting for URA_i^{AT} on the r.h.s. with $M^{LT} \cap UR^{LT}$). Note that if $URA_i^{AT} = \emptyset$, then there is no overlap.

Lemma 2: If $UR = [UR^{Name}, UR^{LT}, UR^{CLS}]$, then $UR^{AT} = \cap_{alli} URA_i^{AT}$, where each URA_i^{AT} is a VURA where $URAM(UR, M_j) = 1$ for some $j = 1..q$.

Proof:

1 Consider URAM as given in Def. 15a. If $URAM(UR, M_j) = 0$ for some j, then UR not authorized to M_j, and there is no need to use this entry to calculate UR^{AT}.

2 Consider all j where $URAM(UR, M_j) = 1$ (VURA of UR to M). If $\exists$ at least one j s.t. $URAM(UR, M_j) = 1$ and $M^{LT} = \emptyset$, then set $UR^{AT} = \emptyset$, and proof completes.

3 Let $URAM(UR, M_j) = 1$ and $URAM(UR, M_k) = 1$ for some j, k. Apply Def. 1a with $UR^{AT} = Compare(URA_{i_j}^{AT}, URA_{i_k}^{AT})$, where i_j/i_k is the VURA for M_j/M_k.

4 Repeat this step for each remaining entry $URAM(UR, M_j) = 1$, apply Def. 1a with $UR^{AT} = Compare(UR^{AT}, URA_{i_k}^{AT})$.

5 If $UR^{AT} \cap ct = \emptyset$, then $UR^{AT} = \emptyset$ and proof completes.

6 Otherwise, $UR^{AT} = \cap_{alli} URA_i^{AT}$.

Lemma 3: If $UA = [U, UR, TC]$ is a VUA, then $UA^{AT} = U^{LT} \cap UR^{AT} \cap TC$.

Proof:

1 By Defs. 16 and 17a, $UA = [U, UR, TC]$ as a VUA means $UAM(UR, U) = 1$. By Def. 9, $U = [U^{UserId}, U^{LT}, U^{CLR}]$. Set $UA^{AT} = U^{LT}$.

2 By Lemma 2, UR^{AT} is the AT of UR for all of its URAs. Apply Def. 1a with UA^{AT} =$Compare(UA^{AT}, UR^{AT})$. UA^{AT} represents the time that U can engage an authorized UR.

3 By Def. 12, a TC is a LT. For $UA = [U, UR, TC]$, apply Def. 1a with UA^{AT} =$Compare(UA^{AT}, TC)$.

4 If $UA^{AT} \cap ct = \emptyset$, then $UA^{AT} = \emptyset$ and proof completes.

5 Otherwise, $UA^{AT} = U^{LT} \cap UR^{AT} \cap TC$ since it is equivalent to $UA^{AT} = UA^{AT} \cap TC$ (by steps 2 and 3 of the proof and substituting for UA^{AT} on the r.h.s. with $U^{LT} \cap UR^{AT}$).

Lemma 4: If OU delegates one of its DUR, UR, to DU, then $DUA = [DU, UR, TC]$ has $DUA^{AT} = OUA^{AT} \cap DU^{LT}$.
Proof:

1 Let $OUA = [U, UR, TC]$ be a VUA for OU. By Lemma 3, OUA^{AT} is the AT for an OU to a UR. Set $DUA^{AT} = OUA^{AT}$.

2 For OU to delegate UR to DU, $UAM(UR, OU) = 1$. When OU delegates UR to DU, then $UAM(UR, DU)$ must be set to 1, and a $DUA = [DU, UR, TC]$ is created. The UR and TC in the DUA are as given in the OUA (Step 1), and thus do not impact DUA^{AT} since they are already in OUA^{AT}.

3 By Def. 9, $DU = [DU^{UserId}, DU^{LT}, DU^{CLR}]$. Apply Def. 1a with $DUA^{AT} = Compare(DUA^{AT}, DU^{LT})$.

4 If $DUA^{AT} \cap ct = \emptyset$, then $DUA^{AT} = \emptyset$ and proof completes.

5 $DUA^{AT} = OUA^{AT} \cap DU^{AT}$ since it is equivalent to $DUA^{AT} = DUA^{AT} \cap DU^{LT}$ (by Step 3 of the proof and substituting for DUA^{AT} on the r.h.s. with OUA^{AT}).

Lemma 5: If $U = [U^{UserId}, U^{LT}, U^{CLR}]$, then $U^{AT} = \cap_{alli} UA_i^{AT}$, where each UA_i^{AT} represents one VUA where $UAM(UR_j, U) = 1$ for some $j = 1..r$. This proof similar to Lemma 2 and omitted.

3.2. MAC Guarantees

Mandatory access controls are governed by strict rules for subjects (users) to access stored information or objects, and include many different properties: *Simple Security Property* [3], the *Strict *-Property* [12], the *Liberal *-Property* [3, 12], and the *Simple Integrity Property* [5]. In this section, we prove that our RBAC/MAC model (see Section 2) satisfies both the Simple Security Property and the Simple Integrity Property as applied to methods, roles, and users. To do so, consider:

Def. 4a: Each $M_{ij} = \{M_{ijk} \mid k = 1..q_{ij}\}$, has read-only methods, $M_{ij}^{RO} = \{M_{ijk}^{RO}\ for\ some\ k\}$ and read-write methods, $M_{ij}^{RW} = \{M_{ijk}^{RW}\ for\ some\ k\}$; $M_{ij}^{RO} \cap M_{ij}^{RW} = \emptyset$ and $M_{ij}^{RO} \cup M_{ij}^{RW} = M_{ij}$.

Def. 28: Let *Dominate*(X, Y) be a boolean function, with X and Y either CLR/CLS (Def. 2) with $U < C < S < T$. *Dominate*$(X, Y) = \{true\ if\ X \geq Y; false\ if\ X < Y\}$.

Given these definitions, we present a series of lemmas on URAs, URs, and UAs in regards to the Simple Security and Integrity Properties.

Lemma 6.1: If $URA_i = [UR, M, TC, SC]$ is a VURA, then URA_i satisfies the Simple Security Property for all M^{RO} and M^{RW}.
Proof by contradiction:

1 By Defs. 14 and 15a, $URA_i = [UR, M, TC, SC]$ as a VURA means $URAM(UR, M) = 1$. By Def. 7, $UR = [UR^{Name}$, UR^{LT}, $UR^{CLS}]$, where UR^{CLS} is the role's CLS. By Def. 4, $M = [M^{Name}$, M^{LT}, M^{CLS}, $M^{Params}]$, where M^{CLS} is the method's CLS. UR is the *subject* and M is the *object*.

2 If $M \in M_{ij}^{RO}$ or $M \in M_{ij}^{RW}$, it has a CLS, M^{CLS}. Suppose *Dominate*$(UR^{CLS}, M^{CLS}) = false$. Set $URAM(UR, M) = 0$ (Defs. 14, 15a, and 15b).

3 This contradicts Step 1 where $URAM(UR, M) = 1$.

4 Then, *Dominate*$(UR^{CLS}, M^{CLS}) = true$ $(UR^{CLS} \geq M^{CLS})$.

5 This is Simple Security (read-down/no-read-up) [3].

Lemma 6.2: If $URA_i = [UR, M, TC, SC]$ is a VURA, then URA_i satisfies the Simple Integrity Property for all M^{RW}.
Proof: Exact Steps as Lemma 6.1 except for Steps 2 and 6 (below).
2. If $M \in M_{ij}^{RW}$, it has a CLS, M^{CLS}. Suppose *Dominate*$(UR^{CLS}$, $M^{CLS}) = false$.
6. This is Simple Integrity (write-down/no-write-up) [5].

Lemma 6.3: Let $UR = [UR^{Name}, UR^{LT}, UR^{CLS}]$ and $\alpha = \cup_{alli} URA_i$, where each URA_i is a VURA $(URAM(UR, M_j) = 1$ for some $j = 1..q)$. If *Dominate*$(UR^{CLS}, M_j^{CLS}) = true$ for all $URA_i \in \alpha$, then UR satisfies the Simple Security Property for all methods and Simple Integrity Property for M^{RW}.
Proof:

1 For each $M \in M_{ij}^{RO}$ and $M \in M_{ij}^{RW}$, *Dominate*$(UR^{CLS}$, $M^{CLS}) = true$ (by Lemma 6.2), and, UR satisfies the Simple Security Property for all methods.

2 For each $M \in M_{ij}^{RW}$, *Dominate*$(UR^{CLS}, M^{CLS}) = true$ (by Lemma 6.2), and, UR satisfies Simple Integrity for all M^{RW}.

3 Steps 1 and 2 means that UR satisfies Simple Security for all methods and Simple integrity for M^{RW}.

Lemma 7: If $UA = [U, UR, TC]$ is a VUA, then UA satisfies the Simple Security and Integrity Properties for U CLR vs. UR CLS. Proof by contradiction:

1 By Lemma 6.3, UR satisfies Simple Security Property for all methods and the Simple Integrity Property for M^{RW}. Hence, $Dominate(UR, M_k) = true$ for all M_k authorized to UR.

2 By Defs. 16 and 17a, $UA = [U, UR, TC]$ as a VUA means $UAM(UR, U) = 1$. By Def. 9, $U = [U^{UserId}, U^{LT}, U^{CLR}]$, with U^{CLR}.

3 Suppose that $Dominate(U^{CLR}, UR^{CLS}) = false$.

4 Then, $UAM(UR, U) = 0$ (Defs. 16, 17a, and 17b), which contradicts Step 2.

5 Thus, $Dominate(U^{CLR}, UR^{CLS}) = true$ $(U^{CLR} \geq UR^{CLS})$.

6 Since UR satisfies both Simple Security and Integrity Properties, UA also does.

Lemma 8: If OU delegates UR in DUR to DU, then a delegated user authorization $DUA = [DU, UR, TC]$ satisfies both the Simple Security and Integrity Properties for delegated user (subject) vs. role (object). Proof similar to Lemma 7 and uses Lemma 4.

3.3. Safety and Liveness Guarantees

In this section, we explore *safety* (nothing bad will happen during a method invocation or delegation) [8] and *liveness* (all good can happen during a method invocation or delegation) [2] for our framework. We begin with a review of *security assurance rules, SARs* [9], which are logical statements that must be satisfied in order for a privilege to be set (design-time) or an action to be performed (runtime). The first four SARs are non-delegation checks at design time (Rule I for when an officer attempts to assign a method to a UR and Rule II for when an officer attempts to authorize a UR to a User) and runtime (Rule III for when a user selects a UR to play for a session and Rule IV for when a user attempts to invoke a method, via a client application).

Rule I: Let $A \in UR$ and M be a method. $URA = [A, M, TC, SC]$ is a VURA iff $A^{CLS} \geq M^{CLS}$, $TC = A^{LT} \cap M^{LT} \cap TC \neq \emptyset$, $TC.et > ct$; Set $URAM(A, M) = 1$, $VURAL = VURAL \cup URA$.

Rule II: Let $A \in UR$ and $X \in UL$. $UA = [X, A, TC]$ is a VUA iff $X^{CLR} \geq A^{CLS}$, $TC = X^{LT} \cap A^{LT} \cap TC \neq \emptyset$, $TC.et > ct$; Set $UAM(A, X) = 1$, $UDAM(A, X) = 1$, $VUAL = VUAL \cup UA$.

Rule III: Let $A \in UR$ and $X \in UL$. A can be authorized to X at runtime iff $UAM(A, X) = 1$ (Rule II is OK), and for the $VUA = [X, A, TC] \in VUAL$, $TC.et > ct$.

Rule IV: Let $A \in UR$, $X \in UL$, and M be a method. X with A can invoke M at runtime iff $UAM(A, X) = 1$ (Rule II is OK), $UDAM(A, M) = 1$ (Rule I is OK), for $VUA = [X, A, TC] \in VUAL$, $TC.et > ct$, for $VURA = [A, M, TC, SC] \in VURAL$, $TC.et > ct$, $SCOracle([M^{Name}, M^{Params}, M^{Values}], SC) = true$.

Note that in support of SCOracle, we assert the following: *There exists a SC Oracle that does not fail. The number and type of parameters vary with each method and SC will accept any combination. SC checks if the Boolean is satisfied, which has a very high expectation of success.*

Rules V and VI are for the assignment of DA and PODA to a user X. Rule VII is for design-time delegation of a UR by a user to another user. Rule VIII is for setting DA or DA/PODA from one user (either OU or DU) to another DU (Rule VII OK). Rule IX is for activating delegation.

Rule V: Let $X \in UL$ and $A \in URL$. X has DA for A ($DAM(A, X) = 1$) iff $UDAM(A, X) = 1$(an OU), $DURV(A) = 1$(a DUR), and $\exists$ a $VUA = [X, A, TC]$.

Rule VI: Let $X \in UL$ and $A \in URL$. X can have DA and PODA for A ($DAM(X, A) = 2$) iff $UDAM(A, X) = 1$(an OU), $DURV(A) = 1$(a DUR), and $\exists$ a $VUA = [X, A, TC]$.

Rule VII: Let $X \in UL$ and $A \in URL$, s.t. $DAM(A, X) \geq 1$ (Rules V or VI). X can delegate A to user Y limited by TC iff $UDAM(A, Y) \neq 1, Y^{CLR} \geq A^{CLS}, TC = (Y^{LT} \cap A^{LT} \cap TC) \neq \emptyset$, and $TC.et > ct$. Set $UAM(A, Y) = 1, UDAM(A, Y) = 2$, and $VUAL = VUAL \cup UA = [Y, A, TC]$.

Rule VIII: Let $X \in UL$ be an OU/DU, $A \in URL$, and $Y \in UL$ be a DU of A. Y can have DA for A (DAM(A,Y) = 1) if X has at least DA for A (DAM(A,X) $\geq$ 1). Y can have DA and PODA for A(DAM(A,Y)=2 if X has both DA and PODA for A (DAM(A,X)=2). Rule VIII limited to 2 levels in our framework.

Rule IX: Let $X \in UL$ be an OU or a DU. Then X can delegate role A to DU Y limited by TC iff (Rule V or VI) and Rule VII.

Now, we present theorems for the safety and liveness of Rules I to IV (delegation omitted). We define: *legal access* as an access authorized by a security policy; *liveness* to mean that every legal access is authorized [2]; and, *safety* to mean that no illegal access is authorized [8].

Theorem I: Rule I meets requirements for liveness and safety.

Proof:

1 Let A be a user role and M a method being authorized.

2 Initially, the URAM is set to all 0s. This is perfect access control as there are no UR authorizations to any methods, M_{ijk}, in this system. This meets safety (no bad things can happen), but not liveness, as no good things can happen.

3 Lemma 1 ensures that a URA is a VURA and $URA_i^{AT} = M^{LT} \cap UR^{LT} \cap TC$. If $URA_i^{AT} \neq \emptyset$ and $URA_i^{AT} \cap ct \neq \emptyset$, then M can be assigned to UR. Otherwise M cannot be assigned to UR because it can never be available.

4 Lemma 6.1 insures $A^{CLS} \geq M^{CLS}$.

5 To change an entry from 0 to 1 in a URAM, there must be a URA (Def. 14).

6 In order to build liveness, yet maintain safety, 0 entries in the URAM must be changed to 1 ($URAM(A, M) = 1$) for only those URs authorized to Ms (Defs. 15a and 15b). Validating changes to URAM allows for both safety and liveness; there is no access except for these specific authorizations and this is precisely Rule I.

Theorem II: Rule II meets requirements for liveness and safety.

Proof:

1 Let X be a user and A be the role being authorized.

2 Initially, the UAM and UDAM are set to all 0s. This is perfect access control as there are no users, U, authorized to any user roles, UR, in this system. This meets safety requirements, but not liveness, as no user can do anything.

3 U and UR must be available for access and $UR^{AT} \cap U^{AT} \cap ct \neq \emptyset$. Lemma 3 insures the maximum AT for a U to a UR. The intersection with the current time assures that available time has not passed, which is obviously a requirement for use.

4 Lemma 7 insures $X^{CLR} \geq A^{CLS}$.

5 To change an entry from 0 to 1 in UAM/UDAM, there must be a UA (Def. 16).

6 In order to build liveness, yet maintain safety, 0 entries in the UAM/UDAM must be changed. Validating changes to UAM and UDAM allows for both safety and liveness, as there is no access allowed except for these specific authorizations and this is precisely Rule II.

The safety/liveness of Theorems III/IV focuses on the runtime authorization of user to role, which is needed since the tranquility of CLR and CLS is not guaranteed, URs can change, and LTs and TCs can expire.

Theorem III: Rule III meets requirements for liveness and safety.

Proof:

1 Let X be a user and A be the role being authorized.

2 If $UAM(A, X) \neq 1$, deny runtime authorization. QED.

3 Revalidate Rule II: $X^{CLR} \geq A^{CLS}$, $TC = X^{LT} \cap A^{LT} \cap TC \neq \emptyset$, $TC.et > ct$. If $X^{CLR} < A^{CLS}$, then Rule II fails. If $TC = X^{LT} \cap A^{LT} \cap TC = \emptyset$, then Rule II fails. If either case is true, deny runtime authorization. QED.

4 Else, Rule II is revalidated at runtime, so by Theorem II, Rule II satisfies safety and liveness. Thus, Rule III does as well.

Theorem IV: Rule IV meets requirements for liveness and safety.

Proof:

1 Let X be a user, A its role, and M the method being called.

2 If $SCOracle([M^{Name}, M^{Params}, M^{Values}], SC) = false$, deny runtime authorization. QED.

3 If $UAM(A, X) \neq 1$, deny runtime authorization. QED.

4 If $URAM(A, M) \neq 1$, deny runtime authorization. QED.

5 If $U^{AT} = \emptyset$, (Lemma 3) deny runtime authorization. QED.

6 If $U^{TC.et} \leq ct$, deny runtime authorization. QED.

7 Otherwise, Rules I and II are revalidated enusring safety and liveness. Thus, Rule IV does as well.

Theorems V to IX correspond are structured in a similar fashion to prove safety and liveness for Rules V to IX

4. Conclusions

This chapter has examined security assurance guarantees for a RBAC and MAC security model and enforcement framework [9, 13, 14]. Section 2 reviewed our RBAC/MAC security model with delegation. Section 3 examined security guarantees with respect to available time (when an invocation can occur), security levels (authorizations of methods to user roles, and user roles to users), and for the attainment of safety and liveness (related to authorization, invocation, and delegation). The main contribution in this chapter is the series of lemmas and theorems that provide validation for the Simple Security and Simple Integrity Properties, which then lead to the stronger properties of insuring safety (nothing bad happens) and liveness (something good happens) as methods are invoked by users playing roles. Please see [16] for further information.

Acknowledgement: Thanks to Prof. C. Reynolds, USMA, Dept. of EE&CS for his input on the various formalisms/notation in Section 3.

References

[1] K. Alford, et al., "Information Assurance Pedagogy," *Proc. of IEEE Info. Assurance Wksp.*, 2001.

[2] B. Alpern and F. Schneider, "Defining Liveness," *Information Processing Letters*, Vol. 21, No. 4, 1985.

[3] D. Bell and L. LaPadula, "Secure Computer Systems: Mathematical Foundations Model," M74-244, Mitre Corp., Bedford, MA, 1975.

[4] E. Bertino, et al., "TRBAC: A Temporal Role-Based Access Control Model," *Proc. of 5th ACM Wksp. on RBAC*, 2000.

[5] K. J. Biba, "Integrity Considerations for Secure Computer Systems," TR-3153, Mitre Corp, Bedford, MA, 1977.

[6] S. Gavrila and J. Barkley, "Formal Specification For Role Based Access Control User/Role and Role/Role Relationship Management," *Proc. of the 3rd ACM Wksp. on RBAC*, 1998.

[7] Joint Operational Support Ctr., http://gccs.disa.mil/gccs/, 1999.

[8] L. Lamport, "Proving the Correctness of Multiprocess Programs," *IEEE Trans. on Software Engineering*, Vol. 3, No. 2, 1977.

[9] M. Liebrand, et al., "Role Delegation for a Resource-Based Security Model," *Data and Applications Security: Developments and Directions II*, E. Gudes and S. Shenoi (eds.), Kluwer, 2003.

[10] W. Maconachy, et al., "A Model for Information Assurance: An Integrated Approach," *Proc. of IEEE Info. Assurance Wksp.*, 2001.

[11] J. McCumber, "Information Systems Security: A Comprehensive Model," *Proc. of the 14th Natl. Computer Security Conf.*, 1991.

[12] S. Osborn, et al., "Configuring Role-Based Access Control to Enforce Mandatory And Discretionary Access Control Policies," *ACM Trans. on Information and System Security*, Vol. 3, No. 2, 2000.

[13] C. Phillips, et al., "Security Engineering for Roles and Resources in a Distributed Environment," *Proc. of 3rd ISSEA Conf.*, 2002.

[14] C. Phillips, et al., "Towards Information Assurance in Dynamic Coalitions," *Proc. of 2002 IEEE Info. Assurance Wksp.*, 2002.

[15] R. Sandhu, "Lattice-Based Access Control Models," *Computer Journal*, Vol. 26, No. 11, 1993.

[16] http://www.engr.uconn.edu/ steve/DSEC/dsec.html

SCHEMA BASED XML SECURITY: RBAC APPROACH

Xinwen Zhang, Jaehong Park, and Ravi Sandhu
George Mason University
{ xzhang6, jpark2, sandhu) } @gmu.edu

Abstract Security of XML instance is a basic problem, especially in enterprise with large number of users and XML objects as well as complex authorizations administration. In this paper, a role-based access control (RBAC) model based on XML Schema is proposed. RBAC has been proven to be efficient to improve security administration with flexible authorization management. XML Schema is a specification to define format and contents of XML instance. Access control based on a schema will be transported to all its instances. As a proposed alternate of XML Document Type Definition (DTD), XML Schema supports complex constraints for XML components, such as elements, attributes, datatypes and groups. Also, XML Schema provides a mechanism to build rich reuse relationships between schemas and elements. These will be applied in reusable permissions in our model, which efficiently simplify the security administration. Based on these features fine-grained access control can be achieved. At the same time, our model also supports instances-level authorization naturally, which provides a uniform mechanism for XML security. A abstract implementation is presented in this paper for our proposed model. "Pure" XML technologies will be applied in the implementation mechanism, which make the system lightweight and can be easily embedded into existing systems.

1. Introduction

Because of its platform-independent characteristics, XML [9] has been increasingly used in many environments to integrate applications and communicate between systems. XML instance is a structured format with meta-data for real data. Because of the ability to express complex reference relationship between data, a XML instance may be generated from various resources with varying security requirements. On the other side, a user can be allowed to access only particular parts of a XML instance. For example in an enterprise, a XML document can consist of information from applications among a few departments and several databases. When an internal or external user tries to access this document, his/her access rights have to be monitored according to security policies in all these departments and databases. The final instance which the user can read or modify is the result of enforcement with overall authorizations.

In this paper, an access control model is proposed to control all accesses to XML instances in such distributed and heterogeneous environment. In an enterprise or organization, there are large number of users and XML objects. Also, there are complex relationships among users, objects, and arbitrary authorizations between users and objects. Each user has identification and attributes. An object can be a XML document, message, dynamically generated XML instance, or any XML elements. Because of the complex data sources with different security policies, authorizations management will be burdensome. Role-based access control model [1, 2] has proven to be efficient in security administration with roles providing a layer of indirection between users and objects. The role-permission assignment is comparatively stable while user-role assignment can be more dynamic. At the same time, RBAC provides strong data type abstraction ability. All the components in the model can be customized and fit into particular applications very easily.

XML Schema [11, 12] is a mechanism to define the content and relationship of elements in an XML instance. A well-validated XML document must follow the format specified by one or several schemas. In our proposed model, permissions a user can invoke are defined on schema or schema element level and will be transported to all XML instances specified by these schema or elements. The permission on a schema component will be transported to all XML instance data which is specified by this component. At the same time, substantial permission reuse can be generated based on the rich relationships between elements, datatypes and attributes in a schema, or between schemas. We will use these relationships to build permission reuse hierarchy. Based on this, fine-grained, flexible, and easy-customized access control model can be achieved. With the unique features of XML Schema, extensible, modular and reusable security policies can be generated in distributed environment.

The remainder of this paper is organized as follows: Section 2 presents the background of XML Schema and the main difference from DTD. Section 3 describes and discusses the model in details. Section 4 briefly presents the high-level implementation of the access control model. Section 5 reviews the previous work on XML document security. The difference between this work to others is presented. Section 6 concludes the paper and outlines the future work to continue on this topic.

2. XML and XML Schema

XML instance has two basic requirements: well-formed and validate-formed. Well-formalization requires XML document to follow some syntax, such as, there is exactly one element that completely contains all other elements, elements may nest but not overlap, etc. Validation requires XML instance to contain specified elements and attributes, following specified datatypes and relationships. Document Type Definition (DTD) and XML Schema are two main validation specification mechanisms.

Document Type Definition(DTD) is the first and earliest language to define the structure and content of XML documents. But it has many limitations which are critical in enterprise and distributed environments. A DTD file is not itself a well-formed and valid XML document. The rules in DTD are not meta-data, but rather some special formats to show the order of elements. The problem with this is that a special process is needed for an XML parser to parse the content in DTD. Another problem is that it is difficult to specify constraints on structure and content of XML instance with DTD. Actually, DTD only specifies the appearance order of element and its subelements and attributes, but cannot define complex relationships and constraints. DTD cannot define datatypes, which make it difficult to be reusable, extensible, and modular. A defined DTD cannot be used by other DTDs, and rules in DTD cannot be reused and extended by other rules within or out of this DTD. All these limitations prevent DTD from being widely applied in distributed and scalable systems. XML Schema is an alternate in modern enterprise environments with some new features. XML Schema is XML document itself, which XML parser can handle just like normal XML instance. Therefore, XPath and XQuery can be applied to specify fine-grained schemas objects. Complex user-defined datatypes can be created in XML Schema. Rich description and relations of schemas and components can be expressed. Hierarchy can be established based on these relationships. This makes schema reusable and extensible. Namespace is supported in XML Schema to solve name conflictions. This helps modular deployment of security administration in our model.

With these reasons, modern XML specifications are all based on schema. At the same time, the improvement of XML Schema results in flexible schema-based access control policy. With DTD's limitations, permission based on DTD is not modular, extensible, and reusable. The access control policy on XML instance documents and DTD have to be implemented separately, since DTD is not XML well-formed and valid-formed. By using schema, we can define and enforce the permissions on schema objects and instance objects with uniform mechanism. Also, in distributed environment, the authorizations from various services and departments can be assembled easily with pure XML technologies, since policy based on schemas is extensile and reusable with schema's characteristics.

3. Extended RBAC Model

Role-based access control is a policy-neutral model studied by many researchers during the past decade. The flexibility and efficiency in security management make it an attractive access control solution in many commercial systems. The main components of RBAC96 model includes users, roles, role-hierarchy, permissions, user-role assignments and permission-role assignment [1].

Figure 1 shows our proposed model extended from original RBAC96 model. The users, roles, role hierarchy, user-role assignment and sessions are the same as that of RBAC96 model. Instead of direct assignment of roles and final permissions, in this model, there are schema-based permissions (SP) and explicit role-permission assignments (EPA) between roles and schema objects. SP are defined by associating some atomic access types with schema components. EPA is the assignment between roles and SP. By the instance mapping (IM) function from schema objects (SO) to instance objects (IO), SP and EPA imply the instance-based permission (IP) and implicit role-permission assignments (IPA). Secure Schema Object Hierarchy (SSOH) is a partial order between schema objects defined by a security administrator , in which the permissions defined on low level objects will be transported to high level objects. Some constraints are specified for the SP and EPA.

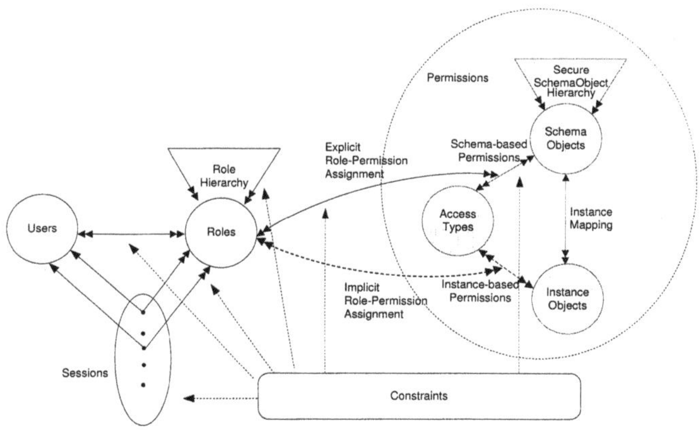

Figure 1. Extended RBAC Model

Extended RBAC Model:

- U (Users), R (Roles), P (Permissions), S (Sessions), AT (Access Types), IO (Instance Objects), SO (Schema Objects), SP (Schema-based Permissions), IP (Instance-based Permisson), IM (Instance Mapping), $SSOH$ (Secure Schema Object Hierarchy)

- S, UA and RH are same as RBAC96
- $SP \subseteq AT \times SO$: Schema-based Permissions
- $IP \subseteq AT \times IO$: Instance-based Permissions
- $IM : SO \rightarrow 2^{IO}$: Instance Mapping
- $P = IP \cup SP$: Permissions
- $SSOH \subseteq SO \times SO$: Secure Schema Object Hierarchy
- $EPA \subseteq R \times SP$: Explicit Role-Permission Assignment
- $IPA \subseteq R \times IP$: Implicit Role-Permission Assignment
  $IPA = \{(r : R, ip : IP) \mid \exists(at : AT, so : SO, io : IO)\cdot[(r, (at, so)) \in EPA] \wedge [ip = (r, (at, io))] \wedge [io \in IM(so)]\}$
- $PA = EPA \cup IPA$: Permission-role Assignment
- $schema\_permissions : R \rightarrow 2^{SP}$, a function mapping a role to a set of explicitly assigned schema-based permissions.
  $schema\_permissions(r) = \{sp : SP \mid (r, sp) \in EPA\}$
- $schema\_permissions^* : R \rightarrow 2^{SP}$, a function mapping a role to a set of explicitly assigned schema-based permissions with $SSOH$.
  $schema\_permissions^*(r) = \{sp : SP \mid \exists(so : SO, so' : SO, at : AT) \cdot [(so' \leq so) \wedge (sp = (at, so)) \wedge (r, (at, so')) \in EPA]\}$
- $schema\_permissions^{**} : R \rightarrow 2^{SP}$, a function mapping a role to a set of explicitly assigned schema-based permissions with $SSOH$ and RH.
  $schema\_permissions^{**}(r) = \{sp : SP \mid (\exists r' : Roles) \cdot [(r' \leq r) \wedge [sp \in schema\_permission^*(r')]\}$
- $instance\_permissions : R \rightarrow 2^{IP}$, a function mapping a role to a set of implicitly assigned instance-based permissions.
  $instance\_permissions(r) = \{ip : IP | (r, ip) \in IPA\}$
- $instance\_permissions^* : R \rightarrow 2^{IP}$, a function mapping a role to a set of implicitly assigned instance-based permissions with $SSOH$.
  $instance\_permissions^*(r) = \{ip : IP \mid \exists(at : AT, so : SO, io : IO) \cdot [(r, (at, so)) \in$
  $schema\_permission^*(r)] \wedge [ip = (r, (at, io))] \wedge [io \in IM(so)]\}$
- $instance\_permissions^{**} : R \rightarrow 2^{IP}$, a function mapping a role to a set of implicitly assigned instance-based permissions with $SSOH$ and

RH.
$instance\_permissions^{**}(r) = \{ip : IP \mid \exists(at : AT, so : SO, io : IO) \cdot [(r, (at, so)) \in schema\_permission^{**}(r)] \wedge [ip = (r, (at, io))] \wedge [io \in IM(so)]\}$

In the following subsections we will explain details of the main components in this extended RBAC model.

3.1. Objects

Definition 1 *(Schema Objects (SO)) A schema object is a XML Schema or schema component(s), may be patterned by an XPath or XQuery expression.*

Definition 2 *(Instance Objects(IO)) A instance object is a XML instance or instance component(s).*

Definition 3 *(Instance Mapping) Instance Mapping (IM) is a mapping between SO and IO:*
$IM : SO \rightarrow 2^{IO}$, *and* $\nexists so_1, so_2 \in SO, io \in IO \cdot (so_1 \neq so_2) \wedge (io \in IM(so_1) \wedge io \in IM(so_2))$

Since it is a well-formed XML document, a XML Schema can be treated as a tree structure, with nodes as the schema elements, attributes and datatypes. XPath can be applied on schema to capture the tree paths with particular conditions. A path can be absolute starting from the root, or relative from current position. For example, "/" is to return the root element of a XML document, while "$customerInfo/name$" selects the child element of "$name$" in "$customerInfo$". Another example, "$customerInfo[@gender = "Male"]$" selects all $customerInfo$ nodes where the value of $gender$ attributes is equal to "Male". XPath can select nodes which satisfy some conditions, such as, "$customerInfo/billingAddress[state = "VA"]$" selects all the $customerInfo$ nodes with Virginia state of billing address. There some built-in functions and in XPath to strengthen the capability of expressions, which can satisfy most of fine-grained specifications.

IM is a one-to-many mapping relationship from SO to IO. In our model, we use IM to implicitly specify the authorization in instance level. Specifically, the permissions defined on schema object will be transported to all its instance objects.

3.2. Secure Schema Object Hierarchy

Definition 4 *(Secure Schema Object Hierarchy ($SSOH$)) SSOH is the partial order relationship between schema objects:* $SSOH \subseteq SO \times SO$

Mostly SSOH is based on reuse relationships between schema objects. The reuse relationships can be regarded as partial order with acyclic, transitive and reflexive relations. Several types of reuse mechanisms have been specified in W3C XML Schema:

1 Datatype library. A datatype library consists of basic schema datatypes as building blocks. Schema elements and attributes can be created with these basic datatypes by specifying their "type" name.

2 Datatype derivation. New datatype or element can be derived from existing datatypes defined in the same schema or other schemas. There are two types of derivations: restriction and extension.

3 Schema element reference. Without duplicated its definition, a new element can be created by referring to another element in the same schema or from other schemas.

Some modularity mechanisms have been specified by W3C XML Schema to reuse datatypes and elements defined in a different schema, specifically including "include", "redefine" and "import". The first two only can be applied under the same namespace, while the third one can be used between different schemas.

Note that it is the security administrator's duty to decide which schema objects will be put in the hierarchy. At the same time, other relationships can be used in $SSOH$ definition by a security administrator.

3.3. Access Types

In this model, four basic access types have been considered to an XML object: $Read$, $Create$, $Update$ and $Delete$.

1 $Read$: "Read" XML information is the most frequent access to external users. A user activates some roles and try to read some instance information. The authorization enforcement point checks the $Read$ permissions defined on the schema objects with these role.

2 $Create$: "Create" access type is particularly for the document composer or source of message. The composition operation has to be verified by the composer's permission on the targeted XML information before storing or transporting. The final version of the created instance may be validated by a schema.

3 $Update$: "Update" permission is to modify the content of a XML object. Also the final version of the modified instance may be validated by a schema.

4 $Delete$: "Delete" is to remove a XML instance or elements in an instance, including the elements and contents. Besides the security check, XML validation check will be launched as well.

3.4. Permissions

Definition 5 *(Schema-based Permissions (SP)) A schema-based permission (explicit permission) is association of a schema object and its allowed access type:* $SP \subseteq AT \times SO$

Definition 6 *(Instance-based Permissions (IP)) An instance-based permission (implicit permission) is association of an instance object and its allowed access type:* $IP \subseteq AT \times IO$

Definition 7 *(Permission Reuse) In* $SSOH$, $\forall so_1, so_2 \in SO, at \in AT$, $(so_1 \leq so_2) \wedge ((at, so_1) \in SP) \Rightarrow (at, so_2) \in SP$

Permission reuse greatly reduces the number and complexity of permissions needed to define. This will simplify the authorization management of the access control system. At the same time, modular and extensible security policy can be achieved by using existing permission based on building block objects. The permissions for new schema objects is extensible with capacity of adding new permissions besides the inherited permissions.

3.5. Constraints

Some constraints are introduced in our model to make it fine-grained and flexible.

1. Recursive

"Recursive" constraint is used when permission based on a schema component will be automatically transported to all its sub-components, such as, a $Read$ permission on an element will transported to all its sub-elements and attributes. Since schema objects are nested meta-data structure, recursive transportation can happen in several levels. We use $r(n)$ to express n level recursiveness. $r(0)$ means permission not transported, while $r(\infty)$ means always nested recursiveness. For example, $(Read, /, r(\infty))$ expresses the permission of $Read$ access to a schema, and to all components in this schema.

2. Recursive Direction

In some cases, permissions on schema component can be transported to its super-component. Sometimes this bottom-up recursive direction is useful. For example, if role CSR (Customer Service Representative) has *"Read"* permission on $CreditCard$ element, the role will have *"Read"* permissions on all other elements or schemas who include this element, since credit card information is normally more sensitive than it's super elements. We use $+$ and $-$ to present top-down and bottom-up directions respectively, such as $r+(n)$, $r-(n)$.

Other constraints can be defined according to the real service and business logic by system designer and security administrator.

3.6. Explicit Permission on XML Instance

So far in our model we assumed that an XML instance is defined by a schema. The explicit permissions defined on schema objects implicitly specify the permission to instance objects. In real world there are two cases that instance-level authorization is desired: one is that there are some *"arbitrary"* XML documents without schema validation; another is that for a schema, the authorization for an instance is different from other instances. For these cases, the permission should be defined based on the instance level. Since XML Schema itself is a well-formed XML document, the permission specification can be easily applied to instance objects without any change. Both schema and instance objects can be expressed in XPath or XQuery. The only thing with extra consideration is to specify which level object is used in explicit permission. This is one of the benefits of the proposed schema based access control model. Generally the permission on instance level will overcome that in schema level.

4. High-level Implementation Mechanism

XML provides a uniform mechanism to solve problems in heterogeneous environment. Figure 2 shows the server-pull [2] implementation architecture. All the messages transported among the services are identified in XML. XML requests and responses are XML messages, whose format will be defined in schemas. We will use some existing XML standard to transport the security information, such as SAML (Security Assertion Markup Language) [13]. With SAML, the messages for user authentication, user-role assignment request/response, permission-role assignment request/response will be in standard format. And the underlying mechanism of user authentication, role server, and policy server can be abstract. That means, the implementation mechanism can be embedded to other systems very easily. This is an important advantage with" pure" XML implementation. Figure 3 shows an algorithm for the process of access control decisions. The algorithm is described in a way for clear exposition rather than efficiency. Implementation details of the XML mechanism will be our future work. As shown in the algorithm, an access request includes a user information (u), a role activated by the user (r), access type (at), and the target XML document ($target.xml$) to be accessed. To make an access control decision, some other related information is needed, such as the schema(s) of $target.xml$ ($target.xsd$), the possible expected output schema ($target'.xsd$), as well as the security information: user-role assignment ($UR.xml$), permission-role assignment ($PR.xml$), role hierarchy ($RH.xml$), and Secure Schema Object Hierarchy ($SSOH.xml$). In some cases, the output of an access control decision is required to satisfy some expected schema. The function $im(target'.xsd)$ is to check if output $target'.xml$ can be validated by $target'.xsd$. Since the authorization process

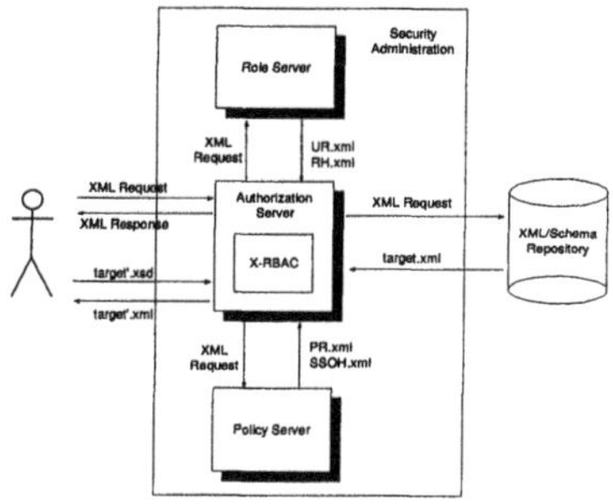

Figure 2. High-level Implementation Architecture

can remove some nodes of the input object, the output may not satisfy some particular schema, which is required by most applications. In this case, the access will be denied.

Function $roles(u)$ returns a set of roles assigned to a user, including direct assignment and inheritance with role hierarchy. Function $parse(target.xml)$ returns a set of data with tree structure. For each instance component i, function $sm(i)$ returns its corresponding schema object. The key part of the algorithm is a recursive method $recursive\_access(t, rootnode)$, which is a depth-first algorithm. For each subtree t, the method first checks the permission to the root node. If the access to it has been permitted, all subtrees will be checked by the same mechanism. Otherwise, access to the whole element and its sub-elements will be denied.

Function $s\_permissions(at, r, PR.xml, RH.xml, SSOH.xml)$ returns a set of schema nodes which is accessible to r or a subrole of r in role hierarchy. $PR.xml$ is defined for each schema. There are different implementations of this permission-role assignment. Here, we just provide a simple and abstract structure as shown in Figure 4. The basic format is similar to a schema document. In this example, each schema component is followed by one or more $< permission >$ tags to specify the permissions. A $< permission >$ tag has two attributes: $role$ and $access$. The value of $< role >$ is a role name, and the value of $access$ is a pre-defined access type. Since RBAC is a close model, any other role which is not specified in the $< permission >$ of a schema component cannot access this object. Because of the large number of schema objects and roles, in the real implementation, a visual tool will be developed to do the permission-role assignment.

$UR.xml$ and $RH.xml$ are more static in real implementation mechanism. $UR.xml$ is very straightforward. The main component is a user information

```
XML-based Algorithm:
Input: Access request: (u, r, at, target.xml)
       Schema of target: target.xsd
       Schema of expected output: target'.xsd
       Security information: PR.xml, UR.xml, RH.xml, SSOH.xml
Output: target'.xml
Method:
    // Verify user-role assignment:
    if r ∉ roles(u, UR.xml, RH.xml)
        ACCESS denied;
    endif
    // Parse and generate instance tree t rooted in rootnode of target.xml:
    t = parse(target.xml)
    recursive_access(t, rootnode)
        so = sm(rootnode)
        if so ∈ s_permissions(at, r, PR.xml, RH.xml, SSOH.xml)
            ACCESS rootnode is permited;
            add(target'.xml, rootnode);
            if (rootnode is not leaf)
                foreach subtree st ∈ t rooted in subnode
                    Recursive_access(st, subnode);
                endfor
            endif
        else
            ACCESS t is denied;
    end recursive_access;
    // Validation check with target'.xml according to target'.xsd if needed;
    if target'.xml ∈ im(target'.xsd)
        Output target'.xml;
    else Access target.xml denied;
    endif
```

Figure 3. Algorithm of XML Access Control

with some sub-nodes of name, department, role name, etc. In the real world, user-role assignment is built on organization structure, maybe be cooperated by some department other than security administrator [3]. So the $UR.xml$ may be derived from other systems. This is out of the range of this paper. What we present here are all very high-level and conceptual. In the next step of this work, we will enrich and finalize the details of this algorithm. Schemas for $UR.xml$, $PR.xml$, $RH.xml$, and $SSOH.xml$ will be defined. Since input and output in the algorithm are all XML documents, open source XML APIs will be applied, such as SAX (Java implemented XML parser).

```
...
<xs:element name="customerInfo">
  <permission role="CSR" access="read"/>
  <permission role="CSR" access="write"/>
  <xs:sequence>
    <xs:element name="ssn" type="xs:string">
      <permission role="CSR" access="read"/>
    </xs:element>
    <xs:element name="name">
      <permission role="CSR" access="read"/>
      <permission role="CSR" access="write"/>
      ...
    </xs:element>
    <xs:element name="creditCardInfo">
      ...
    </xs:element>
  </xs:sequence>
  <xs:attribute name="gender">
    <permission role="CSR" access="read"/>
    <permission role="CSR" access="write"/>
    ...
  </xs:attribute>
</xs:element>
...
```

Figure 4. PR.xml Example

5. Related Work

E.Damiani et al. [6] and E.Bertino et al. [7, 8] did some work in XML document access control, which is close to our work. E.Damiani et al. used organization-level DTD and site-level DTD as objects, built access control model for XML document based on authorization rules of $(subject, object, permission, recursive)$. They only considered $read$ operation in the paper. The algorithm to compute the final view of XML document based on the subject's authorization rules is presented with DOM tree labelling and transformation. E.Bertino et al. provided XML document access control policies, model and implementation based on authorization built on DTD and XML document. The authorization propagations from element-to-subelement, element-to-attribute, DTD-to-instance were considered with recursive options. Based on this, a java-based access control system, named Author-χ, is implemented with discretionary access control (DAC) model . Both Damiani and Bertino's models are based on DTD, using the relationship between XML instance document and DTD to transport authorizations. Another point is that they used DAC model. The main difference between our work and these previous work is that we use RBAC model based on XML Schema. The user-role and permission-role greatly will improve the security administration with vast users and XML objects. Also, the schema based permission and permission reuse enable modular and reusable policy deployment. Another point is that our model is not only for static XML documents, but for dynamically generated XML messages, such as SOAP and other XML protocols.

From industry, mainly there are two projects on XML security motivated by Organization for the Advancement of Structured Information Standards (OASIS): Security Assertion Markup Language (SAML) [13] and eXtensible Access Control Markup Language (XACML) [14]. The motivation of SAML is to define "assertion" for security statements in XML, such as authentication and authorization. Some XML protocols have been specified in SAML to exchange assertion in distributed environment. Our framework is orthogonal to SAML. Actually we will use SAML mechanism in our architecture. As shown in Figure 2, all XML requests and responses will be implemented in SAML messages and protocols. XACML is similar to our work, which applies XML format to specify access control policy with objects identified in XML. The main difference is that XACML focus on policy level, including logical predicates, rules, and policy combining. So in XACML, there is no clear access control model supported. In our model, we focus on model level. A XML-based RBAC model is clearly supported, which is policy neutral.

6. Conclusion and Future Work

This paper presented an extended RBAC model for XML security. Permissions in the model are defined based on XML Schema components and will be transported to all instances. Different from the previous access control model built on DTD, complex object hierarchies can be achieved with rich relationships between schemas components. The permission reuse through these hierarchies greatly improves the security administration by modular, reusable and extensible permissions. Several constraints are presented in the model. The proposed model can be modularly deployed and flexibly administrated in distributed environments. The model can be applied to no-schema based XML instance and instance level authorizations easily. The abstract implementation architecture is presented.

The detail implementation of proposed model is the next step of this work. XML technology is applied in the implementation mechanism. The modular and reusable features of XML will be the benefits to the RBAC model. SAML will be applied in our implementation for all XML messages. In the future we will study the access control in Web Services technologies, where the applications are built from XML protocols. As a service-oriented software environment, Web Services have roles like service provider, registry, requester, deployer, as well as system administrator. The schema based RBAC model can be a solution of Web Services security.

References

[1] R.Sandhu, E.J.Coyne, H.L.Feinstein, Role based access control models, IEEE Computer, 29, (2), pp.38-47, 1996.

[2] Joon S.Park, R.Sandhu, and Gail-Joon Ahn, Role-Based Access Control on the Web, ACM Trans. Information and System Sec., Vol.4, No.1, Feb. 2002.

[3] Sejong Oh, Ravi Sandhu, A Model for Role Administration Using Organization Structure, In Proc. of ACM Symposium on Access Control Models and Technologies, 2002.

[4] E.Bertino, S.Jajodia, and P. Samarati, Supporting Multiple Access Control Policies in Database Systems, IEEE Symposium on Security and Privacy, 1996.

[5] S.Jajodia, P.Samarati, and V.S.Subrahmanian, and E.Bertino, A United Framework for Enforcing Multiple Access Control Policies, ACM SIGMOD International Conference on Management of Data, 1997.

[6] E.Damiani, S.D.C.Vimercati, S.Paraboschi, and P.Samarati, A Fine-grained Access Control System for XML Documents, ACM Trans. Information and System Sec., Vol.5, No.2, May 2002.

[7] E. Beritino, S.Castano, E.Ferrai, and M.Mesiti, Specifying and Enforcing Access Control Policies for XML Document Sources, World Wide Web Journal, Vol.3, No.3, 2000.

[8] E. Beritino, S.Castano, E.Ferrai, and M.Mesiti, Author-x: a Java-Based System for XML Data Protection, 14th IFIP WG 11.3 Working Conference on Database Security, 2000.

[9] World Wide Web Consortium (W3C), Extensible Markup Language (XML), http://www.w3.org/XML, October, 2000

[10] World Wide Web Consortium (W3C), XML Path Language (XPath), http://www.w3.org/TR/xpath20, August, 2002

[11] World Wide Web Consortium (W3C), XML Schema Part 0: Primer, http://www.w3.org/TR/xmlschema-0, May, 2001

[12] World Wide Web Consortium (W3C), XML Schema Part 1: Structures, http://www.w3.org/TR/xmlschema-1, May, 2001

[13] OASIS, Security Services TC, http://www.oasis- open.org/committees/tc_home.php?wg_abbrev=security

[14] OASIS, eXtensible Access Control Markup Language TC, http://www.oasis-open.org/committees/tc_home.php?wg_abbrev=xacml

PERSISTENT VERSUS DYNAMIC ROLE MEMBERSHIP

Jean Bacon, Ken Moody
University of Cambridge Computer Laboratory,
JJ Thomson Avenue, Cambridge CB3 0FD, UK
Firstname.Lastname@cl.cam.ac.uk

David Chadwick, Oleksandr Otenko
IS Institute, University of Salford, Salford, M5 4WT, UK
d.w.chadwick, o.otenko@salford.ac.uk

Abstract Various role-based access control (RBAC) models have evolved along with a small number of implementations. One approach is to make role assignment persistent. After authentication, a principal can exercise the privileges associated with the roles it is assigned to without further action. Another approach is that principals must activate roles explicitly when they need to exercise the privileges associated with the roles. In this paper we outline our models and implementations (PERMIS and OASIS), which provide an example of each style of system. Both are concerned with realistic implementations in large-scale, widely distributed systems. We discuss the advantages and disadvantages of persistent versus dynamic role membership.

Keywords: role-based access control, access control policy

1. Introduction

Access control is a crucial aspect of most computerised systems. Mandatory schemes have been established for military contexts, and discretionary schemes are associated with the design of most operating systems. When distributed systems were first designed, based on emerging local area network technology, encryption-protected, capability-based access control was often used. Over the years this approach has grown in popularity as systems have become larger and more widely distributed. The capabilities have become encryption protected authorisation certificates managed by service providers, often alongside authentication certificates and integrated with a public key infrastructure.

Managing the access rights of principals to objects becomes increasingly difficult as individual systems grow in size and different systems need to interoperate. The privileges associated with a role are largely independent of the principals who may currently fill that role, and these privileges change slowly as an organization evolves. This is the key idea behind role-based access control (RBAC), in which privileges are assigned to roles rather than to individual principals; that is, the service developer specifies access control rights in terms only of roles. There are usually many fewer roles than principals in an organisation, although a large organisation may have several thousand roles. RBAC therefore promises to be an appropriate access control scheme for large-scale systems. When RBAC is used, administrators register principals in the usual way, as students, employees etc. It remains to express and enforce the policy that entitles principals to roles.

An additional requirement for managing access control in widely distributed applications is that heterogeneous, independently developed and administered systems should interwork; that is, principals managed by one system will need to use the services of others. Access to such privileges must be negotiated between the systems. Examples are services associated with e-government, where police, social services or health trusts may be authorised to access certain electronic records managed by another agency. Within the health application, the electronic health records of an individual patient may be shared between management domains such as primary care practices, hospitals, clinics etc.

Various RBAC models have evolved over the years, for example, [8, 9, 12] but there are few architectures and implementations. If RBAC is to be adopted in practice, large-scale engineering issues must be addressed, one of which is the persistence of the binding of principals to roles. Most of the RBAC models assign principals to organisational roles for an indefinite period. The alternative is that a principal activates a role only when it needs to carry out some task for which the privileges associated with the role are needed. In Section 2 we evaluate the approaches in principle then describe two implemented RBAC schemes, PERMIS in Section 3 and OASIS in Section 4. PERMIS uses persistent role-assignment, OASIS uses dynamic role activation, which we shall call P-RBAC and D-RBAC for brevity. In Section 5 we revisit the two approaches, highlighting the differences that remain significant after design decisions have been taken. We conclude in Section 6.

2. Dynamic versus persistent role membership

We aim to evaluate persistent versus dynamic role activation in the abstract and in practice, to the extent that our early implementations allow. Figure 1 gives an abstract architecture for a single service (a) when role membership is persistent (P-RBAC) and (b) when roles must be activated explicitly at the time the service is to be used (D-RBAC). Let us assume that P must be a member of role R in order to have the privilege of invoking service S. Authentication requirements are common to both approaches; let us assume it is carried out by some standard mechanism such as challenge-response.

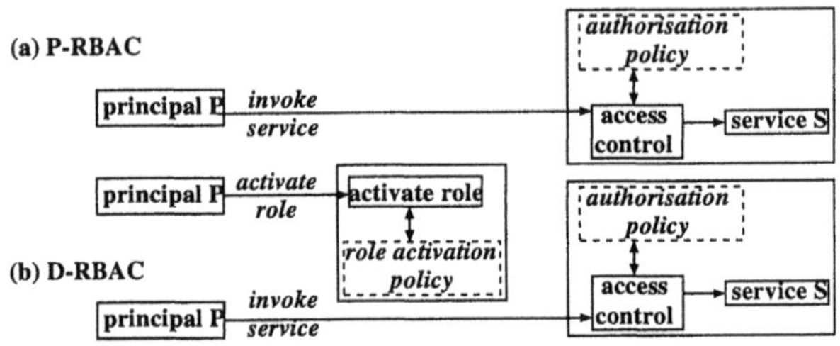

Figure 1. A service architecture with (a) persistent and (b) dynamic role activation

In (a) principal P's right to role R must be established before service S can be invoked by P. Checking of role membership may be carried out as part of access control; either by checking an administrative database that associates roles with principals or by checking a directory in which some form of signed role membership certificate can be associated with P; both are so-called "pull" approaches and require that P is authenticated. Alternatively, P may keep its role certificate for R in its private file space and may present it to S as a parameter on invocation, a "push" approach. If flexibility is required over whether pull or push will be used in a given implementation then some form of encryption-protected role certificates must be used. Note that environmental checks may also be made as part of access control; these include time of day and facts that might be looked up.

In (b) P must first activate role R by establishing its right to R according to R's activation policy. The role activation service may look up (pull) P's credentials or P may present (push) them. In both cases the service will authenticate P, to prove its ownership of them. If the credentials satisfy the role activation policy, the service will record that P is active in role R and may also issue a short-lived role certificate to P. When P invokes S, either P presents the role certificate as a parameter and/or the service checks with the role activation service that P has activated role R. Again, environmental checks can be made as required by role activation and service invocation policy.

2.1. Criteria for comparison

Some criteria for comparison and issues that must be addressed by the two approaches are listed below. Later we show how the design decisions taken in PERMIS and OASIS address these issues. For simplicity of discussion, we assume that role certificates are cryptographically signed or protected by encrypted communication. An alternative is to query secure administrative databases for the information.

Role allocation and activation overhead

In P-RBAC principals persistently hold their maximum number of roles; including those inherited by means of RBAC delegation hierarchies. Certificates are issued at a coarse time-grain, e.g. annually, to all principals entitled to them and may be used on many occasions. Many role certificates may never be used.

In D-RBAC roles are activated at need according to role-activation policy. It is likely that only a small proportion of principals and roles will be active at a given time.

The overhead of certificate issuing is therefore a choice between producing large quantities of long-lived certificates, which can be done in batch, offline or background mode (P-RBAC), or producing small quantities of short-lived certificates in the context of a working session (D-RBAC). The tradeoff is application-dependent and the certificates may not be equivalent. D-RBAC certificates may be passed, unsigned, under encrypted communication, for example.

Credentials

In P-RBAC, a principal's right to a role may be proved once-for-all when the role is first issued. Even paper-based credentials are feasible since the role certificates are issued in background mode. In D-RBAC, entitlement of a principal to a role must be proved by electronic means: certificates, smartcards or database records.

Privacy

Some methods of persistently recording principals' assignments to roles might be considered an invasion of privacy for some applications.

Authentication

Both dynamic and persistent RBAC are authentication agnostic and specific implementations may adopt whatever means are appropriate. Note that some systems (Akenti, CAS) mandate the use of PKIs for authentication so that roles can be linked to the principal's public key rather than to the principal's identity.

Policy expression, enforcement and evolution

P-RBAC and D-RBAC are equivalent with respect to authorisation policy. The policy that entitles principals to roles must also be expressed and enforced in both systems. In P-RBAC, this policy is applied statically, perhaps by a human administrator, and certificates are issued. In D-RBAC, the policy is enforced on role activation.

Policy may require that certain checks must be satisfied, such as time of day, coursework deadlines, relationships between parameters e.g. doctor-patient, and individual exclusions e.g. "all doctors except Fred Smith may read my health record". In P-RBAC assignment of principals to roles is static but environmental checks can be made on service invocation. In D-RBAC environmental checks can be made both on role activation and on service invocation.

Policy will evolve over time, dictated by local and external requirements, and it seems that these changes can be effected more immediately by D-RBAC. There is a need to manage policy change: to control access to policy itself and to ensure consistency as it evolves.

Vulnerability

At first sight it seems that P-RBAC may be more vulnerable to cryptographic attack than D-RBAC. However, the general issue of security of credentials applies to both schemes, involving properties such as the algorithms used and the length of encryption keys. The time available to an attacker should not be an issue if the encryption mechanism is designed well. Vulnerability is more likely to result from theft of keys and certificates. Both approaches are likely to use some long-lived credential, such as a public-private key-pair, for authentication at the start of a session. Vulnerability can be minimised by using session keys instead of persistent keys wherever appropriate, for example to identify a principal within a session.

Revocation

This is a crucial issue for P-RBAC and its importance for D-RBAC depends on how long roles are active. Because few, known principals and roles are active at any time in the latter, revocation seems to be more manageable for it.

Distributed domains

The single-service architecture shown above will in practice require extension to a system of many domains, each comprising many services; for example a national EHR service comprises many primary care practices, hospitals, clinics etc., each with many internal services. A service in some domain must be able to indicate, in its authorisation policy, a role defined in another domain, according to some negotiated agreement.

3. PERMIS overview

PERMIS is a role-based access control infrastructure that is based on standards and driven by policy. Roles are allocated to principals by authorised managers and are held in X.509 attribute certificates. PERMIS has implemented hierarchical RBAC [5], so that a principal who is allocated a superior role will inherit the privileges of all subordinate roles in the role hierarchy. PERMIS has taken a very liberal view of what may be classified as a role. A role is defined by a value of any type (i.e. an attribute in X.509 terminology). So a classical role such as manager, supervisor or employee may be assigned to a principal and, in addition, an application-specific status such as Frequent Flyer Gold, Silver or Bronze. PERMIS provides a Privilege Allocator tool that allows its user to allocate attributes to principals, and to sign the attribute certificates generated with his private key.

Each attribute certificate contains the X.500 distinguished name of the principal (or a pointer to its public key certificate), the attributes (roles) allocated to the principal, the validity period of the certificate, and various other parameters that may limit the applicability of the role assignment. The top level allocating authority is known as the source of authority (SOA) for the embedded attributes. The X.509 standard also specifies mechanisms to control the delegation of authority from the SOA to subordinate attribute authorities, but delegation of authority is not fully supported by the current PERMIS implementation.

3.1. PERMIS Architecture

The integrity and authenticity of attribute certificates are protected by their digital signatures, so they can be stored anywhere without fear of their being modified without detection. Privacy protection is not however provided, so roles of a sensitive nature should not be stored in public repositories. PERMIS has chosen to store the attribute certificates in LDAP directories by default, since LDAP is a popular Internet standard for accessing repositories, and the X.500 standards provide for this. The Privilege Allocator tool can be configured with the URL of an LDAP server, and it will write the attribute certificates directly into the principals' LDAP entries.

PERMIS has been built to support the "pull"or "server pull" model of operation, in which the access control engine pulls a principal's attribute certificates from the LDAP directories whenever it needs to make an access control decision. PERMIS can also support the "push" or "user push model" of operation, in which the principal (or his agent) pushes the attribute certificates to the access control engine whenever a decision is needed (Note that the current release of PERMIS has not implemented the push model fully since it does not check certificate revocation lists, but we plan to add this in a subsequent release.)

The access control engine has been built according to the ISO Access Control Framework (ISO 10181-3) [10]. This splits the access control functionality for an application into two components: the Access Control Enforcement Function (AEF), which is application-specific, and the Access Control Decision Function (ADF), which is application-independent. This architecture ensures that access control decisions within a domain can be consistently enforced by the ADF independently of the application, so that all ADF decisions are based on the access control policy

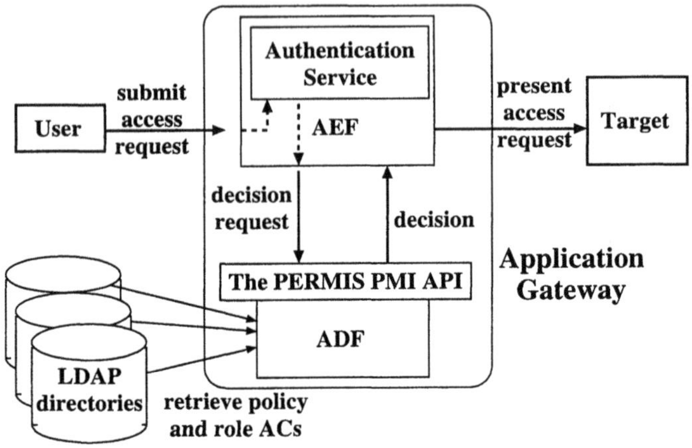

Figure 2. The PERMIS Access Control Architecture

specified for the domain. To support this, PERMIS has defined its own policy grammar (see next section). Each policy of the domain is secured in a policy attribute certificate, digitally signed by the SOA for the domain, and stored in the SOA's LDAP entry (each policy is given a unique object identifier according to the ISO ASN.1 standard). The ADF has been built using Java, and an API has been defined to link the AEF to the ADF. This API comprises three calls (GetCreds, Decision and Finalise) and a constructor. When the ADF is constructed, it reads in the policy for the domain, checks that it has been signed by the SOA for the domain, and that it is the correct policy. Because the AEF and ADF are designed to run as one process, linked via the Java API, there is no need for them to authenticate each other. If they were to run on separate systems with a standalone ADF contacted by multiple AEFs, as in Akenti, then mutual authentication would be necessary. The alternative PERMIS approach is that the ADF runs together with the AEF on each system, and all the ADFs read in the same policy for the domain.

When a user wishes to access an application controlled by PERMIS, he or she must first be authenticated by the application specific AEF. PERMIS has been built to be authentication agnostic. For example, when authenticating a user the AEF could use digital signatures, Kerberos, or even username/password pairs. This is an application specific choice. The only requirement that PERMIS makes is that the principal's distinguished name is passed to the ADF via a call to GetCreds, thus starting a new session. In pull mode, this causes the ADF to retrieve all of the user's attribute certificates from the set of configured LDAP servers. In push mode, the set of ACs is passed at the time of the call to GetCreds. GetCreds validates the user's attribute certificates, discarding any that violate the domain policy, or that have expired, or that have been revoked (in a subsequent release). In addition, any unrecognised or invalid roles/attributes embedded within valid attribute certificates are discarded. When GetCreds has finished, the ADF is left with a set of valid roles that conform to the policy of the domain, and these roles will be used for the duration of the user's session.

Whenever an access request is made by the user, the AEF asks the ADF to make a *granted* or *denied* decision, based on the policy, the target name and the access parameters. In addition to the static policy elements described in Section 3.2 PERMIS includes a plug-in feature so that application specific condition-evaluation objects can be invoked during decision making. Each request that is granted will be passed to the target, whilst each request that is denied will be rejected.

A specific policy is bound to the ADF when it is first constructed. If it is necessary to introduce an alternative policy while an application is executing, the application can destroy the current PERMIS ADF object and construct a replacement. PERMIS also supports an application-defined event object that is called back from the ADF. This allows the AEF to prematurely terminate a user session, for example if the session has been open too long.

3.2. The PERMIS Policy

The PERMIS RBAC Policy [6] comprises the following components:
SubjectPolicy - this specifies the subject domains covered by this policy. Each domain is specified as an LDAP subtree. Only principals with an LDAP distinguished name that falls within a subject domain may be authorised to access targets covered by this policy.
RoleHierarchyPolicy - this specifies the different roles supported by this policy, and their hierarchical relationships to each other.
SOAPolicy - this specifies which SOAs are trusted to allocate roles. The first SOA in the list is the SOA for this domain (and is the one which signs this policy). Subsequent SOAs in the list are remote SOAs which are trusted by the local SOA. This delegates authority to remote SOAs, so supporting distributed role management.
RoleAssignmentPolicy - this specifies which SOAs may allocate which roles to which subjects, whether further delegation of roles may take place, and for how long the roles may be assigned. This sub-policy effectively states who is trusted to allocate which roles to whom, and is central to the distributed management of trust.
TargetPolicy - this specifies the target domains covered by this policy. Each domain is specified as an LDAP subtree. Only domains with an

LDAP distinguished name that falls within a target domain are covered by this policy.

ActionPolicy - this specifies the actions (or methods) supported by the various target domains, along with the parameters that should be passed along with each action, e.g. action *Open* with parameter *Filename.*

TargetAccessPolicy - this specifies which roles may perform which actions on which targets, and under what conditions. Conditions are specified using Boolean logic and may contain constraints such as "IF time is GT 9am AND time is LT 5pm OR IF Calling IP address is of the form 125.67.x.x". All actions that are not specified in a Target Access Policy are denied.

4. OASIS overview

OASIS is an access control system for open, interworking services in a distributed environment, with services being grouped into domains for the purpose of management. Services may be developed independently but service level agreements allow their secure interoperation. OASIS is closely integrated with an active, event-based middleware infrastructure. In this way we can notify applications of any change in their environment, making it possible to ensure that security policy is satisfied at all times. OASIS is role based but has important differences from other RBAC schemes [5, 8, 9, 12]:

- Roles are service-specific; there is no notion of globally centralised administration of role naming and privilege management.
- Roles may be parametrised, as required by applications.
- Roles are activated within sessions. An OASIS session is started by strong authentication of a principal, and an initial role such as *logged_in_user* is created as a side effect of authentication. Roles have activation conditions that may include the requirement for prerequisite roles; a dependency tree of active roles is built up within a session.
- Persistent credentials (as opposed to session-limited RMCs) are implemented as appointment certificates, which do not confer privileges directly; the activation conditions of roles may include appointment certificates. We use appointment instead of delegating roles or privileges.
- Role activation conditions can also include constraints on the context, which must be checked during role activation.
- We provide an *active security environment.* Certain role activation conditions are specified as having to remain satisfied for the role to remain active. These are monitored and a role is deactivated if any becomes false.

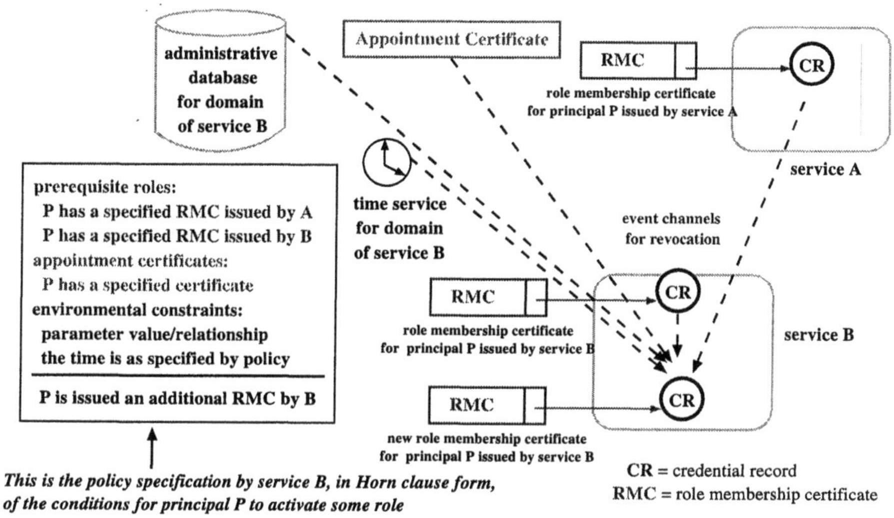

Figure 3. OASIS role activation within a session

An overview of OASIS is given in [1, 2], details of its architecture and engineering can be found in [3] and a formal model is presented in [4]. In this paper we focus on the implications of dynamic role activation. Figure 3 gives an example of a role activation rule. In order to activate a certain role of service B the principal must have activated two specified prerequisite roles (another role of service B and a role of service A); it must present a persistent credential (an appointment certificate) as proof of some long-lasting employment or qualification; and two environmental constraints must be satisfied. One concerns the time at which the role is activated, the other requires the administrative database to be consulted to determine, for example, some value(s) of or relationship between the parameters of the role (not shown). If these conditions are satisfied the new role is activated, and a role membership certificate (RMC) returned to the principal. A new credential record (CR) is set up by service B to record the status of the role that has been activated.

Certain role activation conditions are flagged as **membership conditions**, that is, they must remain true for the principal to remain active in the role. An event channel is set up associated with each of the membership conditions. Should any become false, this is notified immediately to the service that has issued the RMC.

Service level agreements are made to allow principals to invoke services in remote domains from their home domain, or while working temporarily in the remote domains [3]. For example, a hospital doctor may use a national EHR service or may arrange to work temporarily in a Research Clinic.

In our current, web-based implementation, sessions and client RMCs are managed at a web portal under SSL (secure socket layer). X.509 certificates are used for appointments.

4.1. Appointment

Instead of delegating roles or privileges, and to capture long-lived certification of academic qualification or employment, OASIS uses appointment. A function of some roles is to issue appointment certificates to other principals. Appointment certificates in themselves convey no privileges but may be required by policy as credentials, alongside environmental constraints and prerequisite roles, to activate certain roles.

For example, a professional society or academic institution may issue appointment certificates to people who become professionally or academically qualified. At present a paper certificate is typical, backed up by a database record at the issuing body. Such certificates may be required credentials for activating certain roles; for example, to be a member of an appeals panel at the society or institution.

These certificates may be conditions of employment, such as when a doctor is employed at a hospital. Instead of requiring academic and professional certificates in the activation rules of roles in the hospital, it is preferable for the hospital to issue an appointment certificate indicating "employed as doctor" after the professional and academic qualifications have been validated by the issuing bodies. The internal roles of the hospital need then only require the local "employed as doctor" certificate among their activation rules. This long-lived style of credential may be seen as augmenting a database record. The certificates may be issued as machine-readable cards or may be stored in private or public directories.

Appointment may also be used in situations where a technically-qualified stand-in is required; perhaps someone is called away in an emergency and must arrange a substitute. Here, the appointment certificate is unlikely to be long-lived, but its lifetime is not restricted to the session in which it was issued. The receiver may use the appointment certificate to activate appropriate roles within its own sessions.

5. Persistent versus dynamic role membership

We now revisit the issues introduced in Section 2 in the light of the design decisions taken in PERMIS and OASIS. The implemented systems are closer in functionality than we expected; for example, PERMIS requires roles to be used within sessions and checks role activation policy at the start of a session.

This study has made us realise that we have different intuitions about what a role is. In PERMIS roles are generic categories, such as doctor, whereas OASIS deems these to be appointments, that is, credentials for activating service-specific, parametrised roles when the need arises. Examples of roles in OASIS are *doctor-on-duty(Dr-ID)*, an initial role requiring strong authentication and an *employed-as-doctor(Dr-ID)* appointment credential, and *treating-doctor(Dr-ID, patient-ID)*, a role required because only a doctor with whom a patient is registered is permitted to read that patient's health record. Role activation policy is likely to require a *doctor-on-duty* prerequisite role and parameter lookup in an administrative database to check the doctor-patient relationship. OASIS was designed to capture fine-grained, service-specific policies.

Role allocation and activation overhead

Neither implemented system has yet dealt with large numbers of principals and roles e.g. millions of principals and thousands of roles.

For the applications to date, the overhead in PERMIS (P-RBAC), of issuing X.509 role certificates to all principals for all the roles to which they are entitled has been manageable. A Privilege Allocator API allows attribute certificates for all principals to be created automatically from a back-end administrative database e.g. to create "doctor" roles for everyone registered at the General Medical Council. It would not be feasible to create statically the parametrised, service-specific roles envisaged by OASIS, for example a *doctor(Dr-ID, patient-ID)* role for every patient of every doctor.

Allocation and management of OASIS persistent credentials (long-term appointment certificates) involves an overhead comparable with allocation of role certificates in P-RBAC, although database lookup can replace the use of appointments in any implementation. Both systems allow certificate allocation to be partitioned between different sources such as professional bodies and academic institutions. OASIS envisages that some generic employment categories, such as doctor or consultant, will be defined in local domains and appointment certificates will be issued on employment, thus subsuming externally issued credentials, some of which may continue to be paper-based. Short-term but session-independent appointment (to enable the delegation of a role) is likely to be used on a small scale.

Privacy

In the PERMIS pull mode persistent role certificates are stored in public LDAP directories, which potentially compromises the user's privacy. If privacy concerns are paramount, then P-RBAC should use the push model and allow the user or Attribute Authority to hold and control the release of his certificates across a confidential channel. The downside of allowing the user (rather than the AA) to control his role certificates is that revocation checking must now be carried out by the ADF. In D-RBAC the role certificates are not publicly visible when issued or presented and pass within communications that are encrypted under SSL. Thus privacy is ensured.

Vulnerability

Both projects lack experience over a long term of deployment. Both are using standard PKI services: SSL (OASIS), X.509 certificates for roles (PERMIS) and appointments (OASIS).

Revocation

D-RBAC does not necessarily need a revocation mechanism because the roles, and therefore the privileges, are short-lived. But since only a relatively small number of principals are active at any time, it is practicable to have role membership rules (that indicate which role activation conditions must remain true for the principal to remain active in the role) and to monitor that they remain satisfied. Immediate revocation of role certificates is part of the OASIS scheme, effected by invalidating the credential record for the RMC, and notifying any service that has cached its validity and requested call-back.

In P-RBAC it is not feasible to monitor every persistent role certificate in a system continuously, but this is not required, since only currently active certificates need to be monitored. In PERMIS initial monitoring is done at session initialisation time, by either retrieving the latest certificate revocation list or issuing an OCSP (online certificate status protocol) [11] request. Continuous monitoring could be achieved by using a protocol such as OCSP, requiring OCSP queries to the OCSP server immediately prior to each access control decision, but this would be inefficient. It should be necessary only for transactions where the loss associated with accepting a transaction, for a role certificate that has been revoked after initial monitoring, is high. Instead, PERMIS has a callback procedure that allows the AEF to terminate the user's session prematurely in an application-specific way.

Ease of use

The PERMIS P-RBAC pull model is easy for the principal to use, since he does not need to know about his role certificates or where they are stored. The service will pull them from the public repositories. The principal only needs to know how to authenticate to a particular service. The PERMIS push model requires the principal or his AA to know about and to actively manage his role certificates.

The current OASIS implementation, for a web service environment, requires OASIS services and user agents to have PKI facilities. The web portal acts as session manager. For a given authorisation policy it acquires the necessary roles on behalf of the user (validating each role's activation policy) and presents role certificates under SSL.

In both systems, policy is specified by the service developer and may include environmental checks with application and/or domain databases.

As noted above, PERMIS and OASIS roles differ and there may be a tradeoff between simplicity of policy expression and expressiveness/flexibility.

6. Conclusions

Please see our websites for the original paper presented at the conference. Space constraints do not permit a full discussion here. In summary, we believe that the important design decisions for the future will be concerned with scalability and the expression, enforcement and management of complex, evolving, distributed policy. Acceptance by users, application developers and administrators will be critical. Neither system has yet been tested on a realistic scale, for example associated with nationwide systems comprising millions of principals, thousands of domains and many thousands of roles. We look forward to gaining experience from the use of our implementations in large-scale applications.

Acknowledgements

The UK EPSRC has supported two graduate students working on OASIS and a Research Fellow working on the application of PERMIS to Electronic Prescription Processing. The EC ISIS program has partially funded the PERMIS project.

References

[1] J. Bacon, K. Moody, J. Bates, R. Hayton, C. Ma, A. McNeil, O. Seidel, and M. Spiteri. Generic support for distributed applications. *IEEE Computer*, pp.68–76, March 2000.

[2] J. Bacon and K. Moody. Towards open, secure, widely distributed services. Comm ACM, 43(6), pp.59–63, June 2002

[3] J. Bacon, K. Moody and W. Yao. Access Control and Trust in the Use of Widely Distributed Services. In *Middleware 2001*, Springer LNCS 2218, pp.295–310, 2001

[4] J. Bacon, K. Moody, and W. Yao. A model of OASIS role-based access control and its support for active security. ACM Transactions on Information and System Security, Vol. 5, No. 4 (November), pp.492–540, ACM Press, New York, NY, 2002.

[5] E. Barka and R. Sandhu. A role-based delegation model and some extensions. In *23rd National Information Systems Security Conference*, NISSC, Baltimore, MD, Oct 2000.

[6] D. W. Chadwick and A. Otenko. The PERMIS X.509 role-based privilege management infrastructure *Proceedings, Seventh ACM Symposium on Access Control Models and Technologies (SACMAT)*, Monterey CA, pp.135–140, June 2002.

[7] C. Ellison, B. Frantz, B. Lampson, R. Rivest, B. Thomas and T. Ylonen. SPKI Certificate Theory Internet RFC 2693, September 1999

[8] D. F. Ferraiolo, J. F. Barkley, and D. R. Kuhn. A role-based access control model and reference implementation within a corporate intranet. *ACM Transactions on Information and System Security*, 2(1):34–64, Feb. 1999.

[9] L. Giuri and P. Iglio. Role templates for content-based access control. In *Second ACM Workshop on Role-Based Access Control*, pages 153–159, Fairfax, VA. Nov. 1997.

[10] ISO/IEC 10181-3:1996 Open Systems Interconnection, Security frameworks for open systems: Access control framework

[11] M. Myers, R. Ankney, A. Malpani, S. Galperin and C. Adams. X.509 Internet PKI Online Certificate Status Protocol - OCSP. IETF RFC 2560, June 1999.

[12] R. S. Sandhu, E. J. Coyne, H. L. Feinstein, and C. E. Youman. Role-Based Access Control Models. *Computer*, 29(2):38–47, Feb. 1996.

FLEXFLOW: A FLEXIBLE FLOW CONTROL POLICY SPECIFICATION FRAMEWORK

Shiping Chen, Duminda Wijesekera and Sushil Jajodia
Center for Secure Information Systems,
George Mason University,Fairfax, VA 22030

Abstract We propose FlexFlow, a logic based flexible flow control framework to specify data-flow, work-flow and transaction systems policies that go beyond point-to-point flows. Both permissions and prohibitions are specifiable in FlexFlow and meta-policies such as *permissions take precedence* themselves can be specified over the meta-policy neutral policy specification environment of FlexFlow. We show the expressibility of FlexFlow by expressing three existing flow control models which were proposed for different applications and used different mechanisms.

Keywords: Flow control policy, Data flow, Security policy

1. Introduction

Information flow policies govern the exchange of information at various levels in systems. At the lowest levels, information is copied in and out of registers and memory locations inside processors. At a higher level, information is exchanged among variables in programs, methods in object oriented systems and transactions in database systems. In networked systems, messages are copied across system boundaries in order to exchange information. In all of these examples the levels at which information flows, the units of transfer and the number of destinations vary, but the central issue of information flow remains the same. Thus, it is interesting to investigate the commonalities among policies that govern information flow at an abstract level. This paper proposes FlexFlow, a framework to do so.

Being designed to capture properties common across flows, FlexFlow is formulated using abstractions of *nodes* and *trees* of flows among them. Because of this abstractness, FlexFlow has two advantages. Firstly, FlexFlow is not limited to high or low level information exchange policies. Thereby it can be used to reason about and derive consequence of mixing flow control polices at different levels. For example, higher level information exchange policies may govern flows between method calls, and lower level policies may govern data flows inside method calls. Because our framework can model information flow at both levels, it is able to combine policies across both of them.

The second advantage is that our policy specification framework does not depend on any meta policies. Therefore, policies using different meta policies can be modelled and their total effect can be compared using our framework. This is similar to the advantage gained by the *Flexible Authorization Framework* (FAF) of Jajodia et al. [9] over its predecessors in specifying access control policies.

FlexFlow specifies flow control policies as a set of stratified Horn clauses, which is sound and complete, in the sense that every requested flow is either granted or denied, but not both. FlexFlow is based on unique stable model semantics, and therefore FlexFlow rules can be interpreted unambiguously.

The rest of the paper is organized as follows. Section 2 informally introduces abstract concepts of nodes, flow trees and their representations. Section 3 formally describes the FlexFlow framework. Section 4 shows that FlexFlow can be used to express various existing flow control models. Section 5 describes related work and Section 6 concludes the paper.

2. An Informal Description of FlexFlow

This section informally describes the FlexFlow framework and the reasons that went into making our design choices. FlexFlow has trees referred to as *flow trees* build up from *nodes* and *branches.* Nodes represent sources and sinks of information and branches represent pathways taken by information flowing between nodes. Thus, information flows from the leaves of a tree via intermediate nodes to its root. Given that the same node can either send information or refuse to do so under different circumstances, FlexFlow uses *node environments* to capture sufficient data to enforce such *local* decisions. Similarly, a flow tree itself may be acceptable or rejectable due to policies under different global circumstances, despite the nodes enforcing their local policies. Such circumstances are captured by *tree environments* of flow trees. The exact relationship between the environment of a flow tree and those of its nodes is not rigidly fixed by FlexFlow and is therefore application specifiable. Consequently, the flow trees with their environments, consisting of nodes and node environments constitute the basic entities of focus in FlexFlow. In order to specify how to construct acceptable or rejectable flow trees, FlexFlow has rules written in the form of Horn clauses about trees and their structural properties. Our position - one that we put forth in this paper - is that such rules suffice to enforce existing flow control policies in a uniform and meta-policy independent manner.

As an example, consider an abstract syntax tree of the expression $x+(y+z)$. As shown in the left hand side of Figure 1 (the right hand side is its Prolog representation - to be explained shortly), it consists of three leaves with variables (variables are considered named locations that can hold values) x, y and z, one intermediate node R_{temp} and a root node R_{final}. Assume that each variable in this example is accessible by a specified set of subjects. For example, x is accessible by Alice and Bob, y accessible by Bob and Cindy, and z accessible by Alice, Bob and Cindy. We model this situation by making the environment of each node be the access control list. We view each binary addition operation as a computation tree in which the root stores the sum of the values stored in the leaves. Thus, as shown in Figure 1 there is an *intermediate* node R_{temp} holding the value of $x + y$ and the root R_{final} holding $x + (y + z)$. As it is shown in Figure 1, R_{final} holds the value of $x + R_{temp}$. The tree rooted at R_{temp} is said to resemble a *one step* flow, as it has depth one. By piecing together two trees with depth one, (namely the depth-one binary tree rooted at R_{final} and the one rooted at R_{temp}) we get a depth-two flow tree, namely the tree rooted at R_{final} with x, y and z as leaves. Having

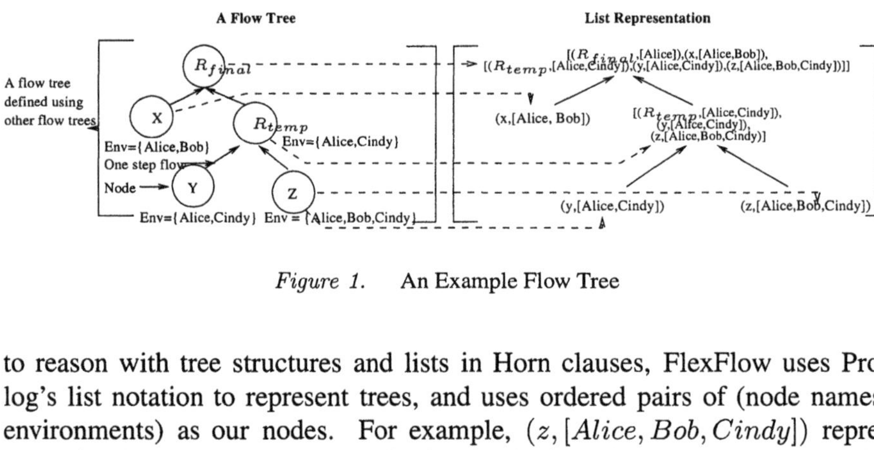

Figure 1. An Example Flow Tree

to reason with tree structures and lists in Horn clauses, FlexFlow uses Prolog's list notation to represent trees, and uses ordered pairs of (node names, environments) as our nodes. For example, $(z, [Alice, Bob, Cindy])$ represents the rightmost bottom (i.e. the last in the in-order representation of the tree) node in Figure 1. And, $[(R_{temp}, [Alice, Cindy]), [(y, [Alice, Cindy]), (z, [Alice, Bob, Cindy])]]$ represents the subtree rooted at R_{temp} with an access control list $[Alice, Cindy]$ and two children y and z.

FlexFlow states flow control policies as Horn clauses using flow trees as individual elements. In order to create these rules we used some predicates. Both rules and predicates used in FlexFlow belong to a five level stratification. FlexFlow use these stratified rules to specify flows that are permitted or prohibited without assuming any meta policies such as the open or closed policy. Formal details are given in Section 3.

2.1. Architecture of FlexFlow

As shown in Figure 2, FlexFlow rules have five stages, numbered zero through four in the figure. The first of them is the structural module (stage 0) containing data structures and functions needed to define flows. These include subject and object hierarchies, predicates necessary to model the environments and list manipulation operations such as adding or removing elements, taking the union of two lists etc.

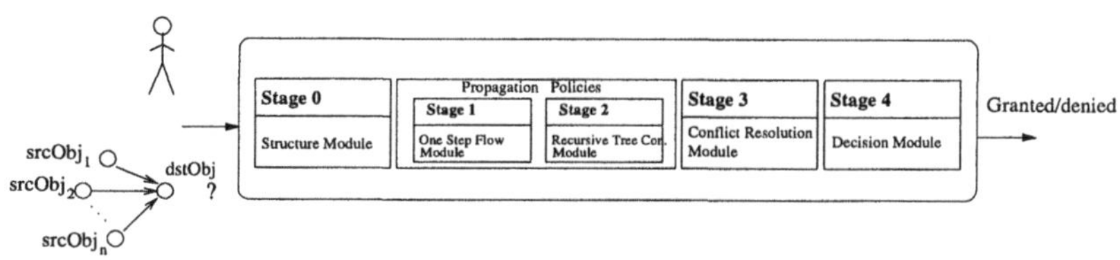

Figure 2. FlexFlow System Architecture

Stage 1 is used to specify one-step flows that are permitted or prohibited based on the structural properties specified at the previous stage. Stage 2 is used to build permitted or prohibited flow trees that may use already defined one-step flows. Recursion is allowed in this step. For example if flows are transitive, they can be specified at this stage, as transitive closure can be defined recursively. Similarly, permissions can be propagated up and down subject, object and role hierarchies using recursive rules.

Although propagation policies are flexible and expressive, they may result in *over specification*. That is, rules could be used to derive both negative and positive flows that may be contradictory. This possible conflict is due to the fact that positive and negative permissions is an application level inconsistency. This kind of inconsistency is not recognized by the underlying stable model semantics of locally stratified logic programs. Similar encodings have been used in the *Flexible Authorization Framework* by Jajodia et al. [9]. In order to weed out contradictive specifications, FlexFlow uses *conflict resolution policies*. They are stated in stage 3.

At stage 4, *decision policies* are applied in order to ensure the completeness of flow specification. That is because every flow request made to FlexFlow must be either granted or denied. This is necessary because, as otherwise the framework makes no assumption about flows that are not derivable only using stated rules.

3. Syntax and Semantics of FlexFlow

3.1. The Language of FlexFlow

Terms of the language: The language of FlexFlow consists of terms that are made up from constants and variables for nodes, environments and actions. It also has constants and variables over lists of (node, environment) pairs. Such lists are considered as flow trees, where the first element is the root and the rest are the children. In addition, FlexFlow allows environments to have application defined structures and predicates. An example of such a structure is an access control list, as used in Figure 1.

Predicates of the language: Predicates in FlexFlow belong to five strata, as summarized in Table 1 and explained below.

Stratum 0: Consists of list manipulation and application-specific predicates. An example of an application specific predicate is role(x_s, x_r) stating that subject x_s plays role x_r. An example list manipulation predicate is isMember((x_n, x_e), X_L) stating that the (node, environment) pair (x_n, x_e) is in the list X_L. More examples are given in section 4.

Stratum 1: Consists of a four-ary predicate safeFlow. The formal parameters x_n, x_e, X_L and x_{action} of safeFlow(x_n, $x_e, X_L, \pm x_{action}$) are respectively the destination node, destination environment, a finite list of source (node, environment) pairs and a name for the one step flow. safeFlow($x_n, x_e, X_L, \pm x_{action}$) holds if the one step flow consisting of the source list X_L and the destination (x_n, x_e) named x_{action} is either permitted or prohibited depending upon the sign (+ or -) appearing in front of x_{action}.

Stratum 2: Consists of a ternary predicate safeFlow*. The formal parameters x_{flowT}, x_{flowE} and x_{action} in safeFlow*($x_{flowT}, x_{flowE}, \pm x_{action}$) are respectively a flow tree, its environment x_{flowE} and its name x_{action}. safeFlow*($x_{flowT}, x_{flowE}, \pm x_{action}$) represents a permitted or prohibited flow tree depending upon the sign (+ or -) appearing in front of x_{action}.

Strata 3 and 4: Consist of a ternary predicate finalSafeFlow, with the same arguments as safeFlow*, representing the flow control decisions finally made by FlexFlow. It is used to express conflict resolution policies. finalSafeFlow($x_{flowT}, x_{flowE}, +x_{action}$) holds when FlexFlow permits the flow tree x_{flowT} and is included in stratum 3. finalSafeFlow(x_{flowT}, $x_{flowE}, -x_{action}$) holds when FlexFlow prohibits the flow tree x_{flowT} and is included in stratum 4.

Table 1. Stratification of FlexFlow and Predicates

Stratum	Predicate	Rules defining predicate
0	application-specific predicates List manipulation predicates	base application-specific relations. recursive list processing rules.
1	safeFlow	Body may contain literals from $\mathbf{SR}_0$.
2	safeFlow$*$	Body may contain safeFlow*and other literals from $\mathbf{SR}_0$ and $\mathbf{SR}_1$. Occurrences of safeFlow$*$ literal must be positive.
3	finalSafeFlow	The head is of the form finalSafeFlow(flowT,_,+_), the body may contain safeFlow, safeFlow*, and literals from $\mathbf{SR}_i$ for $i \leq 2$.
4	finalSafeFlow	The head is of the form safeFlow*(flowT,_,−_), the body contains just one literal ¬safeFlow*(flowT,_,+_).

3.2. Rules used in FlexFlow

A FlexFlow specification consists of a finite set of Horn clauses (rules) constructed using above mentioned predicates. These rules are constructed so that they form a locally stratified logic program. Obtaining a locally stratified logic program requires that the predicates used in the rules belong to a finite set of *strata*, and the rules follow some syntactic constraints. Generally, predicates in the body of any Horn clause are from the lower strata than that of the head of the clause. The only exception to this rule occurs in stratum 2, where safeFlow* is allowed to appear in the head and the body of a rule. Rules that permit the head predicate to appear in the body have to satisfy further syntactic restrictions that they form a *local stratification.* Namely, the occurrence of safeFlow* in the body cannot be negative. Logically, this restriction implies that every instance of the recursive rule can be *unravelled* in a finite number of steps, where negation at any such *unravelling* is interpreted as failure over *previous unravelling*. FlexFlow is stratified by assigning levels to predicates as shown in Table 1, and the level of a rule is the level of its head predicate. Now we explain rules at each stratum with some examples.

Stratum 0: Rules in this stratum consists of basic facts related to application specific predicates and list processing functions. Following facts relate to the syntax tree example in Figure 1.

$$\mathsf{isEnv}(x, [Alice, Bob]) \leftarrow$$
$$\mathsf{isEnv}(y, [Alice, Cindy]) \leftarrow$$
$$\mathsf{isEnv}(z, [Alice, Bob, Cindy]) \leftarrow$$

These rules state that the access control lists of variables x, y and z are $[Alice, Bob]$, $[Alice, Cindy]$ and $[Alice, Bob, Cindy]$ respectively.

Stratum 1: Rules in this stratum have literals from Stratum 0 in their bodies and heads that are instances of safeFlow. Example rules for the syntax tree example of Figure 1 is as follows.

$$\mathsf{safeFlow}(x_n, x_e, X_L, +binaryAdd) \leftarrow \mathsf{union}([(u, u_e)], [(v, v_e)], X_L), \mathsf{isEnv}(u, u_e), \mathsf{isEnv}(v, v_e), \mathsf{intersection}(u_e, v_e, x_e)$$

The rule says that it is safe for the source list X_L to *binaryAdd* into the root (x_n, x_e) provided that X_L has two elements (u, u_e) and (v, v_e), and the environment of x_e is the intersection of access lists of the sources. This rule also uses the list processing predicates union(A,B,C), intersection(A,B,C) that hold when C is the union/intersection of lists A and B respectively.

Stratum 2: Rules in this stratum have literals from Strata 0 and 1 in their bodies and heads that are instances of safeFlow*. Example rules for the syntax tree of Figure 1 are as follows.

$$\mathsf{safeFlow*}(x_t, x_e, +bTree) \leftarrow \mathsf{safeFlow}(x_n, x_e, [(u, u_e), (v, v_e)], +binaryAdd), \mathsf{append}((x_n, x_e), [(u, u_e), (v, v_e)], x_t), \mathsf{union}(u_e, v_e, x_e)$$

$$\mathsf{safeFlow*}(x_t, x_e, +bTree) \leftarrow \mathsf{safeFlow*}(x_1, x_{e_1}, +bTree), \mathsf{mkBinTree}(x_1, x_2, x_t), \mathsf{safeFlow*}(x_2, x_{e_2}, +bTree), \mathsf{union}(x_{e_1}, x_{e_2}, x_e)$$

The first rule says that a one step flow tree is a safe flow tree. The second rule constructs larger flow trees from smaller ones. The larger tree is made by using the predicate mkBinTree. mkBinTree(x_1, x_2, x_t) makes a binary tree x_t with first and second children x_1 and x_2 respectively. In addition, the environment of the new tree is the union of environments of the two trees used to make up the larger tree.

Stratum 3: Rules in this stratum may contain literals from stratum 0 through 2 in their bodies but only finalSafeFlow heads that have (+) action terms. They are used to specify conflicts that are resolved in favor of permissions. Example rules for the syntax tree of Figure 1 is as follows.

$$\mathsf{finalSafeFlow}(x_t, x_e, +bTree) \leftarrow \mathsf{isMember}(Alice, x_e), \mathsf{isMember}(Bob, x_e), \mathsf{safeFlow*}(x_t, x_e, +bTree)$$

The rule says that a flow tree is safe provided that Alice and Bob are included in its environment.

Stratum 4: This stratum has one rule only. It is inserted by the FlexFlow system automatically to ensure the completeness . It reads as follows.

$$\mathsf{finalSafeFlow}(x_t, x_e, -x_{action}) \leftarrow \neg\mathsf{finalSafeFlow}(x_t, x_e, +x_{action})$$

This rule says that permissions not derivable using given rules are prohibited by the system.

3.3. Semantics of FlexFlow

The semantics of FlexFlow is given by the well known stable model semantics [8] and well founded model semantics [7] of logic programs. In fact, as we showed in Section 3.2, FlexFlow specifications are locally stratified. This property guarantees that their stable model semantics is equivalent to their well founded semantics, thus ensuring that they have exactly one stable model (this follows from a result of Baral and Subrahmanian [1]).

4. Using FlexFlow to Express Existing Flow Control Models

This section shows how FlexFlow can express existing flow control models and their flow control policies. We choose three different models from previous literatures. We refer the reader to [3] for the reasons of our choice and the difference between the models and FlexFlow.

4.1. The Lattice Based Flow Control Model of Denning [4]

In [4], an information flow model FM is defined as $< N, P, SC, \oplus, \rightarrow>$, where N is a set of *objects*, P is a set of *processes* and SC is a set of disjoint *security* classes. $\oplus$ is a binary operator on SC and $\rightarrow$ specifies permissible flows among security classes. That is, for security classes A and B, $A \rightarrow B$ iff information in class A is permitted to flow into class B. Under some assumptions, referred to as *Denning's Axioms*, $< SC, \rightarrow, \oplus >$ form a universally bounded lattice where $< SC, \rightarrow>$ forms a partially ordered set.

Suppose f is an n-ary computable function, and a_i are object belonging to security classes $\underline{a_i}$ for all $i \leq n$. Then the flow control policy enforced by FM is as follows. If a value $f(a_1, \ldots, a_n)$ flows to an object b that is bound to a security class $\underline{b}$, then $\underline{a_1} \oplus \ldots \oplus \underline{a_n} \rightarrow \underline{b}$ must hold.

To specify this flow control policy, we use the following sets. C is a set of classes, Obj is a set of objects, P is a set of processes. In this example, we use *objects* as *nodes* and *classes* as *environments of nodes* and the root's environment as the tree's environment. In addition, we define application specific predicates shown in Table 2. For instance, $\mathsf{dominate}(c, c')$ says that the class c dominates class c' in the class set C. The FM policy is now formulated as follows.

Table 2. Predicates used to express Lattice Based Flow Control Model

Predicate	Argument Types	Intended Meaning
$\mathsf{dominate}(c, c')$	(class, class)	Class c dominate class c' in the class set C.
$\mathsf{class}(o, c)$	(object,class)	Object o belongs to class c.
$\mathsf{leastUB}(cList, c)$	(class list,class)	The least upper bound of the elements in the class list $cList$ is c.
$\mathsf{setClass}(X, Y)$	((object,class) pair list, class list)	The classes of objects in X constitute class list Y.

$$
\begin{aligned}
\mathsf{class}(o_1, c_1) &\leftarrow \\
\mathsf{class}(o_2, c_2) &\leftarrow \\
\mathsf{dominate}(c_1, c_2) &\leftarrow \\
\mathsf{dominate}(x_c, z_c) &\leftarrow \mathsf{dominate}(x_c, y_c), \mathsf{dominate}(y_c, z_c) \\
\mathsf{safeFlow}(x_o, x_c, X, +x_{action}) &\leftarrow \mathsf{class}(x_o, x_c), \mathsf{setClass}(X, Y), \mathsf{leastUB}(Y, x), \\
& \quad\ \mathsf{dominate}(x_c, x) \\
\mathsf{safeFlow*}([(x_o, x_c) \mid X], x_c, +x_{action}) &\leftarrow \mathsf{safeFlow}(x_o, x_c, X, +x_{action})
\end{aligned}
$$

$$\mathsf{finalSafeFlow}(X, x_c, +x_{action}) \leftarrow \mathsf{safeFlow*}(X, x_c + x_{action})$$

The first two rules specify that o_1, o_2 are associated with c_1 and c_2 respectively. The third rule says that c_1 dominate c_2 in C. The fourth rule is the transitivity of the dominance relation. The fifth rule says that information from objects in the list X is allowed to flow into x_o iff the least upper bound of the classes of objects of X is dominated by the class of x_o. The sixth rule constructs the depth-one permissible flow tree $[(x_o, x_c) \mid X]$ with environment x_c. Because the flow control policy in this lattice based flow control model has only one-step flows, we don't need to construct flow trees of depth greater that one. Furthermore, the model doesn't allow negative permission, so the conflict resolution policy is simple and given by the last rule.

4.2. The Decentralized Label Model of Mayer and Liskov [11]

The *Decentralized Label Model* [11] of Mayer and Liskov is applied at the runtime data flow analysis level. This model has variables storing values and updating them during a computation. A label contains a list of owners whose data was observed in order to construct the data value in question. Each owner declares a set of principals that may read the value, referred to as the reader set of that owner. Each (owner, reader set) pair is said to constitute a per-principal flow control policy. When a value is read from a variable or an input channel, the value acquires the label of the variable or the input channel. When a value is written to a variable, a new copy of the value is generated with the label of the variable.

The flow control policy used in this model is that when information flows from one object (here, object refers variable or channel) to another, the label of the destination must be more restrictive than the label of the source. A label L_1 is said to be more restrictive than label L_2 iff L_1 contains all the owners of label L_2, and the same or fewer readers for each owner.

To express the policies of [11], we define Obj, P and L as the sets of variables, principals and labels respectively. We use variables (input and output channels included) as nodes of the flow trees and labels of variables as environments of the nodes. Before specifying flow control policies as rules, we define some application specific predicates as shown in Table 3.

$$\begin{aligned}
\mathsf{safeFlow}(x_o, x_l, Y, +x_{action}) &\leftarrow \mathsf{label}(x_o, x_l), \mathsf{listOfRdSet}(Y, Y'), \mathsf{eRdSet}(x_l, X), \\
& \mathsf{allIntersec}(Y', W), \mathsf{cover}(X, W) \\
\mathsf{safeFlow*}([(x_o, x_l) \mid Y], x_l, +x_{action}) &\leftarrow \mathsf{safeFlow}(x_o, x_l, Y, +x_{action}) \\
\mathsf{finalSafeFlow}(X, x_l, +x_{action}) &\leftarrow \mathsf{safeFlow*}(X, x_l, +x_{action})
\end{aligned}$$

The first rule says that information can flow from objects in the list Y to x_o provided that each of principals in the effective reader set of label x_l can act

Table 3. Predicates used to express Decentralized Label Model

Predicate	Parameter Types	Intended Meaning
label(o, l)	(object,label)	l is the label of the object o.
eRdSet(l, X)	(label, principal list)	The effective reader set of label l is X.
cover(X, Y)	(principal list, principal list)	Every principal in X can act for some principals in Y.
listOfRdSet(X, Y)	((obj,label) pair list,RdSet list)	Reader sets of all the labels in X constitute the list Y.
allIntersec(X, Y)	(list of principal list, principal)	The intersection of all the principal lists in X is Y.

for some principals in the intersections of the effective reader sets of labels in Y. The second rule constructs the depth one permissible flow tree. The third rule specifies the conflict resolution policy.

4.3. The Flexible Information Flow Control Model of Ferrari et al. [5]

This model provides an approach to control information flow in object-oriented systems that takes into account, beside authorizations on object, also how the information has been obtained and/or transmitted. They coined a notation of *transaction execution tree* to represent the invocation relations of the methods calls initiated by a user. Figure 3 gives an example *transaction execution tree* simplified from the example in [5], where each node is a execution notated by execution id with the method name and the object on which it executed on, and each directed branch is caller-callee relation between the methods.

Based on the transaction execution tree, they define that there is an *information flow* from o_h to o_k by e_h and e_k, written (o_h, e_h, e_k, o_k) if the method of e_h is *read*, the method of e_k is *write*, and there is a transmission channel between e_h and e_k. For example, there are four information flows in the transaction execution tree example we given, which are (o_3, e_3, e_{17}, o_6), (o_4, e_9, e_{17}, o_6), $(o_5, e_{13}, e_{17}, o_6)$, and $(o_5, e_{16}, e_{17}, o_6)$.

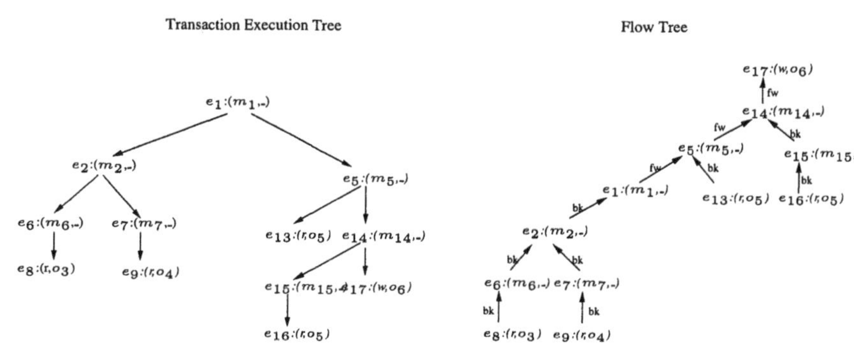

Figure 3. A Transaction Execution Tree and its Flow Tree

In their model, every object has an access control list (ACL) specifying the users allowed to read and write the object. Some methods are associated with waivers. Two kinds of waivers are supported: invoke-waiver (IW), specifying exceptions applicable during a method's execution, and reply (RW), specifying exceptions applicable to the information returned by a method.

Based on the concepts of waivers, they consider each flow under the following policy, referred to as *flexible policy*. A flow (o_h, e_h, e_k, o_k) is safe iff the union of the reader list and the waiver lists for o_h along the transmission channel from o_h up to but excluding o_k subsume the readers list of o_k. The execution of a write method is said to be safe iff all flows ending at it are safe.

In order to express the flexible policy using FlexFlow, we first extract all flow trees from the transaction execution trees using an algorithm called *flow tree generator*[3]. Figure 3 shows a flow tree extracted from the example transaction execution tree. We define four sets, Obj, U, M, E which are sets of objects, users, methods and executions respectively. We also define some application predicates which are shown in Table 4. Some of these are not standard list manipulation predicates. Due to the space limitation we refer the reader to [3] for their definitions. Using these predicates some sample rules that fit in stratum 0 of FlexFlew are as follows.

Table 4. Predicates used to express the Flexible Flow Control Model

Predicate	Attribute Types	Intended Meaning
obj(e, o)	(exec., object)	Execution e is executed on object o.
mtd(e, m)	(exec., method)	The method of execution e is method m.
rAcl(o, X)	(object, list of users)	The access control list of object o is X.
rW(m, X)	(method,waiver list)	X is the reply waiver list associated with method m.
iW(m, X)	(method,waiver list)	X is the invoke waiver list associated with method m.
releaseBK(X, m, X')	(flowE, method, flowE)	The result of applying reply waiver of method m to flow tree environment X is X'.
releaseFW(X, m, X')	(flowE, method, flowE)	The result of applying invoke waiver of method m to flow tree environment X is X'.
unionAdd(X, Z)	(list of flowE, flowE)	The union-add of flow environments in X is Z.
eRdSet(X, Y)	(flowE, user list)	The effective readers set of flow tree environment is Y.
subset(X, Y)	(user list, user list)	User list X is subset of user list Y.
bkFlowCH(e_i, e_j)	(exec., exec.)	There is a backward edge from e_j to e_i.
fwFlowCH(e_i, e_j)	(exec., exec.)	There is a forward edge from e_j to e_i.
listOfSafeFlow$((x, e), Y, a)$	((exec.,env.),list, action)	For all $y_i \in Y$, safeFlow$((x, e), y_i, +a)$ holds.
listOfSafeFlow*(X, Y, E, a)	(list, list, list,action)	For all $(x_i, e_i) \in X$, $y_i \in Y$, and $e_i \in E$, safeFlow*$(y_i, e_i, +a)$ and isHead$((x_i, e_i), y_i)$ hold.
listOfMtd(X, M)	(list, list)	For all $x_i \in X$, $m_i \in M$, mtd(x_i, m_i) holds.
listOfReleaseBK(X, M, Y)	(list, list, list)	For all $x_i \in X$, $m_i \in M$, and $y_i \in Y$, releaseBK(x_i, m_i, y_i) holds.

$$\mathsf{mtd}(e_8, r) \quad \leftarrow$$

$$\mathsf{obj}(e_8, o_3) \quad \leftarrow$$

$$\begin{aligned}
\mathsf{rAcl}(o_3, [Ann, Bob, Carol, David]) &\leftarrow \\
\mathsf{rW}(m_3, [[o_1, Frank], [o_3, Frank]]) &\leftarrow \\
\mathsf{iW}(m_3, [[o_4, David], [o_5, David]]) &\leftarrow \\
\mathsf{fwFlowCH}(e_{14}, e_5) &\leftarrow
\end{aligned}$$

The first two rule specify that e_8 is a read method of o_3. The third rule says that [Ann,Bob,Carol,David] is the read access control list of o_3. The fourth and fifth rules say that m_3's reply and invoke waivers are $[[o_1, Frank], [o_3, Frank]]$ and $[[o_4, David], [o_5, David]]$ respectively. The last rule says that there is a one-step forward flow channel from e_5 to e_{14}. One-step information flows are specified using the following two rules.

$$\begin{aligned}
\mathsf{safeFlow}(x_e, v, [(y_e, v)], +bkChannel) &\leftarrow \mathsf{bkFlowCH}(x_e, y_e) \\
\mathsf{safeFlow}(x_e, v, [(y_e, v)], +fwChannel) &\leftarrow \mathsf{fwFlowCH}(x_e, y_e)
\end{aligned}$$

These two rules say that in order to have one-step forward/backward flow, there must be a one-step forward/backward channel from the source to the sink. Permissible information flow trees are constructed using the following recursive rules.

$$\begin{aligned}
\mathsf{safeFlow*}([x_e], [x_o|X], +u) &\leftarrow \mathsf{obj}(x_e, x_o), \mathsf{mtd}(x_e, r), \mathsf{rAcl}(x_o, X) \\
\mathsf{safeFlow*}(X_{flowT}, X_{flowE}, +n) &\leftarrow \mathsf{listOfSafeFlow}((x_e, v), Y, +bkChannel), \\
&\quad \mathsf{listOfSafeFlow*}(Y, Y_{flowT}, Y_{flowE}), \\
&\quad \mathsf{listOfReleaseBK}(Y_{flowE}, Y_m, Y'_{flowE}), \\
&\quad \neg\mathsf{mtd}(x_m, w), \mathsf{listOfMtd}(Y, Y_m), \\
&\quad \mathsf{unionAdd}(Y'_{flowE}, X_{flowE}), \mathsf{mtd}(x_e, x_m), \\
&\quad \mathsf{append}((x_e, v), Y_{flowT}, X_{flowT}) \\
\mathsf{safeFlow*}(X_{flowT}, X_{flowE}, +n) &\leftarrow \mathsf{safeFlow}(x_e, v, [(z_e, v)], +fwChannel), \\
&\quad \mathsf{safeFlow*}(Z_{flowT}, Z_{flowE}, +n), \\
&\quad \mathsf{listOfSafeFlow}((x_e, v), Y, +bkChannel), \\
&\quad \mathsf{listOfSafeFlow*}(Y, Y_{flowT}, Y_{flowE}), \\
&\quad \mathsf{listOfReleaseBK}(Y_{flowE}, Y_m, Y'_{flowE}), \\
&\quad \mathsf{releaseFW}(Z_{flowE}, z_m, Z'_{flowE}), \\
&\quad \mathsf{append}(Y'_{flowE}, z'_{flowE}, X'_{flowE}), \\
&\quad \mathsf{unionAdd}(X'_{flowE}, X_{flowE}), \\
&\quad \mathsf{append}((x_e, v), Z'_{flowT}, X'_{flowT}), \\
&\quad \mathsf{append}(X'_{flowT}, Y_{flowT}, X_{flowT}), \\
&\quad \mathsf{mtd}(z_e, z_m), \mathsf{isHead}((z_e, v), Z_{flowT}), \\
&\quad \mathsf{listOfMtd}(Y, Y_m) \\
\mathsf{safeFlow*}([x_e, [y_e|Tail], X, +n) &\leftarrow \mathsf{safeFlow}(x_e, v, [(y_e, v)], +fwChannel), \\
&\quad \mathsf{mtd}(x_e, w), \mathsf{safeFlow*}([y_e|Tail], Y, +n), \\
&\quad \mathsf{mtd}(y_e, y_m), \mathsf{releaseFW}(Y, y_m, Y'), \\
&\quad \mathsf{eRdSet}(Y', Y''), \mathsf{obj}(x_e, x_o), \\
&\quad \mathsf{rAcl}(x_o, X), \mathsf{subset}(X, Y'') \\
\mathsf{finalSafeFlow}(X_{flowT}, X_{flowE}, +x_{action}) &\leftarrow \mathsf{safeFlow*}(X_{flowT}, X_{flowE}, +x_{action})
\end{aligned}$$

The first rule says that executing a read method m constructs a one node flow tree that has $[o, X]$ as its environment where X is the ACL of o. Second and third rules recursively constructs flow trees that have non-write roots. Note that for any node in any flow tree extracted from a given transaction execution tree, there is at most one forward channel feeding into it. The fourth rule constructs the whole permissible flow tree whose root is a write execution. The last rule resolves conflicts.

5. Related Work

Flow control is a heavily researched area in the context of multi-level security. In the early days, Bell and LaPadula [2] and Denning [4] proposed the lattice based models of information flow. Some flexibility to Denning's lattice based model was later added by Foley [6], where each entity was associated with a label pair instead of a single label.

McCollum et al. [10] presented an Owner Retained Access Control model (ORAC) to control information dissemination. Based on the same idea, Myers and Liskov [11] provided a language-based information flow control model. Samarati et al. [12] presents an information flow control model for object-oriented system. Ferrari et al. [5] extend that model by allowing waivers associated with methods.

Our work has been influenced by the *Flexible Authorization Framework* (FAF) of Jajodia et al. [9]. FAF is proposed for specification of access control policies, but not flow control policies. To our best knowledge, FlexFlow is the first flexible logic framework for flow control policies specification.

6. Conclusions

The FlexFlow framework specifies flow control policies as stratified logic programs consisting of five levels. Both permissions and prohibitions are specifiable in FlexFlow. By expressing flow control policies at the programming language and transaction specification we have shown the generality of FlexFlow.

Acknowledgments

This work was partially supported by the National Science Foundation under grant CCR-0113515.

References

[1] C. Baral and V.S. Subrahmanian. Stable and extension class theory for logic programs and default theories. *Journal of Automated Reasoning*, 8:345–366, 1992.

[2] D.E. Bell and L.J. LaPadula. Secure computer systems: Mathematical foundations and model. Report M74-244, Mitre Corp., Bedford, MA, 1975.

[3] S. Chen, D. Wijesekera, and S. Jajodia. Flexflow: A flexible flow control policy specification framework. Report ISE-TR-03-04, Center for Secure Information Systems, Fairfax, VA, 2003.

[4] D.E. Denning. A lattice model of secure information flow. *Communication of ACM*, pages 236–243, May 1976.

[5] E. Ferrari, P. Samarati, E. Bertino, and S. Jajodia. Providing flexibility in information flow control for object-oriented systems. In *Proceedings of the IEEE Symposium on Security and Privacy*, pages 130–140, Oakland, CA, May 1997. IEEE.

[6] S.N. Foley. A model for secure information flow. In *Proceedings of the IEEE symposium on Security and Privacy*, Oakland, CA, May 1989.

[7] A.V. Gelder. The alternating fixpoint of logic programs with negation. In *Proc. 8th ACM Symposium on Principles of Database Systems*, pages 1–10, 1989.

[8] M. Gelfond and V. Lifschitz. The stable model semantics for logic programming. In *Proc. Fifth International Conference and Symposium on Logic Programming*, pages 1070–1080, 1988.

[9] S. Jajodia, P. Samarati, M.L. Sapino, and V.S. Subrahmanian. Flexible support for multiple access control policies. *ACM Transactions on Database Systems*, 26(4):1–57, June 2001.

[10] C.J. McCollum, J.R. Messing, and L. Notargiacomo. Beyond the pale of mac and dac-defining new forms of access control. In *Proceedings of the IEEE symposium on Security and Privacy*, pages 190–200, Oakland, CA, May 1990.

[11] A.C. Myers and B. Liskov. A decentralized model for information flow control. In *Proceedings of the 16th ACM Symposium on Operating System Principles*, pages 129–142, Saint-Malo, France, October 1997.

[12] P. Samarati, E. Bertino, A. Ciampichetti, and S. Jajodia. Information flow control in object-oriented systems. *IEEE Transactions on Knowledge and Data Engineering*, 9(4):524–538, July-Aug. 1997.

VII

KEY NOTE

DATA AND APPLICATIONS SECURITY: PAST, PRESENT AND THE FUTURE

Bhavani Thuraisingham
The National Science Foundation, Arlington, VA and The MITRE Corporation, Bedford, MA

Abstract: This paper first describes the developments in data and applications security with a special emphasis on database security. It also discusses current work including security for data warehouses and e-commerce systems. Then it discuses some of the directions for data and applications security which includes secure semantic web, secure dependable information management, and secure sensor information management. Directions for privacy research are also given.

Key words: Database Security, Secure Semantic Web, Secure Dependable Information Management, Secure Sensor Information Management, Privacy

1. INTRODUCTION

Recent developments in information systems technologies have resulted in computerizing many applications in various business areas. Data has become a critical resource in many organizations, and therefore, efficient access to data, sharing the data, extracting information from the data, and making use of the information has become an urgent need. As a result, there have been many efforts on not only integrating the various data sources scattered across several sites, but extracting information from these databases in the form of patterns and trends has also become important. These data sources may be databases managed by database management systems, or they could be data warehoused in a repository from multiple data sources.

The advent of the World Wide Web (WWW) in the mid 1990s has resulted in even greater demand for managing data, information and knowledge effectively. There is now so much data on the web that managing it with conventional tools is becoming almost impossible. New tools and techniques are needed to effectively manage this data. Therefore, to provide interoperability as well as warehousing between the multiple data sources and systems, and to extract information from the databases and warehouses on the web, various tools are being developed.

As the demand for data and information management increases, there is also a critical need for maintaining the security of the databases, applications and information systems. Data and information have to be protected from unauthorized access as well as from malicious corruption. With the advent of the web it is even more important to protect the data and information as numerous individuals now have access to this data and information. Therefore, we need effective mechanisms for securing data and applications.

This paper will review the developments in data and applications security with a special emphasis on database security. Then it will provide directions for data and applications security. These directions include securing emerging applications such as secure semantic web, secure sensor/stream information processing and privacy.

2. DEVELOPMENTS IN DATABASE SECURITY

Initial developments in database security began in the 1970s. For example, as part of the research on System R at IBM Almaden Research Center, there was a lot of work on access control for relational database systems. About the same time, some early work on multilevel secure database management systems (MLS/DBMS) was reported.

However it was only after the Air Force Summer Study in 1982, that much of the developments on secure database systems began (see [1]). There were the early prototypes based on the integrity lock mechanisms developed at the MITRE Corporation. Later in the mid-1980s pioneering research was carried out at SRI International and Honeywell Inc. on systems such as SeaView and Lock Data Views. Some of the technologies developed by these research efforts were transferred to commercial products by corporations such as Oracle, Sybase, and Informix.

The research in the mid 1980s also resulted in exploring some new areas such as the inference problem, secure object database systems, secure transaction processing and secure distributed/federated database systems. In fact Dr. John Campbell of the National Security Agency stated in 1990 is that one of the important developments in database security was the work of Thuraisingham on the unsolvability of the inference problem [6]. This research then led the way to examine various classes of the inference problem. Throughout the early 1990s, there were many efforts reported on these new types of secure database systems by researchers at organizations such as The MITRE Corporation, Naval Research Laboratory, University of

Milano and George Mason University. In addition much work was also carried out on secure transactions processing.

In the mid 1990s, with the advent of the web, there were many new directions for secure data management research. These included secure workflow systems, secure digital libraries, web security, and secure data warehouses. New technologies such as data mining exacerbated the inference problem as even naive users could now use data mining tools and infer sensitive information. However data mining is also a very important technique for solving many security problems such as intrusion detection and auditing. Therefore the challenge is to carry out data mining but at the same time ensuring that the inference problem is limited. Furthermore, with developments in distributed object systems and e-commerce applications, resulted in developments in secure distributed object systems and secure e-commerce applications. In addition, access control also has received a lot of attention especially in the area of role-based access control (RBAC). A fairly comprehensive survey of data management security is reported in the article by Ferrari and Thuraisingham [11]. In this survey, the authors have given numerous references to research in database security starting around the 1970s until around the late 1990s. Also, many of the publications in secure data management have appeared in the Proceedings of the IFIP 11.3 Working Conferences on Data and Applications Security [15] as well as in the proceedings of various security and database conferences. Numerous researchers all over the world have contributed toward the developments in database and applications security. A listing of all the references is beyond the scope of this paper.

3. DIRECTIONS FOR DATA AND APPLICATIONS SECURITY

3.1 Overview

In section 2 we provided a brief overview of the developments in secure data management over a thirty-year period starting around the early 1970s until the late 1990s. While there have been many developments in web security, there is still a lot of work to be done. Every day we are seeing developments on web data management. For example, standards such as XML (extensible Markup Language), RDF (Resource Description Framework) are emerging. Security for these web standards has to be examined. Also, web services are becoming extremely popular and necessary for many applications and therefore we need to examine secure web services.

Semantic web is a concept that will soon become a reality. We need to examine security issues for the semantic web (see for example, [12]).

Security needs to be examined for new application areas such as bioinformatics, peer-to-peer computing, grid computing, and stream/sensor data management. For example, in the case of bioinformatics, it is important that information about the genes of the individuals be protected from unauthorized users. Peer-to-peer computing has received a lot of attention recently. There are numerous security issues for such systems including secure information sharing and collaboration. Furthermore, data is no longer only in structured databases. Data could be streams emanating from sensors and other sources as well as text, images and video. Security for such data has not received much attention. One also has to make tradeoffs between security, data quality and real-time processing. In other words, we need research on quality of service for information processing. Grid computing is developing rapidly especially to develop infrastructures and tools for scientists and engineers to carry out research. We need to ensure that the grids are secure. Finally we need to ensure that individual privacy is maintained especially when tools for data mining are used to extract information for national security purposes.

In summary, as new technologies emerge there are lot of security issues that need to be examined. Furthermore, as technologies are being developed for organizations and societies such as knowledge management and collaboration tools, we need to examine the security impact on these tools and technologies. While we have made a lot of progress in data and applications security the last three decades, there are many more security issues that need to be examined in the next several decades. To address these issues, there are now various research programs being funded in USA and in Europe. A description of the Cyber Trust Theme funded by the National Science Foundation, which includes data, and applications security can be found in [19]. A discussion of some previous efforts can be found in [26]).

The remaining sections will focus on some of the specific directions in secure semantic web, secure dependable information management, and secure sensor information management and privacy. These were some of the direction discussed during the keynote presentation at the IFIP 11.3 Data and Applications Security Conference in Colorado on August 3, 2003 (see [27]. There are many more areas that need work in security including bioinformatics, geoinformatics, and scientific and engineering informatics in general, peer-to-peer information management, and information management for pervasive and mobile computing. A discussion of the security issues for all of these areas is beyond the scope of this paper. Note also that we have not discussed topics such as critical infrastructure protection and information assurance for databases in this paper. For a detailed discussion of database and applications security, we refer to [34].

3.2 Secure Semantic Web

While the current web technologies facilitate the integration of information from a syntactic point of view, there is still a lot to be done to integrate the semantics of various systems and applications. That is, current web technologies depend a lot on the human-in-the-loop for information integration. Tim Berners Lee, the father of WWW, realized the inadequacies of current web technologies and subsequently strived to make the web more intelligent. His goal was to have a web that will essentially alleviate humans from the burden of having to integrate disparate information sources as well as to carry out extensive searches. He then came to the conclusion that one needs machine understandable web pages and the use of ontologies for information integration. This resulted in the notion of the semantic web [17].

Tim Berners Lee has specified various layers for the semantic web. At the lowest level one has the protocols for communication including TCP/IP (Transmission Control Protocol/Internet protocol), HTTP (Hypertext Transfer Protocol) and SSL (Secure Socket Layer). The next level is the XML (eXtensible Markup Language) layer that also includes XML schemas. The next level is the RDF (Resource Description Framework) layer. Next comes the Ontologies and Interoperability layer. Finally at the highest-level one has the Trust Management layer. For the semantic web to operate successfully we need to ensure that security is maintained within and across all of the layers. In this section we provide an overview of the security issues for the semantic web.

As stated earlier, logic, proof and trust are at the highest layers of the semantic web. That is, how can we trust the information that the web gives us? Closely related to trust is security. However security cannot be considered in isolation. That is, there is no one layer that should focus on security. Security cuts across all layers and this is a challenge. For example, consider the lowest layer. One needs secure TCP/IP, secure sockets, and secure HTTP. There are now security protocols for these various lower layer protocols. One needs end-to-end security. That is, one cannot just have secure TCP/IP built on untrusted communication layers. That is, we need network security. Next layer is XML and XML schemas. One needs secure XML (see [4], [5]). That is, access must be controlled to various portions of the document for reading, browsing and modifications. There is research on securing XML and XML schemas. The next step is securing RDF. Now with RDF not only do we need secure XML, we also need security for the interpretations and semantics. For example under certain context, portions of the document may be Unclassified while under certain other context the document may be Classified. As an example one could declassify an RDF document once the war is over. Lot of work has been carried out security constraint processing for relational databases. One needs to determine whether these results could be applied for the semantic web (see [23]).

Once XML and RDF have been secured the next step is to examine security for ontologies and interoperation. That is, ontologies may have security levels attached to them. Certain parts of the ontologies could be Secret while certain other parts may be Unclassified. The challenge is how does one use these ontologies for secure information integration? Researchers have done some work on the secure interoperability of databases. We need to revisit this research and then determine what else needs to be done so that the information on the web can be managed, integrated and exchanged securely.

Closely related to security is privacy. That is, certain portions of the document may be private while certain other portions may be public or semi-private. Privacy has received a lot of attention recently partly due to national security concerns. Privacy for the semantic web may be a critical issue, That is, how does one take advantage of the semantic web and still maintain privacy and sometimes anonymity.

We also need to examine the inference problem for the semantic web. Inference is the process of posing queries and deducing new information. It becomes a problem when the deduced information is something the user is unauthorized to know. With the semantic web, and especially with data mining tools, one can make all kinds of inferences. That is the semantic web exacerbates the inference problem (see [24]). Recently there has been some research on controlling unauthorized inferences on the semantic web. We need to continue with such research (see for example, [10]).

Security should not be an afterthought. We have often heard that one needs to insert security into the system right from the beginning. Similarly security cannot be an afterthought for the semantic web. However, we cannot also make the system inefficient if we must guarantee one hundred percent security at all times. What is needed is a flexible security policy. During some situations we may need one hundred percent security while during some other situations say thirty percent security (whatever that means) may be sufficient.

3.3 Secure Dependable Information Management

Dependable information systems are systems that are secure, survivable, fault tolerant and can process data in real-time. There is quality of service tradeoffs that one needs to make to build dependable information systems. Various information systems including the semantic web have to be dependable. That is, these systems need to be secure, survivable and process data in real-time if needed.

Our previous experience on building next generation command and control systems using real-time objects will form the basis for the discussion on dependable information management. Our infrastructure for the dependable system will consist of objects that have to perform many functions such as interprocess communication as well as memory management. These objects have to incorporate security, real-time processing and fault tolerant computing capabilities. The data managers have to process queries, execute transactions and manage data that may be transient. Data may also be mined to extract information.

The data/information manager will manage various types of data including track data and data for multi-sensor information integration and fusion. The data/information manager will be hosted as an application on the object-based infrastructure. Processing may be distributed among multiple nodes and there has to be coordination between the nodes. Essentially we are proposing a distributed information management system. One could also think of this system as a peer-to-peer system where the nodes are peers that have to work together to solve a problem.

For many applications timing constraints may be associated with data processing. That is, the data may have to be updated within a certain time or it may be invalid. There are tradeoffs between security and real-time processing. That is, it takes time to process the access control rules and as a result, the system may miss the deadlines. Therefore, we need flexible security policies. In certain cases real-time processing may be critical. For example if we are to detect anomalies from the time a person checks in at the ticket counter until he boards the airplane, then this anomaly has to be detected within a certain time. In this case we may have to sacrifice some degree of security. In other cases, we may have a lot of time to say analyze the data and in this case only authorized individuals may access the data.

One possibility for developing dependable infrastructures and data managers for sensor networks is to follow the approach we have developed for real-time command and control systems such as AWACS (Airborne Warning and Control System). Here we developed an infrastructure consisting of a real-time object request broker and services using commercial real-time operating systems. We then developed a real-time data manager and applications hosted on the infrastructure. We used object technology for integrating the various components. We also showed how such an infrastructure could be used to migrate legacy applications (see [3], [25]).

We can take a similar approach to build an integrated system for dependable information systems. We need appropriate operating systems and infrastructures possibly based on object request brokers. We need to host dependable data managers and applications such as multi-sensor data integration and fusion on the infrastructures. We need to ensure that the system is secure and survivable. We also need to ensure that the infrastructure is secure. That is, security has to be built into the system and not considered as an after-thought. Essentially we are proposing a layered architecture for dependable information management. The infrastructure consists of middleware possibly based on object request brokers for sensors. The objects that constitute the middleware include objects for interprocess communication, memory management, and support for data fusion and aggregation. On top of the infrastructure we host a dependable data manager. We also need to examine both centralized and distributed architectures for dependable data management. On the one hand we can aggregate the data and send it to a centralized data management system or we can develop a full-fledged distributed data management system. We need to conduct simulation studies and determine tradeoffs between various architectures and infrastructures.

As part of our work on evolvable real-time command and control systems we examined real-time processing for object request brokers and we were instrumental in establishing a special interest group, which later became a task force within the Object Management Group (OMG). Subsequently commercial real-time object request brokers were developed. The question is, do we need special purpose object request brokers for dependable networks? Our challenge now is to develop object request brokers for dependable systems. We need to examine special features for object request brokers for managing data for dependable systems.

Another aspect that is important is end-to-end dependability. This includes security, real-time processing and fault tolerance for not only all of the components such as infrastructures, data managers, networks, applications and operating systems; we also need to ensure the dependability of the composition of the entire system. This will be a major challenge even if we consider security, real-time processing and fault tolerant computing individually. Integrating all of them will be a complex task and will have to address many research issues and challenges.

3.4 Secure Sensor Information Management

We need to conduct research on security for sensor databases and sensor information systems. Note that sensor information management is one aspect of dependable information management. For example, can we apply various access control techniques for sensor and stream databases? That is, can we give access to the data depending on the roles of the users such as the air port security officer has access to all of the sensor data emanating from the sensors while the airport ticketing agent may have limited access to certain sensor data. Another challenge is granting access to aggregated data. Individual data may be unclassified while the aggregated data may be highly sensitive. This is in a way a form of the inference problem in database systems. Note that inference is the process of posing queries and obtaining unauthorized information from the legitimate responses received. Due to the aggregation and fusion of sensor data, the security levels of the aggregated data may be higher than those of the individual data sets. We also need to be aware of the privacy of the individuals. Much of the sensor data may be about individuals such as video streams about activities and other personal information. This data has to be protected from the general public and from those who are unauthorized to access the data. We have looked at privacy as a subset of security (see for example, [28]). There is also research on privacy preserving data mining and the techniques have to be examined for sensor data mining.

Finally we need to examine security policies for sensor data. These security policies may be dynamic and therefore we need to develop ways to enforce security constraints that vary with time. We also need techniques for integrating security policies especially in a networked and distributed environment. For example, different policies may apply for different sensor databases. These policies have to be integrated when managing distributed databases. One of the major questions here is what are the special considerations for security for sensor and stream data? Do the access control models that have been developed for business data processing applications work for stream data? We need to start a research program on secure sensor networks and secure sensor information management. Some preliminary directions are given in [28].

We need end-to-end security. That is, the infrastructures, data managers, applications, networks and operating systems for sensor information management have to be secure. The Object Management Group has developed standards for securing object request brokers. We need to take advantage of such developments. However, we need to examine security issues specific to object request brokers for sensor information management. We also need to examine composability of the various secure components. For example, are the interfaces between the various components satisfying the security properties? How can we integrate or compose the security policies of the various components. There is little work reported on securing large-scale information systems. Now, we not only have to examine security for such systems, we also need to examine security for such systems that manage and process sensor data. In addition, we need not only secure sensor networks but also sensor networks that are dependable and survivable.

One approach is to develop various features incrementally for data managers and middleware. However this often means that at the end some features are left out. For example, if we build components and examine only security and later on examine real-time processing, then it may be difficult to incorporate real-time processing into the policy. This means that we need to examine all of the features simultaneously. This means security engineering has to be integrated with software engineering.

Other issues include fault tolerant sensors and survivable sensors. Much work has been carried out on fault tolerant data management. We need to examine the fault tolerant data processing techniques for sensor data. Furthermore, these sensor databases have to survive from failures as well as from malicious attacks. Many of our critical infrastructures such as our telephones, power lines, and other systems have embedded sensors. The data emanating from these sensors may be corrupted maliciously or otherwise. For example, how can we ensure that the aggregate data is valid even if the components that constitute the aggregate data may be corrupted? Some directions are given in [20].

3.5 Privacy in Databases

With the World Wide Web, there is now an abundance of information about individuals that one can obtain within seconds. This information could be obtained through mining or just from information retrieval. Data mining is the process of posing queries and extracting information previously unknown machine learning and other reasoning techniques (see [24]). Now, data mining is an important technology for many applications. However data mining also causes privacy concerns as users can now put pieces of information together and extract information that is sensitive or private. Therefore, one needs to enforce controls on databases and data mining tools. That is, while data mining is an important tool for many applications, we do not want the information extracted to be used in an incorrect manner. For example, based on information about a person, an insurance company could deny insurance or a loan agency could deny loans. In many cases these denials may not be legitimate. Therefore, information providers have to be very careful in what they release. Also, data mining researchers have to ensure that privacy aspects are addressed.

We are beginning to realize that many of the techniques that were developed for the past two decades or so on the inference problem can now be used to handle privacy. One of the challenges to securing databases is the inference problem (see [1]). Inference is the process of users posing queries and deducing unauthorized information from the legitimate responses that they receive. This problem has been discussed quite a lot over the past two decades (see [21], [18], [14]). However, data mining makes this problem worse. Users now have sophisticated tools that they can use to get data and deduce patterns that could be sensitive. Without these data mining tools, users would have to be fairly sophisticated in their reasoning to be able to deduce information from posing queries to the databases. That is, data mining tools make the inference problem quite dangerous [7]. While the inference problem mainly deals with secrecy and confidentiality we are beginning to see many parallels between the inference problem and what we now call the privacy problem.

When Inference problem is considered to be a privacy problem, then we can use the inference controller approach to address privacy. For example, we can develop privacy controllers similar to our approach to developing inference controllers [22]. Furthermore, we can also have different degrees of privacy. For example, names and ages together could be less private while names and salaries together could be more private. Names and healthcare records together could be most private. One can then assign some probability or fuzzy value associated with the privacy of an attribute or a collection of attributes. Lot of work has been carried out on the inference problem in the past. We have conducted some research on applying the techniques for handling the inference problem and apply them for the privacy problem. We discuss some of the directions here.

In one area of research we have designed a privacy enhanced database management system (PE-DBMS) where users with different roles access and share a database consisting of data at different privacy levels. A powerful and dynamic approach to assigning privacy levels to data is one, which utilizes privacy constraints. Privacy constraints provide a privacy policy. They can be used to assign privacy levels to the data depending on their content and the context in which the data is displayed. They can also be used to dynamically reclassify the data. In other words, the privacy constraints are useful for describing privacy-enhanced applications. In [29] we have described the design if a PE-DBMS that processes privacy constraints during database design as well as during query and update operations. Recently Jajodia et al have proposed an approach for release control in databases (see [16]. The idea here is to process constraints after the response is computed but before the document is released. This approach could also be adapted for privacy. Another direction for privacy in databases includes using semantic data models for describing the application, reasoning about the application and detecting privacy violations. Some preliminary results are reported in [30].

We have also proved that the general privacy problem is unsolvable and the next step is to examine the complexity of the privacy problem (see [31]). Essentially we have examined our previous work on the inference problem and adapted it to handle the privacy problem.

There is now research at various laboratories on privacy enhanced/sensitive data mining (e.g., Agrawal at IBM Almaden, Gehrke at Cornell University and Clifton at Purdue University, see for example [2], [8], [13], [9]). The idea here is to continue with mining but at the same time ensure privacy as much as possible. For example, Clifton has proposed the use of the multiparty security policy approach for carrying out privacy sensitive data mining. While there is some progress we still have a long way to go. A summary of the developments in privacy preserving data mining is given in [32]. For a detailed discussion of data mining for national security and the implications for privacy we refer to [33].

3.6 Other Security Considerations

As we have mentioned in section 3.1, numerous technologies have emerged over the past few years. These include tools for electronic commerce, gene extraction, geospatial information management, managing moving objects, grid computing, peer-to-peer information management, managing virtual societies and organizations, and pervasive and context aware computing. Security as well as privacy must be examined for these tools and technologies for them to be useful and effective. For example, we could have the best grid computing tools, but if these tools cannot maintain security and privacy at an acceptable level, then they may not be of much use.

We also need to conduct research on usability vs. security. For example, security enforcement techniques may be quite complicated that it takes time to enforcement them. As a result, one could miss deadlines and/or lose valuable information. In other words, often there is a trade-off between security and technologies. How do we evaluate the economic aspects for incorporating security. That is, would it be economically infeasible to enforce all of the access control policies? Do we have to live with partial security? On the other hand by not having security, banks and financial organizations could lose millions of dollars through fraud. Here cyber security helps economic security. In other words, while security may be expensive to incorporate, for many applications we could lose millions of dollars by not enforcing security. We need to carry out trade off studies and examine the return on investment for incorporating security.

4. SUMMARY

This paper has briefly discussed the developments in data and applications security and then described some directions. We first provided a brief overview of the some of the developments in multilevel secure database management systems including relational systems, objects systems, transaction processing, and the inference problem. In the area of directions, we listed many topics such as secure grid computing, secure bioinformatics and secure geospatial information systems and then focussed on some selected topics such as secure semantic web, secure dependable computing, secure sensor information management and privacy in databases. We chose these topics as they are relevant to our current research and also they elaborate on the some of the issues covered during the keynote presentation.

As we have stressed in this paper, all of the topics listed here are important. That is, we need to conduct research on secure pervasive computing as well as examine the economic aspects of incorporating security. We also need to examine the security impact on knowledge management tools for societies and organizations. While we have made good progress, there is still a lot of research that needs to be done on data and applications security. Organizations such as the National Science Foundation now have focussed programs on Cyber security, which includes data and applications security. We can expect some significant developments on security for new generation information management technologies over the next several years.

5. Disclaimer

The views and conclusions expressed in this paper are those of the author and do not reflect the policies of the National Science Foundation or of the MITRE Corporation.

6. Acknowledgements

I thank the National Science Foundation and the MITRE Corporation for their support of my research on data and applications security.

7. REFERENCES

[1] Air Force Summer Study Report on Multilevel Secure Database Systems, Washington DC, 1983.

[2] Agrawal, R, and R. Srikant, "Privacy-preserving Data Mining," Proceedings of the ACM SIGMOD Conference, Dallas, TX, May 2000.

[3] Bensley, E., Thuraisingham, B., et al., Design and Implementation of an Infrastructure and Data Management for Evolvable Real-time Command and Control Systems, proceedings IEEE WORDS, Laguna beach, CA, February 1996.

[4] Bertino, E., E. Ferrari, et al, Access Control for XML Documents, Data and Knowledge Engineering, 2002.

[5] Bertino, E., B. Carminati, E. Ferrari, et al, Secure Third Party Publication of XML Documents, Accepted for publication in IEEE Transactions on Knowledge and Data Engineering, 2003.

[6] Proceedings of the National Computer Security Conference, Developments in Database Security, by Dr. John Campbell, 1990.

[7] Clifton, C. and D. Marks, "Security and Privacy Implications of Data Mining", Proceedings of the ACM SIGMOD Conference Workshop on Research Issues in Data Mining and Knowledge Discovery, Montreal, June 1996.

[8] Clifton, C., M. Kantarcioglu and J. Vaidya, "Defining Privacy for Data Mining," Purdue University, 2002 (see also Next Generation Data Mining Workshop, Baltimore, MD, November 2002).

[9] Evfimievski, A., R. Srikant, R. Agrawal, and J. Gehrke, "Privacy Preserving Mining of Association Rules," In Proceedings of the Eighth ACM SIGKDD International Conference on Knowledge Discovery and Data Mining. Edmonton, Alberta, Canada, July 2002.

[10] Farkas, C., Inference Problem for the Semantic Web, Proceedings of the IFIP Conference on Data and Applications Security, Colorado, August 2003.

[11] Ferrari E., and B. Thuraisingham, "Secure Database Systems," in Advances in Database Management by Artech House, 2000 (Editors: M. Piattini, O. Diaz).

[12] Ferrari, E., and B. Thuraisingham, "Security and Privacy for Web Databases and Web Services," Proceedings of the EDBT Conference, Crete, March 2004.

[13] Gehrke, J., "Research Problems in Data Stream Processing and Privacy-Preserving Data Mining," Proceedings of the Next Generation Data Mining Workshop, Baltimore, MD, November 2002.

[14] Hinke T., "Inference and Aggregation Detection in Database Management Systems," Proceedings of the Security and Privacy Conference, Oakland, CA, April 1988.

[15] Proceedings of the IFIP 11.3 Working Conference on Database Security, 1987 – 2003 (North Holland, Chapman and Hall, Kluwer).

[16] Jajodia, S., et al, "Release Control in Documents," Proceedings of the IFIP Database Integrity and Control Conference, Lausanne, Switzerland, November 2003.

[17] Berners Lee, T., et al., "The Semantic Web," Scientific American, May 2001.

[18] Morgenstern, M., "Security and Inference in Multilevel Database and Knowledge Base Systems," Proceedings of the ACM SIGMOD Conference, San Francisco, CA, June 1987.

[19] Cyber Trust Theme, National Science Foundation, http://www.nsf.gov/pubsys/ods/getpub.cfm?ods_key=nsf04524

[20] A. Perrig, "SIA: Secure Information Aggregation in Sensor Networks," CMU Report, 2003.

[21] Thuraisingham, B., "Multilevel Security for Relational Database Systems Augmented by an Inference Engine," Computers and Security," December 1987.

[22] Thuraisingham, B., W. Ford and M. Collins, "Design and Implementation of a Database Inference Controller," Data and Knowledge Engineering Journal, December 1993.

[23] Thuraisingham B. and W. Ford, "Security Constraint Processing in a Distributed Database Management System," IEEE Transactions on Knowledge and Data Engineering, 1995.

[24] Thuraisingham, B., "Data Mining: Technologies, Techniques, Tools and Trends," CRC Press, 1998.

[25] Thuraisingham, B. and J. Maurer, "Information Survivability for Real-time Command sand Control Systems," IEEE Transactions on Knowledge and Data Engineering, January 1999.

[26] Thuraisingham, B., "Data and Applications Security: Developments and Directions," Proceedings of the IEEE COMPSAC Conference, Oxford, UK, August 2002.

[27] Thuraisingham, B., "Data and Applications Security: Developments and Directions," Keynote Presentation, IFIP 11.3 Conference on Data and Applications Security, Estes Park, Colorado, August 3, 2003.

[28] Thuraisingham, B., "Security and Privacy for Sensor Databases," Accepted for publication in Sensor Letters, 2003.

[29] Thuraisingham, B., "Privacy Constraint Processing in a Privacy Enhanced Database System," Accepted for publication in Data and Knowledge Engineering Journal, 2003.

[30] Thuraisingham, B., "Semantic Data Modeling for Privacy Control in Databases," Submitted for Publication, 2003.

[31] Thuraisingham, B., "On the Unsolvability of the Privacy Problem in Databases," Submitted for Publication, 2003.

[32] Thuraisingham, B., "Privacy-Preserving Data Mining: Developments and Directions" Accepted for publication in Journal of Database Management, Journal, 2003.

[33] Thuraisingham, B., "Web Data Mining and Applications in Business Intelligence and Counter-terrorism, CRC Press," June 2003.

[34] Thuraisingham, B., "Database and Applications Security: Integrating Databases and Information Security," CRC Press, to appear, 2004.

VIII

PANEL

DIGITAL FORENSICS: OPERATIONAL, LEGAL AND RESEARCH ISSUES

M. Pollitt, M. Caloyannides, J. Novotny and S. Shenoi

Abstract With more than 93% of the world's data being computer generated [23], digital forensics offers significant opportunities and challenges. This paper discusses the operational and legal issues related to digital evidence. In addition, it highlights current needs and future research opportunities.

Keywords: Digital Evidence, Computer and Network Forensics, Forensic Processes, Legal Issues, Research Directions

1. Introduction

Digital forensics played a crucial role in the investigations of the 9-11 terrorists, the Enron, WorldCom and Martha Stewart scandals, and the DC sniper attacks. In the sniper case, electronic data extracted from a GPS device in the suspects' automobile provided information about their route across the country. Three unsolved murders along this route, in Louisiana, Alabama and Georgia, which involved weapons of the same caliber as the DC attacks, were connected to the sniper suspects via ballistics and fingerprint evidence. Indeed, due to network convergence and the ubiquity of embedded systems and devices, practically every crime – not just white-collar crime – has a digital forensic component [9,15,21]. Laptops, cell phones and PDAs seized from drug dealers and other violent criminals often yield vital evidence [15,21]. Meanwhile, electronic evidence is playing an increasingly important role in civil litigation. This paper discusses the operational and legal issues related to digital evidence. In addition, it highlights current needs and future research opportunities.

2. Operational Issues

Computers and other electronic devices invariably contain information relevant to investigations. This is the electronic analog of Locard's forensic principle of "exchange," where "every contact leaves a trace" [10]. This section discusses the nature of digital evidence and the forensic process, i.e., the extraction and analysis of digital evidence.

2.1. Digital Evidence

A crime scene contains observable evidence, e.g., blood, which has probative value. However, forensic science has developed techniques, e.g., DNA analysis, that yield information that is not physically observable. Computers, hard drives and flash memory cards are patent (observable) evidence that contain latent information, e.g., files, application metadata, file system debris and operating system debris. Extracting and analyzing latent evidence requires specialized tools and techniques. Moreover, the "forensic specialists" who perform these activities must be well trained and capable of providing expert testimony [18].

The Scientific Working Group on Digital Evidence (SWGDE) has defined digital evidence as: "information of probative value stored or transmitted in digital form" [6]. This definition is now widely accepted by other groups, e.g., the International Organization on Computer Evidence and the G-8 High Tech Crime Subcommittee.

2.2. Digital Forensics

Various terms, e.g., computer forensics, cyber forensics, media analysis and network forensics, are used to refer to the process of acquiring, preserving, examining, analyzing and presenting digital evidence. We prefer "digital evidence forensics," or simply, "digital forensics."

2.2.1 Acquisition. In the acquisition step, electronic devices at the scene are gathered, marked for identification and entered into an evidence control system. When evidence resides on devices that cannot – for legal or practical reasons – be physically collected, e.g., a hospital network containing "live" medical data, it is necessary to create a physical duplicate of the evidence. Dynamic evidence, e.g., network packets in transit, must be captured and recorded on physical media, both accurately and reliably.

2.2.2 Preservation. The preservation step requires the "original" piece of digital evidence to be maintained so that the opposing counsel and the court may be assured that it is both reliable and unaltered [12]. Failure to do so may result in the inadmissibility of evidence. Consequently, forensic examinations are almost always conducted on duplicate media [11].

Thus, preservation has two components: physical preservation of the original and the creation of duplicate media for forensic examination. The former is accomplished via "chain of custody" procedures; the latter by creating either a forensically accurate duplicate or a demonstrably accurate representation of the original. The latter process is often referred to as creating a "forensic image" or a "bit-stream copy."

2.2.3 Examination. Modern computers and data storage devices have huge, ever increasing capacities, making it extremely difficult to identify information of probative value. Examination is the process whereby evidence is subjected to review for its source, origin, and manner of creation, alteration or destruction.

The first step is to document all aspects of the evidence, e.g., physical and logical characteristics, active and deleted file structures, metadata and data contained in unallocated areas. This documentation process assures that both inculpatory and exculpatory information is preserved. Next, the actual examination may begin. Since examinations are usually conducted to support legal proceedings, the nature and specifics of the evidence that would be probative is unique to each examination [20]. Therefore, it is important to define a plan of action and to select forensic software tools based on the goals of an examination.

Numerous forensic tools, including many of dubious quality, are available. Sometimes software not designed for forensic use is pressed into service, but this may raise legal challenges to the evidence or, even worse, render the evidence useless. Collectively, tools seek to include data as potentially probative or to exclude data that would not be probative. Obviously, the more restrictive the filter, the less data there will be to sift through, but it is also more likely that probative information will be missed. The ability to construct a process that invokes the fewest and most appropriate tools in the most efficient way is the artistic part of forensic examination. As storage volume and network bandwidth grow exponentially, it will be increasingly difficult to create tools and processes that are both efficient and accurate.

2.2.4 Analysis. Analysis involves the review of evidence for its content, probative value and usefulness to the investigative or legal objectives. Thus, analysis goes beyond the technical aspects of the original evidence and its constituent parts. While examination attempts to produce information that is potentially probative, it is not until the evidence is evaluated in the context of all of the other evidence that its value can be established. Data recovered from the original evidence may support other information known in the case, it may contradict other information in the case, it may be new information, or it may prove to be non-pertinent. To make these determinations as accurately as possible, it is necessary to have a clear understanding of the investigative process and detailed knowledge of all the investigative material.

2.2.5 Presentation. The output of forensic examination and analysis comprises the data files extracted from the forensic copy of the original evidence and a report documenting the forensic process, pertinent metadata and conclusions. Obviously, the presentation must be complete, concise and clear.

3. Legal Constraints

This section discusses U.S. laws governing the acquisition and use of digital evidence in criminal, civil and intelligence investigations.

3.1. Criminal Investigations

U.S. federal law relating to the acquisition of digital evidence by law enforcement agencies is governed by the Fourth Amendment and statutory privacy laws codified in the Wiretap Statute (18 U.S.C. Sections 2510-22), the Electronic Communications Privacy Act (ECPA) of 1986 (18 U.S.C. Sections 2701-02) and the Pen/Trap Statute (18 U.S.C. Sections 3121-27) [22,27].

The Fourth Amendment limits the ability of government agents to obtain evidence without a warrant. A warrantless search does not violate the Fourth Amendment if: (i) the agents' conduct does not violate an individual's "reasonable expectation of privacy," or (ii) the search falls within an exception to the warrant requirement [5,27,28]. Therefore, agents must consider if a search violates the expectation of privacy. Even if a search does violate this expectation, it may still be reasonable if it falls within an exception to the warrant requirement [27].

Determining what constitutes a reasonable expectation of privacy is difficult in cases involving computers. To assist federal investigators, the U.S. Justice Department recommends that agents treat a computer as a closed container (e.g., a file cabinet) [27]. The Fourth Amendment prohibits law enforcement agents from accessing and viewing computer information without a warrant if they would be prohibited from opening a closed container and examining its contents in the same situation [27]. However, courts have reached differing conclusions on whether or not individual computer files should be treated as separate closed containers.

Warrantless searches that violate a reasonable expectation of privacy comply with the Fourth Amendment if they fall within an established exception to the warrant requirement. For example, agents may conduct a search without a warrant if an individual with authority has consented to the search, if there is an expectation that the evidence will be destroyed, or if the evidence is in plain view [16,27]. Other exceptions occur during searches incident to a lawful arrest, inventory searches and border searches [27].

Because courts may or may not apply an exception, it is advisable to obtain a warrant before searching and seizing evidence. As with any search pursuant to a warrant, law enforcement agents must establish probable cause, and describe the place to be searched and the items to be seized [27]. However, because computer files may be encrypted, misleadingly labeled, stored in unusual formats or commingled with innocuous files, agents cannot simply establish probable cause, describe the files they need, and then go and retrieve the data. Instead, they must understand the technical limits of different search techniques, plan the search carefully and then draft the warrant in a manner that authorizes them to take the steps necessary to obtain the evidence.

Agents should obtain multiple warrants if they have reason to believe that a network search will retrieve data stored in multiple locations. Also, agents should obtain a second warrant to search a computer seized pursuant to a valid warrant if the property targeted by the search is different from that specified in the first warrant.

The incidental seizure of certain materials may implicate the Privacy Protection Act (PPA) or the ECPA [27]. Under the PPA, law enforcement agents must take special steps when planning a search that may result in the seizure of First Amendment materials (e.g., materials posted on the web). The ECPA regulates how agents can obtain the contents of electronic communications stored by third-party service providers. To minimize liability under these statutes, agents should attempt to determine in advance the type of information that may be stored on the computer systems to be searched [27].

Law enforcement agents can conduct "no-knock" warrants if they suspect that announcing their presence would lead to the destruction of evidence [27]. Courts may also authorize "sneak-and-peek" warrants, which do not require agents to notify the person whose premises are searched. The USA PATRIOT Act amended 18 U.S.C. Section 3103a to allow a court to grant a delay of notice associated with the execution of a search warrant if it believes that providing immediate notification will have adverse effects [26]. However, warrants issued under the amended statute still prohibit the seizure of electronic information unless specifically authorized by a court.

In addition to physically seizing computers, agents frequently perform electronic surveillance. In these situations, it is important for agents to act in accord with the Wiretap Statute and the Pen/Trap Statute. The Wiretap Statute (Title III) governs real-time electronic surveillance in federal criminal investigations [7,24]. Title III broadly prohibits the interception of oral, wire and electronic communications. However, Title III contains dozens of exceptions and agents must be familiar with them before performing surveillance. The Pen/Trap Statute governs the use of pen registers and trap and trace devices [27]. The statute authorizes a government attorney to apply for a court order authorizing the installation of a pen register and/or trap and trace device when the information sought is relevant to an investigation. As modified by the USA PATRIOT Act, it now applies to communications on computer networks in addition to telephone communications and gives nationwide effect to pen/trap orders [26].

In addition to the applicable federal laws, state laws must also be considered. In particular, many states have laws regarding privacy, especially with regard to stored electronic information. Unfortunately, laws vary considerably from state to state, and a detailed discussion is beyond the scope of this paper. It is important to note that when there is conflict, federal laws supercede state laws. However, in some instances, state laws are more specific and are, therefore, applicable.

3.2. Civil Investigations

Private corporations investigating their own employees may not adhere to most of the legal constraints discussed above. Frequently, private corporations require employees to sign computer use policies that include stipulations regarding the monitoring of computer activities. In these cases, employees typically resign their privacy rights.

The Fourth Amendment also does not apply to searches conducted by private parties who are not acting as agents of the government [27]. Therefore, no violation of the Fourth Amendment occurs when a private individual acting on his own accord conducts a search and makes the results available to law enforcement. However, law enforcement agents must limit themselves to the scope of the private search. Otherwise, the agents may violate the Fourth Amendment and any evidence gathered may be suppressed.

3.3. Intelligence Investigations

Searching, seizing or otherwise obtaining digital evidence in intelligence investigations can raise difficult questions of both law and policy. For example, the bounds of the Fourth Amendment are less clear than they are for ordinary criminal investigations [27]. Furthermore, the Foreign Intelligence Surveillance Act (FISA) creates a secret court and a legal regime for counterintelligence surveillance inside the United States [25]. When operating outside the United States, agents must be aware of the many laws in other nations that may affect an investigation. The U.S. Department of Justice Computer Crime and Intellectual Property Section (CCIPS) provides guidance on these matters.

4. Current Needs and Research Issues

This section discusses some of the significant areas of opportunity for research in digital forensics.

4.1. Data Storage and Analysis

The amount of data generated and stored in our daily activities is increasing rapidly. A recent University of California at Berkeley study estimated that almost 800 megabytes of data are produced annually for each person in the world; moreover, the per person figure is growing at about 30% per year [2,17]. In this environment, forensic investigators are faced with massive amounts of evidence on digital media and networks. Single cases involving more than one hundred terabytes of data have already been encountered.

Storage area networks (SANs) are an attractive solution [3]. These high-speed special-purpose networks interconnect various data storage devices with massive data servers. SANs permit data from multiple cases to be loaded on networks and accessed, possibly remotely, by investigators. They allow for both physical and logical separation of forensic case files; this prevents evidence from being compromised, as with blood evidence in the well-known O.J. Simpson case. The increased storage capacity and scalability of SANs supports efficient information access, maximized hardware utilization, freedom from vendor dependence and the automation of forensic processes. SANs may also help solve current problems with long-term data storage by providing data redundancy (via RAID) and integrity. Promising research avenues include SAN architectures for large-scale, distributed operations, workflow modeling and analysis, validation and verification of SAN implementations, and the study of the legal ramifications of SAN use.

Another strategy for dealing with massive case files is to apply novel information manipulation techniques that can home in on pertinent data both rapidly and reliably. The main information manipulation techniques are data reduction and data mining. Data reduction methods involving known file filters and hash sets are currently used by forensic investigators, but these are limited in both scope and performance. Data mining employs a combination of machine learning, statistical analysis and modeling techniques to extract relevant information from large data sets. Data mining techniques are just beginning to find applications in digital forensic investigations, and numerous research opportunities exist in this area.

4.2. Specialized Devices

Digital investigations have largely concentrated on computers and networks. However, the ubiquity of hand-held electronic devices and new network appliances requires research on extracting digital evidence from non-traditional, and possibly damaged, equipment. Examples include fax machines, cell phones, smart cards, GPS navigational aids, digital cameras and various consumer electronics devices.

Fax machines store phone numbers of senders and recipients; upscale machines often maintain the actual faxed pages in memory. Cell phones store substantial amounts of data: dialed, received and missed calls as well as contact lists, photographs and MMS files. Information stored in smart cards (and not-so-smart cards) may include toll road access data, ostensibly anonymous prepaid phone cards and supermarket purchases. GPS devices store detailed path information that has been extracted and used successfully in criminal and terrorism investigations. Digital cameras store data in memory chips, which are just as amenable to forensic techniques as traditional computer media, i.e., deleted files are not really deleted and slack space (between end-of-file and end-of-sector) will contain data. Like digital cameras, a multitude of other consumer electronics devices, such as MP3 players and camcorders, have digital memories and may contain useful information.

Embedded devices are an emerging trend. For example, automobiles now incorporate devices that store operational data, e.g., speed, brake status and throttle position, that may be relevant to investigations. The recent fatality accident investigation involving U.S. Rep. William Janklow (R-SD) exemplifies the use of digital evidence extracted from embedded devices in an automobile [1].

Research efforts should seek to identify electronic devices that may contain digital evidence and develop tools and techniques for extracting the evidence. In addition, it is necessary to develop best practices that meet the legal requirements for evidence admissibility.

4.3. Network Forensics

Forensic investigations involving networks languish for practical, jurisdictional and political reasons. Network administrators have no incentive to retain data that may be relevant to investigations outside their networks. This problem is even greater in situations where network nodes are located in foreign countries, especially non-friendly nations or those with different legal systems.

A potential solution is to develop and implement techniques that would make anonymity and pseudoanonymity harder to achieve on global networks like the Internet; this would limit the need for cooperation of foreign parties. IPsec [13], for example, would have resulted in increased sender authentication, but the pressure for its implementation has dissipated due to the popularity of NAT, which removes the urgency for new IP addresses [4], and SSL, which removes the urgency for a broadly accepted means to encrypt select traffic [8].

Clearly, it is difficult to solve the cultural, economic, political and jurisdictional problems that stifle network forensic investigations. However, it may be easier to develop technologies that ride on current IPv4 – and future IPv6 – networks, which could assist in tracing attacks across global networks. These technologies could then be proposed to cognizant organizations, e.g., IETF and IEEE, for possible codification as standards.

Peer-to-peer networks [19] and grid computing [14] are two emerging research areas in network forensics. Peer-to-peer applications create transient Internet-based networks, which are increasingly used to trade copyrighted and other illegal materials. Grid computing networks, on the other hand, utilize transient pools of computing nodes to perform tasks, each node contributing cycles to the collaborative effort. Special techniques and tools must be developed to deal with the scale, jurisdictional and dynamic participation issues in these two types of networks.

4.4. Forensic Tools and Processes

Forensic tools have advanced considerably during the past few years. Nevertheless, the development of highly efficient software that can be utilized on a variety of platforms on a wide range of target systems in a modular fashion could narrow the gap between demand and functionality.

It is equally important to study the forensic process to determine how to conduct examinations most efficiently. Experienced examiners are very efficient, but no efforts have been undertaken to analyze and model their approaches with a view to automating the forensic examination process.

Regardless of the tools and techniques used, it is imperative to ensure the efficiency and effectiveness of forensic examinations. Furthermore, as data, media, forensic tools and investigations become more complex, it is increasingly difficult to demonstrate the "truth" of a forensic examination. To address this issue, research is needed in several directions, including software engineering approaches for trusted forensic software, automated processes and tools, and the validation of software as it applies to a particular platform, data set and forensic procedure.

4.5. Legal Considerations

To ensure that digital evidence will withstand judicial scrutiny, it is necessary to research the reliability and legality of forensic tools, techniques and procedures.

As court proceedings increasingly incorporate digital evidence, judges, juries and attorneys are more likely to test the merit of digital forensic tools and methodologies. In the United States, judicial evaluations of digital evidence – as with other forensic disciplines – will apply the Frye, Daubert and Kumho Tire tests [18]. Under these doctrines, the reliability of the proffered evidence must be demonstrated. This demands comprehensive validation and verification studies of digital forensic tools, techniques and procedures. Unfortunately, with the massive, dynamic electronic landscape, the digital forensics community has had limited success in developing timely and efficient means for validation, let alone verification.

Research on the privacy implications of digital forensic tools and procedures is critical. Even if tools and procedures are reliable and verifiable, investigators cannot wantonly seize digital devices and extract evidence. Electronic devices may store information protected by various privacy laws. Violating privacy laws at any stage during the digital forensic process not only renders the collected evidence useless, but also exposes the investigator to civil action.

5. Conclusions

Sophisticated tools and procedures are sorely needed to acquire, preserve, examine, analyze and present digital evidence in a dynamic electronic landscape. But it is equally important that the tools and procedures be used properly and legally. Digital forensics is indeed a wide open area for research. Its technical, operational and legal dimensions pose myriad challenges and research opportunities.

References

[1] Cable News Network. Prosecutor: Janklow ran stop sign before deadly crash. www.cnn.com, August 20, 2003.

[2] Cable News Network. Scientists report data storage explosion. www.cnn.com, October 29, 2003.

[3] T. Clark. *Designing Storage Area Networks: A Practical Reference for Implementing Fiber Channel and IP SANs*. Addison-Wesley, Reading, Massachusetts, 2003.

[4] K. Egevang and P. Francis. RFC 1631: The IP network address translator. www.faqs.org/rfcs/rfc1631.html, 1994.

[5] M. Elmore. Big brother where art thou? Electronic surveillance and the Internet: Carving away Fourth Amendment privacy protections. *Texas Tech Law Review*, 32:1053-1083, 2001.

[6] Federal Bureau of Investigation. Digital evidence: Standards and principles. *Forensic Science Communications*, 2(2), April 2000.

[7] Federal Bureau of Investigation. *Congressional Statement on Limited Expansion of the Predicate Offenses for Title III Electronic Surveillance*. www.fbi.gov, 2001.

[8] A. Freier, P. Karlton and P. Kocher. The SSL Protocol Version 3.0. IETF (draft-ietf-tls-ssl-version3-00.txt), November 1996.

[9] S. Hinde. The law, cybercrime, risk assessment and cyber protection. *Computers & Security*, 22(2):90-95, 2003.

[10] K. Inman and N. Rudin. *Principles and Practices of Criminalistics: The Profession of Forensic Science*. CRC Press, Boca Raton, Florida, 2001.

[11] International Association of Computer Investigative Specialists. *Forensic Procedures*. www.cops.org, 2001.

[12] International Organization on Computer Evidence. *G8 Proposed Principles for the Procedures Relating to Digital Evidence*. www.ioce.org, 2000.

[13] Internet Engineering Task Force. IP security protocol (IPsec). www.ietf.org /html.charters/ipsec-charter.html.

[14] J. Joseph and C. Fellenstein. *Grid Computing*. Prentice Hall, Upper Saddle River, New Jersey, 2003.

[15] C. Kirby. Cyber sleuths: Computer forensics booms as importance of electronic evidence grows. *San Francisco Chronicle*, February 26, 2001.

[16] J. LaDue. Electronic surveillance and conversations in plain view: Admitting intercepted communications relating to crimes not specified in the surveillance order. *Notre Dame Law Review*, 65:490-533, 1990.

[17] P. Lyman and H. Varian. How much information? www.sims.berkeley.edu/how-much-info-2003, 2003.

[18] A. Moenssens, editor. Amendments to the Federal Rules of Evidence. www.forensic-evidence.com, 2003.

[19] D. Moore and J. Hebeler. *Peer-to-Peer: Building Secure, Scalable and Manageable Networks*. McGraw-Hill/Osborne, Emeryville, California, 2001.

[20] M. Noblett, M. Pollitt and L. Presley. Recovering and examining computer forensic evidence. *Forensic Science Communications*, 2(4), October 2000.

[21] M. Pollitt. Digital evidence. *Proceedings of the Thirteenth Interpol International Forensic Science Symposium*, Lyons, France, 2002.

[22] E. Sinrod, *et al.* Cyber-crimes: A practical approach to the application of federal computer crime laws. *Santa Clara Computer and High Technology Law Journal*, 16:177-232, 2000.

[23] State Bar of Texas. Electronic discovery and computer forensics collection. Computer and Technology Section, www.sbot.org/discovery_library.htm.

[24] R. Strang. Recognizing and meeting Title III concerns in computer investigations. *United States Attorneys' Bulletin*, 49(2):8-13, 2001.

[25] L. Tien. Foreign Intelligence Surveillance Act. Electronic Frontier Foundation, www.eff.org, 2001.

[26] U.S. Department of Justice. *Field Guidance on New Authorities that Relate to Computer Crime and Electronic Evidence Enacted in the USA Patriot Act of 2001*. www.cybercrime.gov, 2001.

[27] U.S. Department of Justice. *Searching and Seizing Computers and Obtaining Electronic Evidence in Criminal Investigations*. www.cybercrime.gov, 2002.

[28] R. Winick. Searches and seizures of computers and computer data. *Harvard Journal of Law & Technology*, 8:75-128, 1994.

www.ingramcontent.com/pod-product-compliance
Ingram Content Group UK Ltd.
Pitfield, Milton Keynes, MK11 3LW, UK
UKHW020131290926
15471UKWH00003B/416
* 9 7 8 1 4 7 5 7 8 0 2 2 2 *